san
francisco

a Virgin guide

First published in 2000
Virgin Publishing Ltd, London w6 9ha
Copyright 2000 © Virgin Publishing Ltd, London

virgin san francisco

Virgin's on-the-spot contributors have selected the best places to shop, eat, hang out, relax, and explore. This San Francisco guide gives an inside take on the city, with an emphasis on what's new, what's in, and what's fun.

contents

the lowdown on the best shops, restaurants, cafés, bars & clubs in each area

Noe Valley ♫*C5–D5*: This appealing little village strikes the right balance with its bohemian flavoured shops and small-town vibe of old-style diners.

North Beach ♫*E1*: Key gathering spot for the 50s Beat poet movement and alternately SF's Little Italy, bustling, boho North Beach exudes Italian warmth and style with scores of superb eateries.

Pacific Heights ♫*C2*: This largely residential area is home to some of the city's most magnificent and intact Victorian mansions. Bustling upper Fillmore Street splits the area in two.

Potrero Hill ♫*F4*: One of San Francisco's best-kept secrets is fast becoming a hip locale for artists and multimedia types, drawn by airy warehouses and great views.

Richmond ♫*A3*: Row upon row of look-alike family homes line these quiet avenues populated largely by a mix of Russian, Japanese, and Chinese residents. Clement Avenue is the lively hub.

Russian Hill ♫*D1–D2*: Steep slopes, well-tended hedges, and an old-meets-new mix of Victorian homes and lavish modern apartments. Eclectic Polk Street grounds the area with a more casual vibe.

SoMa ♫*E3–F3*: This sprawling, industrial area has some of the city's most happening clubs. It's also a cultural hot spot. A burgeoning number of Internet and multi-media companies make their home in and around leafy South Park.

Sunset ♫*A5*: Judah Street at 9th is the buzzing centre of the vast,

fog-strewn Sunset, lined with uniform stucco family homes.

Telegraph Hill ♫*E1*: An upscale area of charming cottages and blossoming gardens boasting some of the city's steepest hills and most breathtaking views.

Tenderloin ♫*D3–E3*: SF's dodgy underbelly is a hotbed for illicit activities (drugs and prostitution head the list).

Theater District/Downtown ♫*D2–E2*: The crowning jewel in this cluster of theatres is the recently renovated Geary Theatre.

Union Square/Downtown ♫*E2*: The heart of Downtown is ringed by some of the city's toniest stores.

Western Addition ♫*C3*: This multi-cultural area is one of the city's poorest and most run down.

getting your bearings

la vida loca

8

mission

A neighbourhood in transition, this hipster haven is the site of a turf war between long-time residents – generations of Hispanics, artists, students – and deeper-pocketed arrivistes, who have brought rising rents and yupscale shops and eateries in their wake.

Mexican and Central American immigrants began settling here in the 60s and the Mission became something of a Latino quarter, with Spanish-language movie theatres, dance clubs, galleries, and a profusion of taquerias. Colourful murals [→76] tell of various triumphs and struggles, and Hispanic residents from all over come to carry candles in the ever-popular Day of the Dead procession (2 Nov). Over the years, the Mission also became a magnet for neo-Bohemians attracted by the low rents, ethnic diversity, and anything-goes attitude, as well as the late-night coffee houses, bars, and clubs. But economic boom times and the steady gentrification have created a growing unease. As a visitor, however, you are likely to indulge your appetites – from a tipple in the hippest bars to shaking it up to salsa, hip-hop, or techno – without ever having to grapple with this political subtext.

day

🛍 Some of the city's most eclectic and inventive clothing (lots of 50s–70s vintage looks) and furnishings boutiques populate the Mission, especially on Valencia Street. Prices are more modest than Downtown.

👁 Pay your respects at Mission Dolores [→71]; catch some rays at Mission Dolores Park [→78]; or check out the myriad murals in the area [→76].

night

🍴 This area is definitely on the cutting-edge of cuisine. Some of SF's most exciting restaurants to open in recent years have opted for Mission addresses.

🍸 The Mission is prime bar crawling territory with innumerable bars and clubs clustered mostly on and around 16th and 22nd Streets. Nightlife starts late and ends later.

getting there

🚌 9, 22, 26, 27, 49
🅱 16th St Mission, 24th St Mission

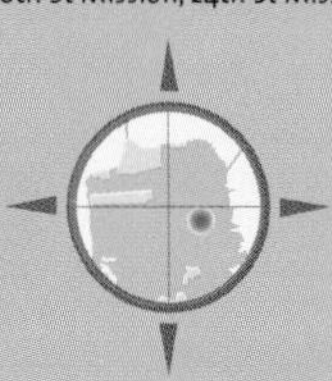

shopping

one-of-a-kind

What better way to soak up the Mission's diversity than to walk the sunny streets in search of worldly goods? *Paxton Gate is like the study of some eccentric

botanist/entomologist with displays of dried and mounted exotic insects, antique gardening tools, butterfly nets, science fiction-like bromeliads, and

bizarre little artefacts. It also features a peace-inducing pond. Kelly Kornegay's flower-and-collectable shop **Rayon Vert** ⌂ has buckets of blooms surrounded by

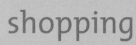

* = featured in the listings section [→88–124]

anything that happens to catch her eye – striped sake bowls, silver julep cups, old paint-by-numbers flowers, and wacky Japanese stationery. For more botanical healing, dip into the apothecary jars at **Currents** and make your own lavender, rosemary, or lemongrass sachet to induce a state of energy or calm. Once relaxed, saunter into *Good Vibrations, the 'clean, well-lighted place for sex toys', which has shrouded windows to protect your identity as you peruse the many gadgets (in colours and sizes not dreamed of), video, and literature devoted to the art of love and self-lovin'. And then you might as well seek salvation at the *Mission Dolores Gift Shop, where they keep rosaries and crosses in addition to books, models, and tiles of all 21 California missions.

vintage clothing

At **Clothes Contact** goods are sold by weight at $8 per pound. Here the young and pierced gather armloads of green leather, fake fur, and neon orange polyfill to concoct outfits to rival the runways. At **Captain Jack's**, they come to plunder the stock of little-seen Levi's (such as old double knits in myriad shades) as well as the more common blue denim varieties. Spanning decades from the 30s to the 70s, **Das Pussycat** seduces with items like a fur-lined women's Nehru Eskimo jacket, a sharkskin Western suit, and an unworn fake patchwork Huggy Bear Wrangler men's suit à la 'Starsky and Hutch'. A popular prop resource, **Retro Fit**

Vintage ⅃ rents and sells shagalicious clothing and collectables from the swinging 60s. But the cream of the vintage crop may well be **Schauplatz**, a chic collection of accessories (Bee-Gees lunch boxes, Lucite purses) and clothing (a 40s Hawaiian halterneck dress, a black velvet floral appliquéd skirt, a dead stock 60s leather coat with inlaid white detailing). The furniture on sale upstairs will transform a mere flat into a pad.

fashion

When designer Dema Grim first opened her eponymous Valencia Street boutique, **Dema**, the audience for her Audrey-inspired, easy-on-the-wallet girlwear consisted mainly of Mission district habitués. Now a destination, Dema is filled with mod little dresses, capri pants, blouses, and skirts rendered in her groovy signature fabrics, as well as stretchy candy-heart pastel sweaters. A little jewel box with pale pink walls and stripped-wood floors, **Laku** is where urban maidens flock for Yaeko Yamashita's handmade fairytale slippers. Each pointy pair is a mad motley of soft fabrics, patterns, and trims (rosettes, pom-poms) – and the teensy leopard-print-and-velvet children's styles are heart wrenching. Luscious hats and antique jewellery are also worth the trip. Hip Brit Adrian Leong's **Fishbowl** is the antithesis of antique, with up-to-the-nanosecond dresses, cropped baggies, jeans and tops by Mooks and Blue Dot, and edgy pieces by Girbaud. Spicing the mix are Leong's own crushed nylon shirts for men and smart little skirts for women.

arts, crafts & voodoo

Mexican and Latin American artists are the focus at **Encantada Gallery**, which is also heavy on domestic textiles, shrines, and folk crafts that honour various saints and holy days (look for the two-headed Frida Kahlo sculpture puffing on a cigarette). For a mixture of art, crafts, and kitsch, *Studio 24 – the gift shop next to the acclaimed Galeria de la Raza – augments its more serious pieces with a bounty of

Day of the Dead ephemera and gift items from Mexico.

Sometimes life requires more than a positive attitude. To cast a spell, induce love, or cause a change in fortune, get thee to the **Lady Luck Candle Shop** or **Botanica Yoruba** for decorative ritual candles to suit every occasion and desire. The Botanica is also a Santeria outlet, stocking incense, oils, and instructional books dedicated to keeping your mojo rising.

books

The Mission's myriad used bookstores are stacked to the rafters with out-of-print and recently published titles, as well as occasional rare and first-editions at much softer prices than in the 'antiquarian' shops. Favourite haunts include **Adobe**, **Abandoned Planet**, and **Dog-Eared Books**, where you can browse for hours. For a deep and thoughtful assortment of new fiction, cultural theory, alternative magazines, Spanish language texts, and revolutionary rhetoric, head for *Modern Times – a favourite of residents all over the city.

music

By-products of the Mission's cultural heritage are two unique music stores, *Discolandia and *Ritmo Latino. The former is a brilliant source of old and new Latin music; the latter stocks all dance genres, including ranchero, salsa, mariachi, merengue, Tex-Mex, norteño, and tango (with never a still body at any of the in-store listening stations). At *Aquarius, let the many hand-written staff recommendations guide you to the richest techno, drum 'n' bass, DJ, and alternative offerings.

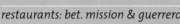

eating & drinking

restaurants: bet. mission & guerrero

Salsa still streams from boom boxes at every corner; taquerias still abound; and a few gritty streets still exist to denote the down-and-out feel of the Mission's past. But only a few. The Latino-dominant neighbourhood was no match for the city's economic boom, and in the mid-90s the Mission became a magnet for Anglo artists and thinkers.... and Silicon Valley moguls. A few years on, the Mission is the city's quirkiest and most exciting restaurant enclave with new eateries opening every month.

The stalwart of the new Mission crew is **Ti Couz** which was one of the first gourmet outposts to open in the area. The line for dirt-cheap French crepes, cider, and giant salads grew so long the owners bought a neighbouring grocery store to house Ti Couz II. Of the same generation, **Flying Saucer** serves dishes that look as space-age as the sobriquet suggests, and they sound as interstellar (duck confit with black chanterelles on coconut-curry lentils). At nearby **Mangiafuoco** – another relative 'old timer' – mismatched furnishings and funky fixtures belie the flawless Italian fare which is imbued with flavour from the wood-burning grill.

These older establishments have quietly made way for three new dynamos, all of national acclaim. *Watergate [→107] is the Mission's most conservative eatery and is one of the few where finery is at all appropriate. Think glossy mahogany tables and chef-Asian cuisine, like prosciutto-wrapped polenta with foie gras. *The* media darling of 99, *Delfina [→105], meanwhile lures with dishes like the swoon-worthy nettles

ravioli, or braised beef cheeks (a Californian approach to Italian food). Critics also laud chef Charles Phan's original take on Vietnamese fare at *Slanted Door [→106]. Herbs taste like they were just plucked from a garden and waiters seem to float through the two-storey, celadon oasis. Locals who can't brook the wait to get in opt for nearby Saigon Saigon where solid Vietnamese fare is a quarter of the price – but without the flourishes.

Slipping onto the scene right before the millenial turnover is the tiny **Neo** where all-white insane-asylum decor could drive you mad if the food and scene weren't so hot. Everything – gourmet comfort food, chic co-diners, conversation – will jump off this white canvas. Another newcomer beginning to create a buzz is **Pintxos**. Founded by one of the city's most successful Spanish restaurateurs, this Basque eaterie looks like a curated annex of the SFMOMA [→73]. Refusing to wait for buzz, and daring to be as flashy as its east Mission neighbours, is the industrial-chic **Tokyo Go Go**. It stands out like a robotic thumb on 16th Street – gun metal and sushi meet under a din of acid-jazz, and yuppies are eating it up. For a dirt cheap and pretension-free alternative, head to **We Be Sushi**.

Locals aren't crazy about all the newcomers descending on their turf, but the frenzy has thankfully drawn attention away from revered standbys. Among them: **Pauline's Pizza Pie** where thin crust pies are topped with gourmet effects like French goat cheese and lamb shoulder; and **Firecracker** which serves inno-

vative Chinese food for foodies, ie no goopy sauce on dishes like fiery shrimp with ginger. You will also hear next to nothing about **Rasoi**, the underrated Indian local, or **El Nuevo Fruitlandia**, one of the few Cuban/Puerto Rican eateries in the city, spinning inspired comfort food out of yucca and plantains.

For more Latin flavours, there's the tiny Mexican *Panchita's Café [→113], as well as numerous lively and colourful tapas/sangria options – all reasonably priced. Dishes at Caribbean-inspired *Cha Cha Cha (at McCarthy's) are the same as at the original Haight Street branch: fried potatoes served with aioli and marinated mushrooms in garlic broth. Alternatively walk a few feet to **Charanga ⚓**; or a few blocks to **Timo's** – both worthy tapas competitors.

Vying for the attention of local Italophiles is **Vineria**, a stylish trattoria/wine bar serving the likes of pumpkin-stuffed ravioli. Only Italian food lovers in the know or those with sensitivity to high emissions of garlic are likely to sniff out the teensy, eight-table **La Villa Poppi** where chef-owner Greg Sweeting does all the prepping, cooking, and dishwashing himself. You'll feel doted upon. Equally unpretentious is *Woodward's Garden [→107] which has to be the best-kept secret in the city. Tender grilled pork chops and a tiny shuttered dining room are the last details you'd expect on this seedy block beneath the freeway.

Thank goodness the media have been diverted from *Herbivore [→117], one of the city's few outstanding vegetarian outposts. Sit up front, watch the passers-by, and savour a carrot juice and low-cal falafel.

Who will rise above the pack old and new in the year 2000? All bets are on **Foreign Cinema**. Foodies and filmgoers have been atwitter over the movie-house bistro since its debut in August 99. Foreign films are screened all year round in an outdoor brick court-yard and accompanied by French vittles (like foie gras atop grilled fruit).

restaurants: east of south van ness

The industrial area east of South Van Ness forms a second restaurant enclave which now claims San Francisco's hottest and most glam new eateries. No neighbourhood trans-formation was more dra-matic than this one during the Internet boom. One day Bryant and Mariposa Streets comprised a vast wasteland of abandoned mayonnaise factories and hollow homes, the next, those buildings had be-come the epitome of industrial chic, filled with TV, advertising and pub-lishing offices, funded by digital largesse. The neighbourhood now has a peaceful but urban hum. The crowd is more Joseph than thrift store chic, and culinary prospectors have been quick to capitalize on this demographic shift by opening ever flashier restaurants. *Gordon's House of Fine Eats [→105] may be the most hyped new member of the pack. The eclectic menu is outrageous: matzo ball soup and fried chicken on the same page as seared-halibut-with-cactus salad. *Blowfish Sushi To Die For, around the corner, is a popular haunt for clubbers seeking fuel for ambient gyrations. Must be something about the restaurant's TV moni-tors flashing Japanese cartoons or the out-there *maki* rolls. For a refined but testosterone-rich environment, vie for a seat at the 30-ft steel and

epoxy bar at **Potrero Brewing Co** and order a house-brewed lager with your hazelnut and blood orange salad. With a chef imported from the Wine Country, the menu is the antithesis of typical pub grub.

Two humble veterans in this crew are the *Univer-sal Café [→108] and the *Slow Club [→108]. At the former, you will feel like you're sitting on a sunny lane in southern Spain as you nibble the newfangled flatbreads (eg topped with portobellos, lemon zest, creamer potatoes, and radish sprouts). The post-industrial chic Slow Club meanwhile feels more like a cement garage. The de-signers have warmed things up with a backlit bar and open kitchen where you can watch chefs racing to rustle up Californian dish-es like rich potato gnocchi.

This east Mission hub even has its own coffee culture. Yuppies sip lattes and make cell calls from the clean, repro-vintage couches at the sprawling Starbucks-owned **Circadia** ♣, while grungy hipsters gather around rickety outdoor tables at **Atlas Café** and feed yam sandwiches to their dogs. Only four blocks apart, these two cafés represent the extreme polarities of the Mission.

cafés & taquerias

Taquerias are the neigh-bourhood's 'fast-food' spe-cialty, and competition for top billing is fierce. **Pancho Villa Taqueria** woos with a dirt-cheap combo platter of grilled prawns and steak tacos. **Taqueria Cancun** is a favourite among Latinos in the 'hood (a priceless endorsement) who prefer their burrito shells lightly grilled instead of soft like everywhere else. Burritos are unattractively soupy at **Puerto Alegre**, but the margaritas are cheap and plentiful and the place is clean and sharp, which you can't say about most of the other taquerias. Arguably the king of the burrito **La Taqueria** packs generous chunks of meat into each savoury torpedo and serves up the freshest guacamole in town. **Papalote Mexican Grill** is the newest in the bunch, offering innova-tions like grilled chicken marinated in spicy *achiote*. Offering the all-American alternative to taquerias is **Jay's Cheese Steak and Burger Joint** where steak sandwiches and burgers are made from Niman Ranch beef (read: hormone and chemical free).

Coffee shops are a neigh-bourhood staple. Sunken couches at **Café La Bohème**; a little Latin spice with your Joe at **Café Que Tal**; or a mini-library and bric-a-brac at the lesbian haven, **Red Dora's Bearded Lady Café**. People-watching galore at them all, of course.

bars & clubs

No area of San Francisco can match the sprawling Mission for sheer volume of places to get bombed. While this is the best Bay Area bar-hopping zone, certain sectors of the Mission can be downright hairy day or night.

Elite among the coolest is the ***Make-Out Room**, a giant, glowing, elegant hall insanely popular with young bohemians. It now offers typically urban local live indie rock or sparse Americana one or two nights weekly. There's sometimes a cover or a wait. Almost as modish is the lively pastiche ***Latin American Club**, the Make-Out's honorary sister-bar nearby. An intriguing blend of poetic types and your average Joe and Jane toss back all manner of blue-collar beers and stylish libations from the bar's impressive selection. Newer but gaining ground in the ongoing race for pole position is idiosyncratic **Sacrifice**, something of a Tiki-gone-techno bar where DJs pump ambient and house grooves on the weekends for the chic coterie chilling on rattan couches. The standby **Uptown** offers final refuge for the super-cool – a plain retro lounge determined to avoid the gentrified fate of nearby taverns. This includes tossing obvious newcomers a healthy serving of who-the-hell-are-you attitude.

Formerly the Mission standard for cool, the ***500 Club** still works for a casual week-night cocktail. Or if you're eager to sardine-cram in, there is a Saturday night singles-get-laid campaign. Similarly, the **Albion** and **Casanova Lounge** are no longer priority pubs amongst the übercool but both still mix a mean drink and attract hearty weekend throngs. Despite having canned their weekly live punk and garage rock, the neon-lit **Kilowatt** ✔ remains curiously popular with the artsy-pierced gang as does the tough, leathery, Harley/bike messenger haunt, **Zeitgeist**. Quietly tucked along the Mission's fringe is the aptly named **Phone Booth**, a mini – and as yet unspoiled – corner bar where a colourful cast of regulars hoist drinks in drunken camaraderie, occasionally breaking out into spontaneous singalongs.

Of the area's scant 'classy' bars, timeless ***Lone Palm** may be the nicest. Candle-lit and sultry like a Bogart flick, it packs with upscale, soigné folk and other such Mission rarities. Boasting cheap grub and few pretensions is homey **Radio Valencia**. Universally championed as the perfect first date joint, you'll get plenty of local suds on tap, casual if loud interiors, and

a live radio station spinning obscure art-rock. More Manhattan than Mission, **The Beauty Bar** (actually imported from NYC) playfully combines 50s-era hair salon decor and bar, serving whimsical potables to hipsters in barber chairs. Long, thin, and mirrored, cosy ***Doc's Clock** recalls a similar epoch for a somewhat less trendy pack of guzzlers. **Shotwell 59**'s simple booze, pool, and popcorn corner bar motif offers comparable Missionites shelter from the torrential trendy storm.

Open on to the one of the more animated blocks in the city **Blondie's Bar & No Grill** gives genuine quality freak watching and a place to sample custom martinis or chat over a microbrewed pint. New kid on the Mission block, **Amnesia**, serves microbrewed beers, to the sounds of experimental musicians and DJs. Another spot to take in some eclectic sounds is the upstairs lounge of the ***Elbo Room**, a popular bar-cum-club Mission hang-out.

🖑 directory

rainbow connection

castro & noe valley

Rainbow flags. Glistening pectorals. Tight jeans. Roving eyes. Pride. Pride. Pride. These are the building blocks of San Francisco's gayest neighbourhood. Less politically erect than in the 60s when it was the sole refuge for homosexuals in the US, today's Castro is almost 100% bacchanalian reverie. Folks come here to see and be seen. Castro and Market streets are lined with coffee houses and bars – social venues for cruising – and by dusk they're throbbing with testosterone and techno. There's no ignoring the sexual electricity. The residential streets are no less vibrant: restored Victorians dressed in light pastels.

Noe Valley, a mellow hamlet on the other side of the hill, is a sort of Castro annex, though the old working class neighbourhood recently gave way to Birkenstocked power-couples, most often seen toting kids to yoga class in minted SUVs. Brunch is prime-time in Noe Valley, if you get the drift.

day

🛍 In the Castro, it's not who you wear, but how you wear it. Clothing shops cater mostly to clubbers and body-conscious men. There's also a good and varied selection of book and record stores.

👁 Head to Mission Dolores Park [→78] to catch some rays. Also within striking distance are Corona Heights and Twin Peaks for top-notch views [→79].

night

🍸 This is gay bar central, with more meat-packing per square foot than any other district in town, plus a smattering of great people-watching cafés and a lively restaurant scene.

☆ The Castro Theatre [→126] plays a year round repertory schedule of new foreign films, mint-print Hollywood revivals, and animation programmes.

getting there

🚌 22, 24, 48
🚈 F, J, K, L, M

shopping

fashion, shoes & accessories

Virtually everything you can find Downtown – but with a hipster spin – is in the Castro. *Rolo ✔ offers two locations: one is chock full of jeans and a colourful selection of trainers; the other offers upscale designer menswear. *Citizen has an

equally diverse selection of relaxed menswear to suit all occasions. Nana stocks men's and women's trend gear from tiny rock 'n' roll T-shirts to sky-high platforms and brothel creepers, plus furry dice, and dashboard saints. *Crossroads

Trading Co has a similar selection of (slightly used) contemporary clothing, along with a fine choice of 50s–80s vintage wear. For vintage shoes to match, swing by *Body Citizen. Over the hill in Noe Valley, Rabat has cute women's

* = featured in the listings section [→88–124]

lines like Betsey Johnson and Anna Sui, plus shoes for both sexes – almost everything in the three figure category. **Designer's Club** has the copycat labels (Free People, Anthologie) as well as sexy party frocks, girlish accessories, and wacky Custo's T's. The tiny but impeccable ***Guys & Dolls Vintage** is a well-kept secret, specializing in 40s and 50s clothing with shop girls dressed to match. **Gallery of Jewels** sparkles with handcrafted jewellery, bags, and hats to top off any outfit, whichever decade's style you favour.

bath & body

Grooming is serious business in the Castro. The **Skin Zone** carries body products from around the world as well as their own soaps and oils in perfumes and flavours from jasmine to chocolate mint. **Gotham** will pierce your bod any place you dare. Afterwards you can stop in at **MMO** for some safe sex supplies. For the more genteel, Noe Valley's **Common Scents** has everything a girl could need for a pampering session, while guys can take their pick from Kiehl's coveted hair and body products.

home & gifts

Since the Castro and Noe Valley are where couples go to nest, it's no wonder the streets are lined with shops catering to the home. **Cliff's Variety** is a neighbourhood institution – drag queens hunt out feather boas and sequins, while the more practical types shop for hammers and nails. For fun, have a look in **Bauerware** where you can find any kind of drawer-pull imaginable – made from chopsticks to cherries. ***Kitty Katty's**, a toy, game, and lifestyle emporium for the devilish gal, and **Under One Roof**

books & records

If you're browsing for new and used books and records, you've come to the right area. For books, ***A Different Light** specializes in gay fiction and non-fiction, and holds regular readings by authors. It serves as a general hub for Castro neighbourhood arts and activism. Noe Valley's **Cover to Cover** has all the best-selling titles with cozy niches and an outdoor patio for reading. Down the block, **Phoenix Books** carries an envi-

provide typically 'only in San Francisco' items, the latter shop's proceeds benefiting AIDS causes.

Over in Noe Valley, **17 Reasons** carries original works by local artists with reasonable price-tags. **Echo Furniture** has everything from luscious cashmere throws to sweet-smelling soaps and scented candles. And if it's candles you're truly after, **Home's** got 'em in all sizes, as well as anything and everything adorned with the image of artist and honorary patron saint, Frida Kahlo.

able selection of secondhand art and photography books while 24th Street's specialty ***Mystery Bookstore** says it all in the name.

For aural inspiration the Castro has ***Record Finder** and ***Medium Rare Records** with hard-to-find vinyl rock, classical, and soundtracks as well as new CDs – from Maria Callas to PJ Harvey. **Street Light Records** carries all genres in all formats, as does ***Tower Records**.

eating & drinking

restaurants

The number one activity in the Castro is hanging out; the number two activity: people watching (let's be honest – it's an open air body bar). For proof, just glance into any jam-packed restaurant or café along Castro or Market Streets. Those windows were cut wide and tall for a reason. Until the late 90s, finding

a good chef in the area was about as easy as finding a virile heterosexual. Then two of the city's best restaurants, Mecca and Zodiac Club, opened up and the neighbourhood's place in the culinary pantheon was clinched. ***Zodiac Club ✓** [→107] has to be the city's oddest restaurant, at least aesthetically. It's almost

pitch black inside; tiny votives and backlit Zodiac signs barely illuminate the food. No matter – anything from the Medi-terranean menu is always amazing, the massive paella platter in particular. Sunday is the night to hit the juggernaut ***Mecca** [→108], when a drag performance complements the innovative

California menu – iced shellfish and shrimp dumplings par excellence. Cherry-stuffed quail is a sure thing at nearby Cal-French restaurant **John Frank**. Everyone, including the waiters wears black – it's that wannabe New York chic – and everyone talks loud.

After those standouts, the fine-dining options drop off dramatically: food elsewhere is more casual. On Friday nights, **2223 Restaurant & Bar** feels like a drunken gay bar mitzvah with everyone switching tables and making small talk across the way. Food tends to be stacked toward the vertical: fish on potatoes on herbs on more fish. The precarious combinations luckily taste great. At *****Chow**, the clientele is decidedly calmer; must be the dirt cheap prices and the heaped portions of fish and pasta that keep them mum. There's no flash or buzz either at **No Name Sushi** (literally, it has no name so navigate by address), just incredibly fresh sashimi and a sense that everyone there is in on one of the best kept food secrets in town. **Firewood Café** is the place to dine alone on scrumptious roast chicken and size up future dates.

Noe Valley's restaurants cater mostly to the DINKY (double income no kids) contingency, and there are a few must-tries. **Alice's** and **Eric's**, owned by the same family, serve some of the freshest, grease-free Chinese in the city, while **Hamano Sushi** is unparalleled in terms of quality (not to mention rude service). The hummus-and-pitta hit, **Fattoush** is now stealing customers from the neighbourhood's most popular weekend brunch spots **Chloe's Café**, **Savor**, and *****Miss Millie's**. And the precious culinary gem is *****Firefly** [→113] where 'home cooking' meets fusion. Innovations like veggie risotto with wild mushrooms are served in a hip Hansel and Gretel dining room tucked between apartments at the foggy tip of 24th Street.

Eyes are on you: everyone is wondering what gender you prefer and if you're available. It's a palpable *joie de vivre*. The mantra: take life by the balls and live it up.

cafés & diners

While the Castro's restaurants mostly cater to a hybrid of customers, the cafés and delis are decidedly gay. That's not to say heteros should avoid the predominantly lesbian **Baghdad Café** at 4am if they're craving eggs, pancakes, or any other form of grease. But someone may just buy you an extra cup of Joe. *****Hot 'n' Hunky** is the same story, except that the touted burgers are served in a shrine to 50s culture – Marilyn Monroe, jukebox et al. Locals have fully embraced **Blue**, where you'll find chichi diner food like gourmet cheeseburgers for inflated prices. **Caffè Luna Piena** offers prime al fresco seating in a manicured Japanese garden, a coveted spot on Sundays, when the almond French toast is in high demand. **Café Flore**'s outdoor seats are even better for people watching; food isn't a strength but no one seems to care. Noe Valley also has some decent cafés and diners. *****Barney's** was named SF's best burger joint by local papers (lots of non-meat choices); and **Herb's Fine Food** looks like the sort of diner Seinfeld would gather the gang. Over at **Diamond Corner Café** you'll want to adopt the cherubic servers and steal their recipe for gingerade – a lemonade with a spicy jolt.

delis & food shops

The **Harvest Market** is the perfect pit stop for groceries and a snack. Serve yourself at the salad and sushi bar and perch on the split-log benches. Or head for **AG Ferrari Foods**, which specializes in homemade Italian deli items (try the risotto balls). **Noe Valley Bakery & Bread Co** comes up with unusual flavours for its fresh baked goods: lemon-almond scones and chocolate and cherry bread. For another sugar-fix try *****Sweet Inspiration**, a dessert café-cum-bakery, or **Chocolate Covered Sweets & Gifts** where you can fill up one of their darling lunch boxes from the dizzying display of chocolates – from insect-shapes to top-of-the-line Godiva.

bars & clubs

The Castro and Noe Valley's watering holes reflect the numerous cliques of the thriving, party-hearty gay community and the yuppie infatuation with Irish pubs. Of the 'boy bars', *Midnight Sun is often the most active. The multiple monitors show a steady stream of gay iconography – Ab Fab, Ricky Martin, etc – while butch college-age kids in tight $100 sweaters play pick-up. Equally cluttered with video screens and fresh meat, **Metro** seems most happening on sunny weekends when the spacious balcony fills up. **The Bar on Castro** is a mildly pretentious lounge where gym-toned club boys take in some techno before their imminent all-night club exploits. Next port of call is often **The Café**, a popular lesbian hang-out which is also surprisingly the area's only pure dance club. There is no cover charge and the popular Sunday T-Dance [→124] assures steady traffic.

Detour ↘ reigns supreme among Castro meat markets. Hunky bartenders pour 'em stiff for near-naked go-go boys, clubsters, and cradle-robbing older dudes hoping to lure a bronzed trophy home. Though they've dropped the politically incorrect tagline, 'for men of colour and men who appreciate them', the **Pendulum**'s theme remains the same. It can hop on

weekends and does well with the snooker set.

The so-called 'Heart of the Castro', breezy **Harvey's** is essentially a so-so bar/restaurant combo with weekly drag revues for yupsters and curious onlookers, but the people watching is world class from the window seats. **Josie's Cabaret & Juice Joint**, besides serving a mean smattering of smoothies, is also SF's premier gay- and sketch-comedy club and often deservedly packed.

Daddy's is ground zero for the mostly 30+, leather and beer crowd, but it is still a far warmer place than you might expect. Likewise for **The Edge**, an easy-going and rarely crowded booze hall where an older gay crew chats over a few frosty ones; and sleepy **Uncle Bert's Place** with its very neighbourhood-ish back barbecue. **Twin Peaks** serves a typically 50 and up, mellower gang – though younger folks are discovering the upstairs balcony. But of all the Castro's kitsch-free hangouts, *The Pilsner Inn** might be the coolest. It's got that simple, gay corner-bar appeal with a huge patio and good boozing company.

Lining Market Street between Church and Sanchez are three hetero haunts. **Expansion Bar** is a homey

little pinball and pool dive catering to serious boozers with a moderate influx of slumming hipsters on the weekends. Discovered by the frat crew, *Lucky 13's ↑ king-of-cool heyday has passed but the bi-level bar still rages on weekends and boasts an awesome New Wave jukebox. Mere steps away, subterranean *Café du Nord is a classy and plush old time speakeasy with red velvet surroundings where you can take in all manner of live swing, afro-jazz, or salsa whilst dining or sipping chic cocktails among the equally chic elite.

Sleepy Noe Valley all but shuts down at night. The underrated **Dubliner** has curt but kind Irish barmaids, often empty back booths, and a mean Guinness. The **Rovers Inn** is more often than not slightly less hectic save occasional drunken outbursts at the foosball table, while **The Peak's**, a decidedly down-and-out joint, has a giant open barbecue, on which patrons roast their own meat as waitresses keep the pitchers coming.

→ map & directory

castro & noe valley

🎵 directory

18

Dubliner *C4*
3838 24th Street
826-2279

Echo Furniture *C5*
3769 24th Street
643-3845

The Edge *A2*
4149 18th Street
863-4027

Eric's *C6*
1500 Church Street
282-0919 $

Expansion Bar *B1*
2126 Market Street
863-4041

Fattoush *B5*
1361 Church Street
641-0678 $–$$

Firefly *A5*
4288 24th Street
821-7652 $$

Firewood Café *A2*
4248 18th Street
252-0999 $

Gallery of Jewels *B5*
4089 24th Street
285-0626

Gotham *A2*
3991 17th Street
701-1970

Guys & Dolls Vintage *C5*
3789 24th Street
285-7174

Hamano Sushi *B5*
1332 Castro Street
826-0825 $$–$$$

Harvest Market *B2*
2285 Market Street
626-0805

Harvey's *A2*
500 Castro Street
431-4278

Herb's Fine Food *B4*
3991 24th Street
826-8937 $

Home *B5*
4028 24th Street
824-8585

Hot 'n' Hunky *A2*
4039 18th Street
621-6365 $

John Frank *B1*
2100 Market Street
503-0333 $$

Josie's Cabaret & Juice Joint *B2*
3583 16th Street
861-7933

Kitty Katty's *B2*
3804 17th Street
864-6543

Lucky 13 *B1*
2140 Market Street
487-1313

Mecca *C1*
2029 Market Street
621-7000 $$–$$$

Medium Rare Records *B2*
2310 Market Street
255-7273

Metro *B2*
3600 16th Street
703-9750

Midnight Sun *A2*
4067 18th Street
861-4186

Miss Millie's *A5*
4123 24th Street
285-5598 $–$$

MMO *A2*
4084 18th Street
621-1188

Mystery Bookstore *A5*
4175 24th Street
282-7444

Nana *B2*
2276 Market Street
861-6262

Noe Valley Bakery & Bread Co *B5*
4073 24th Street
550-1405

No Name Sushi *B1*
314 Church Street
no phone $–$$

The Peak's *A5*
1316 Castro Street
826-0100

Pendulum *A2*
4146 18th Street
863-4441

Phoenix Books *B4*
3850 24th Street
821-3477

The Pilsner Inn *B1*
225 Church Street
621-7058

Rabat *B5*
4001 24th Street
282-7861

Record Finder *B2*
258 Noe Street
431-4443

Rolo *A2*
450 Castro Street
626-7171

Rovers Inn *B5*
4026 24th Street
821-7861

Savor *B5*
3913 24th Street
282-0344 $–$$

17 Reasons *B5*
3961 24th Street
206-1717

Skin Zone *A3*
575 Castro Street
626-7933

Street Light Records *A2*
2350 Market Street
(3979 24th Street)
282-3550

Sweet Inspiration *B2*
2239 Market Street
621-8664 $

Tower Records *B2*
2280 Market Street
431-4443

Twin Peaks *A2*
401 Castro Street
864-9470

2223 Restaurant & Bar *B1*
2223 Market Street
431-0692 $$–$$$

Uncle Bert's Place *A2*
4086 18th Street
431-8616

Under One Roof *A3*
549 Castro Street
252-9430

Zodiac Club *B1*
718 14th Street
626-7827 $$

love 'n' haight

Haight-Ashbury hit the map in the 60s during the 'Summer of Love' when rents were cheap, drugs plentiful, and bands played for free in Golden Gate Park [→78]. Fast forward 30 odd years and the neighbourhood has tied its shoelaces, brushed its hair, and chinos now outnumber bell-bottoms. But the Haight is still hippy dippy. Dreadlocked urchins continue to hock their 'magic herbs' on the street and admire one another's hammer and sickle tattoos. And guitar-toting troubadours still sing Bob Dylan protest songs, though these days they're more likely to spend their change on Ben & Jerry ice-cream than on mind-expanding drugs. Defiance is still in the air, but the focus has shifted to the Lower Haight (past Divisadero), where Gen X slackers prowl the corridors and talk revolution in smoky beer bars.

A more inconspicuous set prefer the dog-and-coffee scene in neighbouring Cole Valley, which offers just enough commercial activity to convenience locals.

day

The city's former hippy bastion is a haven for vintage boutiques and modern-day head shops. Shopping is mostly restricted to Upper Haight Street.

Ogle 'Painted Ladies' in Alamo Square [→71]; satisfy nature pangs in Golden Gate Park [→78]; or find out more about science and fine arts at the park's museums – the California Academy of Sciences [→74], MH De Young Museum [→72], and the Asian Art Museum [→72].

night

This area has mostly funky and ethnic restaurants, plus great morning-after brunch spots. The bar scene shifts from Upper to Lower Haight after hours.

getting there

6, 7, 24, 43, 66, 71

N

more shops | restaurants | cafés

shopping

fashion & shoes

Shop owners in the Haight are as attentive to their sound systems as to their merchandise. Most shops proffer a high-octane blend of streetwear and club garb. For the best interpretations, step into **Behind the Post Office**, with its stacks of popular Michael Stars' stretchy T's in Electric Kool Aid Acid colours and multiple styles. **Ragwood**, **Betty's**, and **Backseat Betty's** also dish up well-priced, urban girl gear, like cropped lavender cargos, pink poplin pedal pushers, rose-appliquéd faded jeans (cheap-and-cheerful homage to a certain fabu designer), and sassy little 'Hello Satan' T-shirts. For pretty, one-of-a-kind pieces, visit **Duchess**, where designers Pedro Olmo and Keri White whip up wrap skirts, simple dresses, and yummy linen frock coats – at perfectly digestible prices.

Taxi's attractive pieces by French imports Paul & Joe and luscious leather items by the Wrights seduce shop-aholics from all over.

* = featured in the listings section [→88–124]

Similarly grown up are the fashions at *Villains Vault, with well-cut separates for both sexes, sporty little pieces by the likes of William B, Helmut Lang, and G-Star and sleek-but-chunky leather shoes by Costume National et al. Looking for something a tad harder-edged? While searching the racks at *Villains ¶, one shopper commented, 'this is the best morning-after ravewear I've ever seen.' And so it is. But lots of non-ravers flock here to cop a bit of urban attitude (baggy pants by Mooks and Kikwear) and gain instant street cred with a pair of purple Pumas. At *Luichiny, slip into a pair of Italian-made sky-high platforms and other X-treme styles, or visit that mad cobbler of the absurd, *John Fluevog, for exaggerated Mary-Janes. If it's unusual trainers you're searching for, the selection at *Shoe Biz is vast and colourful and includes funky slip-on styles by Royal. And don't forget to pop your head into Hoys Sports – where professional athletes come to get shod.

books & music

A fixture for over 20 years, the **Booksmith** keeps a rich and quirky selection of literature and non-fiction (and hosts popular author readings), while revolutionary tracts and conspiracy theories abound at **Bound Together Anarchist Book Collective**. Everything ever published seems to be stocked at **Anubis Warpus**, which also has a tattoo parlour located in the back.

But music is the Haight's main muse. A bowling alley in a former life, *Amoeba Music is the mother of all record stores, with an awesome array of new and used CDs, tapes, DVDs, eight-tracks, and vinyl. Truly a store of last resort – if you can't find it here it might not exist. A couple of times a week touring artists stop by to warm up with a pre-gig set. Bargain music hunters also make a pit stop at *Recycled Records to snap up secondhand jazz, soul, and rock vinyl. Their vintage stock encompasses sounds mostly from the 50s to the early 70s. Vinyl junkies, meanwhile, know *Mobster as the source of new and used rock, jazz, soul, and hip-hop records, as well as CDs. For 'roots' music (nothing too modern) trek down to *Jack's Record Cellar, where jazz, R'n'B, pop vocalists, and country crooners are celebrated – including many rare and hard-to-find faves – almost exclusively on vinyl. And at *Groove Merchant acid jazz reigns supreme.

vintage clothing

The Haight boasts the largest concentration of previously owned garments in the city. For vintage hoarders, the larger emporiums – *Aardvark's Odd Ark, Buffalo Exchange, and *Wasteland – reward patience with a pair of bright orange low-slung pants or a James Dean-era leather jacket. Take in the windows at *Held Over, where the brilliant dioramas have caused pedestrian traffic jams. Calmer (and pricier) are the more selective stores that specialize in party clothes, swing dance outfits, and formal wear. La Rosa has estate clothing and vintage accessories suitable for weddings and Titanic parties, while **Martini Mercantile** and **Martini Men's Shop** stock pretty frocks and skirts from the 30s to the 60s and suits, shoes, hats, and custom-made zoot suits for retro-men. At **Ambiance** old and new pieces with a similar aesthetic hang together.

one-of-a-kind

What would the Haight be without a couple of head shops? **Ashbury Tobacco Center** offers legal smokes with the bongs, pipes, and other implements of euphoria. **Pipe Dreams** has much of the same, along with glow-in-the-dark psychedelic posters.

Conveniently located side by side are **SFO Snowboarding** and **FTC Skateboarding**, sister shops known for the depth of the inventory and expertise of their staff. Rent or buy a board, and stock up on sought-after sportswear. In the Lower Haight, *Used Rubber USA turns yesterday's trashed truck innertubes into today's happening bags, wallets, and organizers oozing with style. For something equally novel, make an appointment at **Dishes Delmar**, a technicolour fantasia of 50s and 60s American dinnerware and glazed pottery displayed in a splendiferous Victorian setting.

The Haight looks like a gypsy wonderland with young boho's re-enacting an era past. In many cases the restaurant scene is equally mischievous.

eating & drinking

restaurants

Chefs in Haight-Ashbury aren't interested in the status quo (ie Cal-cuisine and stark decor) because they know their patrons – cash-challenged cool kids, many fresh out of college – aren't either. Duck into **Kan Zaman** and you may confuse the scene for a bacchanalian orgy. The place is always a crush of young drunken bodies seated cross-legged on the floor. Patrons devour heaps of Middle-Eastern meze, guzzle Greek wine, and puff on fruity tobacco from hookah pipes, while belly dancers gyrate above them (Wed–Sat). **Citrus Club**'s daring is far more subtle: the chef replaces oil with citrus juices in his Pan-Asian specials (Japanese buckwheat noodles in spicy lime and coconut dressing). Both restaurants are bangs for the buck, which is true of many in the locale.

*Cha Cha Cha is the neighbourhood's golden child and diners will wait up to two hours (aided by pitchers of sangria) for a seat. The hot (literally) dining room, decorated with Santeria altars and massive tropical plants, is a perfect complement to the Caribbean tapas. Ethnic options don't stop there. Group dining is advised at **Massawa**, where *sambusa* (samosa) and other Ethiopian classics, such as curried stew on an enormous pancake of *injera*, are served family-style. Eat with your fingers and wash it down with an African beer.

Dine on the secret patio in back at **Zare** where the chef tweaks American cuisine ever-so-slightly with adaptations like hormone-free buffalo and venison burgers. On the same block **Asqew Grill** unites a mishmash of cultures on 6- or 12-inch skewers over the grill.

Flourishing in Cole Valley, an uppercrust annex of the Haight, is ***EOS [→112]** one of the city's best and most refined restaurants. Inside the brightly coloured dining room, wide-eyed patrons fawn over artistic fusion creations and an unparalleled selection of wine. **Zazie** ✔, by contrast, is classic Provence nuzzled into a softly lit storefront. No flash here, just prosaic charm: an antique armoire, vintage French posters, checkered floors. For a more illicit meal, settle in at old-timer **Kezar**: lights are down so low, you can barely see the inspired pub grub. And, because this is San Francisco, and because this enclave must be self-sustaining, there has to be a bustling sushi bar, or two in this case: the charming **Hama-Ko Sushi** feels like someone's steamy basement kitchen, while the more mainstream **Grandeho's Kamekyo** is packed to the gills with upwardly mobile Cole Valley-ites.

Underappreciated but as boho as Upper Haight, the Lower Haight claims two of the city's best Thai and Indian restaurants. **Thep Phanom** has a line at all hours while at the equally refined ***Indian Oven [→114]**, tandooris made in a wood-burning clay oven steal the show.

cafés

Cafés in the Haight probably outnumber restaurants. That's because the civic-minded young people need those home-away-from-home hang-outs where they can linger and debate the state of the nation with their mouths full of cheap but inspired grub – all without reprisal. ***Kate's Kitchen** wins the blue ribbon in this category. Hip-hop music meets soul food (scallion-cheese biscuits and deep-fried cornmeal) in this Lower Haight hotspot. **All You Knead** and **Pork Store Café** tie for second place. Plenty of tattoos and nose rings at both. The former serves a heavenly macadamia nut pancake at their all day breakfast/brunch, the latter an abundance of hash browns. **Spaghetti Western**'s Pesto Scram egg (or tofu) dish gives the restaurant a solid third place standing. The decor – Elvis effigies, cacti, guns – is almost as flavourful. If all you need is fuel in massive quantities, hit **Squat & Gobble Too**. If all you want is eye candy and socializing, **Crepes on Cole** is the place. **Bean There** may be the best coffee shop in all of San Francisco (comfy chairs, massive windows, a tree-lined street); order a French pressed coffee and a bagel, then space-out – the favourite pastime of Haight residents.

Great take-out is equally important in the Haight.

Rosamunde Sausage Grill pays homage to the banger – Italian sausage to Hungarian *kolbas*. **Escape from New York Pizza** serves slices of its pesto pie 'til 2am while **Ali Baba's Cave** and **Truly Mediterranean** compete for falafel customers – the

latter is the hands-down winner. Eat in or take away at the new **Burgermeister**, specialist in gourmet burgers and milkshakes, stick to the classic burrito at **Zona Rosa** (which also has tables), or order a sandwich from **Big Sherm's** blackboard.

bars & clubs

Those seeking the 67 spirit of peace, love, and understanding on legendary Haight Street will find only cheesy head shops and leftover Deadheads begging for beer money, but come to this long, strange strip with a thirst for eclectic and lively bar crawling and you won't be disappointed.

Bike messengers and other pierced folk in combat boots love the grittier Lower Haight where swigging cheap beer and trashing yuppie culture are your best bets for blending in. Home to the tattoo and 'tude crew is neon-lit **Molotov ✔**. Wicked cocktails more than compensate for the lack of warm smiles. The few remaining hippies on the block saunter into *Nickie's BBQ** for all night whirlin' and twirlin' to Grateful Dead mixes, world beats, and deep funk, while those yearning for something more progressive, jam-pack the dark and deafening **Top** where first-class local DJs spin techno, ambient, and jungle wax for hipsters in manic motion. Misunderstood goths, meanwhile, knock back red wine in warped

chairs beneath the melting ceilings and dripping mirrors in cavernous and whimsical *Noc Noc**. *Toronado** has something like 120 different beers, with ales from Algeria, stouts from Scotland, and fruity microbrews from Marin County.

Of the Upper Haight's many dives, none is better than *Gold Cane**, where gin-blossoming barflies and twenty-something workers drink or toss dice together. Runner-up is **Murio's Trophy Room**, a spacious and homey joint that floods with cool cats on weekends but retains its seedy charm most week nights. Grimier still is the **Club Boomerang**, notable mainly for its cheap beer and absurd quantity of live music. Somewhat misplaced and usually none-too-packed, **Trax** is the Haight's resident gay and lesbian dive where the vibe is refreshingly amiable. *Persian Aub Zam Zam** is open on Bruno's whim. You must follow Bruno's strict rules to get your gin (NEVER vodka) martini. Expect to be thrown out on your first few attempts to get in. At

the impossibly hip *Club Deluxe** skilled swing dance revivalists in vintage zoot suits get lit on Bombay Sapphire martinis and jump to live neo-40s acts.

UK and Irish pub fever runs rampant. In the Lower Haight, Eirephiles and homesick Irish head for intimate and cozy **An Bodhran** for well poured Murphy's and spirited conversation with the lads, while even rowdier *Mad Dog in the Fog** packs in the Anglo hooligans for satellite footy matches, rowdy pub quizzes, and authentically greasy pub eats. In the Upper Haight, a cleaner cut preppy crew dig the swankier and tamer **Martin Macks** and have now taken to even cleaner **Hobson's Choice**, a so-called 'Victorian Punch House'. *Finnegan's Wake**, in Cole Valley, however, is primo for those seeking the familial, quasi-Dublin vibe.

♪ directory

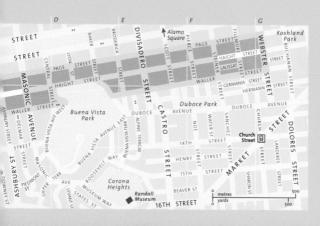

purple hayes

It's typical of San Francisco that as soon as two or three streets acquire some shops and a soupçon of cachet, they instantly become a 'neighbourhood' with a moniker. Such is the case with Hayes Valley which has a few blocks of retail fever. As you take in the new boutiques, bars, and hair salons, or one of the regular Friday evening free-for-all block parties, it's hard to remember that this was once the stomping ground of pimps, prostitutes, and drug dealers. The catalyst for change came from an act of nature rather than legislation, when the earthquake in 89 brought down the overhead freeway that had shrouded the area in gloom. Businesses blossomed and gentrification followed, and not a moment too soon for the politicos and culture vultures of neighbouring Civic Center, whose post-meeting and pre-opera gathering spots used to be limited to one or two dubious dives.

day

📖 Young designers, avant-garde artists, and ultra-hip clothiers crowd two blocks of Hayes Street (bet. Gough & Laguna Sts).

👁 Photo opportunities include the 'Painted Ladies' in Alamo Square [→71], City Hall [→70], and the War Memorial Opera House [→71].

night

🍽 Haute cuisine rules the night-time scene but more casual places and a cluster of bars ensure variety.

☆ The Civic Center, home to numerous theatres and music venues, is also the base for SF Ballet [→129], SF Opera [→130], and SF Symphony [→130].

getting there

🚌 5, 6, 7, 19, 21, 31, 42, 47, 49, 66, 71
🚈 F, J, K, L, M, N
🅑 Civic Center

shopping

fashion

Given an hour (and a credit card), you can easily get outfitted on Hayes Street for the evening of your choice – be it fine dining, attending the opera, or getting down with the DJs.

Feet first. Hayes Valley veteran *Gimme Shoes has all the looks, from retro trainers to high-end heels by Ann Demeulemeester, Dries Van Noten, Clergerie, Costume National, and legions more.

Next door, *Bulo's more eccentric collection of Italian and English designers includes creations such as platform sneaker pumps. At the top of the sartorial heap is the newest kid on the block, Deborah Hampton. This ultra-talented former associate of designer Michael Kors has the clean and sophisticated look perfected, with impeccably tailored dresses, coats, and skirts in urban

shades of grey, ivory, black, and navy and thick cable-knit cashmeres. A few feet away, Darbury Stenderu's ▲ slippery velvet dresses, shirts, and wraps attract artists, neo-hippies, and hair stylists of both sexes with acid-trip colours that are anything but neutral. Cheerful, edgy, and easily priced separates for day and night emerge from Zeni Wear (love the beaded fringe-cuffed William B)

* = featured in the listings section [→88–124]

and *Nomads, which outfits the hombres in trousers from Adriano Goldschmied and big herringbone shirts from Catherine Joseph. And at Haseena there are burnt-velvet slip dresses for days to pair with Chinese dragon platforms that show off those silver painted toenails.

Clubbin' boys get head-to-toe treatment at 3Sixty, with hats, trainers, and comfortable skater-inspired togs, while She is stacked with an impressive array of Custo's ecstatic illustrated T-shirts as well as dress options both sporty and slinky. A kind of showroom for local designers, Asphalt hangs its street and clubland creations on gently swaying ropes. And if it's defunct designers you're searching for, vintage gold mine 560 Hayes is the bomb – swoop in for a 50s cocktail dress, cowboy boots, or Mondrian-print plastic handbag.

accessories

If you're looking for a pre-digital timepiece, strap one on at *Zeitgeist, where the Omegas, Elgins, Gruens, and Rolexes have been lovingly restored by a master watchmaker who also keeps a stellar selection of estate jewellery. Anything but vintage is the deal at Velvet da Vinci, where contemporary pieces range from pretty to provocative (picture a mosquito suspended in rare Baltic amber). The African Outlet imports exotic Berber and Tuareg jewellery as well as Senegalese textiles, Zulu spears, and Kenyan masks. And over at *Mapuche the wall covered in old leather-working tools is almost as lovely as the edgy purses, bags, chokers, and wrist cuffs created by artists-turned-designers Miguel Muñoz Wilson and Damarise Contreras Vrandecic. The 'Long Star' (a black bag with red inlaid star) is quite the rage among fashion fiends on both coasts. Finally, up your sensual quotient at *Alla Prima, where you'll find a tempting selection of designer lingerie.

interiors & antiques

*Alabaster's rich and varied collection of all things ivory (ostrich eggs, Italian alabaster lamps) is complemented by objects of colour and brilliance, such as framed African butterflies and elegant hammered rings of 24K gold or platinum. Across the street at *Zonal rust-kissed bedframes exist in harmony with new chairs covered in clubby leather. Also mixing old and new, Worldware's 'chateau clutter' look is expressed with eco-friendly 620-thread-count bed linens, old water pitchers from Provence, flea market paintings, and scented soaps from France. Back in the new world, Polanco

represents established and worthy up-and-coming artists from Mexico, whose work is mingled with a truly pristine collection of antique and contemporary crafts – from santos figures and retablos to a case full of wonderful silver jewellery. For a spot of antiquing, head down Gough Street and along Market Street and you'll uncover deco- and mid-century splendour (Vintage Modern, Modern Era Decor), kitsch (Other Shop), relics from the wild west (One-Eyed Jack's), and piles of plunder from bygone eras (Beaver Brothers Antiques et al) at stores that double as prop rental resources.

books & records

Richard Hilkert is the kind of cozy endangered bookstore that makes you weary of 'dot-com'. The carefully curated collection includes books on interior design and architecture, as well as new and used fiction, belles lettres, and children's books. At the other end of Hayes Street, *Borderlands specializes in the hair-raising, with old and new science fiction,

fantasy, and horror by the masters of menace. Also at opposite ends of the block and spectrum are Star Classics, where audiophiles browse for classical, jazz, and Latin sounds, under the gaze of divas as diverse as Bartoli and Barbra; and BPM, a merchant of the latest vinyl doubling as a live chat room for local DJs.

eating & drinking

restaurants

The only people that used to eat in this district were employees of nearby city agencies or tony mink-and-sequin patrons of the opera and symphony halls. Proximity was of the essence and people took what they could get. The area's urban renaissance, however, has enticed risk-taking restaurateurs to move in and food-lovers now come out of their way to dine here. Most restaurants

fall into one of two categories: palatial and exorbitant, or hip and pricey. *Jardinière [→106] eclipses the first – foodies adore gossiping about this place. Can Traci des Jardins compete with the 'big boys'? Absolutely. Even the 'old boys' approve of her lobster strudel served to the sounds of live jazz, beneath that gilded, domed ceiling. Reservations are scarce so if you're spurned, consider

Ovation at the Opera which sneaked onto the palatial scene last year when new owners revamped the French menu but left the opulent decor intact. *Hayes Street Grill [→116] is yet another option in this category, the sort of conservative establishment which can do no wrong. The kitchen turns out some of the city's most perfect mesquite- grilled seafood – swordfish to tuna – depending on the season.

The blue bloods, meanwhile, are starting to take notice of the area's trendsetters. At *Zuni Café [→109] sun-kissed diners seated along the giant front window get a kick out of being on display. Everyone seems to be sipping a pink cocktail (ordered at the copper bar) and pealing with laughter. Amazing that after 20 years it's still a scene: even the food – canonized Mediterranean fare – is still innovative. Food at **Absinthe** ✓, however, struggles to draw attention away from the beautiful belle époque detailing: burgundy velvet curtains, rattan chairs, a stamped-tin ceiling. Enjoy the set from the bar, then walk over to **Piaf's** for a pristine French meal (escargots in Champagne) and boisterous, live renditions of Edith Piaf covers, and cabaret on Friday and Saturday nights. Patrons also create the buzz at *Suppenkuche. This casual eatery with 5-star German food feels like a Munich boarding house (bench tables, low ceilings, and take-your-shoes-off joviality). Best of all, you don't leave feeling like you've just eaten an entire heifer soaked in beer and cream – the chef even has a light touch with the Wiener schnitzel.

Some trendsetters are quieter than others. **Indigo**, for example, is passed unnoticed every day by most Gough Street commuters. Only a splash of blue light draws the eye to this tiny restaurant. Sophisticated diners rest against velour banquettes in preparation for chef John Gilbert's spry

New American dishes such as wild boar-cranberry sausage with succotash. At *Carta [→113], another sleepy spot, chef Rob Zaborny focuses on a different national cuisine (Belgian, Mexican, Brazilian etc) every month. Gimmicky perhaps, but he's so talented and does such extensive research that he pulls it off. Zaborny should, however, lay off the Brazilian for Hayes Valley is San Francisco's Brazilian culinary seat. **Canto do Brasil** is the place to go for fried plantains and authentic feijoada. However, for a Californian spin on the often heavy South American fare, settle in at **Terra Brazilis**. It wasn't until Terra's debut in 99 that the city's yuppie population took an interest in the cooking style. Here dishes like curried shellfish stew are paired with an erudite selection of international wines and whimsical decor befitting the area.

*Millennium [→117] is the perfect spot for a romantic evening with the vegetarian in your life. Housed in the Abigail Hotel, the restaurant even offers a package including a meal and a swanky suite for two. If all else fails, there is always classic Italian at **Caffè delle Stelle** or greaseless Chinese at **Eliza's**. You won't be let down at either, but the titillation factor won't be off the charts.

cafés & delis

Cafés and delis in this neighbourhood are universally quirky. At Belgian coffee house **FRJTZ** you can get your tea leaves, tarot cards, and palms read while waiting for soup, salad, a focaccia sandwich, or Belgian fries. **Moishe's Pippic Inc** is a Jewish deli where every item has a namesake in the Midwest (eg The Michigan Avenue, their bagel and lox combo). *Baristi* are gruff at **Momi Toby's Revolution Café**, the quintessential coffee house replete with board games, books, and dishevelled characters. **Powell's Place** feels like it was plucked out of Mississippi and dropped on Hayes Street – the fried chicken is magical. **Flipper's** is a great burger joint with meat, chicken, and veggie 'garden' varieties by the dozen. Hungry opera-goers will drop into **Vicolo Pizzeria**, a glamorized shack near the War Memorial Opera House [→71], for a piece of the acclaimed corn-meal crust pizza, while **Tartine Café Français** is a French linen closet where you'll want to get ensconced.

bars

Most local bars line impossibly cute Hayes Street and cater to a relaxed mix of amiable young couples, trendy artists, and finely suited older folk out for a night of Mozart and

Merlot. **Absinthe** is a lush slice of 20s elegance, an ornate upscale brasserie serving Cabernets and a famous mint-infused cocktail. Similarly chic is the ***Hayes & Vine Wine Bar**, a surprisingly unpretentious sip spot with an extensive selection of vintages, perfect for a pre- or post-sym-phony visit. Even more well-bred is **Stars**, a fancy, lively, and pricey restaurant-cocktail lounge combo where those with fat wallets sample from the top shelf at the city's longest bar. Intimate and dimly lit, **Marlena's** pours cocktails for the older gay and drag queen set, while **Place Pigalle** furnish-es libations for the young creative collective who chat over friendly pool or critique the rotating art displays. **The Orbit Room** attracts budding writers by day and mod kids by night, while **Bahia Cabana** is a slice of Miami Vice where Latin hombres in white suits lambada the noche away.

🏷 directory

hayes valley & the civic center

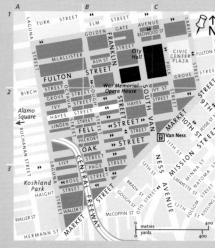

haute heights

pacific heights

Strolling through the tree-lined streets of Pacific Heights – non-fat, decaf latte, or soy chai tea in hand – world hunger, global warming, and civil strife seem as distant as the days of disco or affordable housing. Always a privileged and protected enclave, this wealthy hilltop area, with its million dollar houses and views, was spared much of the devastation that followed the 1906 earthquake, and today boasts more mansions per city block than any other 'hood. While some come to swoon over the charming Victorian houses, the truth is most come to shop, to see, and to be seen.

Pacific Heights proper encompasses a fairly wide area including Japantown, but upper Fillmore Street is its main retail aorta and lifeblood. In recent years a charming and quirky mix of shops has sprung up, many catering to the pedigreed and somewhat homogeneous population who pay extraordinary rents for studio apartments so they can call this neighbourhood home.

day

Though it's a relatively short stretch of about eight blocks, Fillmore Street has all the fixings to fill a shopping bag – from of-the-moment fashions to offbeat furnishings and home decor.

When it's time for a break indulge in an impromptu picnic at Alta Plaza or Lafayette Parks or some serious relaxation at the Kabuki Hot Springs & Spa [→84]. For an insider's view of a 'painted lady' head to Haas Lilienthal House [→76] and for some ultra-modern architecture take a look at St Mary's Cathedral [→71].

night

Have a grown-up cocktail to the sounds of smooth jazz or venture into one of the numerous intimate eateries – but be prepared to say good night by midnight. Pacific Heights shuts up early.

☆ Cinema options include AMC Kabuki 8 Theatres (1881 Post Street) and Clay Theatre [→126]; all types of music can be heard at the Fillmore [→132], while the Boom Boom Room [→132] is a magnet for blues lovers.

getting there

🚌 1, 2, 3, 22, 24, 38

shopping

fashion

Even if you plan to 'just look' during your Fillmore crawl, bring plenty of cash. By the time you end up at Japantown for sushi, you'll probably have acquired enough shopping bags to open your own small boutique.

The award for freshness goes straight to **Annies**, a joint venture of two clothes horses who have their fingers pressed firmly on the racing pulse of fashion, with an especially good eye for funky fabrics and flattering

shapes. Their cheerful store overflows with Rozae Nichols' trendy drawstring skirts, hand-knit Souchi sweaters, Chaiken & Capone jeans, Phare frocks, and their own house line of frothy cashmere. If price

* = featured in the listings section [→88–124]

is no object, brace yourself for the very determined salesfolk at **Cielo** for a peek at the latest collections from Ann Demeulemeester, Dries Van Noten, Strenesse, and others, and ogle the small but smouldering selection of shoes and boots by the same designers. Sporty separates by Jenne Maag and the Chanel of the streets – Katayone Adeli – line the racks at **Zoe**. And locally based chain **Bebe** has the club-kitten-morning-after looks down to a T. For choices from slinky to sweetly slutty, check out the Victorian bordello-chic ambiance of *****Betsey Johnson ✔** where tatty faux-lizard evening dresses hang next to rose-patterned skirts and cardigans that even your mother would love. To go under all that, **Toujours Lingerie** sells stockings, garters, camisoles, and sweet nothings both stretchy and lacy, as well as soft and sensible chenille robes. And the latest outpost of *****Gimme Shoes**, the city's premier shoe palace, offers addictive foot candy from Miu Miu, Dries, Espace, Costume National, and many many more.

It's virtually impossible to walk through Pacific Heights without getting a case of mansion-envy. Console yourself with rich pickings from one of the many thrift stores.

one-of-a-kind

Don't even think of coming home to a pining pet without stocking up at *****George ✔**, the hippest pet shop on the planet. The collection of baked-from-scratch treats, 'good dog' towels, lucky charm collars, screen-printed bowls, and T-shirts (for bipeds) is the bomb. Another San Francisco retail landmark is **Brown Bag**, a stationery store but so much more, with citrus-coloured mesh bags, tiny satellite TV clocks from Tokyo Bay, and a plethora of miniature amusements. If you feel like a good read, settle down in the overstuffed armchairs at **Browser Books**, which keeps a lively and literate general collection.

Mother-magnet **Yountville** imports much of its

precious children's gear from France, with tiny sweaters, overalls, and other styles for coddled infants through eight-year olds.

vintage & thrift

When you think about who actually lives in Pacific Heights (new and old money intermingled on the same streets), it's clear why this 'hood boasts some of the best thrift stores in town. Barely worn shoes by Ferragamo, Blahnik, and Charles Jourdan bask in the windows of the **Victorian House**, whose profits benefit a nearby medical centre. The trophy label donations (Donna Karan, Ralph Lauren, Armani et al) at **Seconds-To-Go**, meanwhile, help supplement the scholarship fund of the local private school. Many a nearly virginal Brioni and Chanel suit have been snatched up at the Junior League's **Next-to-New Shop**, which also has a consignment boutique for those who can't quite donate outright. Twenty-somethings flock to *****Crossroads Trading Co** to exchange one season's cropped tops and boot-flared pants for the next year's similar-yet-different profiles. Down at *****Departures – From the Past** the mood is more theatrical, with vintage styles, formal attire, and creative costumes, while at **Trixie's** high-end vintage spans the gamut from the turn of the century to the early 70s.

pacific heights

interiors

From recherché to chrome cool, Pacific Heights can satisfy most design zeitgeists. With three city stores, the local branch of *****Zonal** expands its empire of nostalgia with painted metal bedframes and weathered wood tables mellowed by time, as well as a stellar collection of burnished leather chairs, beds, and sofas that are made and delivered to order. At the eponymous furniture emporium **Mike**, classic couches and chairs inspired by Jean-Michel Frank are surrounded by lamps, tables, and a cache of glitzy gifts. And *****Fillamento** is famous for its trendy-eclectic stew of post-modern office supplies, zen-inspired housewares, architect-designed dishes, furniture, and exotic body potions made from ingredients like kelp and roses.

*****Nest**, a repository of riches, tops every gift-wrapped package with a miniature bird's nest. Inside might reside white-glazed French pottery, Tin-Tin bowls, Tocca linens, crystal sconces, Moroccan tea glasses with gilded rims, and pink or yellow Chinese lanterns that fold for packing. At **Zinc Details** organic and undulating shapes and forms characterize the modern, artist-designed goods – from the Danish Moon light line to hand-wrought Japanese bud vases and dishware by local design guru Tom Bonnauro. And for over-the-top revisionist Victoriana, trek down Sacramento Street to **Shabby Chic**, whose name perfectly sums up the slip-covered couches, flea-market flower paintings, and striped poplin linens it stocks.

eating & drinking

pacific heights

restaurants

Nightlife at the top of SF's most stately neighbourhood is fairly tame. After walking their Dalmatians and bichons frisées up and down Fillmore Street, denizens rest at one of the dozen or so boutique eateries, most as charming as the Victorian homes that lord over this part of the city.

Just recently, Pacific Heights began stealing diners away from Cow Hollow's bustling commercial drag, Union Street. New restaurants like **Florio**, poised to be the best French bistro in town, and ***The Meetinghouse** [→106], a dainty gem specializing in innovative American cuisine, explain why. No one expected much from Florio, but Chef Richie Rosen's simple bistro food – particularly the moules marinières – are bowling over sceptics. The waitstaff is garrulous to the point of flirtation. The bright and friendly Meetinghouse, located in a former apothecary, could be renamed the doll house and may be the city's most adorable restaurant.

There are a few veteran restaurants that also buoy the area's reputation. Among them, the 18-year-old Cajun-Creole **Elite Café** which appeases even hipster foodies. Order the classic Bloody Mary and a plate of raw oysters from one of the handsome waiters and kick back in the high-backed wood booths. Patrons walk all the way from Russian Hill to test the grilled meats and nibble the free bruschetta at **Jackson Fillmore**. Friendly to its core, it's the sort of place you could take your parents to. **Laghi** is another old reliable; the namesake owner-chef is almost always in the kitchen ensuring quality; his risotto with red wine and black truffles will make you sigh with delight. And then there's the tiny ***Café Kati** [→112] where every night is a culinary surprise. Chef Webber believes in hybrid food, delicious crossbreeds like blackthorn cider-marinated pork with smoky grits and ginger apple chutney.

For an authentic Asian food experience, lace up your trainers and walk over to nearby Japantown. Unlike Chinatown, the food here doesn't get enough hype. Yes, there's **Sushi-A** ⌐ if you're hankering for the raw stuff but, in this part of town, sushi is the boring option. Diners, not chefs, grill tongue, tripe, and steak over communal grills at **Juban** and **Korea House**. At ***Mifune**, the area's most acclaimed noodle house, patrons wait for a table while dithering over which of the 55 types of noodles to order. **Sapporo-Ya** gets less attention but the noodles are also made fresh daily. For California-Fusion cuisine, dine at the sleek **Dot** (formerly YoYo Bistro) a new cutting-edge restaurant within the Miyako Hotel.

bars

This area is generally more concerned with quality shopping and wheatgrass smoothies than cocktails, but there are a few gems. **Frankie's Bohemian**, a consistently popular ersatz-Czech eatery/pub, resembles a respectable Eastern European corner bar – the illusion, however, is shattered only by the throngs of local thirtysomethings dropping cash on beers and 'bramborg' (piles of hash brown potatoes with various toppings). **Divisadero Ale House** draws a similar crew but for freshly tapped keg beers and slightly more casual chats. Thematically less thrilling but endearing in its timeless simplicity is **Harry's on Fillmore**, a dark and intimate little slice of yesteryear with

cafés & delis

If you don't snack you're going to run out of shopping stamina in this hilly neighbourhood. There are plenty of drop-in coffee shops, the famous ***Peet's Coffee & Tea** among them (super strong brew), but for gourmet snacks, pitstop at ***Vivande Porta Via** [→112] where a deli case takes up most of the floor and is jammed with hard-to-find Italian ingredients, seasonal breads, and modern renditions of Italian classics. Stay for an eat-in

lunch if you can grab one of the few tables. **Food Inc Trattoria** is on a par, selling expensive oils and jams in addition to all the deli items that you can take out or eat there. Yuppies swarm the tiny **Curbside Café** especially on Sunday mornings – if you don't finish the Sunday *Times* waiting in line, finish it inside while munching on California-styled fresh spinach salad with spinach pasta, pine nuts, feta cheese, and vinaigrette.

friendly old bartenders and suitably sultry blues and jazz. The new star of the area though is blues icon John Lee Hooker's **Boom Boom Room** [→132]. Granted, it lacks the time-worn soul of the older blues joints in the East Bay, but the nightly live jams with the odd greats on stage (occasionally Hooker himself), and ample dancefloor, where older Fillmore folk shake rump beside white-as-Wonderbread young couples, ranks this among the brighter area options. Strangely, the best (and arguably only) guzzling spot in Japantown is the surprisingly good time **Japantown Bowl** [→82], where kind-hearted wait-resses serve amply potent potables (and bowling pin-shaped Budweisers) to a curious cross-section of eager ball rollers.

🎧 directory

pacific heights

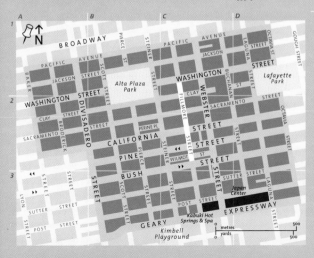

on the waterfront

marina & cow hollow

Money, money, money. That's what will be on your mind as you walk through these two neighbourhoods. Everybody looks like they've got some – just count the BMWs and Kate Spades – and every vista is worth a million bucks. Both areas are magnets for the parvenu which undoubtedly has something to do with the Bay views, bobbing sailboats, and proximity to the Golden Gate Bridge [→70]. The entire commercial infrastructure is geared toward the wealthy, but thankfully money hasn't bred gluttony. Almost every store and restaurant is petite: charming boutiques are stocked to their circa-1906 ceilings; and candle-lit eateries exude intimacy. That humility is key as it means romance lives on, particularly at night when you can wander through Fort Mason, along the Marina Green ▲ and covet thy neighbour's yacht and Victorian mansion, before finding a bistro with just the right plat du jour.

day

🛍 Boutique shopping doesn't get much better than Union Street with *tchotchkes*, housewares, and women's clothing. Chestnut Street offers similar fare.

👁 Sun yourself on Marina Green or in the Presidio [→78] and take in views of the Golden Gate Bridge [→70]. Soak up science at the Exploratorium [→74], and a world of cultures at the Mexican [→76] and Fort Mason Museums [→75]. Or get ship shape at the Maritime National Historical Park [→74].

night

🍸 Charming Euro bistros abound alongside twenty-something drinking haunts.

☆ Entertainment options include the Magic Theatre [→128] and two cinemas: the United Artists Metro and Cinema 21.

getting there

🚌 22, 28, 30, 42, 43, 45, 47, 49

shopping
fashion, accessories & kids

This tony district is a paradise for big spenders with big bucks. Shopaholics will splurge on Cow Hollow's Union Street with its wellspring of womenswear boutiques. **Vie Vie** entices with minimalist tops and sleek trousers, **Culot SF** lures with fun and chic styles, and *Canyon Beachwear vies for attention with an impressive range of swimwear. At *Dosa, any girl will succumb to the up-to-the-minute shoes and accessories and one-of-a-kind pieces. Its sister location, *Workshop, has a larger selection of fine womenswear (and lingerie), every piece fit for a fashionista. For the finishing touches **Cara Mia** ✔ specializes in the extras: straw purses and daisy-design sandals for summer and sumptuous scarves for winter. Sexy, girlish items can be snapped up at **Bisou Bisou** and **Bebe**, while **Girlfriends** flaunts everything a woman dreams of having in her boudoir – from sweet smelling lotions and salts to maribou-trimmed bags: check the 100% cotton pjs with the lovely, Indochine embroideries. For men and women, it's viva Italia at **Nida** where Prada, Miu Miu, and D&G rule the racks. **Uko** has an Eastern eye for delicate, timeless mens-and womenswear (often by Japanese designers). Giorgio's most casual store, **Armani Exchange** and urban chic *Kenneth Cole

*= featured in the listings section [→88–124]

have already won aficionados around the world; both draw devotees to this classically chic Marina corner.

Meet the kids' needs and your own if you are an expectant mother at **Minis Kids & Maternity**, where everything is made in SF. You'll find those oh-so-cute knit caps in fruit and veg designs fit for your pumpkin or strawberry blonde.

Neighbouring Chestnut Street, **Smash** and **Rabat** take care of trend-conscious feet. Capri is also the lone outpost here for fashion-forward quality womenswear. And for specs, seek and ye shall see at ***City Optix** where the latest frames from favourite eyeglass architects are on eye-catching display.

food & drink

*Peet's Coffee & Tea, a Bay Area institution, is the place to tank up on your wicked brew and some sweet treats to go. If you're after a wider selection of tea, nearby **Dragon Well** is one of the many tea-bars to have sprouted in the wake of the coffee explosion.

Among the area's oldest and best-loved food stores, **Lucca Delicatessen** is an old-fashioned Italian joint famous for its fresh ravioli. Put together a picnic and then pick up some fine Merlot or a Chardonnay from **PlumpJack Wines** too wash it all down with.

interiors

Design-conscious San Franciscans love to decorate their homes with goods from **John Wheatman** which has an eye for mixing the antique with the new. One block along at **Loft**, you'll find San Francisco-centric items like cookbooks and things to jazz up your pad like lemon grass candles, or a velvet leopard-print pillow. Locals rely on Chestnut

Street stalwarts **Pottery Barn** and **Williams Sonoma** for functional but eminently attractive home and kitchen goods. For some retail and creative therapy in one, join the growing Union Street throng who've taken to designing their own crockery: **Terra Mia** and **Color Me Mine** both offer this unique, DIY shopping experience.

books & stationery

Solar Light Books, a quintessentially San Franciscan neighbourhood bookstore, is ironically located in a basement. A selection of art, political, and metaphysical titles takes up most of the shelf-space, while quirky new releases fill the front racks. The store is the scene of regular author readings and its assistants are happy to recommend material. **Kozo** specializes in decorative

paper and bookbinding for the discerning customer who knows what they're looking for. On the other hand, Chestnut Street's **Kimmel's Stationery** is the kind of shop filled with things you didn't even know you needed. This old-fashioned place is where you are likely to find the very same kind of desk-items your grand-dad once had.

make-up & beauty

*Benefit is one of the city's finest exports. The two sisters who came up with the skin care and cosmetics line have made their company a top-pick among stylists and beauty experts. In no small part this is owing to products that really do magic. Hundreds of brilliant ideas include the cleverly named Lip Plump

and Brow Ling, or the Benetint, a liquid lip stain that won't come off no matter what you bite. National brand ***MAC** has one of their rare free-standing stores on Union Street. Shop assistants will make you over – appointments are recommended for the full monty.

marina & cow hollow

33

→ more restaurants | cafés & diners | bars | map & directory

eating & drinking

restaurants

Considering the neighbourhood's yuppie contingent and their constant demand for new, different, and BIGGER (especially when it comes to cars), it comes as a surprise that residents

seem content with small and subtle restaurants.

In the early 90s, two locals – foxy city supervisor Gavin Newsom and son-of-a-mogul Bill Getty – opened

*PlumpJack Café [→110] ▲ the area's most sophisticated restaurant. The chef manages to offset the stark grey motif with risotto and other Cal-bistro concoctions that levitate the palate.

Rose's Café, another venue from the prolific restaurateur Reed Hearon, also manages to be quietly successful. Even breakfast is impressive when they serve a sublime and simple polenta with mascarpone. Complementing the food are waitstaff that look plucked from a modelling agency. Zinzino is another Italian eatery that has found a home outside North Beach. Decorated with twinkling lights and a hodgepodge of vintage furnishings, it may be the area's best. Bonta, with a pastiche of murals and flowers out front, beckons ladies in search of a lite bite. Pane e Vino and Via Vai, at opposite ends of Union Street, are equally quaint and popular; both look like authentic trattorias. The former excels at wood-fired pizzas; the latter at homemade pasta and gnocchi.

There are plenty of outlets for Francophiles too; you'll be charmed by the Provençal feel at Cassis Bistro even before you see the menu, which almost gives away the food ($6 for escargots). By contrast, the dark and moody Brazen Head feels like a quirky throwback to bygone days.

bars

The Marina and Cow Hollow's bars are consistently crammed with booze thirsty, twentysomethings – many single, mostly white, but all less judgmental than the SoMa and Mission attitudinal cool crews. Anyone who likes to drink is welcome here. For a shameless meat-market experience, toss on a baseball cap and head into either the *Horseshoe Tavern or the Blue Light Café, which will be equally jam-packed every weekend. Both deliver plenty of microbrews on tap and some form of bar-sport, not to mention the potential for drunken kisses from horny young professionals. Single women beware – you're deep in testosterone country. Mick's Lounge, with its wide selection of potent 'Micktails', offers much the same, only

*Baker Street Bistro [→110] and Bistro Aix offer excellent value prix-fixe French meals for under $15; both are romantic. For a more vivacious ambience and near-to-perfect pommes frites, visit Café de Paris L'Entrecôte on a weekend night when patrons break into French song, goaded by the piano player.

Cow Hollow is home to much of San Francisco's old money, and Balboa Café and Eastside West are doing most of the 'old-boy' glad-handing – dark mahogany woods and whisky ad nauseum. Ground zero for a younger 'establishment' crowd is *Perry's [→111], the social HQ in Armistead Maupin's Tales of the City. Izzy's Steak & Chop House, meanwhile, is the Cheers of the Marina where regulars come for giant steaks and friendly banter. Old boys are nowhere to be seen at *Café Marimba [→113] (yet another Reed Hearon outpost), instead you'll find foodies from all over the city savouring sophisticated Mexican food. Vibrant Day-of-the-Dead murals cover every inch of wall space in this appealing, upbeat spot.

with a stage where cheesy funk and 80s cover bands set butts in motion.

Somewhat more refined though still occasionally given to festive nights are Delaney's, the Marina version of a corner bar, and Liverpool Lil's, a quasi-Anglo pub where an older set nurse Newcastle and chomp hearty shepherd's pies. Certainly the smallest bar in the Bay, the wonderful Black Horse London Pub recreates a London corner inn circa WWII and invites strangers to chat over warm ale. Last call is at 7pm. Another area gem is the externally bland but internally elegant Marina Lounge, where smartly clad folk sip martinis and casually two-step to the old school swing flavoured jukebox.

Filling the sushi quota are two above-par restaurants. Yakatori (skewered meats) is the specialty at Yoshida Ya, where you'll find fewer yuppies and more Japanese than at the industrial-chic Ace Wasabi. For a more unique culinary experience, kick off your shoes, recline in a sunken booth, and tuck into authentic Burmese creations at *Irrawaddy [→114], or head for *Lhasa Moon [→115], SF's only Tibetan restaurant. For fusion cuisine in more decadent, sumptuous surroundings, wait in line for a table at *Betelnut Pejiu Wu [→112].

Probably the most famous restaurant of all in the Marina is the vegetarian mecca *Greens [→117]. Even meat-eaters flock to this converted army barrack overlooking the Bay to test chef Annie Sommerville's Zen-like creations.

cafés & diners

Denizens of this chichi neighbourhood don't cook. Why should they when inexpensive cafés and diners are turning out a plenitude of gourmet grub? Harken back to your college years and you might be able to picture the young cafeteria scene at Pluto's. Instead of chipped beef, however, you'll find flank steak sandwiches and mesclun green salads; instead of peeling wallpaper, look for gunmetal fixtures and clean lines.

Even pizza is a gourmet snack around here. The owner of SF Pizza hired a 5-star chef to develop his crunchy/chewy crust; offbeat toppings include lobster and avocado. Take a slice to a grassy knoll at Fort Mason and watch the world go by. For a hearty start to your Sunday make a reservation at homely *Doidge's where the French toast is legendary. If you cannot get a table, try Bechelli's where the diner interior looks like it was imported from Brooklyn, or grab a latte-to-go from the Coffee Roastery.

🔖 directory

Ace Wasabi *C2*
3339 Steiner Street
567-4903 $

Armani Exchange *C3*
2090 Union Street
749-0891

Baker Street Bistro *A3*
2953 Baker Street
931-1475 $–$$

Balboa Café *C3*
3199 Fillmore Street
921-3944 $–$$$

Bebe *C3*
2095 Union Street
563-2323

Bechelli's *B2*
2346 Chestnut Street
346-1801 $

Benefit *B2*
2219 Chestnut Street
567-1173

Betelnut Pejiu Wu *D3*
2026 Union Street
929-8855 $$

Bisou Bisou *C3*
2116 Union Street
775-1633

Bistro Aix *C2*
3340 Steiner Street
202-0100 $–$$

Black Horse London Pub *E3*
514 Union Street
928-2414

Blue Light Café *D3*
1979 Union Street
922-5510

Bonta *C3*
2223 Union Street
929-0407 $$

Brazen Head *D3*
3166 Buchanan Street
921-7600 $–$$

Café de Paris L'Entrecôte *C3*
2032 Union Street
931-5006 $$–$$$

Café Marimba *B2*
2317 Chestnut Street
776-1506 $–$$

Canyon Beachwear *D3*
1728 Union Street
885-5070

Cara Mia *D3*
1814 Union Street
922-2272

Cassis Bistro *C3*
2120 Greenwich Street
292-0770 $–$$

City Optix *B2*
2154 Chestnut Street
921-1188

Coffee Roastery *B2*
2331 Chestnut Street
931-5282

Color Me Mine *D3*
2030 Union Street
474-7076

Culot SF *D3*
1969 Union Street
931-2413

Delaney's *B2*
2241 Chestnut Street
673-9383

Doidge's *C3*
2217 Union Street
921-2149 $–$$

Dosa *D3*
2063 Union Street
931-9939

Dragon Well *B2*
2142 Chestnut Street
474-6888

Eastside West *C3*
3154 Fillmore Street
885-4000 $$–$$$

Girlfriends *D3*
1824 Union Street
673-9544

Greens *D1*
Building A, Fort Mason
771-6222 $$

Horseshoe Tavern *C2*
2024 Chestnut Street
346-1430

Irrawaddy *D2*
1769 Lombard Street
931-2830 $–$$

Izzy's Steak & Chop House *C2*
3345 Steiner Street
563-0487 $–$$$

John Wheatman *D3*
1933 Union Street
346-8300

Kenneth Cole *C3*
2078 Union Street
346-2161

Kimmel's Stationery *B2*
2144 Chestnut Street
921-2294

Kozo *D3*
1969a Union Street
351-2114

Lhasa Moon *B3*
2420 Lombard Street
674-9898 $–$$

Liverpool Lil's *A3*
2942 Lyon Street
921-6664

Loft *D3*
1823 Union Street
674-0470

Lucca Delicatessen *C2*
2120 Chestnut Street
921-7873

MAC *D3*
1833 Union Street
771-6113

Marina Lounge *C2*
2138 Chestnut Street
922-1475

Mick's Lounge *E3*
2513 Van Ness Avenue
928-0404

Minis Kids & Maternity *D3*
2042 Union Street
567-9537

Nida *C3*
2163 Union Street
928-4670

Pane e Vino *C3*
3011 Steiner Street
346-2111 $–$$

Peet's Coffee & Tea *B2*
2156 Chestnut Street
931-8302

Perry's *D3*
1944 Union Street
922-9022 $–$$

PlumpJack Café *C3*
3127 Fillmore Street
563-4755 $$–$$$

PlumpJack Wines *C3*
3201 Fillmore Street
346-9870

Pluto's *B2*
3258 Scott Street
775-8867 $

Pottery Barn *C2*
2100 Chestnut Street
441-1787

Rabat *C3*
2080 Chestnut Street
929-8868

Rose's Café *C3*
2298 Union Street
775-2200 $–$$

SF Pizza *D2*
1602 Lombard Street
567-8646 $–$$$

Smash *C2*
2030 Chestnut Street
673-4736

Solar Light Books *D3*
2068 Union Street
567-6082

Terra Mia *C3*
2122 Union Street
351-2529

Uko *C3*
2070 Union Street
563-0330

Vie Vie *D3*
1977 Union Street
346-4416

Via Vai *D3*
1715 Union Street
441-2111 $–$$

Williams Sonoma *C2*
2000 Chestnut Street
929-2520

Workshop *C3*
2254 Union Street
561-9551

Yoshida-Ya *C3*
2909 Webster Street
346-3431 $$–$$$

Zinzino *B2*
2355 Chestnut Street
346-6623 $$

marina & cow hollow

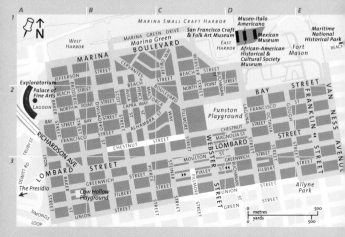

social climbing

russian hill & nob hill

As the sun sets and street lights begin to illuminate the cable car tracks, Hyde Street may be the most charmed spot in San Francisco. Cable car passengers look longingly at the Russian Hill bustle: dog-walkers yanked along by a multitude of pooches, couples leaned in close over candlelit vittles, work-a-day Joes loaded down with laptop and groceries, willing themselves to ascend some of the steepest grades in the city. Locals know that everything good is up: hidden stairways and terraced gardens; views of the Bay and Alcatraz; extravagant mansions and humble, million-dollar cottages. Most residents of this tony hillock would refuse to live anywhere else. The boho population has dwindled, and the yuppies now rule the roost. Still, novelist Jack London would love to know that his former haunt is dotted with boutique bookstores and affordable bistros.

Neighbouring Nob Hill offers much of the same. A rarefied air of wealth pervades and services revolve around the moneyed class. They're a hoot to watch but if you follow them inside the posh hotels be prepared to blow the limits of your credit card.

day

🛍 Polk Street is home to antique shops and quirky home-furnishing boutiques. In the loftier climes of upper Russian Hill and Nob Hill, there's very little retail action, except within the lobbies of the grande dame hotels.

👁 Drive down SF's famous crooked corkscrew, Lombard Street [→71]; get spiritual at the Gothic Grace Cathedral [→75]; and take a peek at the very first cable car inside the Cable Car Barn & Museum [→80].

night

🍴 Russian Hill has a good cache of intimate restaurants for one-to-one dining. The bar scene is fairly tame and closes down early.

☆ Pick up a repertory calendar for films at the cozy Lumiere cinema [→126].

getting there

🚌 1, 19, 27, 42, 45
🚋 C, PH, PM

shopping

If antiquing is your thing, poke around in the numerous shops dotted on lower Russian Hill's Polk Street. The cream of the area's vintage-heavy retailers are *Zonal, specializing in original folk art and American furniture; Swallowtail ✓, which gives a distinctly San Francisco spin on French flea market fare; and **Molte Cose**, which stocks everything from Victoriana to 70s kitsch.

The top of Nob Hill is largely a shopping-free zone, save for the gift shops in the large luxury hotels. However, tucked inside the magnificent **Grace Cathedral** [→75] complex, you'll find a heavenly emporium of spiritual matter – beautiful handmade icons, books, and jewellery.

* = featured in the listings section [→88–124]

Hyde & Seek is a traditional antique treasury located on a picture postcard block of Hyde Street. Next door, dressmaker's studio **Atelier des Modistes** specializes in sleek urban fashion and elegant wedding gowns. To create a more exotic impression, make your way to **In My Dreams** and recreate your image from a surreal collection of new and old chinoiserie, silks, and saris.

Smoke Signals will satisfy even the most unusual request with a wide selection of newspapers, magazines, and cigarettes from around the globe. Decision making can be equally time consuming at **Swensen's Ice Cream**, the city's oldest ice-cream store and original flavour-maker. From peppermint to coffee with almonds and fudge, they've got it – on a double-dipped sugar cone, of course.

Burn some calories trudging up and down the neighbourhood's awesome grades and inspect the precariously perched residences and the tiny restaurants tucked above, behind, and below every other home.

eating & drinking

restaurants

Discreet, sophisticated, and intimate hideaways lure a recherché crowd to dine in Russian and Nob Hill. **Hyde Street Bistro** ✓ is a gem: the portly chef greets diners with a French accent and an *amuse-gueule* that will foreshadow the exquisite yet inexpensive bistro fare to come. Nab the table in the window or the painted nook in the back and you will feel like he is cooking just for you. Thirty-seat **Elan Vital Restaurant & Wine Bar** across the street puts a more contemporary spin on French fare. Only seven (thin) bodies can fit at the wine bar where an endless scroll of seasonal dishes awaits. Run by the same chef-owners is **Frascati** where the maître d' places happy couples in the window to attract attention to the innovative California cuisine. Often confused with Frascati is **I Fratelli** which is across the street on Hyde. Consistently good, if predictable, Italian favourites are served in a sanguine setting that makes any Chianti taste blessed.

Universally attractive diners are drawn to *Sushi Groove where a happening vibe has been created by co-owners Martel and Nabel, two of the city's most prominent party and club planners. This is a place to be seen: the line to get in is a scene in itself. And once inside, even the sushi chefs are tapping their feet to the ambient music, while rolling funky combinations like eel, sea urchin, and avocado. **Zarzuela**, a nearby Spanish restaurant, is a good alternative. Expect fewer hipsters and some of the best paella in town.

Two blocks west on Polk Street is Russian Hill's second restaurant troupe, this one larger and more highly acclaimed than the Hyde Street set. Polk Street is louder in general, with a few bar, café, and club options for those who want to go on after dinner. Chef Roland Passot rustles up magical French food, utilizing luxurious ingredients such as lobster, foie gras, and caviar at his family-run *La Folie [→105] – one of the city's best and most exclusive restaurants. Patrons tend to be slightly younger and slicker at *Yabbie's Coastal Kitchen [→117] where fish is the main attraction; you may wait up to an hour to be served the one you ordered, but the informed waitstaff will keep you occupied. If you're in the mood for innovative (but not gimmicky) Italian fare head to **Antica Trattoria**. No tired classics on the frequently changing menu here. Pricier and more luxurious is *Acquerello [→107] where beautifully presented regional Italian gems are served in a former chapel. Heading south on Polk Street, there is a slew of eateries. Most are run-of-the-mill and inexpensive, but the charming new **Bistro Zare** promises to sophisticate the stretch with a Mediterranean-influenced menu that includes many pastas and fresh seafood dishes.

The best Nob Hill restaurants tend to be tucked away in the bejewelled hotels that decorate the famous hilltop. *The Terrace at the Ritz-Carlton is dazzling on Sundays when a four-piece jazz band serenades brunch-goers for upwards of $50 per person. You are paying for the name, the American caviar buffet station, and the views. Wear a tie and bring a flexible credit line to *The Dining Room [→104], a formal French affair in the same hotel. The same applies to *Charles Nob Hill [→104], where chef Ron Siegal is the only American to have taken part in and won the tele-vised 'Iron Chef' competition in Japan – his artistic nouvelle creations are breathtaking. Venticello is easily mistaken for just another apartment on Taylor Street, but this trat-toria is one of the few upscale Nob Hill restau-rants to survive outside a hotel. It draws locals with its Tuscan motif (cobalt blue tiles, ochre walls) and grappa sauces.

cafés & delis

A few trendy but inexpen-sive cafés and delis serve Russian Hill's struggling (and dwindling) artist community. Everyone at **Royal Ground Coffees** looks to be writing a treatise or painting a masterwork, and help is notoriously grouchy to well-heeled customers who are too lazy to walk the extra block to **Peet's Coffee & Tea** (where they belong). A few stools are all that decorate the famous counter at **Swan Oyster Depot**, where the idea is slurp- or crack-and-

go (as in the raw oysters, and Dungeness crab). By contrast **Polkers American Café** caters to the grease-loving crowd, and **Rex Café** overflows with brunch tak-ers on Sunday – most over eager to show off their Patagonia and Nike pur-chases. **Za Gourmet Pizza** belongs in a college town – the guys tossing dough behind the counter are built like volunteer fire-men (ie salt-of-the-earth beau hunks) and patrons are dressed down in fleece and plaid.

bars

Boozing establishments tend to be mixed affairs – some classy, calm, and collected, others revved up with the promise of late-night assignations. At the Fairmont Hotel's irresistibly kitsch **Tonga Room** ✓ hourly indoor tropical squalls rage with pseudo thunder. Patrons guzzle vibrant tropical poison beneath rows of bam-boo and palm fronds, sere-naded by live tiki tunes from the floating stage. Along similarly surreal lines, **Buccaneer** is a swashbuckling pirate's lounge where seafaring limeys chat beside the fire-place. It's a different, if no less historic, story at near-by *Top of the Mark (in the Mark Hopkins Hotel), where you'll need far

finer clothing to get in and sip a $10 sidecar or gimlet. Caviar is optional. Smooth jazz is the sound-track to what is arguably the finest 360-degree vista in the western hemi-sphere. Echoing a bygone time, the ever-sophisti-cated, cozy, and colourful **Royal Oak** serves swanky cocktails to soignée folk on plush sofas and at gorgeous oak tables. Dimly lit and velvet-draped **Tonic** does more of the same, and often seems more relaxed.

At the homely **John Barley-corn** neo-speakeasy, Bass, whisky, and friendly chats flow freely for a cadre of neighbourhood drin-kers. From upstairs at the **Hyde-Out**, enjoy kick-ass martinis among a cross

section of recent grads and amiable older folk.

Greens Sports Bar rages on game day, serving up pitchers of the frothy stuff to thirsty gamers cheering and jeering as they take in any- and everything athletic from myriad TVs. Even frattier is the shame-less but ultra-festive meat-market called **Shanghai Kelly's**, where eager, Gap-clad co-eds bolstered by liquid courage scour the bar for willing bedmates, or do the infamous white-man-overbite dance to the jukebox's fine array of top 40 cheese.

ꝏ directory

Acquerello ✗A4
1722 Sacramento Street
567-5432 $$$

Antica Trattoria ✗A2
2400 Polk Street
928-5797 $–$$

Atelier des Modistes ✗B2
1903 Hyde Street
775-0545

Bistro Zare ✗A4
1507 Polk Street
775-4304 $–$$

Buccaneer ✗A3
2155 Polk Street
673-8023

Charles Nob Hill ✗C3
1250 Jones Street
771-5400 $$–$$$

The Dining Room ✗D4
Ritz-Carlton Hotel,
600 Stockton Street
296-7465 $$$

Elan Vital Restaurant & Wine Bar ✗B3
1556 Hyde Street
929-7309 $$–$$$

Frascati ✗B2
1901 Hyde Street
928-1406 $$

Grace Cathedral ✗C4
1100 California Street
749-6300

Greens Sports Bar ✗A2
2239 Polk Street
775-4287

Hyde & Seek ✗B2
1913 Hyde Street
776-8865

Hyde-Out ✗B4
1068 Hyde Street
441-1914

Hyde Street Bistro ✗B3
1521 Hyde Street
292-4415 $–$$

I Fratelli ✗B2
1896 Hyde Street
474-8240 $$

In My Dreams ✗B3
1300 Pacific Avenue
885-6696

John Barleycorn ✗B4
1415 Larkin Street
771-1620

La Folie ✗A2
2316 Polk Street
776-5577 $$$

Molte Cose ✗A3
2044 Polk Street
921-5374

Peet's Coffee & Tea ✗A3
2139c Polk Street
474-1871

Polkers American Café ✗A2
2226 Polk Street
885-1000 $

Rex Café ✗A2
2323 Polk Street
441-2244 $–$$

Royal Ground Coffees ✗A2
2216 Polk Street
474-5957

Royal Oak ✗A2
2201 Polk Street
928-2303

Shanghai Kelly's ✗A3
2064 Polk Street
771-3300

Smoke Signals ✗A2
2223 Polk Street
292-6025

Sushi Groove ✗B2
1916 Hyde Street
440-1905 $

Swallowtail ✗A2
2217 Polk Street
567-1555

Swan Oyster Depot ✗A4
1517 Polk Street
673-1101 $–$$$

Swensen's Ice Cream ✗B2
1999 Hyde Street
775-6818

The Terrace at the Ritz-Carlton ✗D4
600 Stockton Street
773-6198 $$–$$$

Tonga Room ✗D4
Fairmont Hotel,
950 Mason Street
772-5278

Tonic ✗A2
2360 Polk Street
771-5535

Top of the Mark ✗D4
Mark Hopkins
Inter-Continental,
999 California Street
392-3434

Venticello ✗C3
1257 Taylor Street
922-2545 $–$$$

Yabbie's Coastal Kitchen ✗A2
2237 Polk Street
474-4088 $–$$

Za Gourmet Pizza ✗B2
1919 Hyde Street
771-3100 $$

Zarzuela ✗B2
2000 Hyde Street
346-0800 $–$$

Zonal ✗A3
2139 Polk Street
563-2220

39

russian hill & nob hill

northern beat

north beach

A traditional working class Italian neighbourhood that became the epicentre of the San Francisco Beat Movement of the 50s, North Beach has somehow retained its quixotic charm in the face of rising rents, tourist invasions, and the subsequent exodus to the suburbs.

Almost half-a-century may have passed since tour buses stormed the area in search of real live 'beatniks', but North Beach has maintained something of its bohemian aura. Radical artists and experimental poets have decamped for cheaper digs, but writers still gather in the many cafés. And when the wind blows, you can still discern a refreshing whiff of political insurgency mingling with the irresistible aroma of steamy espresso.

Today, the unique melange – historic watering holes, European-style cafés, strip clubs, and a fresh new wave of creative retailers – maintains the area's reputation as San Francisco's left bank.

day

🛍 Upper Grant Avenue is a haven for local clothing designers and one-of-a-kind furnishing shops. SF's upscale antiques ghetto is located at nearby Jackson Sq.

👁 Orientate yourself: look up for the Transamerica Pyramid [→71]; look down from Coit Tower [→71]. For bay vistas and the Alcatraz [→74] experience, hop on a ferry from nearby Fisherman's Wharf.

night

☕ Outdoor cafés and restaurants line Columbus Avenue, with many more tempting choices on Washington Square and Grant Avenue. Many stay open late.

☆ A few music [→131] and dance venues populate the area round Broadway and Columbus Avenue.

getting there

🚌 15, 30, 42, 45
🚃 PM

shopping

fashion & accessories

In the past few years, a scant stretch of Upper Grant Avenue (between Green and Filbert Streets) has blossomed into a shopping destination akin to New York's happening NoLita district. Young designers and merchants, encouraged by the free-spirited atmosphere and availability of small storefronts, have moved in and created a nirvana for fashionistas with a few dollars to drop.

The proprietors at *MAC have an uncanny eye for what's fresh, flattering, and just plain pretty. The salon-like store stocks wispy tie-dyed slip dresses and camisoles, flower-embroidered evening bags, and Italian girly knits. Across the street at Lilith, French-designed separates in smoky colours are made for layering – ideal in this city of perverse temperatures. *AB Fits offers one-stop shopping

for the perfect pair of jeans, with more than 20 brands (Replay, Aviatic, and hand-loomed Hollywood Ranch Market from Japan) and expert fit counselling. The shop also stocks cool suede kerchiefs and cowboy hats in screaming colours like chartreuse. At Fife, Scottish designer/DJ Andrew Linton is the king of stretch – his simple cropped pants and slit skirts move with you not against you – and the

* = featured in the listings section [→88–124]

traffic-stopping colours are a welcome antidote to khaki. The dead stock (unworn) collection of 40s and 50s ties is reason alone to turn into **Martini Mercantile**, where vintage originals and reproduction Hawaiian shirts, Chinese dragon lady dresses, and flowery 40s frocks hang cheek by jowl – along with requisite attire for the swing dance set who frequent the clubs on nearby Broadway.

For a wedding or posh occasion, chat up resident couturiers Ivana Ristic and Lynn Rosenzweig at **Ristarose**, where silk organza, chiffon, and satin are whipped into bias-cut gowns and dresses that cling and drape in all the right places without a trace of cheesy bridal poufferie. The past plays muse to mens- and womenswear designer **Martha Egan**, who favours vintage and vintage-looking fabrics that evoke Calder and Miró and pretty profiles from previous eras. Shoe fetishists slip into sexy Sigerson Morrison sling-backs, Mare loafers, and chunky Paraboots at ***Insolent**. A few doors down at ***Alla Prima** the bustiers, bras, panties, and camisoles by Leigh Bantivoglio, Chantal Thomas, and La Perla beckon in basic black and candy colours. The owner is a fiend about fit and stocks all sizes, so no one leaves feeling like a freak of nature.

furnishings

Flower-shop-cum-curio-emporium **Columbine Design** is home to seashell-studded sailor's valentines, gothic crosses, and fascinating taxidermy rendered from roadkill: squirrels bearing gilded crowns and black ravens (used by one customer to add zest to her Christmas tree). ***Aria** ⬈ is like some dusty dream attic come to life – it's crammed full of flea market

books & stationery

Founded by poet Lawrence Ferlinghetti during the 50s Beat Movement, ***City Lights** is as much a landmark as a generalist bookstore. It remains a shrine for readers, writers, and lovers of the printed word. A few blocks away at ***Quantity Postcards** hundreds of new and vintage postcards are displayed in a funhouse atmosphere, along with a stellar collection of psychedelic poster art by the likes of Frank Kozik. More writing options are offered at **Planet**, which has a quirky mix of photographic cards and funky writing journals, in addition to Tokyo Bay sunglasses, scented candles, and DVDs.

finds: old sports trophies, vintage photos, lamps, stainless steel furniture, and old Mexican Santos figures. Down on Columbus, **Biordi Italian Imports** also channels Old World Italian craftsmanship with Renaissance-style Majolica ceramic. Shipment of the hand-painted crockery, candlesticks, and bowls can be organized for you.

antiques

The red-bricked, ivy-covered buildings around historic Jackson Square tell tales of the Barbary Coast days, when bordellos, dance halls, and saloons once raised hell. Today, Jackson Square plays host to about a dozen of the city's poshest antique stores. Of note are: **Foster-Gwin Antiques** (English country and formal); **Hunt Antiques** (set up like an old English town house and filled with furniture, clocks, paintings, and silver); **John Doughty Antiques** (desks from the 18th century to Edwardian eras); and **Robert Domergue & Co** (European furniture, drawings, screens, and precious *objets d'art*).

more restaurants | cafés & pizzerias | bars & clubs

eating & drinking

restaurants

Prepare for a crush of bodies in SF's Italian food district. The spicy flavours mingled with the heat from throngs of young bodies breeds a certain sexual energy. The Italians who laid claim to the area in the late 19th-century are still dishing up their flavourful fare here –

osso bucco to drunken *tiramisu* – and Italian is still bandied about. But, in the 90s, restaurateurs and movie moguls began to speculate in the area. They brought flash, they brought leg room, and in many cases they brought something other than Italian food.

Celebrity chef Reed Hearon opened ***Rose Pistola** [→112] in the early 90s. His sprawling restaurant is the show-pony on Columbus. Well-heeled patrons wait in line for roast rabbit with fresh shell-bean ragout and other family-style Cal-Ital fare served in the earthy but

sleek dining room. His other media darling, **Black Cat** [→107], is flashier (it has to be next to all those neon XXX sex signs). Everyone is yacking away on their cell phone about an IPO or the eclectic menu – from Singapore noodles to wok-cooked lobster. After dinner, hep cats head downstairs to the luminescent Blue Bar to listen to cutting-edge jazz, or a poetry reading.

Francis Ford Coppola of *Godfather* fame joined the culinary cosa nostra in 99 with his own juggernaut, **Café Niebaum-Coppola**, located beneath his production offices (and Sean Penn's studio). Part deli, part café, it offers the best al fresco seats on Columbus. The crowds here all look like movie stars or agents of movie stars or starlets. Before opening his own café, Coppola patronized **Tommaso's**, a divey Italian restaurant nearby with excellent wood-fired pizzas.

*Enrico's [→110] supper club is also in the limelight. Financial District folk strip off their sport coats and climb the hill to the coveted seats on the heated patio. With the opening of Black Cat across the way they've finally got something to look at other than the strippers parading Broadway. Still it's best as a pit-stop – a few minty *mojitos* and a nibble from the Cal-Med menu. Enrico's chef, Rick Hackett, also introduced locals to Italian *chicchetti* (tapas) with the opening of **Tavolino** nearby.

Old-fashioned power-brokers – stockbrokers, bankers – prefer veteran establishments like ***Moose's** [→109], where they can clinch deals over monstrous slabs of meat and some of the best fish dishes in town. Moose's and **Washington Square Bar & Grill** (aka Washbag), another old boys' 'den', both overlook Washington Square. To catch the morning martial arts in the park, however, you'll need a window seat and 'momelet' at the comically churlish **Mama's on Washington Square**.

Don't let the flashier establishments steer you away from more intimate eateries. ***Café Jacqueline** [→107], tucked away on a narrow lane, is the soufflé specialist, while at ***L'Osteria del Forno** homemade pumpkin ravioli fly from a pea-sized kitchen to a pea-sized dining room. **Caffè Macaroni** and **Caffè Sport** are a step down on the culinary scale, but both offset the loss with outrageous decorative effects.

Off the European map, ***Helmand** [→114] blends classical austerity with ornate fixtures and intensely flavoured Afghan foods like leek ravioli and baby pumpkin with yoghurt and mint sauce. The less formal **Maykadeh Persian Cuisine** serves standard Middle Eastern dishes like hummus and kebabs. **The House** and **La Moone** fill out the area's fusion quota. The latter will scare away claustrophobes; small metal booths block diners from watching each other slurp down noodle dishes like one with sake-spiced raisins. And nowhere else prepares sea bass like The House, where the design is a lesson in feng shui.

Nestled between boutique law firms and art galleries around Jackson Square, another restaurant enclave has taken hold. Leader of the pack, the ***Cypress Club** [→109] looks like a cave out of the Flintstones if Dali had decorated it, but the food is far from Neanderthal and the impressive

cheese selection indicates sophistication. Wear your Prada with pride to ***MC²** [→106], another design feat in industrial chic, and expect unpronounceable, mostly seafood delicacies. If you like the pastries, pick up more at **Zero Degrees**, MC²'s sister bakery next door. **Bix** is best if you're looking for a handsome stranger to share a martini with; the moody, speakeasy ambience overshadows the food. Also in the Jackson Square hinterland is ***Kokkari** [→106], SF's token gourmet Greek restaurant where there isn't an ouzo-besotted patron to be found. ***Globe** [→108] is more remote, but the tiny bistro is packed and jumping 'til close, often with chefs seeking to unwind over seafood appetizers and great Californian wines. Lending a bit of rural charm to this otherwise flashy nexus is **Elizabeth Daniel**. The former Wine Country restaurateur immigrated back to the city to open this 56-seat French eaterie. The circa-1850 storefront is embellished with huge windows and a glass enclosed kitchen so diners can watch the prix-fix (around $65) dinners being concocted.

Hidden at the opposite end of Columbus sits **Zax**, where you can savour a cumin-crusted pork tenderloin and watch cable cars slip by en route to Fisherman's Wharf. Nearby ***Albona Ristorante Istriano** [→114] is more old-fashioned, but even hipsters swear by the Italian/Croatian food.

cafés & pizzerias

A truly great North Beach café must have: 1) strong espresso and 2) numerous perches for people-watching. **Caffè Greco** and **Caffè Roma** really make the grade. There's always an Adonis framed in the window at Greco; at Roma, the beans bring you back for more. If you want something savoury with your coffee, **Caffè Malvina** is the place, plus there are good views onto Washington Square – you'll bring a book and never open it. *Mario's Bohemian Cigar

Store Café, meanwhile, is a hip local classic that feels like it never left the Beat era. It specializes in giant, grilled focaccia sandwiches (there are no cigars). *Caffè Trieste is another popular option with a similarly bohemian feel. Closer to Downtown, expats pack the colourful **Café Prague** where bagels and goulash are served on mismatched tablecloths and there is often live music.

And what of North Beach's famous pizzas? Well, **Golden Boy Pizza** serves up soft squares to go. They are so loaded with toppings, you're handed a knife and fork with your slice. And there's no throwing away a **North Beach Pizza** crust, particularly if it's attached to that pesto topping. For true, mouth-watering focaccia bread made in traditional brick ovens, there's only **Liguria**. Opened in 1911 by three brothers from Genoa, the tiny family-run bakery opens at 8am and closes around mid-afternoon when they sell out.

43

bars & clubs

Stylish upper-shelf joints, storied old-timer blues haunts, collegiate pick-up bars, seedy strip clubs, and working class pool pubs ensure North Beach night crawling will be a strange and colourful experience. Don your best slacks and sport coat to sip bubbly with the business set at the ultra swank and velvety **Bubble Lounge**, West Coast partner to the same-named bar in NYC's TriBeCa. Smooth and sophisticated nightclub jazz fills the place while sexy young waitresses serve the predominantly 30 and over singles club. Meanwhile at the elegant, Havana-styled **850 Cigar Bar**, shameless yuppies puff cigars and pray for better trade relations with Cuba. A rare patio offers refuge from the smoky but classy interior. **15 Romolo** may highlight Bay Area cocktails du jour, but it is less pretentious if no less ornate than other similarly styled bars. All that and only steps from all the porn you'd ever wish for! Local luminaries have for years sipped expertly mixed martinis at somewhat legendary *Tosca Café. While the odd Metallica member or Sean Penn might sometimes hide out in the back room, most nights this hotspot hosts a cross section of the hard-drinking 'in' crowd. Their 'cappuccino' (coffee, cream, and brandy) will blow you away. Even

more famous is nearby *Vesuvio ►, one time bar-of-choice for Kerouac, Ginsberg, and their Beat pals, whose literary movement began at City Lights bookstore next door. Insanely popular, Vesuvio remains surprisingly unspoiled and a fine place to sip a pint and wax poetic with pals.

A shadow of its former 60s self – when folks like Janis Joplin used to jam there – the humble **Lost & Found Saloon** today attracts a clientele of career drinkers. Second-rate alternative rock and generic R'n'B hit the stage these days but the back bar, fashioned from the hull of an old ship, is still pretty neat. Equally old but far cooler, **Gino & Carlo** is a must. This 50+ year-old timeless joint has a pair of pool tables and is justifiably sardine-packed on weekends. Continuing the old-school theme, **The Saloon** is often similarly crowded with hard workin' folks looking to blow the froth off a few and hip shake to danceable blues bands. The dark and divey **Club Cocodrie** boasts nightly rock, punk, and alternative bands which vary wildly from night to night. The large dance floor occasionally fills up but the music usually serves as a background soundtrack for the cavalcade of long-haired, leathery locals guzzling Bud at the bar or

shooting stick. *Bimbo's 365 Club is a plusher, swankier club option where live music rocks the place on most nights. Tiny **Columbus Café** is not a café, nor is it on Columbus, but it is one of the better lowbrow boozing rooms, sporting a colourful cast of deadly serious but friendly drinkers, bartenders likely named Charley or Hank, and dim, flickering lights.

Frat boys pound tequila shots, get competitive at the foosball table, and hone their cheesy pick-up lines on giggly blondes at the immensely popular **Savoy-Tivoli**. You must check your IQ at the door here (and pay a cover on weekends) but you will likely have a blast and probably get laid. Though not the Irish heart of the city, **O'Reilly's** does a respectable job of mimicking a Dublin pub, slow pouring a thick Guinness, and dishing up crispy and flaky fish 'n' chips. And for arguably the city's best microbrew pub, **San Francisco Brewing Co** serves a tasty array of stouts and lagers across a gorgeous mahogany bar in a century-old building.

♫ directory

AB Fits ♫B2
1519 Grant Avenue
982-5726

Albona Ristorante Istriano ♫A1
545 Francisco Street
397-4077 $$

Alla Prima ♫C2
1420 Grant Avenue
397-4077

Aria ♫C2
1522 Grant Avenue
433-0219

Bimbo's 365 Club ♫A1
1025 Columbus Ave
474-0365 $$–$$$

Biordi Italian Imports ♫B2
412 Columbus Avenue
392-8096

Bix ♫D3
56 Gold Street
433-6300 $$–$$$

Black Cat ♫C3
501 Broadway
981-2233 $–$$

Bubble Lounge ♫D3
714 Montgomery Street
434-4204

Café Jacqueline ♫C2
1454 Grant Avenue
981-5565 $$$

Café Niebaum-Coppola ♫C3
916 Kearny Street
291-1700 $–$$

Café Prague ♫C2
584 Pacific Avenue
433-3811 $

Caffè Greco ♫B2
423 Columbus Avenue
397-6261 $

Caffè Macaroni ♫C3
59 Columbus Avenue
956-9737 $–$$

Caffè Malvina ♫B2
1600 Stockton Street
391-1290 $–$$

Caffè Roma ♫B2
526 Columbus Avenue
296-7942 $–$$

Caffè Sport ♫B2
574 Green Street
981-1251 $$–$$$

Caffè Trieste ♫C3
601 Vallejo Street
392-6739 $

City Lights ♫C3
262 Columbus Avenue
362-8193

Club Cocodrie ♫C3
1024 Kearny Street
986-6678

Columbine Design ♫B2
1541 Grant Avenue
434-3016

Columbus Café ♫B2
562 Green Street
291-0818

Cypress Club ♫C3
500 Jackson Street
296-8555 $$$

850 Cigar Bar ♫D3
850 Montgomery St
291-0850

Elizabeth Daniel ♫D3
550 Washington Street
397-6129 $$$

Enrico's ♫C3
504 Broadway
982-6223 $–$$$

Fife ♫C2
1450 Grant Avenue
677-9744

15 Romolo ♫C3
15 Romolo Place
398-1359

Foster-Gwin Antiques ♫D3
38 Hotaling Place
397-4986

Gino & Carlo ♫B2
548 Green Street
421-0896

Globe ♫D3
290 Pacific Avenue
391-4132 $$–$$$

Golden Boy Pizza ♫C2
542 Green Street
982-9738 $

Helmand ♫C3
430 Broadway
362-0641 $–$$

The House ♫C3
1230 Grant Avenue
986-8612 $$

Hunt Antiques ♫D3
478 Jackson Street
989-9531

Insolent ♫C2
1418 Grant Avenue
788-3334

John Doughty Antiques ♫D3
619 Sansome Street
398-6849

Kokkari ♫D4
200 Jackson Street
981-0983 $$–$$$

La Moone ♫D3
533 Jackson Street
392-1999 $–$$

Liguria ♫B2
1700 Stockton Street
421-3786 $

Lilith ♫C2
1528 Grant Avenue
781-6171

Lost & Found Saloon ♫C2
1353 Grant Avenue
392-9126

L'Osteria del Forno ♫B2
519 Columbus Avenue
982-1124 $–$$

MAC ♫B2
1543 Grant Avenue
837-1604

Mama's on Washington Square ♫B2
1701 Stockton Street
362-6421 $–$$

Mario's Bohemian Cigar Store Café ♫B2
566 Columbus Avenue
362-0536 $–$$

Martha Egan ♫C3
1 Columbus Avenue
397-5451

Martini Mercantile ♫C2
1453 Grant Avenue
362-1944

Maykadeh Persian Cuisine ♫C2
470 Green Street
362-8286 $$

MC² ♫C3
470 Pacific Avenue
956-0666 $$$

Moose's ♫B2
1652 Stockton Street
989-7800 $$–$$$

North Beach Pizza ♫C2
1499 Grant Avenue
433-2444 $–$$

O'Reilly's ♫B2
622 Green Street
989-6222

Planet ♫B2
552 Columbus Avenue
392-7641

Quantity Postcards ♫B2
1441 Grant Avenue
986-8866

Ristarose ♫C2
1422 Grant Avenue
781-8559

Robert Domergue & Co ♫C3
560 Jackson Street
781-4034

Rose Pistola ♫B2
532 Columbus Avenue
399-0499 $$–$$$

The Saloon ♫B2
1232 Grant Avenue
989-7666

San Francisco Brewing Co ♫C3
155 Columbus Avenue
434-3344

Savoy-Tivoli ♫C2
1434 Grant Avenue
362-7023

Tavolino ♫C2
401 Columbus Avenue
392-1472 $$–$$$

Tommaso's ♫C3
1042 Kearny Street
398-9696 $–$$$

Tosca Café ♫C3
242 Columbus Avenue
391-1244

Vesuvio ♫C3
255 Columbus Avenue
362-3370

Washington Square Bar & Grill ♫B2
1707 Powell Street
982-8123 $–$$$

Zax ♫A1
2330 Taylor Street
563-6266 $$

Zero Degrees ♫D3
490 Pacific Avenue
788-9376 $

orient express

This dense network of streets is home to one of the largest Chinese communities outside Asia. English is a second language, Starbucks is nowhere to be seen, bagels are replaced by dim sum dumplings, and a spicy aroma infuses the air. San Francisco's Chinatown is rough round the edges: many of its residents live ten to an apartment in tenement conditions; cars sit in gridlock; and every available space is crammed with curio shops, fish and produce markets, and restaurants pungent with sizzling pot-stickers, good luck incense, and exotic spices. During the two-week long Chinese New Year celebrations [→134] the area reaches peak intensity. Give in to the idea that nothing happens quickly here and instead soak up the authentic flavours of this Asia in miniature.

day

🛍 Trading companies line Grant Avenue, selling everything from silk robes and jade figurines, to penny candy and trinkets.

👁 For greater insight into Chinese culture head to the Chinese Historical Society of America [→75].

night

🍲 The streets are teeming with Chinese eateries including R&G Lounge and Yuet Lee which both stay open late. A few oddball bars fuel the adventurous and the thirsty.

getting there

🚌 1, 15, 30, 45

🚋 C, PH, PM

chinatown

shopping

From precious green jade to crisp ginger, you'll find it in Chinatown. The back alleys have the herbalists while the side streets are for the dressmakers – like **Hung Chong Co** where you can have a *cheongsam* made to order (in a week or two). The real action is along Grant, with its ornately designed and neon-lit storefronts. For clothing – like simple silk and cotton pajamas and brocade tops – head to **Mandarin Fashions**, and for delicate, hand-embroidered linen, stop by **Imperial Fashion**. At **Suey Chong Co**, East and West meet old and new: the old-fashioned store is

filled with vintage chinoiserie as well as 'take-away carton' silk purses and platform slippers emblazoned with dragons. Across the street at **Fat Ming & Co**, there are racks of traditional, bright red and gold gift cards, beautiful paper goods, and writing implements. And don't miss the souvenir chopsticks, wallets, toys, and paper parasols at **Canton Bazaar**.

If you feel a spiritual calling, the **Paulist Center Bookstore** attached to historic Old St Mary's Church carries all the Catholic goods you'll ever need. And when you feel peckish,

there's **Eastern Bakery** for a lotus ball or egg custard tart – President Clinton tucked into a pastry here and they've proudly displayed the photos to prove it. Wash it all down with a spot of tea across the street at **Ten Ren Tea Co** where you'll sample the *oolong* or *dragonwell* before they pack up your tea leaves or ginseng to go. Will it be some fine jewellery from one of the many dealers on Grant? Or will you head to the beach once you've grabbed a flying paper fish from **Chinatown Kite Shop**? Hard to say what will find its way into the carry-all after a trip to Chinatown.

restaurants | bars | map & directory

---

* = featured in the listings section [→88–124]

eating
& drinking

restaurants

Sit down at one of Chinatown's dim sum huts, point at a shrimp-and-scallop pastry and have it ladled directly onto your plate. That's the way dim sum works here – point and ye shall receive. At the hidden **Oriental Pearl** the dim sum is so fresh the chef makes it to order. The sparsely decorated **Kowloon**, meanwhile, deserves a blue ribbon for its devotion to the vegetarian cause. All the dim sum and entrées here are meat free, a culinary ethos in keeping with the regimen of Buddhist monks.

Not every restaurant serves dim sum. **Hing Lung** packs in diners 'til 1am, most of whom are craving noodles and a pasty gruel called *jook*, a combination of rice, meat, fish, and herbs. **Yuet Lee Seafood** stays open even later ('til 3am) – catering to the club-goer with a discerning palate. Who wouldn't sacrifice a basket of fries for incredibly fresh oysters in black bean sauce? **House of Nanking** shines with hyperkinetic energy. Join the eternal line for a table, ignore the bland decor, and nudge your waiter for unlisted specials like duck dumplings or shrimp with peas and yam. Salt and pepper crab is indicative of the authentic Cantonese cuisine served in the formal shoji-screened dining room at the **R&G Lounge**, a favourite among Financial District types. **Golden Flower Vietnamese Restaurant** specializes in *pho*, an intense Vietnamese noodle soup packed with fish or meats and fresh herbs.

bars

Deep within Chinatown's dark streets lurk a pair of hidden gems as yet known only to the keenest of the hip, and old Chinese men who lurk in the lantern's shadows. The unspoiled ***Buddha Lounge** with its shiny black lacquer walls and vibrant, flowery murals belongs, on weekdays, to the hardcore locals. On weekends, a steady stream of trailblazing hipsters have begun venturing in, making for a strange and drunken cultural exchange. Even cooler is ***Li Po's**. From the glowing red cave entrance to the bright red booths, this supposedly haunted former opium den is nothing if not surreal. Old Chinese barflies throw dice while the younger set soak in the wonderful weirdness compounded by Frank Sinatra on the jukebox.

directory

bank on it

The Transamerica Pyramid rises out of the fog like a Goliath sword, its triangular tip recognized the world over as the aerial vortex of San Francisco's commercial aorta. This is where the deals go down: where the stocks are traded (the Pacific Stock Exchange is hopping by 4am); where ambulance chasers calculate their billable hours over seared halibut and kir royal. The streets are swarming with suits and ties... and shopping bags. Banana Republic takes up almost an entire city block. Macy's and Neiman-Marcus jockey for space with high-rise hotels. But don't be fooled by Downtown's serious countenance, this neighbourhood is as quirky and surprising as any in the city. Hidden alleys harbour moody French cafés and elite boutiques. Dainty ladies decked out in Prada skitter nervously past iconoclastic bible-beaters preaching the gospel into megaphones in Union Square. Just bring an open mind, a full wallet, and watch where you're going – this is bike messenger turf.

day

🏛 Post Street is a who's who of big-name designers, SF's answer to New York's 5th Avenue. Union Square offers one-stop department store shopping.

👁 Numerous commercial galleries [→77] are dotted around the area. Landmarks include the Transamerica Pyramid [→71] and the Ferry Building [→70].

night

🍷 Drinking and eating options tend to be refined, upscale affairs: dress up and bring your platinum card.

☆ The city's major theatres [→127] are clustered around Geary Street. The latest art-house films play at the Embarcadero Center cinema [→126].

getting there

🚌 1, 2, 3, 5, 6, 7, 9, 15, 27, 30, 32, 38, 42, 45, 66, 71

🚃 F, J, K, L, M, N

🚐 C, PH, PM

Ⓑ Embarcadero, Montgomery St, Powell St

shopping

department stores & shopping centres

If you only have time to peruse one department store, get thee to *Saks Fifth Avenue ✔ and soak up the *haute* and happening mix of designer threads, baubles, and luscious lingerie. Also worth a peek is *Neiman-Marcus, the Dallas-based homage to excess, and the favourite haunt of accessory queens hot on the trail of Prada bags and Miu Miu shoes. Fashionistas do not flock to *Macy's, but others wander the olympic-sized floors which include a basement food hall and the West Coast's largest shoe department. The vast and varied shoe offerings at *Nordstrom might stretch to the moon laid end to end (a future Christo project?) while the clothing itself is largely hit or miss. The store opens out into the San Francisco Shopping Centre – the closest Downtown SF has to a

* = featured in the listings section [→88–124]

bona fide mall – where post-preppy clothier **J Crew** stocks denims and chinos.

A short hike from Union Square are the towers of the **Embarcadero Center**, a shopping/office complex whose jewel in the crown is a five-screen art movie house. A blandly tasteful round-up of the usual suspects, the boutiques include **Williams-Sonoma** (cooking equipment), **Pottery Barn** (mass-market interior design), and a great European newsstand. And for a picture postcard snapshot of SF, zip up to the SkyDeck.

interiors

The kind of store that gets featured in *Architectural Digest*, *de Vera is arrayed like a shrine, with uncommon objects and singular artefacts from old Murano art glass to Tibetan buddhas. Known for its jade and freshwater pearl collection, *Gumps is also a repository for unusual tableware, local crafts, antique furniture, and antique garden ornaments. And for a change of culture stroll through the entryway to Chinatown [→45–46].

For shoppers seeking retail nirvana, Union Square is the shining path to sartorial enlightenment.

fashion: only in san francisco

Planted amidst the chains and eponymous designer shops are a handful of home-grown stores run by hip mixmasters who work with silk and cotton rather than vinyl. At the top of the list is *Metier, favourite haunt for both artsy and career types who find personal expression through a pony-print skirt, pale lavender poncho, and a pair of Cathy Waterman diamond hoops. The hand-knit cashmere, mohair, and chenille at Margaret O' Leary help cut the chill of a San Francisco summer, while next door *Diana Slavin's haberdashery-inspired suits and separates are smart without being severe (ditto the selection of Clergerie shoes). Men get equal fashion time just down the lane at *MAC (Modern Appealing Clothing), where even sales folks from other stores come to check out the wares – relaxed modern with a vintage subtext. Nearby *Billy Blue supplies the smooth guys with unflappable Italian suits, sweaters, and ties.

Larger in scale and often too *haut* to handle is *Wilkes Bashford, clothier to SF society and the occasional ageing rock star. Less stuffy *Ultimo hangs big guns like Marc Jacobs, Dolce & Gabbana, and Randolph Duke next to accessible hipsters such as Daryl K and Katayone Adeli. And many younger style-mongers take field trips to *Rolo, where the music never stops during the hunt for cutting edge threads from Trina Turk, Margiela 6, and the lords of denim. For the *dernier cri*, *Gimme Shoes stocks the cream of the footwear crop for him and her.

mini-chains & superstores

Who can resist *Agnès B, with its timeless *Breathless*-inspired (Belmondo, not Gere) profiles for men and women interpreted through classic and comfortable fabrics? The hyper cool buy their denim and streetgear at *Diesel ✓, while *Levi's new hip-hopped image is on show at their hometown megastore, where you can chill out in a tub while your new jeans shrink to fit. Black leather is the textile of choice at *Kenneth Cole's flagship store, which keeps his entire line of grown-up, street-hep threads, and well-priced shoes and accessories. And for a quick pick-me-up, shimmy into one of *Betsey Johnson's deliciously stretchy beflowered creations and rediscover your inner bad girl.

Urban Outfitters does a bang-up job of reinterpreting styles for home and body at student prices. For ramped up modern looks with pared-down detailing (and price tags), **Club Monaco** and **Laundry Industry** lead the pack, along with local heroes **Gap**, **Banana Republic**, and **Old Navy** who churn out well-priced clothing (and irresistible toddlers' togs) with unflagging consistency. *Nine West has a knack for knocking off the latest shoes, while footwear from *Joan & David balance a bit of flair with a lot of craftsmanship. Finally, if bargain-hunting is in your blood, many a discounted diamond-in-the-rough has been unearthed at *Loehmann's, though not without saintly patience.

books & music

While away a few hours at *Virgin Megastore which has numerous CD listening stations as well as books, videos, and a café. *Borders is the bookstore equivalent with an equally vast selection. The literati browse at *Rizzoli, which specializes in art books but also keeps a decent choice of fiction. For magazines to service any fetish from *haute couture* to British bikes, **Harolds International Bookstand** is a browser's paradise.

international designers

Compared to New York or LA, where most top designers have a bricks-and-mortar edifice, understated San Francisco has relatively few. Congregated Downtown, they do a brisk traffic in pure, undiluted luxe.

Much closer geographically than aesthetically, sartorial sisters **Chanel** and **Jil Sander** offer the season's highlights, the former flogging handbags like hotcakes and the latter staking her claim on a 'less is more' credo. Classicists intent on cut and drape saunter into **Giorgio Armani**, home of his Black label and **Emporio Armani**, while American mythologizer **Ralph Lauren**'s retail empire can outfit you for an evening at the opera or a picnic on the polo field – and give your house a facelift with faux and real

antiques. A stone's throw away, **Versace**'s 'dress for excess' mantra is realized with street theatre costumes for the bold and the buff. And neo-bohemian chic permeates the goods at **Gucci** – the attitude is optional. Cashmere-addicts haunt **TSE Cashmere**, where creative direction from Hussein Chalayan is warming things up as much as the goat's hair. For the best pashminas, those in the know wrap it up at *N Peal, where the cloud-weight shawls come in more colours than a deluxe crayon box. And those with no credit limit needn't work up a sweat in their search for bags, belts, and multi-carat rocks: **Hermès**, **Tiffany**, **Louis Vuitton**, and **Bottega Veneta** are all located within a few blocks radius.

one-of-a-kind

Old World meets New with **Jacqueline Perfumery**, a family-run shop that has been scenting San Franciscans for three decades, and *Sephora, the millennial beauty megastore where you can sample your way through almost any make of scent or *maquillage*. And if the thought of four floors of fabrics, notions, trims, buttons, and tassels makes your blood race, welcome to **Britex**.

Kidlets in tow or waiting at home? Toys, games, dolls, and child-oriented diversions fill up at **FAO Schwarz** and **Sanrio**, not to mention the monolithic *Disney Store, a fascinating study in the art of science and pure marketing. Equally shameless in their mass marketing technique is teen nirvana *Niketown.

49

downtown

eating & drinking

restaurants

There's only one semi-formal neighbourhood left in San Francisco and this is it. Finance, shopping, theatre, and hotels all intersect in this compact node. For foodies, this confluence augurs most of the city's finest restaurants. There are so many people vying for reservations that even eateries tucked away in dark alleys flourish.

In fact, alley restaurants are where ex-pats and hipsters hole up Downtown – far away from the flashy consultant. French and moody describes the majority of alley dwellers, **Café Bastille** and *Café Claude ✔ the most famous among them. French posters, French waiters, French food – they are perfect bistro replicas. Both

excel at the classics (pommes frites, mussels, salade niçoise etc) and both overflow with patrons seeking coveted alfresco seats. Bastille shares its alley with *Plouf [→116], a Cal-French bistro with spare decor and award-winning mussels ($10 buys you a boatload), and **B44**, a new restaurant from renowned Spanish chef Daniel Olivella where the margaritas flow freely. All serve food outside, turning Belden Place into a veritable street fest at night, particularly when jazz trios come to serenade. **Anjou** is more private, though noise tends to reverberate off the brick walls and brass fittings. Not French but equally of note are popular alley dwellers: **Rumpus**, a perky California-style

café, and **Café Akimbo**, an Asian bistro perched three-storeys above Maiden Lane.

French chefs love to set up shop Downtown, and some of the city's best French eateries are here – and not just in the backstreets. *Rubicon [→105] is the media darling in the group. Acclaimed sommelier Larry Stone and investors Robert De Niro, Francis Ford Coppola, and Robin Williams certainly don't hinder its reputation. Amazingly, the Cal-French cuisine keeps pace with the hype. King Louis XIV would have approved of **The Grand Café** with its vaulted ceilings which must be over 50-ft high. The classically trained French chef has a fondness for braised beef

more restaurants | cafés & delis | bars | directory

cheeks with white beans. French kings of the old guard are **Le Central** and *****Fleur de Lys** ▸ [→104]. Powerbrokers and VIPs such as mayor Willie Brown prefer to hide away and grouse about the bad service in the dark grottos of Le Central, while foodies at Fleur de Lys shell out big bucks for culinary grandeur. A tuxedo isn't out of place set against the festoons of gold wall fabric. Only a few restaurants share Fleur's pedigree of grandeur. And *****Masa's** [→105], the Mount Olympus of food and extravagance, is one of them. Those who get a reservation must pay a small fortune for the sublime French-Cal cuisine (medallions of fallow deer with caramelized apples and Zinfandel sauce) served in equally sumptuous surroundings.

Other juggernauts include *****Aqua** [→116], arguably the best fish restaurant in town. Even chefs gossip about this place. Standards are supposedly so high that only the most steely ego can survive in the kitchen here. Diners benefit from such ambition and dishes like savoury mussel soufflé are transporting. *****Campton Place** [→104] is another high-end, high-concept dining experience, one of the few luxury hotel restaurants with a local following. Some of America's most prolific chefs apprenticed here. Alternatively **Silks** is the super-sophisticated hotel restaurant serving outstanding Pacific Rim treasures such as seared tuna and foie gras terrine, and crab ravioli in saffron-infused broth.

For a contemporary breath of fresh air head to *****Faralon** [→116] where restaurant-designer-about-town, Pat Kuleto, has created an OTT underwater theme (jellyfish lamps et al). The seafood delicacies come from chef Mark Franz who leans heavily (and brilliantly) on truffles and caviar. Equally dramatic and filled with modern art is *****Postrio California** [→110]. Wolfgang Puck came up from LA to launch this

Cal-Asian-Italian hybrid in 89 and the place hasn't faltered since.

The Italian presence Downtown is less auspicious than in other neighbourhoods, but there are a few standouts. *****Oritalia** [→113] is flourishing in its new off-Union Square location and chef Jon Nelson continues to woo diners with Italian/Asian cuisine. His high notes include the signature tuna tartar on sticky rice cakes. Theatre-goers are always sneaking into **Kuleto's** before curtain call for drinks and antipasto. The Cal-Ital fare is first rate if slightly clichéd. Expect innovative Italian menus at **Palio d'Asti** and **Zare**. Palio's industrial-chic interior looks like something Armani might sponsor while the tiny Zare is more illicit and *au naturel*.

Old time restaurants dating back to the 1800s also manage to thrive here. At **Sam's Grill** the cigar smoke of generations of Financial District 'old boys' still lingers in the dark corridors; hefty burgers and lamb chops are the order of the day. **Tadich Grill** draws both loyal locals and intrepid tourists to its enormous wooden dining bar and discreet curtained booths, probably because it's the only place in town that still makes

dishes like crab Newberg and sole Florentine.

Two old-timers underwent major construction last year. No telling if **Jack's**, the city's oldest operating restaurant, has lost its culinary prowess – not all chefs are thrilled at the prospect of making petrale sole and turtle soup every day – but the beautifully restored room with its gilt embellishments and perfect little dining terraces is atmospheric enough to make most diners overlook menu flaws. *****Le Colonial** [→114], formerly Polynesian stalwart Trader Vic's, is packed with the parvenu. It's *the* new blue-blooded establishment for Gen-Xers. The food, exotic French/Vietnamese, is impeccable. You'll save dollars and get similar flavours at **E&O Trading Co**, where an after-work singles crowd nibble lamb and potato-mint naan bread. Meanwhile, Indian food-lovers in the know are drawn to the dirt cheap *****Shalimar** [→115], the anomaly in this upscale district.

cafés & delis

There are literally hundreds of lunch stands and shops Downtown, most designed to serve anxious traders and lawyers and shoppers who need food and NEED IT NOW! **Ur**'s gimmick is a Mediterranean salad bar filled with gourmet trifles like barbecued quail, grilled eggplant, and fatoosh salad. **YaYa Cuisine** is a bigger, full-service Iraqi restaurant, popular among business folk who have more time for lunch. Ex-pats linger and ravage foreign newspapers at **Café de la Presse** a French coffee-house. *****Sear's Fine Food** meanwhile feels like a scene out of the TV show *Alice*. Waitresses in pink bibs take

orders for Swedish pancakes. If you can't stomach the wait hit **Dottie's True Blue Café** instead – the decor is a 50s throwback and everything, including the ginger and cinnamon pancakes, is homemade. Alternatively puff pastry topped with Gruyère and marinara sauce at the **Emporio Armani Café** will cost a fraction of the jacket you've got your eye on there. *****Original Joe's** is great for a burger fix and at **David's Delicatessen**, one of the few Jewish delis in town, sandwiches overflow with pastrami and corn beef, and the pastry case is jammed with over 100 European pastries.

bars

From the sex shop section of Market to the brisk Financial District and the tourist throngs around Union Square, Downtown does it all. Most of the activity takes place during the day and this area can be a ghost town late at night when many of these bars close and drinkers in need scatter up to North Beach or down SoMa way.

However unappealing the seedy Tenderloin district may seem, numerous bars merit mention, most notably ***C Bobby's Owl Tree**, a quirky, relatively unspoiled joint curiously decorated with all manner of stuffed and painted barnyard hooters that attracts a mixed clientele of career boozers and slumming hipsters. Despite its squalid exterior, **Hollywood Billiards** is much nicer inside and probably the best pool hall in town with dozens of tables and a fine view of bustling Market Street. Beware hustlers.

Harrington's is a 60-year old Downtown institution,

often crowded from 5–9pm with suited men relaxing after a hard day of litigation and stock trading. ***The Irish Bank** also sees most of its action early in the evening, with a similar if slightly livelier crowd nursing expertly poured Guinness and enjoying perfectly authentic UK pub grub. Enophiles in suits sip fine Merlot from a dizzy selection at the **London Wine Bar**, a classy and pricey establishment of brick and wood. Lower-rung Downtowners – mailroom rats and temps – share an afterwork swill and basket of popcorn at ever amiable **Sutter Station** or duck into offbeat **Ginger's Trois**, where drag queens and Internet whiz kids drink together beneath a dormant disco ball.

Named for the 30s SF Seals manager, **Lefty O'Doul's** is all about baseball. Major league aficionados cram in to dig photos of old Lefty himself, gulp a cold one, or join in a round of *I left my heart*.... at the piano bar. Nearby, the Cajun-inspired

Biscuits & Blues supper club serves up fine local and national blues in a suitably moody, though hardly gritty, environment. The biscuits themselves are authentic even if the absence of home-bottled moonshine at the bar isn't. ***Harry Denton's Starlight Room**, on the 21st floor of the Sir Francis Drake hotel, is an institution of old school glitz and glam, drawing local celebs and other rich folk for its luxury, snazzy views, infamous chocolate martinis, and big band dancin'. Less flashy but more refined is the Clift Hotel's high society **Redwood Room**. Considered one of the grandest of SF cocktail lounges, this art deco wonder of redwood and marble invites the smartly dressed, top-shelf drinker.

downtown

♫ directory

map & directory

Hermès *B2*
212 Stockton Street
391-7200

Hollywood Billiards *A3*
61 Golden Gate Ave
252-9643

The Irish Bank *B2*
10 Mark Lane
788-7152

Jack's *B1*
615 Sacramento Street
421-7355 $$–$$$

Jacqueline Perfumery *B2*
103 Geary Street
981-0858

J Crew *B3*
865 Market Street
546-6262

Jil Sander *B2*
135 Maiden Lane
273-7070

Joan & David *B2*
172 Geary Street
397-1958

Kenneth Cole *B2*
166 Grant Ave.
981-2653

Kuleto's *A2*
221 Powell Street
397-7720 $–$$$

Laundry Industry *B2*
59 Grant Avenue
576-0720

Le Central *B2*
453 Bush Street
391-2233 $–$$

Le Colonial *A2*
20 Cosmo Place
931-3600 $$–$$$

Lefty O'Doul's *A2*
333 Geary Street
982-8900

Levi's *B2*
300 Post Street
501-0100

Loehmann's *B2*
222 Sutter Street
982-3215

London Wine Bar *C1*
415 Sansome Street
788-4811

Louis Vuitton *B2*
230 Post Street
391-6200

MAC *B2*
5 Claude Lane
837-0615

Macy's *B2*
Stockton & O'Farrell Streets (at Union Square) 397-3333

Margaret O'Leary *B2*
1 Claude Lane
391-1010

Masa's *B2*
648 Bush Street
989-7154 $$

Metier *B2*
355 Sutter Street
989-5395

Neiman-Marcus *B2*
150 Stockton Street
362-3900

Niketown *B2*
278 Post Street
392-6453

Nine West *B2*
250 Stockton Street
772-1924

Nordstrom *B3*
865 Market Street
243-8500

N Peal *B2*
110 Geary Street
421-2713

Old Navy *B3*
801 Market Street
344-0376

Original Joe's *A3*
144 Taylor Street
775-4877 $–$$$

Oritalia *B2*
586 Bush Street
782-8122 $$–$$$

Palio d'Asti *B1*
640 Sacramento Street
395-9800 $$–$$$

Plouf *B2*
40 Belden Place
986-6491 $$–$$$

Postrio California *A2*
545 Post Street
776-7825 $$–$$$

Pottery Barn *B2*
1 Embarcadero Center
788-6810

Ralph Lauren *B2*
90 Post Street
788-7656

Redwood Room *A3*
495 Geary Street
775-4700

Rizzoli *B2*
117 Post Street
984-0225

Rolo *B3*
21 Stockton Street
989-7656

Rubicon *B1*
558 Sacramento Street
434-4100 $$–$$$

Rumpus *B2*
1 Tillman Place
421-2300 $–$$

Saks Fifth Avenue *B2*
384 Post Street
986-4300

Sam's Grill *B2*
374 Bush Street
421-0594 $–$$$

San Francisco Shopping Centre *B3*
865 Market Street
495-5656

Sanrio *B3*
30 Stockton Street
981-5568

Sear's Fine Food *A2*
439 Powell Street
986-1160 $–$$

Sephora *B3*
1 Stockton Street
392-1545

Shalimar *A3*
532 Jones Street
928-6654 $

Silks *C1*
222 Sansome Street
986-2020 $$$

Sutter Station *C2*
554 Market Street
434-4768

Tadich Grill *C1*
240 California Street
391-1849 $$–$$$

Tiffany *B2*
350 Post Street
781-7000

TSE Cashmere *B2*
60 Maiden Lane
391-1112

Ultimo *B2*
140 Geary Street
273-7077

Ur *B1*
663 Clay Street
434-3567 $$

Urban Outfitters *B3*
80 Powell Street
989-1515

Versace *B2*
60 Post Street
616-0604

Virgin Megastore *B3*
2 Stockton Street
397-4525

Wilkes Bashford *B2*
375 Sutter Street
986-4380

Williams-Sonoma *C1*
2 Embarcadero Center
362-6904

YaYa Cuisine *B1*
663 Clay Street
434-3567 $$

Zare *B1*
568 Sacramento St
291-9145 $$–$$$

somarvellous

The area known as SoMa was just plain old 'South of Market' before coming down with a serious case of Manhattan envy. And before that, the no-man's land was simply 'South of the Slot' (the 'slot' being the streetcar track running down Market Street). A once-dicey destination studded with industrial buildings, artists' studios, nightclubs, and a sprawling flower mart, SoMa today is caught up in the city's relentless zeal to commercialize every square inch of space. Comprised of numerous micro-neighbourhoods, its developments have left varying footprints on the landscape. The Yerba Buena arts and cultural centre replaced former fleabag hotels and flophouses with an urban oasis. A few blocks down Third Street (birthplace of Jack London) is South Park, a once-sleepy oval of grass designed during the Gold Rush to resemble a classic London square. Today it is the caffeinated epicentre of the 'hood known as Multimedia Gulch – stomping ground of young techno-wizards. But the true heart and soul of SoMa is the stretch of Folsom Street that's abundant with music clubs, bars, cafés, and late-night restaurants.

day

🏛 The industrial warehouses of SoMa are rapidly being converted, many into discount designer outlets.

👁 The Yerba Buena cultural hub includes SFMOMA [→73]; Yerba Buena Center for the Arts [→73]; Metreon [→80]; and ZEUM [→80]. Nearby are the Ansel Adams Center for Photography [→75]; the Cartoon Art Museum [→75]; and a few commercial galleries [→77].

night

🍴 SoMa is dotted with culinary treasures: most lie to the east of 4th Street; and a few cluster around South Park.

☆ The Metreon's 15 cinemas [→80], Yerba Buena Center for the Arts, a couple of theatres, as well as comedy, poetry, and music venues ensure variety.

🌙 This is SF's nightlife mecca, with clubs clustered around 11th and Folsom Streets.

getting there

🚌 1, 2, 3, 5, 6, 7, 9, 14, 15, 19, 26, 30, 42, 45, 66, 71

🚇 F, J, K, L, M, N

Ⓑ Embarcadero, Montgomery St, Powell St, Civic Center

more shopping | restaurants | cafés & eateries

shopping

interiors, books & music

Within easy strolling distance of one another are four stores whose offerings cross oceans, span centuries, and embrace contrary aesthetics. Purist's paradise *Limn is a shrine to modernism – the vast, multi-level space is filled with furnishings and housewares by most of the major players of the 20th century. Small but pristine, The Magazine's two-storey loft space houses Mies van der Rohe's Barcelona Chair and classics by Le Corbusier and the Eames', as well as a covetable Mueller fridge available in 200 colours. Tucked beneath the freeway a time warp away is *Interieur Perdu, crammed to the rafters with rustic treasures

54

from the French countryside. And for an artful blending of past and present, **Maison d'Etre** retrofits vintage rococo chandeliers with colour-dipped crystals that illuminate ever-changing curiosities: antique circus tarps, cool stainless steel lab furniture, prints of moody photos from the 40s, and a cache of delicious-smelling candles and soaps.

One of the city's best independent bookstores, *Alexander Book Co offers three floors of titles, literate help, and no slavish pandering to the bestseller list. Across the street travellers pick up maps, guidebooks, gadgets, and globes at the *Rand McNally Map & Travel Store. Shooters should check out the *Friends of Photography Bookstore at the Ansel Adams Center [→75] for unusual finds and catalogues. More photography and art books as well as cards, posters, videos, jewellery, toys, and hyper-designed gifts are gathered under one roof at the *SFMOMA Store ↗

Old music doesn't die, it just gets moved to the *Tower Records Outlet Store, where thousands of overstocked CDs are sold for a song. And to listen before you buy, venture into the Metreon's [→80] **Hear Music** to discover dozens of brilliant titles set up at listening stations throughout the store.

fashion

'Designer' outlets supposedly thrive in SoMa but there are only a handful of shining examples. On a corner of South Park is the light and airy *Jeremy's, where the season's unsold treasures – from Valentino to Voyage – are snapped up for prices worth gloating about. Also housed in one of the park's turn-of-the-century converted brick warehouses is ISDA & Co, where racks are heavy with discounted 'Shaker-inspired' clothing for men and women – clean, spare, and woven with just the right

one-of-a-kind

One of the city's quirkiest haunts is Bell'Occhio where spools of fairy-tale ribbons, private label perfumes (including Violet, Marie Antoinette's favourite), French face powder, fuschia silk matador's stockings, milliner's flowers, and other essentials fill the shelves.

For an aphrodisiacal and indulgent afternoon, start out at the **San Francisco Flower Mart** (open 10am–3pm Mon–Sat) where the city's florists come to procure their blooms. Primarily

amount of urban stretch. North on Howard Street, the outlet store for hip haberdashers **Rolo** feeds in bargains from its four SF boutiques for perennial sale days. Next door the **North Face** outlet attracts discount-hunting adventurers bound for field, stream, and snow. And for brand new (and full price) women's fashion with that critical SoMa edge, seek out *Six Brady where candy-coloured T-shirts, cashmere sweaters, embroidered shawls, and street-smart skirts and trousers beckon.

a trade market, many of the vendors sell to the public as well. From here it's a short stroll to **The Wine Club**, for unnaturally friendly and informed advice along with an outstanding (and discounted!) selection of pinots and clarets from California and abroad. And wrap it up at **Pandora's Box**, where European-style chocolates in fantastical packages put a sweet end to a day spent roaming SoMa's streets, or ensure an even sweeter night.

eating
& drinking

restaurants

Ever since restaurateurs figured out that neighbourhood webheads would rather starve than trek across Market Street for fuel, SoMa has been flush with phenomenal food. *Restaurant LuLu ✔ [→111] was the icebreaker. When Reed Hearon opened the

Mediterranean eatery with vaulted ceilings and exposed brick ovens in 93, there was almost no culinary panache South of Market. Seven years later, and under new leadership, LuLu is as noisy and flirtatious a scene as when it first opened. **Azie**, LuLu's French-

Asian spin-off next door, is set to be as popular – LuLu's spill-over alone could fill the seats. *Boulevard [→109] is deliberately less playful. Chef Nancy Oakes is a self-taught prodigy, stylizing crab and mascarpone ravioli with truffle beurre blanc in a sumptuous dining room. Nearby, overlooking the bay, *One Market [→109] is a contrast in styles: cosmopolitan aesthetic as a backdrop for gourmet Midwestern cuisine. Chef Bradley Ogden has elevated stick-to-your-ribs fare to a form of art. The equally lush *Hawthorne Lane [→106] competes for the same clientele. The husband and wife team is electric in the kitchen – try the roast Sonoma lamb with crispy eggplant spring rolls. It's not clear yet if the Mexican restaurant Maya will join this coterie. The outposts in New York were instant hits but San Franciscans aren't accustomed to paying big bucks for guacamole and chillis *rellenos*, however intoxicating the renditions.

There are a few other restaurants that deserve a spot in SoMa's culinary pantheon but fail to create such media buzz. Palomino, for instance, has the best bread pudding this side of the Mason-Dixon line. It's a singles magnet filled with hot bodies from the chichi gym next-door, and has a flaming oven that is probably also responsible for kindling relationships. The best basket of bread in the city and 'alterered egg dishes' await brunch-goers at Town's End, just off the Embarcadero. *Le Charm [→111], meanwhile, is a rare breed in SoMa, a tiny bistro belonging in a Pacific Heights Victorian mansion. Romantic. Darling. Cheap (less than $30 for a prix fixe meal). Tu Lan, hidden along one of the most unsavoury strips in SF, is one of those holes-in-the-wall you hardly dare enter. The Vietnamese food is arguably better and more filling, and certainly cheaper than Manora's Thai or Cha-Am, two excellent Thai options for those seeking safer surroundings and contemporary decor. But it's Red Herring that is scratching at the high-heels of the culinary monoliths. Chef James Ormsby is masterful and his mussels-in-orange-saffron-mint broth are a primary lure. A recent makeover and the Bay views add to the restaurant's appeal.

South Park's restaurants are another story entirely. The mellow *South Park Café could be transplanted to the Luxembourg Gardens in Paris and fit right in. Newspapers are draped on wooden racks for customers to peruse while nibbling pommes frites and grilled steak with red wine sauce. Ristorante Ecco, the other biggie in the park, is also fail safe. Enlightened Italian fare is served in what feels like an igloo, with a limestone floor and skylit bar.

If you are willing to sacrifice park views, there are three restaurants nearby that are worth a look. *Bizou [→110] and *Fringale [→111] compete for Francophiles in search of innovative variations of beef cheeks and cassoulet. At both, the chefs are intrepid, the settings charmed. *Infusion ✔ entices twentysomethings with its live bands and gimmicky fruit-and-vegetable infused vodkas. Vials of the stuff ring the bar (mint, watermelon etc), but it's the food that seals the deal – creamy spinach salads and anise-laced mussels.

SoMa restaurants pop up in the strangest places. There's the industrial Elroy's which could easily double as an airplane hangar. With chef Mark Valiani now on board there are more reasons to go than beautiful crowds and dinosaur cocktails. Follow the locals and you may find the hidden Fly Trap – a resurrection of one of the city's old-time restaurants where diners broker deals over classic French food with a California twist. You'll also struggle to find Buca di Beppo where all your senses will be indulged with generous amounts of Italian food, wine, and kitsch – pure gluttony. Thirsty Bear, on the same street, is an industrial fortress warmed up by garlic and spice and young bodies. Authentic Spanish tapas and home-brewed beer are served. With the opening of the new ballpark, Momo's may have the most coveted seats in the city. Fans who prefer Caesar salad to hot dogs

will soon discover they can run to Momo's and back during the seventh inning stretch. Patently corporate Montage and XYZ are two new eateries. The former is the kingpin in Metreon – see if you can concentrate on 'global cuisine' with ten video screens flashing ads and animation. XYZ, at the new W hotel [→138], feels as stark as its name, but the French food and star-studded scenery offset the sterility. Thank goodness for George Morrone and the new Fifth Floor. No corporate presence here. Just smashing renditions of suckling pig and beef Wellington served in intimate, zebra-carpetted alcoves.

cafés & eateries

Most tech-execs are too busy coding software to have a leisurely lunch. As a result, a thriving café and take-out scene has developed. Lunchtime lines form at Caffè Centro for its salty panini and lemonade. The panini are twice the size at Mondo Café where waiters exchange flirtations (*ciao bella!*) with all the ladies. Café Museo at the SFMOMA charges inflated prices for similar panini combos, but the art-deco setting makes it worth it; plus you're patronizing the arts. You can feel similarly philanthropic at Delancey Street where *spanikopita* and barbecued ribs are prepared by ex-convicts and addicts. You would never guess that this friendly reliable restaurant doubles as a rehab centre. Service is cooler at *Hamburger Mary's, but it wins with grit charm (this is bike messenger territory) and great burgers. To contrast these all-American options, Long Life Noodle Co capitalizes on the Asian craze of the early 90s for bottomless bowls of *jook*.

bars & clubs | map & directory

bars & clubs

Techno club-hopping, rock 'n'roll raging, micro-brew sipping, supper-club swanking, and gay and lesbian cavorting – it all happens in the wide, open SoMa streets. Folsom at 11th is SF's clubbing epicentre, a fun-zone matched only by the Mission for afterhours liveliness [→clubs 122–124].

At the ***Covered Wagon Saloon**, the grittiest of SoMa music clubs, rowdy bike messengers swill Pabst Blue Ribbon and mosh to death metal or high octane punk. Dig the Thursday 'Stinky's Peep Show' for a twisted marriage of trash rock and comical backroom sex show. On any night, at least one of the bands at ***Paradise Lounge** will merit the door charge. The cavernous and labyrinthine venue is a haven for local pop rockers and those who love them. Amiable throngs descend upon the slender but ornate ***Hotel Utah** for twangy Americana acts. Elsewhere local loft dwellers wash their rags, sip pints, and soak up folk and rock unplugged at the quirky **Brain Wash Café & Laundromat**. Jazz junkies head for the stylish ***Up & Down Club**, where younger, experimental/fusion acts work out their chops for packs of well-dressed cats sipping potions du jour. Bridge-and-tunnel twentysomethings quaff award-winning suds at the roomy and airy ***Twenty Tank Brewery** before and after

shmoozing at the slough of clubs nearby. Both the **Gordon Biersch** and **Thirsty Bear** breweries attract yuppier, Financial District Janes and Joes for after-work eats, superior stouts, and sports watching. Affable **Dave's** and the **4th Street Bar & Deli** cater to a similar set who unwind over a cold microbrew and break from casual conversation when someone homers or nails a clutch three-pointer.

Ground zero for the SoMa lesbian clique is the subterranean **CoCo Club ✔** which hosts all manner of festivity from erotic 'Ladies Only' cabaret, to indie rock and techno danceathons. Mostly older gay bikers duck into **Hole in the Wall** to talk Harley and swill draft Bud, but the **Eagle Tavern** attracts hog enthusiasts of a younger, hunkier variety. Boys and daddies rock the leather here daily, cramming the place on Sunday for the spirited beer bust. Made famous in Armistead Maupin's *Tales of the City*, ***The Stud** is perennially popular and ranks among the better SoMa gay haunts. Butch, queen, and young buck alike shake it side by side here, particularly at the Tuesday 'Trannyshack' gig [→123].

Young tech-execs head for the vibrant **Café Mars** which serves fanciful, interstellar creations and libations. Equally gimmicky but some-

what divier is **Pow!**, where a grungier, cooler crew sample the Truth Serum, Ooze, and other such superhero mixtures. Despite their side-by-sideness, **El Bobo** and **Holy Cow** entice different crowds. Somewhat older sophisticates gather in the post-modern El Bobo for pricey imported beers and well-behaved revelling, while few over 30 would dare step foot inside the Holy Cow, a party-till-you-get-laid joint replete with mandatory New Wave tunes and a disco ball. **Julie's Supper Club** is old world refined and classy sans the haughtiness (and some of the luxury) of other supper clubs. It is a good middle ground for those dressed up but not necessarily grown up. For an afternoon nip, step into the bustling **M&M Tavern** where hard drinking beat writers from the two major newspapers nearby plant phoney leads and scoops to run their competitors afoul. Despite its curious out-of-the-way locale, **Annie's Cocktail Lounge** remains an après-gig favourite for local rock gods, while Tuesdays draw Mission-esque greasers for drunken, rousing rounds of punk karaoke.

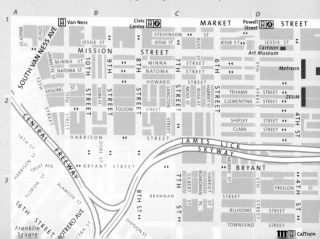

♗ directory

Alexander Book Co ♗E1
50 2nd Street
495-2992

**Annie's Cocktail
Lounge** ♗C3
15 Boardman Place
703-0865

Azie ♗D2
816 Folsom Street
495-5775 $–$$

Bell'Occhio ♗A1
8 Brady Street
864-4048

Bizou ♗D3
598 4th Street
543-2222 $$–$$$

Boulevard ♗G1
1 Mission Street
543-6084 $$–$$$

**Brain Wash Café &
Laundromat** ♗B2
1122 Folsom Street
861-3663

Buca di Beppo ♗D1
855 Howard Street
543-7673 $–$$

Café Mars ♗C3
798 Brannan Street
621-6277

Café Museo ♗E1
151 3rd Street
357-4500 $

Caffè Centro ♗E3
102 South Park
882-1500 $

Cha-Am ♗D2
701 Folsom Street
546-9710 $–$$

CoCo Club ♗B1
139 8th Street
626-2337

**Covered Wagon
Saloon** ♗C2
917 Folsom Street
974-1585

Dave's ♗E1
29 3rd Street
495-6726

Delancey Street ♗F3
600 Embarcadero St
512-5179 $–$$

Eagle Tavern ♗A2
398 12th Street
626-0880

El Bobo ♗A2
1539 Folsom Street
861-6822

Elroy's ♗F2
300 Beale Street
882-7989 $$

Fifth Floor ♗D1
Hotel Palomar,
12 4th Street
348-1555 $–$$$

Fly Trap ♗F2
606 Folsom Street
243-0580 $–$$$

**4th Street
Bar & Deli** ♗D1
55 4th Street
442-6734

**Friends of
Photography
Bookstore** ♗E1
655 Mission Street
495-7000

Fringale ♗D3
570 4th Street
543-0573 $$–$$$

Gordon Biersch ♗F2
2 Harrison Street
243-8246

Hamburger Mary's
♗A2
1582 Folsom Street
626-5767 $–$$

Hawthorne Lane ♗E1
22 Hawthorne Street
777-9779 $$$

Hear Music ♗D1
832 Mission Street
487-1822

**Hole in
the Wall** ♗B2
289 8th Street
431-4695

Holy Cow ♗A2
1535 Folsom Street
621-6087

Hotel Utah ♗D2
500 4th Street
421-8308

Infusion ♗E3
555 2nd Street
543-2282 $$

Interieur Perdu ♗E2
340 Bryant Street
543-1616

ISDA & Co ♗E3
29 South Park
512-0313

Jeremy's ♗E3
2 South Park
882-4929

Julie's Supper Club
♗B2
1123 Folsom Street
861-0707

Le Charm ♗D2
315 5th Street
546-6128 $$

Limn ♗D3
290 Townsend Street
543-5466

**Long Life
Noodle Co** ♗G1
139 Steuart Street
281-3818 $

The Magazine ♗E2
528 Folsom Street
777-4707

Maison d'Etre ♗E3
92 South Park
357-1747

M&M Tavern ♗D1
198 5th Street
362-6386

Manora's Thai ♗A2
1600 Folsom Street
861-6224 $–$$

Maya ♗E2
303 2nd Street
621-8025 $$–$$$

Momo's ♗E3
760 2nd Street
227-8660 $$–$$$

Mondo Cafè ♗E1
602 Mission Street
882-1682 $

Montage ♗D1
Metreon, 4th &
Mission Sts
369-6111 $$–$$$

North Face ♗B1
1325 Howard Street
626-6444

One Market ♗F1
1 Market Street
777-5577 $$$

Palomino ♗F1
345 Spear Street
512-7400 $–$$$

Pandora's Box ♗E3
543 2nd Street
543-3829

Paradise Lounge ♗A2
1501 Folsom Street
621-1912

Pow! ♗C1
101 6th Street
278-0940

**Rand McNally Map &
Travel Store** ♗E1
595 Market Street
777-3131

Red Herring ♗F1
155 Steuart Street
495-6500 $$–$$$

Restaurant LuLu ♗D2
816 Folsom Street
495-5775 $$

Ristorante Ecco ♗E3
101 South Park
495-3291 $$

Rolo ♗B1
1301 Howard Street
861-1999

**San Francisco Flower
Mart** ♗C3
640 Brannan Street
392-7944

SFMOMA Store ♗E1
151 3rd Street
357-4000

Six Brady ♗A1
6 Brady Street
626-6678

South Park Café ♗E3
108 South Park
495-7275 $$

The Stud ♗B1
399 9th Street
863-6623

Thirsty Bear ♗E1
661 Howard Street
974-0905 $$

**Tower Records Outlet
Store** ♗D3
660 3rd Street
957-9660

Town's End ♗E3
2 Townsend Street
512-0749 $–$$

Tu Lan ♗C1
8 6th Street
626-0927 $

**Twenty Tank
Brewery** ♗A2
316 11th Street
255-9455

Up & Down Club ♗B2
1151 Folsom Street
626-2388

The Wine Club ♗C2
953 Harrison Street
512-9086

XYZ ♗E1
181 3rd Street
817-7836 $–$$$

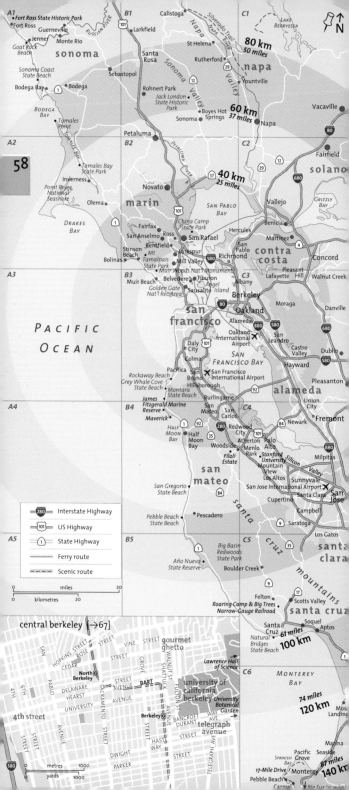

around san francisco

hiking & biking

marin county

What outdoor enthusiasts love
about San Francisco is that rugged Marin is its backyard. Hikers
and bikers stream over the Golden Gate Bridge every weekend
to partake in the splendour of
Marin, with trails that meander
through towering redwoods,
past windswept fields and
crashing waves. Just across the
bridge are the Marin Headlands.
Stop by the Ranger Station
(☎ 331-1540) to pick up a trail
map. Mt Tamalpais also abounds
with trails, and its rough terrain
makes it a particular favourite
among mountain bikers.
The reward for tackling the
mountain is stunning views
from the top. Angel Island is
another choice destination for
hikers and bikers. Bikes can be
hired in Sausalito from:
Sausalito Bike & Skate Rental
803 Bridgeway ☎ 331-4448
🚲 approx $5/hr; $25/day

wine country

The Wine Country's level terrain,
warm weather, and gorgeous
scenery make it ideal cycling
territory. Rent a bike in the area
and head out on your own, or
join a guided bike tour.
Napa Valley Bike Tours &
Rentals 4080 Byway East, Napa
☎ 1-800-707-2453 🚲 $7/hr;
$22/day; tours from $85

berkeley & the east bay

The East Bay offers ample
opportunities for hiking and
biking. Tilden Park (in the Berkeley
Hills) and neighbouring Wildcat
Canyon and Park are covered
with trails. Redwood Regional
Park in the Oakland Hills is
another great outdoors spot.
The 31-mile Skyline Trail, open to
hikers and horseback riders,
traverses all the East Bay Parks.
Missing Link Mountain Bikes
1988 Shattuck St, Berkeley
☎ 1-510-843-7471 🚲 $20–$35/day

south of the city

Some of the best strolling and
biking spots are in and around
beachy Pacifica and Montara.
If it's the wide outdoors that
you're in search of, head further
south to the state beaches, parks,
and reserves along the coast
towards Half Moon Bay, Santa
Cruz, and Monterey.

Bicycle Rental Center
131 Center Street, Santa Cruz
☎ 1-831-426-8687
🚲 $7/hr; $25/day

transport options

marin county

To fully explore Marin County it is
definitely best to have your own
wheels. Alternatively travel by
ferry. Ferries can get booked up,
so reserve by phone in advance.
🚢 **Blue & Gold Fleet:** Pier 41 to
Alcatraz ($12.25), Angel Island
($11), Sausalito ($12), Tiburon
($12); Pier 39 for bay cruises ($17).
They also run boat/bus trips to
other parts of Marin ☎ 773-1188.
🚢 **Golden Gate Ferries:** Ferry
Building, Pier 1 to Sausalito
($9.60) and Larkspur ($5.70)
☎ 923-2000
🚢 **Red & White Fleet:** Pier 43.5
to Sausalito ($9.60) and for bay
cruises ($17) ☎ 673-2900
🚌 **Golden Gate Transit:** an extensive bus system throughout
Marin County from the Transbay
Terminal – guided bus trips are
also offered ☎ 923-2000

wine country

The best way to enjoy the
scenery and the wineries at your
own pace is by car. Several bus
systems also make the trek.
🚌 **Golden Gate Transit:** buses
between SF and Santa Rosa once
an hour daily ☎ 923-2000
🚌 **Sonoma County Transit:** buses
throughout Sonoma
☎ 1-707-576-7433 or 1-800-345-7433
🚌 **Napa Valley Transit:** buses
throughout the Wine Country
☎ 1-800-696-6443
🚌 **Greyhound:** from the Transbay
Terminal to Calistoga ($28) and
Sonoma ($21) ☎ 1-800-231-2222
☞ **Gray Line:** one-day guided
tours of Napa and Sonoma ($46)
☎ 558-9400
☞ **Blue & Gold Fleet:** boat and
bus tours from Pier 41 to the
Wine Country ($52) ☎ 773-1188

berkeley & the east bay

The simplest way to get to
Berkeley is on the BART. For a
more scenic route take the bus.
🅱 **BART:** the downtown Berkeley
stop is two blocks from the university campus ☎ 1-650-992-2278
🚌 **AC Transit:** the East Bay area is
covered by over 100 bus routes
☎ 1-510-817-1717

south of the city

The public transportation system
is comprehensive and well-main-
tained, but if you plan to get away
from the city, a car is necessary.
🅱 **BART:** trains south to Daly
City and Colma ☎ 992-2278

🚌 **Greyhound buses:** from SF's
Transbay Terminal to San Jose
($10), Monterey ($30), and Santa
Cruz ($12) ☎ 1-800-231-2222
🚌 **Blue & Gold Fleet:** buses from
Fisherman's Wharf to Monterey
($52) and Carmel ($52) ☎ 773-1188
🚌 **Red & White Fleet:** buses from
Transbay Terminal to Monterey
($50) ☎ 673-2900
🚌 **Santa Clara Valley Transporta-
tion Authority:** buses and light
railways throughout Santa Clara
County, including Menlo Park
and San Jose ☎ 1-408-321-2300
🚌 **SamTrans:** buses throughout the
peninsula. Services run from Daly
City, Downtown SF, and SF Interna-
tional Airport ☎ 1-800-660-4287
🚊 **CalTrain:** from SF CalTrain
Depot to Palo Alto ($4) and San
Jose ($5.25) ☎ 1-800-660-4287
🚊 **Amtrak:** from Emeryville to
Santa Cruz ($13.50); and from
Oakland to Carmel ($26) and
Monterey ($25) ☎ 1-800-872-7245

information points

Berkeley ☎ 1-510-549-7040
w www.berkeleycvb.com
Bodega Bay ☎ 1-707-875-3422
w www.bodegabay.com
Calistoga ☎ 1-707-942-6333
w www.calistogafun.com
Carmel ☎ 1-831-624-2522
Marin County ☎ 499-5000
w www.visitmarin.org
Marin Headlands ☎ 331-1540
w www.ups.gov\goga
Mill Valley ☎ 388-9700
w www.millvalley.org
Monterey Peninsula
☎ 1-831-648-5350
w www.monterey.com
Russian River Region
☎ 1-707-869-9212
w www.russianriver.org
Sausalito ☎ 332-0505
w www.sausalito.org
San Jose & Silicon Valley
☎ 1-408-291-5250
w www.sjchamber.com
San Mateo County
☎ 1-650-348-7600
w www.sanmateocountycvb.com
Santa Cruz ☎ 1-831-425-1234
w www.santacruzca.org
Santa Rosa ☎ 1-707-577-8674
w www.visitsantarosa.com
Sonoma Valley
☎ 1-707-996-1090
w www.sonomavalley.com
Tiburon ☎ 435-5633

getting your bearings

mellow marin

Organic alfalfa sprouts wait patiently on store shelves for housewives in bell-bottoms to drive them home in $100,000 cars. One of America's wealthiest yet quirkiest counties – where rock stars chat with Zen monks over the backyard fence – Marin personifies every facet of the California Dream. Golden crescents of beach flank forests and a fully-fledged mountain; mansions perch on every bluff and hillside, boasting walls of glass; hot tubs sparkle like scattered diamonds. Envy-struck San Franciscans mock the smug self-indulgence of those visionary hippies who settled here seeking casual chic in the 60s and 70s only to watch their property values skyrocket. Today egrets still soar over Marin's wide wetlands, and the casual spirit that once lured Janis Joplin and the Grateful Dead still prevails down its country lanes. But the unspoken truth is that nearly everyone you see is ridiculously rich.

around sausalito   ♫B3

Crossing the Golden Gate Bridge [→70] is never so satisfying as when you're using it to go somewhere. Windswept Vista Point, at the spot where the bridge finally alights on solid ground, commands a gull's-eye view ✓ of San Francisco, but savvy photographers cross over to Conzelman Road for its jaw-dropping bridge-and-city panoramas. The surrounding *Golden Gate National Recreation Area is honeycombed with hidden coves and eerie, abandoned military garrisons built to guard San Francisco from invaders that never dared show up.

Charming and chichi Sausalito likes nothing better than to be compared to the Italian Riviera. Ferries to and from SF offer facefuls of salt air and the sparkle of bridges and blue sky and bay, with dark hills brooding beyond. The town's checkered history as a brawlers' lair is long forgotten; today chic boutiques, restaurants, and cafés claim the waterfront. With its owner-built vessels ranging from the palatial to the silly, Sausalito's vibrant houseboat community spotlights the 70s-style eccentricity that fuels Marin's reputation. For a giant's perspective of tides, currents, and local geography, the US Army Corps of Engineers' 1.5-acre *SF Bay & Delta Model is a working replica whose waters really move in and out just like the flowing tides.

Further along the wannabe Riviera's bayshore are quaint Tiburon ✓ and posh Belvedere with their real estate ranking among the nation's priciest. City kids flock to Tiburon for weekend brunch on the deck at places like *Sam's Anchor Café and *Guaymas, soaking up the sun and sipping margaritas as they gaze across the bay. From Tiburon, ferries skim to *Angel Island. Now a state park with heavenly vistas, it was purgatory for boatloads of Chinese immigrants detained here within sight of their goal, San Francisco. Many were deported, never reaching the mainland. Today hiking trails thread the peaceful undeveloped island's slopes and coves, while military barracks still show Chinese poems chiselled into their walls.

inland marin ♫B2

Eastern Marin's upscale bedroom communities ooze laid-back luxury. Mill Valley's name evokes a sleepy village of shady streets and cozy shops. And it is, but the streets are lined with million-dollar cottages and the shoppers browsing the boutiques sometimes make appearances on the cover of *Vanity Fair*. Vintage-vinyl collectors from across the globe make pilgrimages to 33-rpm shrine *Village Music, while those hungry for classic American food settle in at the popular *Buckeye Roadhouse. To the north, old-fashioned Larkspur is home to *Lark Creek Inn, an elegant restaurant set amidst pines and redwoods, serving hearty regional fare. Nearby, at Larkspur ferry docks, the forbidding San Quentin State Prison is the antithesis of everything Marin stands for. This is home to celebs

* = featured in the directory

mount tamalpais state park
$B2, B3

Legends say the outline of Mount Tamalpais seen from a distance is the silhouette of a recumbent enchanted Indian princess. Up close, 2600-ft-high 'Mt Tam' is the Bay Area's answer to an alp. Within *Mount Tamalpais State Park, hiking trails thrust and wriggle for hundreds of miles through towering redwoods and emerald meadows, with expansive views of the open sea. A loop trail rings the summit, whose vast stone amphitheatre bathes in sunshine above ghostly coils of fog. Other trails of varying difficulty run alongside creeks, cross the chaparral, and sweep down to Stinson Beach below. This is also mountain bike terrain –

the mountain bike was invented in Marin and Mount Tamalpais probably had a lot to do with it. Excellent trails criss-cross the mountain: two of the most popular are the Old Stage Road and the Old Railroad Grade [→145 for bike hire]. The Ranger Station Office sells trail maps. Also within the park is the popular *Muir Woods National Monument, whose trails wander among a virgin stand of old-growth redwood trees hundreds of feet tall, ten feet thick, and nearly a thousand years old. Sunlight scarcely pierces the canopy of this last vestige of the once-magnificent forest that blanketed the continent's Pacific coast.

of a different kind: the psychopaths on Death Row. Northwards, the backroads wind through Kentfield, Ross, and San Anselmo, studded with folksy enclaves of the rich and sometimes famous. Beyond bustling San Rafael lie the oakwoods and green marshes of *China Camp State Park. Clinging to a golden slip of shore, its deserted fishing village still boasts the pier and shanties where hundreds of Chinese once caught and processed shrimp.

→ wine country

the pacific coast
$A2, B2, B3

From Sausalito or Mount Tamalpais, Highway 1 runs westward to the ocean. A mile inland from **Muir Beach**, Zen Buddhist retreat *Green Gulch Farm offers lodgings, lessons, and meditation sessions, and has a Sunday market selling produce from the organic gardens. The less ascetic sip sherry, mead, and ale at the Elizabethan-inspired *Pelican Inn, where cottage pie, bangers, and a game of darts persuade homesick Brits to stay overnight (B&B from $174). If Muir Beach's parking lot is full, the nearby Muir Beach Overlook offers inspirational coastal views. **Stinson Beach** is the most popular destination on the Marin coast and on sunny days, thousands flock here to lie on the sand and dream of owning one of the opulent bungalows that line the strand. Reclusive residents of **Bolinas** uproot highway signs directing outsiders to their close-knit community; those who find it can decide whether its secluded beach and bluffs are worth the town's unsettling ambience.

The informative *Bear Valley Visitor Center in **Olema** sits atop the San Andreas Fault and is the starting point

for the Earthquake Trail, a short walk traversing the exact epicentre of the monster 1906 quake that destroyed San Francisco. Beyond are Czech-flavoured **Inverness**, the calm waters of flower-fringed *Tomales Bay State Park, and the 70,000 acres of *Point Reyes National Seashore which feels like the rim of the world. Lordly Tule elks roam free around northern Tomales Point, while on brackish inlets oyster farms offer picnickers their catches, raw and barbecued. In 1579, Sir Francis Drake spent five weeks here repairing the *Golden Hind*. The white cliffs overlooking what is now named Drake's Beach so resembled Dover's that he dubbed California 'Nova Albion' – 'New England' – and claimed it for the queen. Awesome Pacific waves pounding a seemingly endless beach along Point Reyes' western shore will shake the knees and cleanse the soul. From December to April, heavily bundled figures stake out one of the world's best whalewatching spots around Point Reyes Lighthouse at the peninsula's outermost tip.

directory

around sausalito

Angel Island State Park ☎ 897-0715

Golden Gate National Recreation Area ☎ 556-0560

Guaymas
5 Main Street, Tiburon ☎ 435-6300 $$

Sam's Anchor Café
27 Main Street, Tiburon ☎ 435-4527 $$

SF Bay & Delta Model
2100 Bridgeway ☎ 332-3871
◑ 9am–4pm Tue–Sat. ▣ free

inland marin

Buckeye Roadhouse
15 Shoreline Hwy, Mill Valley ☎ 388-7400 $$–$$$

China Camp State Park ☎ 456-0766

Lark Creek Inn
234 Magnolia Ave, Larkspur ☎ 924-7766 $$–$$$

Village Music
9E Blithedale Ave, Mill Valley ☎ 388-7400

mount tamalpais state park

Mount Tamalpais State Park ☎ 388-2070

Muir Woods National Monument ☎ 388-2595

the pacific coast

Bear Valley Visitor Center
Bear Valley Rd, near Hwy 1, Olema ☎ 663-1092

Green Gulch Farm
1601 Shoreline Hwy, near Muir Beach ☎ 383-3134

Pelican Inn
10 Pacific Way (at Hwy 1), Muir Beach ☎ 383-6000 $$

Point Reyes National Seashore ☎ 669-1250

Tomales Bay State Park ☎ 669-1140

fruit of the vine

Rolling hills like recumbent lions cradle the Wine Country's alluring valleys. Vineyards bask under cloudless skies while hot springs gurgle invitingly from the earth. Picnic baskets overflow with locally grown fruit and cheese. At faux chateau after faux chateau, welcoming vintners pour glasses of Zinfandel, Riesling, Chardonnay, Pinot Noir, Merlot, and more – even Champagne. And it's all California-style. Even San Franciscans who prefer hops to grapes sit in their offices dreaming of Sonoma's paradisical river and coastline.

wine country

napa valley   ♇B1, C1

Hundreds of visitor-friendly wineries throng Napa Valley's vine-blanketed lowlands, and more vintners and tourists seem to crowd into the valley every year. Each winery strives to distinguish itself with its own trademark: Minoan columns here, a wishing well there, bocce-ball courts, and sculpture gardens over there. If the panoply of choices is daunting, hop aboard the *Napa Valley Wine Train, featuring gourmet meals and local wines in restored 1917 Pullman dining cars that cruise alongside the valley's main drag **Highway 29**. Most visitors take to Highway 29 which is lined with wineries, testing their driving skills against as much wine as they can guzzle. Booklets describing Napa's wineries are free at the larger establishments and visitor centres.

Since 1876, *Beringer Vineyards' reds and whites have been mellowing along miles of cool tunnels that still bear the pick-marks of Chinese labourers – its expansive gardens and ornate mansion make it a popular stop. The **Silverado Trail** (a road running parallel to' Highway 29) is less crowded and holds some of Napa's most respected wineries, including award-winning *Stag's Leap Wine Cellars and the trés Gaulois *Clos du Val Wine Co.

At the north end of the valley around cozy **Calistoga** with its *fin-de-siècle* storefronts erected directly above hot subterranean springs, no less than a dozen spas [→84] vie to immerse visitors in steaming mineral pools and medicinal volcanic mud. Furious but punctual, Calistoga's *Old Faithful Geyser is one of only three around the world that spout on schedule.

Deep in the woods near the pleasant small town of **St Helena**, *White Sulphur Springs Spa with its creekside cottages is the region's first, attracting exfoliate-starved San Franciscans since 1852. The town is also home to *Tra Vigne, an upscale restaurant and more modestly priced *cantinetta* which has long made bright Tuscan dishes relevant in the Napa Valley setting. Other fine dining options can be found in **Yountville**, a bend along the Wine Country road where several big-name chefs have hung their toques. Foodies from around the world flock to *French Laundry, a vine-covered farmhouse where Cal-French concoctions are to be marvelled at. Gutsy cassoulet and *coq au vin* at *Bistro Jeanty are decidedly more affordable. And for a luxurious overnight Napa experience book a table and a room at *Auberge du Soleil [→143].

sonoma valley   ♇B1

For all Napa's yuppie appeal, its sister-county Sonoma enjoys a slightly more non-conformist heritage. Malcontents have always fled big cities for these lush slopes, including author Jack London and proponents of 1846's Bear Flag Rebellion, which for a brief time established California as an independent nation. London's former ranch is now the 800-acre *Jack London State Historic Park where riders and hikers can roam its hills and ruined mansion. Sonoma's wineries, not packed in quite as tightly as Napa's, have more of a family feel (and wine tasting is almost always free). At *Buena Vista, the state's oldest premium winery, one parking space is earmarked for a descendant of the Hungarian count who launched California's wine industry in 1857. *Sebastiani offers a popular tour with a peek at its 60,000-gallon wine cask, the world's largest. Bustling *Viansa features a vast delicatessen and a terrace with lovely views – an idyllic lunch spot in summer. Just south of Sonoma, Winona Ryder's hometown, **Petaluma** – so perfect a slice of retro-USA that they used it in *American Graffiti* – hosts annual arm-wrestling championships.

Sonoma's recent surge of Euro-inspired restaurants

* = featured in the directory

russian river

⚡A1

West of Sonoma Valley, the lazy **Russian River** winds through redwoods, orchards, and yet more vineyards before meeting the sea at **Jenner**. Funky resorts lining the riverbanks cater mainly to gay partyers but also to vacationing families, campers, and hippies, and on summer weekends the shoreline is thick with (often naked) bodies lolling in the sun. Huckleberry Finns dream away long days here drifting downstream on innertubes and canoes. **Guerneville** is ground zero for picnic supplies, cafés, and information, where at the *Chamber of Commerce you can find maps and

is giving Napa's a run for their mushrooms. Among the tantalizing choices are *Deuce and *Café la Haye, located just off the main town plaza. Fresh-off-the-farm produce and regional wines are emphasized at Deuce, while regulars at tiny, casual Café la Haye salivate over daily risotto or dishes such as pan-roasted chicken breast with goat cheese herb stuffing.

lists of the region's many B&Bs, canoe rentals, resorts, and restaurants. The Russian River's most notorious attractions, however, are off-limits: Monte Rio's ultra-exclusive Bohemian Grove is where the world's most powerful men – US presidents, billionaires, heads of state – frolic wantonly in a private forest. And the area's numerous illegal marijuana plantations are often hidden away on public land. Come in August and September for the apple harvest, but stay away during rainy winters, when the river becomes a frothing torrent.

63

sonoma coast

⚡A1

Sonoma's moody coast, a far cry from *Baywatch*, was the flashpoint where two vast empires finally collided: by the early 19th century, fur-happy Russians had expanded their hunting grounds all the way down the Pacific coast to this northernmost outpost of Spanish California. Thus Sonoma County is the world's only place where a Spanish mission (downtown Sonoma) exists a few miles from an old Russian Orthodox chapel (Fort Ross). Today these wild coves, cliffs, dunes, and headlands draw beachcombers, birdwatchers, anglers, and hermits. If you plan to spend more

than a day exploring the area's natural beauty, **Bodega Bay**'s many B&Bs and seafood restaurants make it a natural home port. From this fishing village, a series of spectacular beaches with the collective name Sonoma Coast State Beaches sweep northward up to Jenner. Each of the ten strands has a personality of its own. **Goat Rock Beach**, at the mouth of the Russian River, plays host to a colony of harbour seals. Twelve miles north of tiny Jenner, along a coastal highway whose panoramas are as gut-wrenching as its zigzags *Fort Ross State Historic Park** eerily rises from the

customary fog. This faithfully reconstructed Russian settlement, with its rustic Orthodox church and shivery barracks, evokes the tzarist fur trappers who colonized the area and nearly wiped out the otter population. Miles from civilization, exclusive *Sea Ranch Lodge offers total isolation inside a private seaside community, with sleek 70s architecture, beaches, a golf course, and a country-club sensibility.

directory

napa valley

Auberge du Soleil
18300 Highway 12, Boyes Hot Springs ☎ 1-707-963-1211 $$$

Beringer Vineyards
2000 Main Street, St Helena
☎ 1-707-963-7115

Bistro Jeanty
6510 Washington St, Yountville
☎ 1-707-944-0103 $$

Clos du Val Wine Company
5330 Silverado Trail
☎ 1-707-252-6711

French Laundry
6640 Washington St, Yountville
☎ 1-707-944-2380 $$$

Napa Valley Wine Train
1275 McKinstry Street, Napa
☎ 1-800-427-4124 Ⓡ Ⓢ $30–$90 ♿ w www.winetrain.com

Old Faithful Geyser
1299 Tubbs Lane, Calistoga
☎ 1-707-942-6463 Ⓢ $6

Stag's Leap Wine Cellars
5766 Silverado Trail
☎ 1-707-944-2020

Tra Vigne
1050 Charter Oak Avenue, St Helena
☎ 1-707-963-4444 $$

White Sulphur Springs Spa
3100 White Sulphur Springs Rd, St Helena ☎ 1-707-963-4361

sonoma valley

Buena Vista Winery
18000 Old Winery Rd, Sonoma
☎ 1-800-926-1266

Café la Haye
140 E Napa Street, Sonoma
☎ 1-707-935-5994 $–$$

Deuce
691 Broadway, Sonoma
☎ 1-707-933-3823 $–$$

Jack London State Historic Park
☎ 1-707-938-5216

Sebastiani Vineyards
389 4th Street, E Sonoma
☎ 1-707-938-5532

Viansa Winery
25200 Arnold Drive, Sonoma
☎ 1-707-935-4700

russian river

Chamber of Commerce
16200 1st Street, Guerneville
☎ 1-707-869-9000

sonoma coast

Fort Ross State Historic Park
☎ 1-707-847-3286

Sea Ranch Lodge
60 Seawalk Drive, (north of Fort Ross, on Hwy 1) ☎ 1-707-785-2371 $$–$$$

wine country

south of the city ⊙

surf & silicon

Head south on Highway 1, and a continuous fringe of beaches stretches for hours, the pale sand mostly deserted save the occasional seal. Alternatively, take Highway 101, just parallel, to plunge into suburban Shangri-La: sprawling ranch-style homes, strip malls, and then the black glass blockhouses of secretive Silicon Valley. Two worlds could scarcely be more spiritually remote than those of Santa Cruz's surfers and San Jose's software titans. Both roads meet in Monterey, where shades of California history still flit against a spectacular waterfront, shameless tourist snares, and a world-famous aquarium.

san mateo county coast $\square$ B3, B4, B5

Starting just south of San Francisco and easier to reach than those of Sonoma [→62–63] or Marin County [→60–61], San Mateo County's 40-plus miles of beaches are just as rugged and just as vast. And the vibe in its towns, like **Pacifica**, which hosts a sardonic annual Fog Festival, is a tad folksier. Brisk walkers find paradise on the smooth sands of Pacifica's convenient **Rockaway Beach**, the lovely and lonesome stretches of **Montara State Beach**, and the seething, anemone-studded tidepools of *James Fitzgerald Marine Reserve. Meanwhile, white-sanded **Gray Whale Cove State Beach** ranks among the state's strands where nudity is allowed. The strategically situated *Point Montara Lighthouse doubles as a friendly hostel, where for peanuts, free spirits are lulled to sleep by the sound of the sea.

Surfers worldwide speak in hushed tones of **Maverick**, where every winter daredevil waveriders risk death on towering, tsunami-like swells. Walk from West Point

Avenue in Princeton along the shore to the western breakwater of Pillar Point Harbor. **Half Moon Bay** stands as the last outpost of civilization before Santa Cruz, far to the south, so pause for snacks and supplies. From here the beaches get wilder and lonelier all the way down to towering *Pigeon Point Lighthouse where the adjacent building serves as a hostel.

*Año Nuevo State Reserve ▲ is home to a colony of rare elephant seals. The only way to view these gigantic pinnipeds fighting, making whoopee, and giving birth from December through March is on guided walks (reservations required). There are no tours at other times of the year, when the seals are fewer and lazier.

the peninsula & silicon valley $\square$ B3, C4

A few years after the Great 1906 Quake, San Francisco decided to rebury all its dead beyond its boundaries, thereby creating the all-cemetery town of **Colma**. Country churchyards they're not, but the monument-studded rolling green acres that comprise the surreal landscape of this 'City of the Dead' are an intriguing and easy getaway from SF.

South of San Francisco International Airport, the millionaire enclaves of **Hillsborough** and **Atherton** are a northern Beverly Hills, their columned manses sheltering the Bay Area's uppermost crust – baseball legend Willie Mays had to fight bigots to be allowed to live in Atherton. Adjacent **Burlingame** hosts the unexpected *Burlingame Museum of Pez Memorabilia, displaying the world's largest collection of Pez candy dispensers.

Peninsula towns give a hint of the self-satisfied commuter's life. In **Palo Alto**, Spanish roofs shield well-bred brains like Chelsea Clinton's from the sun at *Stanford University. At the university's Rodin Sculpture Garden an edition of *The Thinker* forms part of the largest Rodin collection outside Paris. For information and free tours of the country's most prestigious

The South Bay is an odd marriage of surfers and silicon chips, of newly minted software millionaires and old-money establishment – all vying for a piece of the action.

*= featured in the directory

private university, head to the Romanesque main quad. On and around University Avenue you'll find all the accoutrements of a college town: overflowing beer gardens, trendy clothing stores, quirky music venues, budget restaurants, and ubiquitous coffeehouse cum bookstores. Of particular note is *Evvia which brings glamour and style to Greek cuisine, and *L'Amie Donia which draws a huge contingent of gastronomes to savour boldly flavoured French food.

Elegant *Filoli Estate near haughty **Woodside** is recognizable as the setting for TV's *Dynasty*. The lavish mansion is ringed with a vast year-round flower garden. For a rather different slice of American life, make your way to the heart of **Silicon Valley**. Techies touring this stretch between Palo Alto and San Jose often come away mystified as there's no focal point for the widely scattered and architecturally undistinguished computer firms, which don't encourage prying eyes anyway. Instead, **San Jose**'s stirring *Tech Museum of Innovation [→81] gives a hands-on feel for the wizardry that goes on behind those high-security doors. From a time before modern technology, *Winchester Mystery House is a zigzaggy 160-room puzzle of a mansion. The

house was erected by a Victorian rifle heiress who believed she could only satisfy the ghosts of those killed by her family's guns if she never stopped building this house. Craftsmen thus laboured 24 hours a day for 38 years. Stairways lead nowhere, windows are set into floors, and doors open to reveal solid walls. Also in San Jose, is the *Rosicrucian Egyptian Museum ↘. Run by a sect that claims a 4000-year lineage, it displays the largest collection of mummies and Egyptian artefacts in the western United States.

Cognitive powers fall by the wayside at **Santa Clara**'s *Paramount's Great America, one of the nation's largest and silliest theme parks, with thrill rides based loosely on Paramount films.

santa cruz   *C5*

Boasting a graceful sylvan University of California campus, an antique wooden roller coaster, and miles of swimmable beaches is Santa Cruz. Year-round, surfers congregate just off shore, where their sport, fresh from Hawaii, first took root on the mainland. Bone up on local culture at the tiny *Santa Cruz Surfing Museum, housed in a lighthouse, then step outside to watch wet-suited bodies cruise the waves just below.

Natural Bridges State Beach and its adjoining park are a winter haven for orange-and-black monarch butterflies, their bright wings fluttering by the thousands. Further along, the *Santa Cruz Beach Boardwalk, an old-fashioned seaside funfair, recalls an earlier era with cotton candy, penny arcades, and a carousel so old it's been declared a national landmark. Vegetarian fast food, a local staple, is a bargain at *Dharma's Natural Foods, which takes pride in never serving 'anything that had a mother'. Downtown Santa Cruz, centred on Pacific Avenue, reveals an amiable pedestrian-friendly district

of bookshops, boutiques, restaurants, and health-food emporia. The *Visitor Information Center can fill you in on the area's many upscale B&Bs.

The thickly forested Santa Cruz Mountains, north of town, shelter more than their share of surprises. The *Mystery Spot is an all-American roadside tourist attraction where optical illusions and/or gravitational anomalies have people and buildings leaning at odd angles, balls rolling uphill, and bumper stickers appearing magically on visitors' cars. The *Roaring Camp & Big Trees Narrow-Gauge Railroad retraces its

hundred-year-old route from Felton through colossal redwoods, a canyon, and over river rapids high into the mountains. A connecting line runs all the way to the Beach Boardwalk and back. Round off the ride at the depot's Wild West saloon and chuck wagon barbecue.

Deep in the forest beyond Boulder Creek, *Big Basin Redwoods State Park's trails wind among enormous sequoia trees nearly 2000 years old. This is perhaps the best place in the Bay Area to appreciate what some consider to be the most magnificent trees on the planet.

monterey peninsula
♪C6

Eighteenth-century Spanish friars could no more resist this moody peninsula with its wind-gnarled pines and cypress than the whalers, artists, and tourist hordes who later arrived, in succession. Today the stink and scum of John Steinbeck's beloved Cannery Row in **Monterey** have been transformed into souvenir malls of an antiseptic slickness. Yet in their midst is *Monterey Bay Aquarium ▼, among the world's very best, with its hundreds of thousands of creatures, its kelp forest, and frenzied otters, iridescent kingdoms of jellyfish, and sharks gliding past vast sheets of glass.

From **Pacific Grove**, a former Methodist utopian community, the 17-Mile Drive curves through exclusive gated communities and along the most scenic stretches of the Monterey Peninsula – though drivers must pay a $9 toll. The Drive and nearby *Pebble Beach Golf Links have just been purchased by Clint Eastwood, who was formerly the mayor of Carmel. Golfers from Canberra to Cape Cod hyperventilate at the thought of getting a chance to play the legendary links at Pebble Beach, Spyglass Hill, Cypress Point, and Spanish Bay. Many are actually public courses, open to everyone and all it takes is a reservation and a big pile of cash.

Clinging to the bottom of the peninsula is **Carmel**, a fabled getaway whose beach, cypresses, and tearoom-dotted lanes call out for easel and palette. For fussiness, however, the laws of this relentlessly quaint town rival Singapore's: you can't chew gum on the streets or play live music in the bars and restaurants. Southward, Highway 1 descends into **Big Sur**, whose misty cliffs beetling over crashing surf sent Henry Miller, Jack Kerouac, and his Beatnik pals around the twist.

directory

san mateo county coast

Año Nuevo State Reserve
New Years Creek Road, Pescadero (off Hwy 1, south of Half Moon Bay)
☎ 1-650-879-0227 🅿 $5 🅳 $4 per person (walking tour)
🕐 8am–sunset daily. ♿

James Fitzgerald Marine Reserve
California Avenue (or Cypress Ave off Hwy 1), Moss Beach
☎ 1-650-728-3584
🕐 dawn–dusk daily.

Pigeon Point Lighthouse
210 Pigeon Point Road (at Hwy 1), Pescadero
☎ 1-650-879-0633
🅳 $15–$17 (non-members) ♿

Point Montara Lighthouse
Highway 1 (at 16th St), Montara
☎ 1-650-728-7177
🅳 $15–$17 (non-members) ♿

the peninsula & silicon valley

Burlingame Museum of Pez Memorabilia
214 California Drive, Burlingame
☎ 1-650-347-2301 🅳 free
🕐 10am–6pm Tue–Sat. ♿

Evvia
420 Emerson Road, Palo Alto
☎ 1-650-326-0983 $$

Filoli Estate
86 Canada Road, Woodside
☎ 1-650-364-2880 🅳 $10

🕐 mid-Feb–mid-Oct: 10am–3pm Tue–Sat. ♿

L'Amie Donia
530 Bryant Street, Palo Alto
☎ 1-650-323-7614 $$

Paramount's Great America
Great American Parkway
2401 Agnew Road, Santa Clara
☎ 1-408-988-1776 🅳 $33
🕐 Apr–Oct: 10am–8pm daily. ♿

Rosicrucian Egyptian Museum
1342 Naglee Avenue, San Jose
☎ 1-408-947-3635 🅳 $7
🕐 10am–5pm daily.

Stanford University
Memorial Editorium,
551 Serra Mall, Stanford
☎ 1-650-723-2560 🅳 free
☞ 11am & 3.15pm daily. ♿

Tech Museum of Innovation
201 S Market Street, San Jose
☎ 1-408-294-8324 🅳 $8
🕐 10am–6pm daily (to 8pm Thu). ♿

Winchester Mystery House
525 S Winchester Boulevard, San Jose ☎ 1-408-247-2101
🅳 $13.95 🕐 65-min tours from 9.30am–5pm daily.

santa cruz

Big Basin Redwoods State Park
☎ 1-831-338-8860

Dharma's Natural Foods
4250 Capitola Road, Capitola
☎ 1-831-462-1717 $

Mystery Spot
465 Mystery Spot Road (off Branciforte Drive) Santa Cruz
☎ 1-831-423-8897 🅳 $4
🕐 9am–5pm daily (to 6pm Sat & Sun).

Roaring Camp & Big Trees Narrow-Gauge Railroad
Roaring Camp Road (off Graham Hill Rd) Felton
☎ 1-831-335-4484 🅳 $14
🕐 ring for schedule. ♿

Santa Cruz Beach Boardwalk
400 Beach Street, Santa Cruz
☎ 1-831-426-7433 ♿

Santa Cruz Surfing Museum
West Cliff Drive, Mark Abbott Lighthouse, Santa Cruz
☎ 1-831-420-6289 🅳 free
🕐 12–4pm Thu–Mon. ♿

Santa Cruz Visitors Information Center
701 Front Street (at Water St), Santa Cruz
☎ 1-800-833-3494 ♿

monterey peninsula

Monterey Bay Aquarium
886 Cannery Row, Monterey
☎ 1-831-648-4888 🅳 $16
🕐 10am–6pm daily. ♿

Pebble Beach Golf Links
17-Mile Drive, Pebble Beach
☎ 1-800-654-9300 🅳 $305 (if not staying at resort)
🕐 dawn–dusk daily. ♿

athens west

The tang of espresso wafts across marble tabletops, snaking around cranberry scones, laptops, and dog-eared copies of *Soul on Ice*. Cafés in this sunny nest of sonnets and revolt outnumber nearly everything else, except perhaps bookshops. Locals are less fond of the nickname 'Berserkley' than of their city's earlier appellation – 'Athens West'.

berkeley

gourmet ghetto

Few neighbourhoods take food so seriously as Berkeley's Gourmet Ghetto. All around world-famous *Chez Panisse restaurant, with its anise parfaits and wine-boysenberry soup, bakeries and delis sprout like chanterelles. Allusions to Provence and Tuscany abound in the tiled entryways and basil-scented air, but the merging of salmon tartare with politics is purely Berkeley. Potent, locally roasted, and the Bay Area's coffee of choice, *Peet's sells by the cup and the pedigreed pound. When nothing will do but noodles crafted with squid ink, rose petals, cocoa, or habañero chilis, *Phoenix Pastificio satisfies, while nearby *Poulet supplies gourmet picnic makings like mango-jicama-corn salad. At the petite *French Hotel, locals schmooze over madeleines in the sidewalk café while awaiting evening readings at *Black Oak Books.

4th street

On 4th Street, a high-end yet funky shopping mecca which *Metropolis* magazine ranks among the nation's top five, trash bins masquerade as outsize Greek amphorae. Designer doorknobs, gardening clogs, and telescopes share a pastel landscape with aristocratic pet supplies, toddlers' *haute couture*, and a *Market Plaza whose cheeses, baked goods, and jams span the planet. California cuisine reigns; at assertively 'east-west' *O'Chamé, shiitake and seaweed befriend Belgian endive and smoked trout. For herbal medicine

that tastes like a banquet, trendy *Xanadu serves 'RestorAsian Cuisine'. Relief from relentless chic resides at *Brennan's, a cavernous blue collar cafeteria/pub whose roast beef and Irish coffees have been cheerful Berkeley institutions for 50 years.

university of california

At the other end of town, a rippling creek, redwood groves, and elegant pale stone architecture including a lofty campanile, mark the UC Berkeley campus, 30,000-student strong and the flashpoint for cultural and scientific revolutions that have changed the world. Lush landscaping and stately buildings invite strollers. In the hills above the campus are a palm-shaded *University Botanical Garden and the hands-on *Lawrence Hall of Science, with shimmering views of SF.

telegraph avenue

Running southwards from the campus, Telegraph Avenue is a shopper's Shangri-La where generations of students have pondered existentialism over cups of java. Street vendors proffer hash pipes, handcrafted hair ornaments, tie-dye, tarot readings, and T-shirts with slogans like *I Am An Angry Girl*. Beggars, Maoists, legalize-pot activists, buskers, tattoo artists, and Hare Krishnas vie for attention while music blares from emporia stocked with all the fuel of tomorrow's trends. Bookstores include the four-storey, mainly secondhand *Moe's and

the vast *Cody's. For a crisp pint of microbrew, retire to *Bison Brewing Co, where fermentation vats are part of the ambience.

*= featured in the directory

san francisco's top sights

A1 / B1 / C1 / D1
GOLDEN GATE BRIDGE
Marin County
SAN FRANCISCO
Crissy Field · Exploratorium
GOLDEN GATE BRIDGE FREEWAY
LINCOLN BOULEVARD
· Palace of Fine Arts
presidio
A2 / B2 / C2 / D2
PACIFIC OCEAN
Baker Beach
Coastal Trail
Lincoln Boulevard
28
The Presidio
presidio heights
China Beach
CLAY ST
laurel heights
CALIFORNIA STREET
Lobos Creek Valley
Lincoln Park
· California Palace of the Legion of Honor
A3 / B3 / C3 / D3
POINT LOBOS AVENUE
18
GEARY 38 BOULEVARD
GEARY BOULEVARD
· Columbarium
TURK
FULTON
· Cliff House & Musée Mécanique
18
38
45TH AVENUE
40TH AVENUE
21ST AVENUE
19TH AVENUE
BALBOA STREET
richmond
FULTON STREET
Asian Art Museum of San Francisco
MH de Young Memorial Museum
Conservatory of Flowers
· Laserium
California Academy of Sciences
upper haight-ashbury
A4 / B4 / C4 / D4
Golden Gate Park
LINCOLN WAY
28
IRVING STREET
PARNASSUS AVENUE
Muni Metro N
JUDAH STREET
sunset
MORAGA STREET
30TH 24TH 19TH
Mount Sutro
Tank Hill Park
Muni Metro K·L·M
42ND AVENUE
SUNSET BOULEVARD
NORIEGA STREET
twin peaks
A5 / B5 / C5 / D5
GREAT HIGHWAY
PACIFIC Beach
Sunset Reservoir
QUINTARA STREET
Forest Hill
WOODSIDE AVE
O'SHAUGHNESSY BOULEVARD
Coastal Trail
18
TARAVAL STREET
Muni Metro L
parkside
VICENTE STREET
Pine Lake Park
Stern Grove
West Portal
PORTOLA DRIVE
Mount Davidson Park
SANTA CLARA AVE
kilometres
SLOAT BOULEVARD
OCEAN AVENUE
Fort Funston
miles
San Francisco Zoo
18

68

getting your bearings

69

- Mission [→8–13]
- Castro & Noe Valley [→14–18]
- Haight-Ashbury [→19–23]
- Hayes Valley & the Civic Center [→24–27]
- Pacific Heights [→28–31]
- Marina & Cow Hollow [→32–35]
- Russian Hill & Nob Hill [→36–39]
- North Beach [→40–44]
- Chinatown [→45–46]
- Downtown [→47–52]
- SoMa [→53–57]
- good bus routes
- Muni Metro route (surface)
- Muni Metro route (underground)
- cable car route
- BART route
- ferry route
- 49-Mile Scenic Drive

tours

walking tours

City Guides operate numerous walking tours of the city: these include Victorian San Francisco and art-deco Marina [→145].
☎ 557-4266
w www.wenet.net/users/jhum
⌧ free ◑ daily.

Cruisin' the Castro focuses on the history of gay San Francisco.
☎ 550-8110 ⌧ $40 (includes brunch) ◑ 10am–2pm Tue–Sat.

bicycle tours

Bay Bicycle Tours & Rentals: join the three-hour bike tour across the Golden Gate Bridge to Sausalito and return by ferry.
☎ 436-0633 ⌧ $35 (includes bike and a ferry ticket)

Wheel Escapes run custom bike tours for large groups and sometimes for families [→145].
☎ 586-2377
w www.wheelescapes.com
⌧ $65–£110 (includes bike rental and lunch)

ferry tours

The Red & White and Blue & Gold Fleets both organize tours of the Bay Area [→ 146–147].
☎ 673-2900 (Red & White Fleet)
☎ 705-5555 (Blue & Gold Fleet)

49-Mile Scenic Drive

For San Francisco's most scenic drive, follow the blue-and-white seagull indicators starting from the Civic Center. Maps are available from the SF Visitors Bureau [→151].

admission charges

admission charges

Admission ranges from $3 to $11. Most SF museums offer a free day each month [→148].

discount tickets

CityPass allows half-price entry to seven SF attractions.
☎ 1-800-824-4795
w www.citypass.net ⌧ $27.75

Golden Gate Explorer Pass gives free entry to all the museums in Golden Gate Park.
☎ 750-7145 ⌧ $14

Muni Travel Passport offers discounts on the Muni system and to many SF attractions.
☎ 923-6050 ⌧ $6–$15

getting your bearings

the city seen

From a bridge painted a most unlikely shade of red, to an art deco movie theatre that still plays live organ music, SF's sights reflect the irresistible whimsy of the city by the bay.

↓ hi-lo culture

Cable Cars
Unique to San Francisco, these cars are attached to underground cables and travel up gradients too steep for buses to handle. So, when your feet are weary, hop on and be whisked up the next steep hill. The cars operate on three routes, the Powell-Hyde line has the best views (and the most tourists).

Castro Theatre | 429 Castro St (at Market St)
Arguably the best revival house in the city, this 1600-seat movie palace is also an architectural and cultural landmark. The elaborate exterior and interior were both designed by late local wunderkind Timothy Pflueger. The Wurlitzer organ plays nightly before films and in June, the Gay and Lesbian Film Festival [→126] is held here.

City Hall | 200 Polk St (at Van Ness Ave)
This beaux-arts marvel at the centre of the Civic Center complex displays a grandiosity appropriate to Mayor Willie Brown, under whose reign the entire building was recently renovated. Memorable events under the grand dome include the marriage of Marilyn Monroe and Joe DiMaggio in 1954.

Coit Tower | 1 Telegraph Hill (at Greenwich St)
Eccentric philanthropist Lillie Hitchcock Coit financed this concrete fire nozzle which was built in 1933. The murals on the first floor depict scenes from Depression-era San Francisco. The tower tops Telegraph Hill and the view from the observation platform is terrific, especially at sunset.

Ferry Building | Market St (at Embarcadero)
In the minds of many old-timers, the Ferry Building (1896), with its distinctive clock tower, is the true gateway to San Francisco. Prior to the construction of the Bay Bridge in 1936, some 50 million commuters passed through the building each year to and from Bay Area cities.

Golden Gate Bridge | Toll Plaza (The Presidio)
The web of cables is a visual masterpiece; the colour a stroke of genius; and the structure (completed in 1937) an astonishing engineering feat. In high winds, the roadway can swing up to 27 ft in each direction. And even large earthquakes have made no mark on SF's quintessential landmark.

Lombard Street | bet. Hyde & Leavenworth Sts

It may or may not be the 'crookedest street in the world', but this short stretch of Lombard is certainly twisty. It was built this way in the 1920s, because there was no way a Model T or horse-drawn coach could climb such a steep hill in a straight line. The novelty factor and the bay views ensure a steady stream of visitors.

Mission Dolores | Dolores St (at 16th St)

The oldest building in the city, Mission Dolores was one of 21 Franciscan missions built by Spanish settlers in the late 1700s. Survivor of three major earthquakes and one fire, it is likely to withstand something the gentrification of the area that is its namesake. Thick adobe walls block noise and strife, while the garden soothes the soul.

'Painted Ladies' | Steiner St (at Alamo Square)

The Queen Anne-style houses near Alamo Square – most notably the 'Painted Ladies' on Steiner Street – make for a favourite San Francisco snapshot. Their Victorian splendour is enhanced by the view beyond of the Civic Center and Downtown.

Palace of Fine Arts | 3601 Lyon St
(bet. Jefferson & Bay Sts)

A clear triumph for California architect Bernard Maybeck, the Palace of Fine Arts replicates Greek and Roman ruins. The lagoon in front is the backdrop for hundreds of wedding photographs; the adjacent Exploratorium science museum [→71] is an interactive delight.

St Mary's Cathedral | 1111 Gough St (at Geary Blvd)

It's hard to miss this ultra-modern building. The roof is something architects call 'four-part arching paraboloid', but many people say it looks like the agitator in an old-fashioned washing machine. At any rate, the inside looks wonderful in a 1970s way: the canopy made of aluminium rods gleams above a stone altar.

Transamerica Pyramid | 600 Montgomery St
(bet. Clay & Washington Sts)

An eyesore to some but an inspiration for millions, this 853-ft structure defines the city from a distance. The 27th-floor observation area is now closed to visitors, so you have three choices: gawk skyward, enjoy the art displays in the lobby, or relax at the Redwood Park nearby.

War Memorial Opera House | 401 Van Ness Ave
(bet. Fulton & Grove Sts)

The 1932 building looks pretty impressive from the outside (it was designed by Arthur Brown, architect of City Hall), but what goes on inside counts even more. It is home to the San Francisco Ballet [→129], America's oldest professional dance company, and the San Francisco Opera [→130], beloved by aficionados.

sights, museums & galleries

more sights, museums & galleries

↓ well hung

Asian Art Museum of San Francisco ►

One of the largest institutions of its kind outside Asia, this museum provides a key view into Asian art. The core of the holdings – some 12,000 objects spanning 6000 years – was the bequest of Chicago industrialist Avery Brundage who donated his substantial collection on the condition that San Francisco build a museum to house it. Today, some 40 Asian countries are represented, with Chinese, Japanese, and Korean art and artefacts being the most visible. Other areas are devoted to the Near East and southeast Asia. Like the de Young Museum, which is housed in the same building in Golden Gate Park [→78], the Asian has run out of room and a new expanded facility will open on the site of the old Main Library in the Civic Center in 2001.

✿ Spectacular jade collection.

❶ Occasional evening events bring in younger, more fashionable crowds.

Tea Garden Drive, Golden Gate Park
☎ 668-8921 🖷 379-8801
w www.asianart.org 🚌 5, 21, 71 🚈 N
🅿 $7 🖃 MC/V ◑ 9.30am–5pm Wed–Sun.
❑ ♿ ☞ ❡ ⛪
[→Haight-Ashbury 19–23]

California Palace of the Legion of Honor

This stately beaux-arts museum which opened in 1924, sits high atop Lincoln Park, offering spectacular views of Downtown and the Golden Gate Bridge [→70]. Alma deBretteville Spreckels, a poor art student who climbed her way to the top of San Francisco society by first being mistress to, and then wife of sugar millionaire Adolph Spreckels, was the obsessive force behind the museum. Alma had a passion for French art, specifically Rodin sculpture, and spent much of her time – and her husband's money – flitting around Europe buying up as much of it as she could find. Good thing for San Francisco: the museum's collections, which include large holdings of Rodin sculpture (among which is one of five original castings of *The Thinker*), 19th-century European painting, 18th-century decorative arts, and more than 70,000 works from the Achenbach Foundation for Graphic Arts, are due largely to Alma's devotion. Today special exhibitions tend toward big names such as Francis Bacon and Picasso, as well as artists with local ties.

✿ Café with lovely outdoor patio.

Legion of Honor Drive, Lincoln Park
☎ 750-3600 🖷 863-3330 w www.thinker.org
🚌 18, 38 🅿 $7 🖃 AE/MC/V ◑ 9.30am–5pm
Tue–Sun. ❑ ♿ ☞ ❡ ⛪

MH de Young Memorial Museum

A museum of San Francisco for all San Franciscans, the de Young is the prime cultural attraction in Golden Gate Park [→78] and its broad popularity befits the location. It was built to showcase art and artefacts for the California Midwinter Exposition of 1894, and afterwards was used as a sort of clearing house for oddities left over from the fair. Eventually what grew from this random collection of Gold Rush equipment, decorative doodahs, stuffed birds, and paintings of the American West was a focus on American art. Today, substantial sections of the museum are devoted to an impressive collection of paintings by 19th- and early-20th century American artists, including works by Winslow Homer, Albert Bierstadt, Grant Wood, and Wayne Thiebaud (*Three Machines*, 1963 ◄), as well as to the arts of Africa, Oceania, and the Americas

san francisco's key areas

(Map labels)

Fort Point
Golden Gate Bridge

B1 | C1

MARINA SMALL CRAFT HARBOR

Marina Green
MARINA BLVD

Fort Mason
Golden Gate National Recreation Area

D1

marina
BAY STREET
Funston Playground

The Presidio

presidio

UNION BLVD

PRESIDIO BLVD

LOMBARD STREET

cow hollow

B2 | C2 | D2

BROADWAY

WASHINGTON STREET

Alta Plaza Park

Lafayette Park

pacific heights

CALIFORNIA

PINE

BUSH

japantown

The Presidio

Presidio Golf Course

WEST PACIFIC AVENUE

WASHINGTON

PRESIDIO AVENUE

Mountain Lake

laurel heights

GEARY EXPRESSWAY

Kimbell Playground

western addition

EDDY

Jefferson Square

PARK PRESIDIO BOULEVARD

CALIFORNIA

B3 | C3

GEARY BOULEVARD

10TH

7TH

AVE

richmond

Angelo Rossi Playground

TURK STREET

MASONIC AVENUE

TURK STREET

McAllister

FULTON

Alamo Square

STEINER

FILLMORE

WEBSTER

hayes valley

D4

Koshland Park

BALBOA BOULEVARD

STREET

FULTON STREET

STANYAN STREET

Panhandle

B4 | C4

HAYES STREET

FELL

OAK

lower haight-ashbury

Stow Lake

Golden Gate Park

LILY POND

upper haight-ashbury

HAIGHT STREET

Buena Vista Park

Duboce Park

Church Street

DOLORES STREET

LINCOLN WAY

cole valley

Corona Heights

CASTRO STREET

MARKET

Castro Street

IRVING STREET

JUDAH STREET

7TH AVENUE

PARNASSUS STREET

17TH

ASHBURY STREET

STREET

castro

D5

sunset

B5 | C5

University of California Grounds

Tank Hill Park

Mission Dolores Park

CHURCH

10TH AVENUE

Mount Sutro

CLARENDON AVENUE

SUTRO RESERVOIR

twin peaks

MARKET STREET

CASTRO STREET

noe valley

24TH STREET

kilometres 0

miles 0

6

2

3

4

5

♫ directory

Castro ♫*C4–C5*: A fierce sense of community and gay pride is evident at every turn in this bustling, compact gay mecca of the city – if not the world.

Chinatown ♫*E2*: This tiny area pulsates with a palpable Pacific Rim energy as more than 80,000 residents go about their business.

Civic Center ♫*D3*: The impressive City Hall and Beaux Arts government buildings loom in contrast to the homeless population who camp out here. Evening brings the dressy cultural cadre to the nearby symphony and opera.

Cow Hollow ♫*C2*: Union Street is the focus of this swanky quarter.

Financial District/Downtown ♫*E2–F2*: By day, this 'Wall Street of the West' is abuzz with all forms of financial wheeling and

dealing. By night, the area is an abandoned shell.

Fisherman's Wharf ♫*D1–E1*: A touristy kitsch-fest by the bay offering cheesy museums, tacky T-shirt stands, piers-turned-mini-malls, and seafood restaurants with crowds of tourists.

Haight-Ashbury ♫*B4–C4*: Once the epicentre of 60s hippy culture, this neighbourhood is still largely propelled by its past. Stores appeal to counterculture tastes, while further afield are tree-lined streets of Victorian homes. Lower Haight is the new hang-out spot for those who think Upper Haight has become too gentrified.

Hayes Valley ♫*D3*: A tiny but proudly eclectic sliver of a neighbourhood, Hayes Valley draws a mix of arty types and pre-symphony diners to its eateries.

Japantown ♫*C2–D2*: Japantown comprises a few blocks dominated by the 5-acre Japan Center and the Peace Plaza, with a pagoda.

Marina ♫*C1*: A gorgeous, glossy swath of waterfront awash with expensive Mediterranean-style homes. From the boutique-and-café-lined Chestnut Street to the Marina Green this is where SF yuppies live, shop, play, and flirt.

Mission ♫*D5–E5*: The exuberant, multi-cultural Mission is a study in contrasts: an hispanic populace lives alongside young, urban artists and professionals who have trickled in over the last decade.

Nob Hill ♫*E2*: Suitably called 'the hill of palaces' and 'snob hill', this classy neighbourhood is home to four ritzy hotels perched atop one of the city's highest hills.

(South and Central). A large textile collection, with tapestry, lace, silks, *haute couture* fashion, and Eastern and Asian rugs, is one of the finest in the country. The oldest museum in San Francisco, the de Young is finally getting a long overdue seismic and structural overhaul, scheduled for completion in 2004.

Tea Garden Drive, Golden Gate Park
☎ 750-3600 📠 863-3330 **w** www.thinker.org
🚌 5, 21, 71 🚃 🚋 💲 $7 🅿 MC/V
⏰ 9.30am–5pm Tue–Sun. ♿ 🚻 ☞ 🎧 (for big shows) ⛳ 🏛
[→Haight-Ashbury 19–23]

San Francisco Museum of Modern Art

Since appearing in 1995, like a giant punctuation mark on the city's skyline, SFMOMA has been doing its damnedest to position San Francisco as a major player on the art world map. The striking building, designed by Mario Botta, has become a cultural landmark with its brick façade and striped, cylindrical skylight, and what's inside reveals a museum on the fast track to a high profile. There are some 50,000 sq ft of sleek gallery space, a good portion given to travelling exhibitions of modern works (recent blockbusters have included Alexander Calder and Bill Viola).

A light-filled atrium spans the building's five floors, with a vertigo-inducing bridge at its apex. Filling banks of sky-lit gallery spaces is SFMOMA's rapidly growing permanent collection of painting and sculpture with the likes of Monet, Duchamp, Lichtenstein, and Paul Klee. Two galleries are devoted to 14 recently acquired seminal works by Robert Rauschenberg. Strong photography, media arts, and architecture and design departments have their own galleries, while the more architecturally dramatic upper-floor galleries house contemporary works and special exhibitions.

♿ Matisse's *Femme au Chapeau*; Koons' *Michael Jackson and Bubbles*; the Rauschenberg works.
♿ Caffè Museo and SFMOMA Store [→95].

151 Third Street (bet. Mission & Howard Sts)
☎ 357-4000 **w** www.sfmoma.org
🚌 5, 9, 14, 15, 30, 38, 45 🚇 J, K, L, M, N
💲 $8 🅿 none ⏰ 11am–6pm Thu–Tue (to 9pm Thu). ♿ 🚻 ☞ 🎧 ⛳ 🏛
[→SoMa 54–57]

Yerba Buena Center for the Arts

The city's most culture-intensive district is defined by the Yerba Buena Gardens, a civic oasis opposite SFMOMA, that includes the Yerba Buena Center for the Arts. Part museum, commercial gallery, and community centre, the arts complex is housed in a striking modern structure designed by Japanese architect Fumihiko Maki and built in 1993. It is a spiffy facility with galleries of various scales, a small screening room, and a multipurpose forum space. The programming is eclectic, sometimes concentrating on local artists and subcultures, at other times introducing international artists into the mix. There are usually a few exhibitions running simultaneously which are wide-ranging in medium and subject matter, but a more consistent film and video programme explores unexamined veins of (once) popular media (Italian horror films, 1970s sexploitation, etc). A large and wonderfully appointed theatre, designed by American James Stewart Polshek, presents performances of theatre, dance, and music.

The Yerba Buena Gardens themselves, which partially reside on top of the cavernous Moscone Convention Center, feature a large grassy knoll, the Martin Luther King memorial fountain, and the massive Metreon [→80] entertainment complex that deals in more populist forms of diversion such as Hollywood film, virtual arcades, and shopping for high-tech electronics.

♿ The Seven01 Multimedia Café [→112] has free internet access.

701 Mission Street (at Third Street)
☎ 978-2787 **w** www.yerbabuenaarts.org
🚌 15, 30, 45 🚇 F, J, K, L, M, N 💲 $5 🅿 all
⏰ 11am–6pm Tue– Sun (to 8pm Thu–Sat). ♿ 🚻
☞ (by arrangement) 🎧 ⛳ 🏛
[→SoMa 54–57]

sights, museums & galleries

more sights, museums & galleries

↓ top tickets

Alcatraz ►

The windswept and menacing 'Rock' continues to rule as the Bay Area's most popular attraction. Named after the Spanish word for 'pelican', Alcatraz is inhabited by these birds which are returning in huge colonies. The island, the most famous prison setting in the world, was the Bay's maximum security jail from 1934 to 1963, housing some of history's nastiest characters. The ghosts of the 'Birdman', Al Capone, and 'Machine Gun' Kelly haunt the bleak cellblocks on the jagged, surf-splashed outcrop, giving Alcatraz a sinister glamour that the genial guides and rangers – some ex-guards, all fascinating – may capitalize on by slamming the occasional door or hitting the lights.

Excellent audio tours tell tales of how desperate men tried to swim towards the whiff of seafood from Fisherman's Wharf, sometimes never to be seen again. Since over a million people visit Alcatraz annually, you need to book way in advance. Weekday late-afternoon trips are often less busy. The effort is worthwhile – it is a chilly, thrilling experience.

Alcatraz Island ☎ 705-5555 or 1-800-229-2784 ☎ 773-1188 w www.nps.gov/alcatraz/ ⚓ from Pier 41 ⬚ $12.25 (return ticket with audio tour) ☐ AE/D/MC/V ⏰ departures: 9.30am–2.15pm daily (to 4.15pm Jun–Sep). ☐ ♿ ☞ 🎧 🎦
[→North Beach 40–44]

California Academy of Sciences ◄

Colourful 'Earth, Ocean, Space' banners hang over the entrance to this vast multi-faceted science complex which encompasses an aquarium, a natural history museum, and a planetarium. The Steinhart Aquarium is the big attraction here. A giant swamplike reptile pit full of snapping alligators, snakes, and turtles entices kids and never fails to thrill. Other highlights include the Touch Tidepool, and feeding times at the Fish Roundabout (2pm) and penguins (11.30am & 4pm).

In the Natural History Museum, visitors marvel over convincing lifesize dinosaur replicas and a Tyrannosaurus Rex skeleton, a simulated earthquake which recreates the 1906 and 1989 tremors, and dioramas that adorn the African Hall. There are also displays of California's varied flora and fauna and micro-climates, and a snake and reptile special called Venom – the newest exhibit for 2000. In the Morrison Planetarium there are daily astronomy shows and laserium light displays (Mon–Thu) set to rock or classical music [→80].

Music Concourse Drive, Golden Gate Park ☎ 221-5100 📠 750-7145 w www.calacademy.org ⬚ 5, 21, 28, 71 🚇 N ⬚ $8.50; Morrison Planetarium $5 ☐ AE/MC/V ⏰ Sep–Jun: 10am–5pm daily; Jul–Aug: 9am–6pm daily. ☐ ♿ ☞ 🎦
[→Haight-Ashbury 19–23]

Exploratorium

This hands-on museum fills 100,000 sq ft in a hangar-like building next to the Palace of Fine Arts [→71]. The Bernard Maybeck-designed structure was left over from the 1915 Panama Pacific Exposition and is now packed with hundreds of perceptual phenomena, trippy visuals, and science facts that test your knowledge and perceptions of the physical world. There's a distorted room with no angles, bathroom tiles that form shape-shifting MC Escher-like patterns, and a wall that holds your shadow. There are also biological displays with gooey, gross-out appeal – see the popular cow's eye dissection booth. Temporary exhibitions address specific topics, and pull artists and scientists into the design process. Kick off your shoes, enter the geodesic dome, and try to find your way through the pitch black using just your sense of touch. The Exploratorium may be geared towards young audiences, and it's a space filled with kids' shrieks of delight, but adults will also need to be dragged out at the end of the day.

☐ Mid-Mar–Sep 2000: 'Revealing Bodies' documents the way we have imaged human bodies over time.

Marina Boulevard (at Lyon St) ☎ 561-0360 📠 397-5673 w www.exploratorium.edu ⬚ 28, 30 ⬚ $9 ☐ AE/MC/V ⏰ 10am–5pm daily (to 6pm Jun–Aug; to 9pm Wed). ☐ ♿ ☞ 🎥
[→Marina & Cow Hollow 32–35]

Maritime National Historical Park

The term 'park' is loosely applied: no trees or duck ponds here. Instead, the ship-shape hulk of the Maritime Museum with its collection of seafaring artefacts and oddities spills out onto the steps of the Inner Harbor and down to Hyde Street Pier, home to a number of historic ships. Elegantly curved like a 1930s luxury liner, complete with porthole-style chrome windows, the Maritime Museum testifies to the project that helped to build it in the Depression as well as to the bustling waterfront of the Barbary Coast era. A huge marine mural of Atlantis by deco-era artist Hilaire Hiler completes the whole effect. Best of all, it's free – and so are its excellent special exhibits. Ask to see the relics from writer Jack London's boat The Snark.

Next door, Hyde Street Pier (which isn't free) is where the 1886 three-masted Balclutha, veteran of many trips around the Horn, is moored. You can even haul on the sheets with a 'Heave ho!' and test out the rigging. Also tied up at the dock are the ferryboat Eureka and three-masted schooner CA Thayer. Their later companion, the World War II submarine USS Pampanito, is located further down at Pier 45 and has a separate entrance fee.

Jefferson Street (at Hyde St) ☎ 556-3002 w www.nps.gov/safr ⬚ Museum free; Hyde Street Pier $5; USS Pampanito $6 ⏰ Museum: 9am–5pm daily; Pier: 9.30am–5.30pm daily. ☐ ♿ 🏛
[→Marina & Cow Hollow 32–35]

↓ one-of-a-kind

Ansel Adams Center for Photography

One of the first arts organizations to open in the now culturally overflowing Yerba Buena area, the Ansel Adams Center has just relocated to a spiffed-up new location. Adams' luminous Yosemite landscapes are frequently on view at this sleek photography showcase, but a wider range of images is the mainstay of the programming here. Along with work by classic photographers such as Imogen Cunningham, visitors are likely to see a Cindy Sherman or Irving Penn print. It's modestly scaled, but tightly focused in its vision of presenting photography in its various historical and contemporary guises. Lectures are sometimes held here and the bookstore is well-stocked with glossy coffee-table tomes and books of visual theory.

655 Mission St (bet. 3rd & New Montgomery Sts) ☎ 495-7000 w www.friendsof photography.org 🚍 9, 15, 30, 45 🚇 F, J, K, L, M, N 🚊 $5 🚇 AE/MC/V 🕐 11am–5pm daily. 🚱 🔊 💺
[→SoMa 53–57]

Cartoon Art Museum

Since so many famous cartoonists have lived in San Francisco, it is fitting that the city is home to a museum devoted entirely to cartoon art. While Robert Crumb was working on *Fritz the Cat* in the late 1960s, Charles Schultz's *Peanuts* was already prevalent. The *Fabulous Furry Freak Brothers* and *Last Gasp Comics* also spread knowledge of the new art form and, by the late 1980s, San Francisco had its own impromptu cartoon art collection, now housed in these tiny upstairs premises. The gallery puts on revolving shows consisting of its 10,000-plus collection as well as outside sources. The museum also offers kids cartooning classes, generally once a month. Check out the well-stocked gift shop.

2nd Fl, 814 Mission Street (bet. 4th & 5th Sts) ☎ 227-8666 w www.cartoonart.org

🚍 14, 27, 30, 45 🚇 F, J, K, L, M, N 🚊 $5 🚇 MC/V 🕐 11am–5pm Wed–Sat (from 10am Sat); 1–5pm Sun. 🚱 🔊 💺
[→SoMa 53–57]

Chinese Historical Society of America

Musty and dusty this small, temporarily located museum may be, but plans are afoot to relocate to a gorgeous old Arts and Crafts building in Chinatown. Also, it's free, its atmosphere is authentic, and its bilingual displays are sincere in their attempts to tell the tale of the earliest Chinese immigrants on the railroads and in the opium dens of Chinatown. The antique Buddhist altar, original hand-written Chinese telephone book, and other items give a genuine whiff of the Gold Rush era, when Asian immigrants fell victim to the 'Exclusion' law.

4th Fl, 644 Broadway (bet. Stockton & Columbus Sts) ☎ 391-1188 w www.chsa.org 🚍 15, 30, 45 🚇 C 🚊 free 🚇 MC/V 🕐 10.30am–4pm Mon–Fri (from 1pm Mon). 🚱 🔊 💺
[→Chinatown 45–46]

Columbarium

This 1898 temple enshrining the ashes of thousands of San Franciscans is an architectural poem within a garden. Decorated with thousands of hand-laid Portuguese tiles and fanciful funerary urns that might be Ming or directoire-style bronze, the Columbarium replaced a graveyard which was forced out by the living population in the 19th century. Tier upon tier of niches, and galleries for more cremation urns, reflect thousands of lives – usually couples together, often gay, a sizeable number victims of the AIDS scourge. Many founding families are also interred here – the Folgers of coffee fame, Magnins, Brannans, Hayeses, and dozens of others who were important enough in their lifetime to have streets named after them. Poker packs, baseball cards, Hawaiian hula dolls, and effusions of kitsch photos and heartfelt love letters furnish intriguing clues to the departed around this curious rotunda of solemn stained glass. Piped Bach and mosaics contrast strangely with the sheer exuberance of all the memorabilia.

1 Loraine Court, Anza St ☎ 752-7891 🚍 38 🚊 free 🕐 10am–5pm daily (to 2pm Sat & Sun). 🚱 limited
[→Chinatown 45–46]

Fort Mason Museums

The former army base on the waterfront houses several mini-museums including the Mexican Museum [→76]. Across the way, the Museo Italo-Americano reflects the artistic contributions of Italian Americans, while the African-American Historical & Cultural Society has a collection of drums, provoking photographic shows, and occasional touring displays, plus a fascinating walking tour about the black experience in 19th-century San Francisco. Everything from baskets and textiles to masks and sculpture makes its way into the SF Craft & Folk Art Museum, which focuses on local artists.

Fort Mason Center (at Buchanan St & Marina Blvd) 🚍 28 🚇 PH

Museo Italo-Americano ☎ 673-2200 🚊 $2 🚇 MC/V 🕐 12–5pm Wed–Sun. 🚱 🔊 💺

African-American Historical & Cultural Society ☎ 441-0640 🚊 $2 🚇 MC/V 🕐 12–5pm Wed–Sun. 🚱 🔊 💺

SF Craft & Folk Art Museum ☎ 775-0990 🚊 $3 🚇 none 🕐 11am–5pm Tue–Sun; 10am–5pm Sat. 🚱 🔊 💺

Grace Cathedral

Remind you of anything? Yes, SF's Episcopalian headquarters is a concrete replica of Paris' Notre Dame. Built on the site of railroad baron Charles Crocker's mansion and completed in 1964, the cathedral took over half a century to construct. A French rose window and organ add a certain grandeur, but this being California, it also has a couple of whimsical additions, including a copy of Ghiberti's giant bronze 'Doors of Paradise' from the Baptistry in Florence, and the Labyrinth Walk, a carpet copy of the meditational floor in Chartres Cathedral that is strangely soothing: devotees plod around it in circles to enhance their contemplation. The startling Aids Memorial triptych, by contemporary artist Keith Haring, adds to the effect. The basement hosts a discreet museum where you can trace the recent $14 million renovation. Catch the Men and Boys Choir evensong (5.15pm Thu & 3.30pm Sun).

1100 California St (at Taylor St) ☎ 749-6300 📠 749-6310 w www.gracecom.org 🚍 1 🚇 C 🚊 donations 🕐 1–3pm Mon–Fri; 11.30am–1.30pm Sat; 12.30–2pm Sun. 🚱 🔊 🤝 💺
[→Russian Hill & Nob Hill 36–39]

sights, museums & galleries

more sights, museums & galleries

sights, museums & galleries

Haas Lilienthal House

The most extravagant of all the 'Painted Ladies' are those in Queen Anne style, and William Haas' abode, with its cupolas, balustrades, and carved, curved windows, sums up those lavishly ornamented Victorian houses. A Jewish grocer from Bavaria who made good in the 1880s by peddling food to miners, Haas Lilienthal built this house of 28 rooms, and 7 bathrooms including a bidet and a shower. Subsequent generations made their millions on Levi-Strauss jeans.

Lilienthal's abode was a modest effort compared to the other Victorian mansions which once lined Van Ness Avenue. After the 1906 quake many of these were dynamited to make a fire break, but period photographs record their grandeur. The Haas Lilienthal House is the only such house on public show and it is open two afternoons a week thanks to volunteers.

2007 Franklin Street (bet. Washington & Jackson Sts) ☎ 441-3004 w www.sfheritage.org 🚌 42 💳 $5 🕐 12–3pm Wed; 11am–4pm Sun. ♿ 🚻 🛍 [→Russian Hill & Nob Hill 36–39]

Mexican Museum

California's relationship to Mexico is deep, complex, and full of veiled histories, which is one reason why this cultural institution is so important. The museum is devoted to presenting art, artefacts, and folk art from Mexico, Central and South America as well as works by Chicano and other related artists, and has amassed an impressive permanent collection in that vein. Exhibits of religious artefacts, terracotta figures, paintings and sculptures by artists such as Diego Rivera, Frida Kahlo, Miguel Covarrubias, and Patssi Valdez are presented in the diminutive galleries. An annual Dia de Los Muertos exhibition held in November is an energetic event that combines historical and contemporary material. One of the best reasons to visit the museum is the substantial bookstore and gift shop where you'll find *retablos*, Frida paraphernalia, tin ornaments, jewellery, and books on Mexican art and culture. To resolve their space issues, the Mexican Museum will be relocating to brand-new expanded digs in the Yerba Buena Gardens in late 2001.

Building D, Fort Mason Center (at Buchanan St & Marina Blvd) ☎ 202-9700 📠 441-0404 w www.mexicanmuseum.com 🚌 28 🚡 PH 💳 $4 🕐 12–5pm Wed–Sun (from 11am Sat & Sun). ♿ 🚻 🛍 🎁 🛍 [→Marina & Cow Hollow 32–35]

Musée Mécanique

If the little kid in you is screaming to get out, appease the little rascal with a visit to this fun-house of delights filled to capacity with a dizzying array of over 130 mechanical games from the early 1900s. For a quarter, you can peek into one of the many teasing come-on peep shows ('See What The Belly Dancer Does On Her Day Off!'), have your fortune read by the all-knowing Gypsy Queen, or catch a glimpse of the world's most horrible monster. On your way out, pump some quarters into the beloved Laughing Sal to hear her wicked guffaw. Sal, along with many of the games, was moved here when Playland-at-the-Beach, one of San Francisco's most popular amusement parks of the 40s and 50s, closed in 1972.

Next door, venture into the quirky little Camera Obscura, a rare optical device that shows a projected panorama of the surrounding ocean and cliffs. It's based on one of the oldest forms of photography, initially sketched by Leonardo da Vinci and others in the late 15th century.

1090 Point Lobos Avenue (at Pacific Ocean) ☎ 386-1170 🚌 38 💳 free 🕐 10am–8pm daily (Oct–May: 11am–7pm Mon–Fri; 10am–8pm Sat & Sun). ♿ 🚻 🛍

mission murals

One of San Francisco's most vibrant and accessible art galleries shares its space with Muni buses, cars, and pedestrians: the Mission, with over 200 lively murals splashed liberally across walls and garage doors everywhere, ensures that SF more than lives up to its name as mural capital of the world. Murals initially flourished in Mexico in the 1920s as a celebration of indigenous history and pride, and then travelled north to San Francisco via the famed muralist Diego Rivera and others who passed on their mural styles and techniques to local artists. Funding from the federal

government helped keep the legacy alive, so that today the Mission lives on as an open air mural museum. **The Precita Eyes Mural Arts & Visitors Center** offers mural walks led by experienced guides that depart from the centre and cover over 75 Mission murals. Or take to the streets on your own: start with **24th Street** which teems with murals between Mission Street and Potrero Avenue. Along the way is **Balmy Alley** (bet. Harrison St & Treat Ave), one of the centrepieces of the mural movement, where nearly all the murals, some dating from the early 1970s, portray Central American themes. Look for the mural called *Indigenous Eyes: War or Peace*, depicting a giant pair of piercing eyes looking into the future, crowned by images of a Central American homeland. This mural is by Susan Cervantes, a long-time muralist and activist, and founder of the mural centre. Another must-see is the **Cesar Chavez Elementary School** (825 Shotwell Street, bet. 21st & 22nd Sts) where the entire building is bedecked in stunning interconnected murals exploring the power of education, with the theme of school children blossoming like flowers into adults. The corner **Women's Building** (3543 18th Street, bet. Valencia & Guerrero Sts) is awash in a swirl of richly-hued murals celebrating the achievements of women worldwide. Reigning from the roof is Guatemalan activist and Nobel Peace Prize winner Rigoberta Menchu, with ancient gods sprouting from her outstretched hands. To bring your mural experience full-circle, duck into **Clarion Alley** (bet. Valencia & Guerrero Sts, 17th & 18th Sts) where a new generation of muralists are wielding their paint brushes. The murals here reflect the hip-hop aesthetics of today, blending together everything from graffiti to cartoon characters to stencil art.

The Precita Eyes Mural Arts and Visitors Center
2981 24th Street (bet. Folsom & Harrison Sts) ☎ 285-2287 🕐 10am–5pm Mon–Fri; 11am–4pm Sat & Sun. 🚶 Walks: every Sat & Sun at 1.30pm 💳 $7 🚶 Bicycle mural tours: third Sun of every month at 11am from 348 Precita Avenue (at Folsom St) 💳 $10

↓ commercial galleries

The highest concentration of dealers is to be found Downtown and the prime spot is the 49 Geary Building, which houses more than a dozen of the city's best commercial galleries. One of the nation's finest photography dealers, **Fraenkel Gallery** is housed in swanky quarters on the fourth floor and shows a range of major contemporary photographers as well as vintage work dating to the 1800s. Contemporary art is well represented by the **Haines Gallery**, with a mix of conceptual works, luminous monochromatic painting, and artists who work with natural elements, and the spacious **Stephen Wirtz Gallery**, which showcases painting, sculpture, and photography. **871 Fine Arts**, meanwhile, concentrates on printed matter such as artist books, old gallery announcements, and other ephemera. Other notable Downtown addresses include **Gallery Paule Anglim**, which shows quite a range of modern works – including the Bay Area conceptual school (David Ireland, Tom Marioni, Paul Kos et al) – and **Rena**

Bransten Gallery which favours lush, large scale photography, pop abstract painting, and the occasional large scale video installation. The city's only certifiable blue chip dealer, **John Berggruen**, uses three floors to show off works by Willem de Kooning, Francis Bacon, Elizabeth Murray, Sol LeWitt, and others. A funkier fourth floor space serves as a project room, featuring works by younger and edgier artists, both local and international.

SFMOMA [→73] and the cultural density of the adjacent Yerba Buena district have given the local commercial gallery scene a shot in the arm by offering galleries who couldn't afford Union Square rents a chance to strut their stuff. Two galleries in a converted warehouse have formed a mini-enclave here. **Hosfelt Gallery** is larger and focuses on pattern painting and drawing, and the occasional site-specific installation, while **Braunstein-Quay Gallery** features more eclectic work, with surrealist and craft-referencing influences.

Braunstein-Quay Gallery
430 Clementina Street
(at 5th St) ☎ 392-5532

871 Fine Arts
4th Fl, 49 Geary Street
(at Kearny St) ☎ 543-5155

Fraenkel Gallery
4th Fl, 49 Geary Street
(at Kearny St) ☎ 981-2661

Gallery Paule Anglim
14 Geary Street (at Kearny St)
☎ 433-2710

Haines Gallery
5th Fl, 49 Geary Street
(at Kearny St) ☎ 397-8114

Hosfelt Gallery
430 Clementina Street
(at 5th St) ☎ 495-5454

John Berggruen Gallery
228 Grant Avenue (bet. Post & Sutter Sts) ☎ 781-4629

Rena Bransten Gallery
77 Geary Street (at Kearny St)
☎ 982-3292

Stephen Wirtz Gallery
3rd Fl, 49 Geary Street
(at Kearny St) ☎ 433-6879

↓ alternative galleries

San Francisco is also a pioneer in the realm of alternative and non-profit art spaces. Many began and flourished here in the 1970s, presenting artwork with limited commercial potential – installation, performance, sound pieces, video, and difficult images. These galleries have maintained their independent spirit. The cavernous **Southern Exposure** in the Mission – an area that has recently become a burgeoning new digital media hub – offers first group show opportunities to young, mostly American artists, as well as operating some heartening community-based artist and inner city teen projects. **New Langton Arts** also deals in group shows for younger artists, but its small structure makes it more conducive to solo exhibitions, sometimes by mid-career artists of international repute. New music, performance, video, and literary events are frequently presented in a downstairs theatre. **SF Camerawork** is an enduring institution that stretches the definition of photo-based art with group and solo shows that push the limits of the medium. A sturdy roster of lectures and events accompanies most shows. **The Lab**, founded in 1983, is a younger relation to the

aforementioned spaces and shows a similar range of media. It has an appealing funky edge that provides a contrast to the spiffy new **Logan Galleries**. The complex of three gallery spaces opened in 1999 in a renovated modernist bus terminal (also housing the California College of Arts & Crafts). Its programming suggests an emphasis on international artists, as well as design and architectural exhibitions.

The non-profit legacy has most recently spawned a type of gallery that exists somewhere between commercial and alternative. **Four Walls**, a large space in the middle of a hip Mission block, features younger artists engaged with experimental media and highly appealing colour schemes. Unlike most commercial galleries, artist talks and live music often accompany the exhibitions. The boisterous wine and cheese opening receptions here are most reflective of the local artist community. The nearby **ESP** is a more intimate storefront site that deals in edgy but entertaining work. And finally, **Gallery 16**, an offshoot of a digital colour lab, presents a variety of ambitious

exhibitions, usually with an accompanying print edition, that have less a commercial feeling than one of artistic integrity. At the turn of the century, there is no need for big promotions, sponsors, and patrons; the alternative ethos is simply to do it yourself.

ESP
305 Valencia Street (at 14th St)
☎ 252-8191

Four Walls
316oa 16th Street (bet. Green & Vallejo Sts) ☎ 626-8515

Gallery 16
1616 16th Street (at Kansas St)
☎ 626-8403

The Lab
2948 16th Street (at Capp St)
☎ 864-8855

Logan Galleries
California College of Arts & Crafts, 450 Irwin Street
☎ 551-9207

New Langton Arts
1246 Folsom Street (bet. 8th & 9th Sts) ☎ 626-5416

SF Camerawork
115 Natoma Street (bet. New Montgomery & 2nd Sts)
☎ 764-1001

Southern Exposure
401 Alabama Street (at 17th St)
☎ 863-2141

sights, museums & galleries

parks, beaches & views

The credo of most locals is they would rather do it than watch it: this means getting outdoors even when swirling fog banks and freezing water make surfers don 10mm wetsuits. Of course, San Franciscans get the last laugh come winter.........

↓ turf 'n' surf

parks

Buena Vista Park

For lovers who want to explore their inner, um, child, this park offers privacy (if not the occasional gay tryst). From its 570-ft summit, it also has a 360-degree view of the Bay as far as Mount Diablo to the east and Mount Tamalpais [→61] to the north. Scramble up along paths and through undergrowth from the Haight's depths, and voilà – a private paradise with a view, appropriately named Buena Vista. The park was established in 1870 by Adolph Sutro of Sutro Baths fame. Best avoided after dark.

Entrances on: Haight St; Buena Vista Ave East; & Buena Vista Ave West ⬛ 6, 7, 24, 43, 66, 71 🚹 N ◑ dawn–dusk daily. [→Haight-Ashbury 19–23]

Golden Gate Park ▼

No matter how many joggers and bicyclists take to its leafy trails, the world-famed, three-mile-long park still has room for everything in its 1000-plus acres. This skinny strip originally planted on sand dunes by Scots gardener John McLaren is the lungs, if not the heart, of the city. At one end buffaloes frolic not far from an old Dutch Windmill; at the other, rollerbladers rub elbows with culture vultures contemplating art and science at the park's cluster of museums. In between, the oldest municipal band in the nation plays Sousa marches in the bandshell as sight-impaired visitors soak up aromas along special trails in the Strybing Arboretum fragrance gardens. If you have but one day to go, make it Sunday, when the park is closed to cars, and the only traffic you'll find will be a conga line of rollerbladers. From the Panhandle in the east down all the horse, hiking, biking, and blading trails west to the Beach Chalet (a restaurant/brewery cum visitors centre) overlooking the ocean, it is all waiting for you. And every time you go you will find new surprises.

Entrances on: Fulton St; Stanyan St; Lincoln Way; & Great Highway ☎ 831-2700 ⬛ 5, 7, 21, 28, 31, 66, 71 🚹 N ◑ 24 hours daily. ◐ archery; baseball; basketball; boating; bowls; cycling; fishing; golf; handball; horseriding; polo; rollerblading; soccer. ◔
[→Haight-Ashbury 19–23]

Mission Dolores Park

Any unexpected ray brings out bare-breasted boys and ab-sporting babes to this sloping Mission meadow known as 'Dolores Beach'. Infamous for pick-ups and questionable nightlife, the park is a favourite place with locals who savour its view of Downtown.

Entrances on: 18th; Dolores; 20th; & Church Sts ☎ 554-9529 ⬛ 22 J ◐ 24 hours daily. ◐ basketball; tennis. [→Mission 8–13]

The Presidio

Location, location, location: 1500 acres of enchanted eucalyptus groves and Bay-watching panoramas make The Presidio a hiking, biking haven. From its earliest days in the 1770s as Captain de Anza's Spanish garrison – a tiny museum testifies to his era – The Presidio was army property. It holds over 600 army buildings of every imaginable shape, date, and size. Lurking in the shadows of the Golden Gate Bridge [→70] is Fort Point, a brick, civil war fortress built to protect San Francisco Bay from invaders who never showed up. Ironically, its cannons are regularly set off these days for visitors and schoolchildren, as part of the park's programme to illustrate military life in early California.

This billion dollars-worth of real estate is now a national park. Trail-wise, the choices are endless: coastal cliff tops; Crissy Field meadow; Lobos Creek Valley, where you can birdwatch rare species like the California Quail; and numerous guided tours such as the Ecology Walk (contact the information centre).

Entrances on: Presidio Blvd; West Pacific Ave; Lyon St; & Marine Drive ☎ 561-4000 ⬛ 28, 43, 45 ◑ 24 hours daily. ◐ bowling; cycling; fishing; golf; hiking; swimming; tennis; walking trails; windsurfing. [→Pacific Heights & Fillmore 28–31; Marina & Cow Hollow 32–36]

Stern Grove

Way out in the foggy Sunset district, this pocket Eden of pines, eucalyptus, redwoods, and raccoons harbours a grassy open air theatre where free performances take place in summer. Each Sunday around 2pm you can enjoy everything from world music and rock to ballet and opera. Arrive early for a prime spot clutching picnic, sunscreen, shades, and sweater, and don't let gophers steal your sandwiches.

Entrances on: 19th Ave & Sloat Blvd ☎ 252-6252 ⬛ 28 K, L, M ◑ 24 hours daily. ◐ croquet; putting green; walking trails.

parks, beaches & views

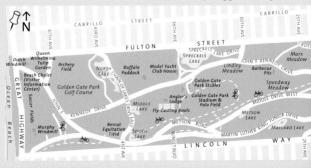

beaches

Baker Beach

Nude and gay at the north end, with fishermen and families at its south section, this mile-long beach has the best view of the Golden Gate Bridge [→70]. It can only be reached by the Presidio's Lincoln Boulevard, making it ideal for cyclists or hikers on the Coastal Trail. Don't risk swimming: the currents and cold are dangerous.

Lincoln Boulevard, The Presidio
☎ 556-8371 🚌 29

The Coastal Trail

For spectacular windswept Pacific vistas, some fresh air, and peace and quiet, walk a stretch of the nine-mile Coastal Trail running from Fort Funston to Fort Point. Cliff House, mid-way along the trail, is the perfect place to sip a sundowner as the sun sets over the ocean or to watch the seals frolic at Seal Rocks. Alternatively head downstairs to the charming Musée Mécanique [→76] with its antique token-operated amusements, or explore the ruins of nearby Sutro Baths, a vast bathing resort built by engineer Adolph Sutro.

Up the Coastal Trail, the jagged rocks at Point Lobos mark the point where many a foolhardy surfer has ventured too far. Further north, Lincoln Park winds around 275 acres of challenging cliff paths (a mountain biker's dream), and an 18-hole golf course. At its apex, with Emerald City views of Downtown, is the California Palace of the Legion of Honor [→72].

Point Lobos Avenue (at Great Highway) ☎ Cliff House: 556-8642 🚌 5, 31, 38 🕐 Cliff House: 10am–5pm daily. ✆

China Beach

The smallest, cleanest, and safest of the city beaches is named after Chinese fishermen who once lived here. Nestling under cliffs, it is quite sheltered, offers good swimming, and boasts showers, sunbathing decks, and changing rooms (nudity is not allowed). Despite its convenient location, it remains uncrowded.

Lincoln Boulevard, The Presidio
☎ 556-8371 🚌 1

Ocean Beach & Fort Funston

Fog-veiled Pacific breakers make for dangerous surfing and only hardened pros chance the waves at Ocean Beach. Instead, the beach is home to locals, joggers, and frisbee-loving dogs. It is also the venue for occasional midnight bashes. It runs three miles south down to Fort Funston's ruins where the sand is powdery fine, and you can lie on your back to watch the hang-gliders leap off the bluffs, collect driftwood, spot nesting petrels, or observe windsurfers and boardsurfers around Mussel Rocks.

off Great Highway & Skyline Blvd ☎ 239-2366 🚌 48

getting high

Francis Drake logged an entry on 'stynkinge fogges' from the Golden Hind while missing the Bay entirely back in 1579. You may be just as unlucky in summertime, when marine mists often mean pea-souper panoramas. But on clearer days there's plenty of choice. Citizens debate the merits of **Angel Island** [→60] versus the top of Russian Hill's **Lombard Street** [→71] or the esoteric charms of **Potrero Hill** (Vermont at 20th) versus photogenic **Filbert Steps** (Telegraph Hill) where wild gardens and split-level cottages recall Armistead Maupin's saga *Tales of the City*. **Twin Peaks** (to the south west) is still the classic choice, a sprawling, blustery double summit known to the Spanish as 'the breasts of the Indian girl'. Night-time, when the city is spread before you like an embroidered tablecloth of light, is a special pilgrimage here; but, sadly, it attracts too many tour buses to be a private idyll by day. You want privacy? Then climb **Tank Hill Park**, off Twin Peaks Boulevard or try nearby raw and windy **Corona Heights**, reached via a tiny path off Roosevelt Way. New Agers reckon this is a 'chakra' or magic pulse point and at sunset or full moon, you'll sometimes find a bunch of Deadheads here.

The cityscape across the Bay from **Marin County** [→60–61] by night is particularly spectacular. And back in the city, firehose-shaped **Coit Tower** [→70], atop Telegraph Hill, offers wonderful nocturnal views. This was the favourite view of Robert Louis Stevenson while he lived here in the 1880s. When the next 'Big One' comes, citizens will flock to posh uptown **Huntington Park** beside Grace Cathedral [→75], the safest spot in the city. People come for its air of heady privilege and the views from one of the legendary if wallet-squeezing skyrooms, such as Top of the Mark [→118].

And for another perspective, get low. Stroll the **Embarcadero** (from Golden Gate Bridge to the Oakland Bay Bridge) and take in the Bay and its bridges from a different, but equally enchanting angle.

parks, beaches & views

In addition to all the kid-oriented attractions, San Francisco yields many spontaneous thrills: gawp at the seals; hop on a cable car; cruise the bay by ferry; picnic on a beach; or join a game in one of the many parks [→78].

↓ kids' corner

great adventures

Bay Area Discovery Museum

Six former army barracks have been converted to this exciting interactive learning environment for kids. Major exhibits change every few months; permanent facilities include an art room, a science lab, and a media centre with organized activities.

557 McReynolds Road, Fort Baker, Sausalito ☎ 289-7266 📠 487-4398 🌐 www.badm.org 🚢 from Pier 41, then taxi 🎫 $7 adults; $6 1–18yrs; free under 1yr ◐ Oct–May: 9am–4pm Tue–Thu; 10am–5pm Fri–Sun; Jun–Sep: 10am–5pm Tue–Sun. ☒ 0–10 ♿ ☕ 🛍

Cable Car Barn & Museum

Cable cars are fun to ride, but they're even more fascinating once you understand the unusual mechanism that keeps them moving. From a viewing platform in this 1887 powerhouse building, watch the underground cable endlessly wind around giant spools. Exhibits illustrate the history of the beloved cars.

1201 Mason St (at Washington St) ☎ 474-1887 🚌 1, 30, 45 ⏺ PH, PM 🎫 free ◐ Apr–Sep: 10am–6pm daily; Oct–Mar: 10am–5pm daily. ☒ 3yrs & up ♿ 🛍

Exploratorium ✓

In this noisy, warehouse-like space, kids and curious adults can bounce from one interactive science exhibit to the next. A favourite among the hundreds here is the Shadow Box, where silhouettes are momentarily captured by a flash of light. Take home tools and toys from the store [→74].

3601 Lyon Street (bet. Marina Blvd & Bay St) ☎ 561-0360 🌐 www.exploratorium.edu 🚌 28, 30, 43 🎫 $9 adult; $5 6–17yrs; $2.50 3–5yrs; free under 3yrs ◐ Apr–Sep: 10am–6pm daily (to 9pm Wed); Oct–Mar: 10am–5pm Tue–Sun (to 9pm Wed). ☒ all ages ♿ ☕ 🛍

Golden Gate Park

This 1000-acre park [→78] is sprinkled with playing fields and playgrounds. The most extensive is the Children's Playground near its eastern end, with elaborate climbing frames, slides, and plenty of sand to dig in. A beautifully restored 1914 carousel provides musical accompaniment.

Golden Gate Park (off Waller St) ☎ 831-2700 🚌 7, 66 🚇 N 🎫 free ◐ 24 hrs ☒ all ages

Laserium

Four nights a week, Morrison Planetarium, in the California Academy of Sciences [→74], becomes a performance dome where laser lights dance, choreographed to rock, pop, and classical music. Teens especially love this one-hour show; not recommended for those under six.

California Academy of Sciences, Music Concourse, Golden Gate Park ☎ 750-7138 🚌 5, 21, 71 🚇 N 🎫 $7 adults; $4 6–12yrs ◐ 5pm Mon–Thu. ☒ 6yrs & up ♿ 🛍

Marine Mammal Center

Environmentally conscious Californians help protect dolphins, whales, and seals at this non-profit wildlife veterinary centre. Watch marine biologists and volunteers nurse sick, injured, and orphaned sea creatures to health, eventually to be released into their native habitat.

Fort Cronkite (near Sausalito) ☎ 289-7325 🚢 from Pier 41, then taxi 🎫 free ◐ 10am–4pm daily. ☒ 5yrs & up ♿ 🛍

Metreon

With 15 cinemas, restaurants, stores, an IMAX® theatre, and high-tech special attractions, Sony's new entertainment complex will fill an exhausting day. Smaller kids can romp through a magical forest based on the famous picture book Where The Wild Things Are by Maurice Sendak; older ones will dive into the Airtight Garage, a state-of-the-art game arcade. Browse for books, videos, and educational toys with science and nature themes under the Discovery Channel Store's giant video wall.

4th Street (bet. Mission & Howard Sts) ☎ 1-800-638-7366 🚌 14, 15, 30, 45 🚇 F, J, K, L, M, N

🎫 free entry (attractions vary in price) ◐ 10am–10pm daily. ☒ all ages ♿ ☕ 🛍

Pier 39

Shopping here can be fun, but kids may prefer Underwater World, where they can view local sea life; Turbo Ride, a 'motion simulation theatre'; Namcoland and Cyberstation, arcades for younger and older kids respectively; and San Francisco – The Movie, a Cinemax presentation on the city's colourful past and present. Swing by to say hi to the sea lions who hang around the pier's west marina.

Embarcadero (at Beach St) ☎ 981-7437 🚌 15, 32, 42 ⏺ PH, PM ◐ 10.30am–9pm daily. ☒ all ages ♿ ☕ 🛍

Rooftop at Yerba Buena Gardens

Adjacent to the Metreon, and above the Moscone Center, this arts and recreation complex is geared toward older kids. There are outdoor gardens, bowling lanes, and an indoor ice rink, plus ZEUM, a hands-on multimedia art centre where kids can dabble in animation and video arts among other things.

4th Street (bet. Howard & Folsom Sts) ☎ 247-6500 🚌 14, 15, 30, 45 🚇 F, J, K, L, M, N 🎫 varies ◐ 9am–10pm daily. ☒ 5–18yrs ♿ ☕ 🛍

San Francisco Zoo

See 1000 animal favourites, many grouped in natural settings like the Primate Discovery Centre and the Australian WalkAbout and don't miss feeding time at the Lion House (2pm Tue–Sun). The Children's Zoo has barnyard animals to pet plus an Insect Zoo. Dress warmly; chilly oceanside fog lingers here.

Sloat Boulevard (at 45th Ave) ☎ 753-7080 🚇 L 🎫 $9 adults; $6 12–17yrs; $3 3–11 yrs; free under 2yrs ◐ 10am–5pm daily. ☒ all ages ♿ 🛍

kids' shopping

Popular **FAO Schwarz** is a three-storey madhouse stocked with the usual favourites (Steiff bears, Barbie) and other playthings. Toys, T-shirts, and other products starring Disney characters fill the **Disney Store**. Fans of Bugs Bunny and Daffy Duck will find a parallel universe of cartoon merchandise at the **Warner Brothers Studio Store**. At **Sanrio** mini-shoppers scoop up mini-goods bearing ultra-cute Japanese characters like punky penguin Badtz Maru. You can watch, or even be involved in, the making of cuddly toys at the **Basic Brown Bear Factory & Store** and then take one home with you.

Gap Kids is the place for newborns-through-teens to update their casual jean-and-khaki wardrobes while **Mudpie** offers a dressier, classic look (as well as plenty of children's books and toys). **Zutopia** targets what it calls

'Generation Z,' pre-teen boys and girls. Heaven for teenage girls is the **Esprit Outlet**, a giant space full of discounted trendy wear. There are also clothes, shoes, and purses for women, younger girls, and unisex clothing for toddlers.

Basic Brown Bear Factory & Store
444 DeHaro Street (at Mariposa St) ☎ 626-0781 🚌 19, 22 🚊 22nd Street ◐ 10am–5pm daily (from 12pm Sun). ⛎ 3–18yrs

Disney Store
400 Post Street (at Union Sq) ☎ 391-6866 🚌 2, 3, 30, 45 ⍟ PH, PM ◐ 10am–6pm Mon–Sat (to 7pm Fri); 11am–5pm Sun. ⛎ all ages

Esprit Outlet
499 Illinois Street (at 16th St) ☎ 957-2550 🚌 15, 22, 48 🚊 22nd Street ◐ 10am–8pm Mon–Sat (to 7pm Sat); 11am–6pm Sun. ⛎ 1–12yrs

FAO Schwarz
48 Stockton Street (at O'Farrell St) ☎ 394-8700 🚌 30, 38, 45 🚇 F, J, K, L,

M, N ⍟ PH, PM ◐ 10am–7pm Mon–Sat; 11am–6pm Sun. ⛎ all ages

Gap Kids
100 Post Street (at Kearny St) ☎ 989-1266 🚌 2, 3, 15, 30, 45 ◐ 9am–8pm Mon–Sat; 11am–6pm Sun. ⛎ 4–16yrs

Mudpie
1694 Union Street (at Gough St) ☎ 771-9262 🚌 41, 45 ◐ 10am–6pm Mon–Sat; 11am–5pm Sun. ⛎ 0–12yrs

Sanrio
30 Stockton Street (at O'Farrell St) ☎ 981-5568 🚌 30, 38, 45 🚇 F, J, K, L, M, N ⍟ PH, PM ◐ 10am–8pm daily (to 6pm Sun). ⛎ all ages

Warner Brothers Studio Store
865 Market Street (at Powell St) ☎ 974-5254 🚌 6, 7, 9, 21, 66 🚇 F, J, K, L, M, N ⍟ PH, PM ◐ 9.30am–8pm Mon–Sat; 11am–6pm Sun. ⛎ all ages

Zutopia
Stonestown Galleria (bet. 19th Ave & Winston Drive) ☎ 681-9140 🚌 28 🚇 M ◐ 10am–9pm. ⛎ 5–15yrs

children

kids' eats

Nostalgia isn't the only reason families find 50s-style diner-theme restaurants so appealing. The burgers and milkshakes are comfortingly familiar, the oldies blasting from the jukebox drown out the whines of cranky kids, and the chrome-and-formica decor makes it easy to wipe up spills. Two favourites are **Johnny Rockets**, with a short-and-sweet menu of burgerjoint classics, and **Mel's Drive-In** which branches out with salads, espresso drinks, and Elvis egg scramble. If the kids demand spaghetti, try **Buca di Beppo**, conveniently located near the Metreon centre

[→80]. It captures the 'Mama Mia!' mood of Italian-American restaurants a generation ago, with zany decor and food served up in huge portions to share. It's popular, so make a reservation. If you're loco for cocoa, splurge on a giant hotfudge sundae or other treats at the **Ghirardelli Chocolate Manufactory & Soda Fountain**. The mini-chocolate-factory at the rear of the shop is a smaller version of the manufacturing plant that once occupied this entire building.

Buca di Beppo
855 Howard Street (bet. 4th & 5th Sts) ☎ 543-7673 🚌 15, 22, 30, 45, 76 🚇 F, J, K, L, M, N ◐ 5–10pm

Mon–Fri (to 11pm Fri); 4–11pm Sat & Sun (to 10pm Sun). ⛎

Ghirardelli Chocolate Manufactory & Soda Fountain
900 North Point Street (at Larkin St) ☎ 474-3938 🚌 19, 30, 42 ⍟ PH ◐ 9am–11.30pm daily (Soda fountain from 10.30am). ⛎

Johnny Rockets
81 Jefferson Street (at Fisherman's Wharf) ☎ 693-9120 🚌 19, 30 ⍟ PH ◐ 7am–midnight daily (to 2am Fri & Sat). ⛎

Mel's Drive-In
3355 Geary Boulevard (bet. Parker & Beaumont Sts) ☎ 387-2255 🚌 38 ◐ 6–3am Fri–Sat; 6–1am Sun–Thu. ⛎

silicon valley

An hour south of San Francisco and easily accessible by train [→143 for transport details], lies Silicon Valley, the centre of today's booming Internet and new media industries. Appropriately, the newest attraction here is a state-of-the-art museum exploring technology's impact on our daily lives. The **Tech Museum of Innovation** has over 250 interactive exhibits, plus a remarkable IMAX® theatre with an eight-storey domed screen. While designed for all-ages appeal, older kids and teens will enjoy it most. Younger learners can explore the basics of science, history, and the arts through drumming, climbing, and blowing bubbles at the **Children's Discovery Museum**. Over 150 hands-on exhibits plus the Early Childhood Center, a

calmer playspace set aside for those under four. Shift from the flashy and futuristic to the mysterious and ancient at the **Rosicrucian Egyptian Museum**. Inside its Egyptian-styled building, discover artefacts of this fascinating civilization, including human and animal mummies, and tour a replica of a 4000-year-old tomb.

Fill a day with fun at **Paramount's Great America**. This family amusement park features many thrill rides (including eight rollercoasters), an IMAX® theatre, live stage shows, roving performers, and KidZville, with 18 scaled-down rides and play areas for youngsters.

Children's Discovery Museum
180 Woz Way, San Jose ☎ 1-408-298-5437

w www.cdm.org 💲 $6 adults; $4 2–18yrs; free under 2yrs ◐ 10am–5pm (from 12pm Sun); (winter: 10am–5pm Tue–Sat). ⛎ 12yrs & under ♿ ♻ 🎁

Paramount's Great America
Great America Parkway, 2401 Agnew Road, Santa Clara ☎ 1-408-988-1776 **w** www.pgathrills.com 💲 $33 adults; $19.50 children ◐ Apr–Oct: 10am–8pm daily. ⛎ all ages ♿ ♻ 🎁

Rosicrucian Egyptian Museum
1342 Naglee Avenue, San Jose ☎ 1-408-947-3635 **w** www.rosicrucian.org 💲 $7 adults; $3.50 children; free under 6yrs ◐ 10am–5pm daily. ⛎ 8yrs & up 🎁

Tech Museum of Innovation
201 S Market Street, San Jose ☎ 1-408-294-8324 **w** www.thetech.org 💲 $8 adults; $6 3–12 yrs ◐ 10am–6pm daily (to 8pm Thu). ⛎ 8yrs & up ♿ ♻ 🎁

The real fun begins when you delve into the city's quirky underbelly, where all you have to lose are your inhibitions. From midnight rollerblading to virtual bowling, the offerings are as diverse and weird as you could want.

↓ have a blast

Balloon Trips ►

Rise above it all with a balloon ride over the Wine Country [→62–63]. At **Air Flambuoyant**, Captain Wim – an adventurous Hollander known to all as the Flying Dutchman – will sail you over the rolling vineyards of the Sonoma region. Balloon trips depart from Santa Rosa, last for an hour, and include brunch at a nearby café. **Above the Wine Country Balloons & Tours** has been taking to the skies since the late 70s, and their flights, which leave from Santa Rosa, include views of geysers and the Russian River, and a champagne brunch.

Air Flambuoyant
250 Pleasant Ave, Santa Rosa
☎ 1-800-456-4711
w www.airflambuoyant.com
🚗 63 miles north of SF 💲 $185 per person ◐ at sunrise daily.

Above the Wine Country Balloons & Tours
2508 Burnside Road, Sebastopol
☎ 1-800-759-5638
w www.balloontours.com
🚗 64 miles north of SF 💲 $175 per person ◐ at sunrise daily.

Baseball Batting Cages

Bases are loaded, and you're up to bat in front of a screaming crowd. At **Triple Play USA**'s batting cages, you get as many chances as you have tokens to hit that ball right out of the park. There's also air hockey, half-court basketball, and champagne games.

Triple Play USA
5892 Christie Ave (at 59th St), Emeryville 🚗 12 miles east of SF
☎ 1-510-652-4487
w www.tripleplayusa.com
💲 $2.25 for 20 pitches
◐ 3–9pm Mon–Sat (from 11am Sat); 11am–6pm Sun. ♿

Bowling

For the quintessential bowling experience, head to the 40-lane **Japantown Bowl**, where an enthusiastic crowd fills the place every night. When you're ready to take it to the next dimension, book ahead for cyberbowling (Tue, Sat & Sun night) when the whole place is bathed in an ultra-violet light, so that balls, pins, and lanes glow in the dark. Add a trippy light show and piped-in music and you're set for the night.

If you've ever wondered what it would be like to send a bowling ball careering down one of San Francisco's hills, now's your chance with virtual bowling

'Hyperbowl' at **Metreon**'s Airtight Garage, a high-end computer arcade. The sprawling Sony complex boasts four floors of games, restaurants, stores, and movie theatres [→80].

Japantown Bowl
1790 Post Street (at Webster St)
☎ 921-6200 🚌 2, 3, 22, 38
💲 $1.80–$3.60 a game; cyberbowling: $60–$75 per lane
◐ 9am–1am Sun–Thu; 24 hours Fri & Sat. Cyberbowling: 9–11pm Tue & Sun; 8.30–11pm Sat. 🚻

Metreon
4th St (bet. Mission & Howard Sts) ☎ 1-800-638-7366
w www.metreon.com
🚌 14, 15, 27, 30, 45 🚇 F, J, K, L, M, N
💲 $6 ◐ 10am–10pm daily (to midnight Fri & Sat). ♿ 🚻 ♂

Dancing

If you think men should be wearing fedoras, and women sporting cigarette holders, head for **Hi-Ball** for some swing dancing lessons. You're guaranteed to work up a sweat and, if nothing else, you can impress your grandparents with your new (old) moves. Or, hit the dance floor Latin-style with a vigorous hour of salsa lessons at **El Rio** [→120] a longtime Mission bar with a fabulous outdoor patio.

Hi-Ball
473 Broadway (bet. Kearny & Montgomery Sts) ☎ 397-9464
w www.hiball.com 🚌 15, 30, 41
💲 $5–$7 ◐ classes 7pm (basic) & 8pm (intermediate) Sun–Tue; 8pm Fri (basic).

El Rio
3158 Mission St (bet. Cesar Chavez & Valencia Sts)
☎ 282-3325 🚌 14, 49 💲 free (Wed); $5 Sun ◐ classes: 6.30pm Wed; 3.15pm Sun.

Golf

If there were golf courses in heaven, they'd probably look like the 18-hole **Lincoln Park Golf Course**, where you're surrounded by amazing views of the Golden Gate Bridge [→70], the Bay, and the Marin Headlands [→59]. Also top-notch are the wooded hilly greens of the 18-hole **Presidio Golf Course**. Of course, if golfing is your passion, you should really make a pilgrimage south to Carmel, home of the world-famous **Pebble Beach Course** [→66].

Lincoln Park Golf Course
34th Avenue (at Clement St)
☎ 750-4653 🚌 1, 2, 38
💲 $23–$27 ◐ dawn–dusk daily. ♂ 🚻

Pebble Beach Course
17-Mile Drive, Pebble Beach
☎ 1-800-654-9300 💲 $305
◐ dawn–dusk daily. ♿ ♂

Presidio Golf Course
300 Finley Rd (at Arguello Gate)
☎ 561-4653 w www.presidio-golf.com 🚌 28 💲 $42–$72
◐ dawn–dusk daily. 🚻 ♂

Hiking & Biking

The Bay Area's lush and varied scenery – coupled with the year-round pleasant weather – makes it a haven for outdoor activities. To get started, hikers and bikers can check out the *San Francisco Bike Map & Walking Guide* ($2.50), sold at most bookstores. The newly completed Bay Area Ridge Trail is open to hikers, bikers, horses, and even wheelchair users. One of the most popular legs of the trail runs from Arguello Gate through the Presidio [→78] to the Golden Gate Bridge [→70]. Still feeling spry? Then continue across the bridge and into the Marin Headlands [→60], where the trail continues. Contact the **Bay Area Ridge Trail Council** for detailed maps and directions on how to get to the nearest trail head from any address. Bikes can be hired from Park Cyclery [→145] on the edge of Golden Gate Park.

Bay Area Ridge Trail
☎ 391-9300
w www.ridgetrail.org.

Hire a Limousine

If fame has eluded you thus far, who says you can't pretend? After all, it's not who you are, but how you look, and a stretch limo helps considerably. **Bauer's Transportation** will have you outfitted in one of their luxury limos in no time, so pass the bubbly, would you? **Falcon Limousine** is another good bet, and – art lovers take note – they offer an art and gallery tour of the Bay Area.

Bauer's Transportation
Pier 27, Embarcadero
☎ 522-1212 w www.bauers limousine.com
💲 $80/hr (3 hr minimum)

Falcon Limousine

20 Hemlock St (bet. Polk & Larkin Sts) ☎ 1-800-990-4546
w www.falconlimo.com
⬛ $85/hr (4 hr minimum)

Karaoke

When you feel like belting out your own version of Sinatra's *My Way* to an appreciative (and mostly gay) audience, it's time to make for the **Mint Karaoke Lounge** where the slogan is 'Karaoke... 365 days a year!' Of course, part of the deal – and most of the fun – is that you have to listen to all other Cher (or Madonna, or Streisand) wannabes. On the other side of town is **Silver Clouds**, a casual neighbourhood restaurant and bar that transforms into a karaoke lounge at the stroke of ten.

Mint Karaoke Lounge

1942 Market St (bet. Laguna St & Duboce Ave) ☎ 626-4726
w www.themint.net ⬛ 26
🚇 F, J, N ◑ *karaoke: 7pm–2am daily (from 4pm Sat & Sun).*

Silver Clouds

1994 Lombard St (at Webster St) ☎ 922-1977 ⬛ 22, 28, 43
◑ *karaoke: 10pm–1.30am daily.*

Pool & Billiards

The aptly named **Great Entertainer**, with over 43 pool tables, a video arcade, a football bar (rigged with a widescreen TV for some serious game watching), shuffleboard, table tennis, and foosball, has something for everyone, as the boisterous crowds will attest. If your tastes run more to the classy billiards halls of yesteryear – think Paul Newman in *The Hustler* – head to **Chalkers**, a joint with over 30 custom and antique pool tables that is popular among the 9-to-5 set.

Great Entertainer

975 Bryant Street (bet. 7th & 8th Sts) ☎ 861-8833
w www.tge.com ⬛ 19, 27, 42
⬛ pool: $6.50/hr per table
◑ *11am–2am daily (to 3am Sat & Sun).* 🚻 🍴 🖥

Chalkers

Rincon Center, 101 Spear Street (at Mission St) ☎ 512-0450
w www.chalkers.com ⬛ 1, 14, 42
🚇 F, J, K, L, M, N ⬛ *approx $5 per person* ◑ *11.30–1am Mon–Fri (to 2am Thu & Fri); 2pm–2am Sat; 3–11pm Sun.* 🚻 🖥

Rollerblading

Adventurous rollerbladers are in luck: the 200-strong **Midnight Rollerbladers** skate a 12-mile loop through the city every Friday night. This fun, sociable event is an excellent way to meet San Franciscans. Or, test your mettle at **Bladium**, a huge indoor stadium where you can join in pick-up hockey games. You can rent inline skates at **Skates on Haight**.

Midnight Rollerbladers

Departs from Embarcadero in parking lot across from Pier 32
☎ 752-1967 ◑ *8pm Fri.*

Bladium

1050 3rd St (bet. Berry & 4th Sts) ☎ 442-5060 ◑ *games: 4.30–6pm Mon–Wed; 4–6pm Fri; 12–1.30pm Sat.*

Skates on Haight

1818 Haight St (at Stanyan St) ☎ 752 8374 ◑ *11am–7pm Mon–Fri; 10am–6pm Sat & Sun.*

Skateboarding

SF is one of the biggest skateboard parks in the world. It is illegal to skateboard on the sidewalk, but the rules are often bent, and the city is hopping with hot spots drawing skateboarders like a magnet. Among them are 9th Ave (at Judah St) and the Downtown area near Pier 7, where you can get fancy on steps and blocks. A skateboard park is due to open in early 2000 at Crocker Amazon playground, on Geneva Street. For more information, check with staff at DLX [→95] or at FTC Skateboarding [→20] when you buy or rent skateboards.

Watersports

With all the water around the Bay Area, sooner or later you'll want to experience it first-hand. **Spinnaker Sailing** offers a two-hour sunset sail in the bay three times a week, with the setting sun providing a gorgeous backdrop to views of the Golden Gate Bridge [→70], the city skyline, and Alcatraz [→74]. Keep in mind that the Bay Area is at its foggiest in June and August, when views may be obscured. Make reservations at least a week in advance. At **Adventure Cat**, you can cruise the Bay in a customized sailing catamaran, outfitted with two built-in trampolines. Sunset tours include snacks and two drinks. If what you really want is a roll in the Bay, **Sea Trek Kayaks** offers guided starlight kayak tours around the placid and beautiful Richardson Bay near Sausalito – and – how's this for romantic – full moon paddles. Most of these paddle tours are accessible to first-time kayakers. Guided tours are available during the day, when kayaks can also be hired privately with all the gear included.

Spinnaker Sailing

Pier 40, Embarcadero (at Townsend St) ☎ 543-7333
w www.spinnakersailing.com
🚇 N ⬛ 42 ◑ *2-hr trips depart at approx 5.30pm (depending on season) Wed, Fri & Sat.*
⬛ $22.50 per person ♿

Adventure Cat

Dock J, Pier 39 ☎ 777-1630
w www.adventurecat.com

⬛ 15, 42 ◑ *1 1/2-hr tours leave at 1pm, 3pm & sunset tour between 5–6.30pm.*
⬛ $25; $30 (sunset tour) ♿

Sea Trek Kayaks

Schoonmaker Point Marina (at Harbor Drive), Sausalito
☎ 488-1000
w www.seatrekkayak.com
⬛ from Pier 41 ⬛ $15/hr; $65 (starlight paddle); $85 (full moon paddle) ◑ *10am–6pm daily (from 8am Sat & Sun); 3-hr starlight paddle: 7pm Fri & Sat (times vary with season).*

WestCoast Live

Back in the days when radio was king, the overwhelming majority of American households tuned in nightly for their favourite shows. Then along came television and the rest, as they say, is history. Enter WestCoast Live, a popular San Francisco-based show that has been successfully reviving the lost art of the radio variety show for over 15 years. The nationally and internationally syndicated two-hour show is hosted by long-time local hero Sedge Thomson, and every Saturday from 10am 'til midday it beams out to the world from varying locations throughout the city, including SFMOMA [→73]. As part of the audience, you'll enjoy a range of musical and comedy acts, and interviews with authors and artists.

WestCoast Live

Fort Mason Bayfront Theatre
☎ 664-9500 call to reserve tickets and check location
w www.wcl.org ⬛ $12–$14

Whale Watching

When the human race starts getting you down it's time to commune with animals, and the **Oceanic Society** offers an unparalleled opportunity to do so. Whale-watching trips (Dec–mid-May), led by expert naturalists, head under the Golden Gate Bridge [→70] and north along the Marin coast [→60–61], where whale and bird sightings abound. You might catch glimpses of grey and humpback whales, dolphins, porpoises, and up to 30 different species of birds. The society also offers cruises to the Farallon Islands (end Jun–end Nov) 27 miles west of SF, where you can find marine life of all kinds, from tiny plankton to blue whales.

Oceanic Society

Trips depart from Building E, Fort Mason Center ☎ 474-3385
w www.oceanic-society.org
⬛ 19, 28, 42, 47, 49 ⬛ $48–$50; $60–$65 (Farallon Islands trip)
◑ *tours leave at 9.30am and returns at 4pm Fri–Sun; Farallon Islands trips leave at 8.30am and return at 4.30pm Fri–Sun.*

games & activities

Now it's time to get in on some of that peace and lovin' the city is known for with a feelgood foray into the choicest spas in town – along with prime work-out spots where you can get physical all over again.

↓ the feelgood factor

spas

Kabuki Springs & Spa ►

For a slice of heaven – Japanese style – in the middle of the city, this is the spot. One step through the silk curtains and you'll find there's nothing that an effervescent bath and massage ($90), or seaweed wrap and scrub ($65) can't cure. Or, for $10 ($15 after 5pm and on weekends) lounge blissfully in their communal bathing facility, with hot pool, cold plunge, sauna, and steam room.

Japan Center, 1750 Geary Boulevard (at Fillmore St) ☎ 922-6000 w www.kabukisprings.com 🚌 2, 3, 22, 38 ◑ 10am–10pm daily. 🖃 AE/MC/V ♿

Osento

This women-only spa (particularly popular among lesbians) attracts a steady stream of regulars who come as much for the reasonable prices ($50–$70 for an invigorating one-hour massage) as for the strong sense of community which is bolstered, no doubt, by the spa's late hours. Where else can you relax in a steam room at midnight? Other pluses are the outdoor deck and the cool-down room where you can repose among flickering candles.

955 Valencia Street (at 20th St) ☎ 282-6333 🚌 14, 26, 49 ◑ 1pm–1am daily. 🖃 none

Osmosis

The rejuvenating, one-of-a-kind Osmosis experience begins when you shed your clothes for a Japanese robe and are ushered into an exquisite tea garden, complete with bonsai trees and a trickling waterfall. Only then are you ready for the specialty of the house, a 20-minute soak in a steaming enzyme-therapy bath of fermenting rice bran and white cedar mulch. A bath and blanket wrap is $65; with a massage, it's $140. Osmosis is a one-hour drive from San Francisco.

209 Bohemian Highway (at Broadway High), Freestone ☎ 1-707-823-8231 w www.osmosis.com 🚗 most easily accessible by car (off Highway 12) ◑ 9am–9pm daily. 🖃 AE/MC/V ♿ ⛩

Sonoma Mission Inn & Spa

In the heart of the Wine Country, this elegant 198-room inn and newly renovated spa have been doling out decadence for decades. They offer all the usual massages ($89–$198), a unique Watsu water experience in their natural mineral pool ($105), and all forms of body wraps, including a grape seed body polish ($92). At less than an hour away from San Francisco, it makes for an ideal day trip or overnight getaway. Rooms at the inn start at $195 (weekdays) and $275 (weekends). It's best to make a reservation two months in advance in summer.

18140 Sonoma Highway (at Boyes Blvd), Boyes Hot Springs ☎ 1-707-938-9000 w www.sonomamissioninn.com 🚗 most easily accessible by car (on Highway 12) ◑ 7am–9pm daily. 🖃 AE/DC/MC/V ♿ ⛩ ⛩

Spa Nordstrom

Nordstrom [→88] has become synonymous with expert service, and its spa embodies this with sophisticated panache. Tucked away from the rest of the store, this peaceful oasis provides a perfect respite from the shopping masses. Attentive therapists will cater to your every whim, including a rich milk whey bath ($50) or a penetrating hot stone massage ($80).

Nordstrom, SF Shopping Centre, 865 Market Street (at 5th St) ☎ 977-5102 🚌 6, 7, 9, 66, 71 🚇 F, J, K, L, M, N ◑ 9am–9pm Mon–Sat (from 7.45am Wed–Fri); 10.15am–7pm Sun. 🖃 AE/D/MC/V ♿ ⛩ ⛩

Spa Radiance

The intoxicating wafts of vanilla and ginger that greet you at the door are just a hint of the delights that await in this fab spa. It's been family-run for nearly 20 years, and owner Angelina will see to it that you are pamperedt with a range of creative treatments including a 2 1/2-hour rose petal body scrub and massage ($195) or an aromatherapy facial ($110).

3061 Fillmore Street (at Filbert St) ☎ 346-6281 w www.sparadiance.com 🚌 22, 45 ◑ 9am–7pm daily (to 9pm Wed–Fri). 🖃 AE/D/MC/V ♿ ⛩

calistoga

Forget the wines, Calistoga's real draw is the water – naturally hot mineral water that bubbles up from deep within the earth, and is widely believed to possess soothing restorative powers. Scores of visitors descend upon the Calistoga spas every weekend. One of the oldest and consistently highest rated spas in town is **Indian Springs**. Here you can sink into a luxurious mud or mineral bath in their 1913 bath house, followed by a 1-hour massage for $140. Private bungalows start at $175 a night. Another fixture is the casual **Dr Wilkinson's Hot Springs Resort** where you can get the works (mud and mineral bath, blanket wrap and massage) for $129, rooms from $89. For a step up in personalized care, try **Mount View Spa**. Any of their luxurious European-style treatments (including a purifying seaweed bath for $30) will leave you glowing and grinning, and wondering how you lived without it for so long. Rooms from $130.

Dr Wilkinson's Hot Springs
1507 Lincoln Ave (at Fairway St), Calistoga ☎ 1-707-942-4102 ◑ 8.30am–3.45pm daily. 🖃 AE/MC/V ⛩

Indian Springs
1712 Lincoln Ave (at Silverado Trail), Calistoga ☎ 1-707-942-4913 ◑ 9am–8pm daily. 🖃 D/MC/V ♿ ⛩

Mount View Spa
1457 Lincoln Ave (at Washington St), Calistoga ☎ 1-707-942-5789 ◑ 9am–9pm daily (to 9.30pm Sat). 🖃 AE/MC/V ♿ ⛩ ⛩

hair & nail care

With stylish salons sprouting up all over the place, San Francisco has become a city with quite a flair for hair. Some, however, are a cut above the rest. Having a haircut at *Salon Andres* is like being queen for a day. The salon's sensual look – a burgundy velvet motif, high ceilings, ornate mirrors – coupled with a comp glass of wine and their oh-so-attentive staff make for an experience to savour. Haircuts start at $35. To round things off, have a manicure ($14) or a massage ($75). The trend-setting stylists at *diPietro Todd Salon* are as skilled with their shears as they are at updating your hairdo. Cuts are $40 and up. The minimalist-chic *Elevation Salon & Café* has friendly, chatty stylists who'll make you feel at home and then give you one of the best haircuts in town. Sip an espresso in their full-service café while waiting. As for nails, ask for Naly at *Nail Pretty*: after a half-hour of her tough love treatment, you'll walk away with the smoothest, softest feet and toes in town (a pedicure is $15).

diPietro Todd Salon
177 Post Street (bet. Kearny & Market Sts) ☎ 397-0177
◑ 9am–5pm Tue–Sat (to 7pm Thu).

Elevation Salon & Café
451 Bush Street (bet. Geary & Kearny Sts) ☎ 392-2969
◑ 9am–5pm Tue, Wed & Sat; 10am–6pm Thu & Fri.

Nail Pretty
3315 Sacramento St (bet. Walnut & Presidio Sts) ☎ 673-9818
◑ 9.30am–7.30pm daily.

Salon Andres
55 Grant St (bet. Geary & O'Farrell Sts) ☎ 397-9767 ◑ 10am–6pm daily (from 9am Tue, Wed & Sat; to 7pm Wed; to 8pm Thu & Fri).

yoga, meditation & tai chi

Integral Yoga

It's easier to get in touch with your spiritual centre when you're doing it in a gorgeous Victorian mansion with spacious, sunny rooms all done up in lush pastel carpets. The stunning views of the city also help. Classes ($8) are taught in the traditional Hatha style. Every weekday they also host a noon meditation followed by a vegetarian lunch.

770 Dolores Street (at 21st St) ☎ 827-1117 w www.users.aol. com/iyisf/iyi.html ◪ J ◑ 9.30am–7.30pm Mon–Fri; 8am–11am Sat & Sun (class times vary). ⊟ none ◫

Iyengar Yoga Institute

As the oldest Iyengar yoga school in the US, this place was around long before yoga became the popular gym alternative that it is today. Most of the instructors have been teaching for over ten years, and its stellar reputation draws devoted followers from all over the city. They offer classes ($12–$15) for all levels, and for children, pregnant women, and seniors. Drop-ins are welcome.

2404 27th Ave (at Taraval Ave) ☎ 753-0909 w www.iyisf.org ◪ L ◑ 8am–9pm daily (class times vary). ⊟ M/V/◇ ◫

Tai Chi, Mission Dolores Park

East meets west in Mission Dolores Park [→78], where every Tuesday and Saturday morning you'll see people practising the ancient martial art of Tai Chi. Newcomers are welcome ($10–$12 per class). Based on the yin yang concept, Tai Chi focuses on relaxation and balance, working the muscles and the mind. Classes are run throughout the city – contact the Tai Chi Dance Association.

Mission Dolores Park ☎ 671-0120 (Tai Chi Dance Association) w www.taichisf.com ◪ J ◑ Classes: 7am Tue; 9am Sat. ⊟ none

fitness & dance

Crunch

It's one-stop shopping at the cutting-edge Crunch, where under one roof you'll find a rock-climbing wall, a boxing ring, and classes such as urban stick fighting and the firefighter workout, along with the usual stairmasters and exercycles. It's $22 for the day, and $69 for the month.

1000 Van Ness Ave (bet. Geary Blvd & O'Farrell St) ☎ 931-3345 w www.crunchfitness.com ◪ 19, 38, 42, 47, 49 ◑ 5.30am–11pm Mon–Fri (to 9.30pm Fri); 8am–8pm Sat & Sun (to 6pm Sun). ⊟ AE/MC/V ♿ ◕ ◫

Gorilla Sports

Train like an athlete is the motto at Gorilla Sports' two locations, and there's always some serious sweating going on, whether on the state-of-the-art machines or in the high-energy kick boxing classes. So long as it's trendy, they have it: spinning, pilates, and the latest exercise-du-jour, Kwando (a version of the ultra-popular Tae Bo, a martial arts aerobics). It's $15 for the day, and $54 for the month.

2324 Chestnut Street (bet. Scott & Divisadero Sts) ☎ 292-8470 ◪ 30 2450 Sutter St (at Divisadero St) ☎ 474-2699 ◪ 2, 24 w www.gorillasports.com ◑ 5.30am–11pm Mon–Fri; 7am–8pm Sat & Sun (from 8am Sun). ⊟ AE/D/MC/V ♿

Metronome Ballroom

Move over Fred and Ginger. After a few classes here you'll be dancing with the best of them. The choices are endless, including waltz, foxtrot, tango, rumba, merengue, samba, salsa, and swing. No matter if you're a beginner or a seasoned pro, the festive come-one-come-all spirit of the place is infectious. Drop-ins are welcome ($12–$15 a class) and there are regular gay nights. Call ahead for the schedule.

1830 17th Street (at De Haro St) ☎ 252-9000 w www. metronomeballroom.com ◪ 19, 22 ◑ 12–9pm Mon–Sat (from 10am Sat); 10am–6pm Sun. ⊟ MC/V ◫

body art

Body Manipulations

Are your ear lobes feeling a little bare? How about your tongue or navel? The possibilities are endless at this Mission piercing joint. The amiable staff will answer all questions and offer suggestions, or you can just hang out in the waiting room and check out the newly pierced for ideas. Piercings start at $25.

3234 16th Street (at Guerrero St) ☎ 621-0408 w www. bodym.com ◪ 22, 26 ◪ J ◷ 16th Street ◑ 12–6.30pm daily. ⊟ AE/MC/V ♿ ◫

Gotham

The nonconformist Castro neighbourhood is a fitting location for this popular tattoo and piercing shop (formerly Gauntlet) where anything goes. Vince the tattooist (his specialty is tribal tattoos) charges $100 an hour. Piercings start at $20.

3991 17th Street (at Market & Castro Sts) ☎ 701-1970 w www.gothamworld.com ◪ 24 ◪ K, L, M ◑ 12–8pm daily. ⊟ D/MC/V ◫

san francisco's top shopping streets

Map labels: Fort Point, Golden Gate Bridge, Marina Small Craft Harbor, Fort Mason, Marina Green, Golden Gate National Recreation Area, Funston Playground, marina, BAY STREET, CHESTNUT STREET, LOMBARD STREET, FILLMORE STREET, cow hollow, UNION STREET, WEBSTER STREET, BROADWAY, DIVISADERO STREET, The Presidio, Presidio Blvd, WASHINGTON STREET, Lafayette Park, Alta Plaza Park, FILLMORE STREET, PINE ST, BUSH, Presidio Golf Course, WEST PACIFIC AVENUE, ARGUELLO BOULEVARD, PRESIDIO AVE, SACRAMENTO STREET, pacific heights, CALIFORNIA STREET, Mountain Lake, PARK PRESIDIO BOULEVARD, CALIFORNIA, GEARY EXPRESSWAY, JAPAN CENTER, GEARY, EDDY STREET, Jeffers Squa, 10TH AVENUE, 7TH AVENUE, GEARY BOULEVARD, MASONIC AVENUE, DIVISADERO STREET, TURK STREET, FILLMORE STREET, WEBSTER STREET, haye valle, BALBOA, Angelo Rossi Playground, TURK BOULEVARD, McALLISTER STREET, FULTON, Alamo Square, HAYES STR, richmond, FULTON STREET, STANYAN STREET, Panhandle, HAYES STREET, FELL STREET, OAK STREET, D4, Lily Pond, Golden Gate Park, HAIGHT STREET, Buena Vista Park, Duboce Park, Church Street, Stow Lake, haight-ashbury, CASTRO STREET, MARKET, Muni Metro N, LINCOLN WAY, Corona Heights, Castro Street, Muni Metro J, IRVING STREET, PARNASSUS AVENUE, Castro, JUDAH STREET, 17TH STREET, castro, DOLORES STREET, CHURCH STREET, sunset, University of California Grounds, Muni Metro K-L-M, CLARENDON AVENUE, ASHBURY STREET, D5, Mission Dolores Park, Mount Sutro, noe valley, SUTRO RESERVOIR, twin peaks, MARKET STREET, 24TH STREET, kilometres, miles

♟ directory

getting your bearings

Castro & Market Streets | Castro
♟ C4–C5: The heart of gay culture, the Castro is the place to get ultra-trendy men's clothing – from suits to workwear to leathers – cool shades, gifts sublime and quirky, furnishings, books, flowers, records, and other desirables of urban life.

Chestnut Street | Marina ♟ C1: This yuppie high street is lined with a generic collection of shops and chain stores – and a strangely large collection of ultra-trendy eyeglass outlets.

Grant Avenue | Chinatown ♟ E2: The chaotic streets here are packed with fish and produce markets and shops selling trinkets, lanterns, woks, pottery, embroidered silk coats, Dragon Lady dresses, parasols, pearls, jade,

artefacts – and mystical jars of ancient healing herbs.

Fillmore Street | Pacific Heights
♟ C2: This tree-lined street made for strolling is lined with yummy urban-girl clothing boutiques, high-end vintage and consignment shops, and a number of trendy interior design stores.

Haight Street | Haight-Ashbury
♟ B4: Clothing stores galore sell a melange of tie-dyed hippy era items, rave wear, recycled and vintage threads, club clothes, and of-the-moment street garb. Head shops, record stores, tattoo and piercing parlours, and outfitters of radical skate- and snowboarding gear also line the street.

Hayes Street | Hayes Valley ♟ D3: A hipster haven on the cusp of becoming mainstream, Hayes

Valley is a magnet for shoe worshippers, clothes horses, designer types – and anyone who likes to consider him- or herself on the alternative side of the cutting edge.

Japan Center | Japantown
♟ C3–D3: This five-acre complex in the heart of Japantown is overflowing with oriental gifts, artefacts, crafts, books and magazines, Hello Kitty! oddities, kimonos – and a restorative, Japanese-style spa.

Market Street | Hayes Valley
♟ D4: A short hop from Hayes Valley, this compact antiques row attracts decorators and stylists and sells everything from pristine examples of mid-century splendour to Western kitsch.

Mission [→8–13]

Castro & Noe Valley [→14–18]

Haight-Ashbury [→19–23]

Hayes Valley & the Civic Center [→24–27]

Pacific Heights [→28–31]

Marina & Cow Hollow [→32–35]

Russian Hill & Nob Hill [→36–39]

North Beach [→40–44]

Chinatown [→45–46]

Downtown [→47–52]

SoMa [→53–57]

═ Muni Metro route (surface)

= = Muni Metro route (underground)

— cable car route

▬ BART route

═ good shopping street

getting your bearings

Polk Street | Russian Hill
⚲D1–D2: A condensed stretch of newly swank Polk Gulch where antiques, collectables, home furnishings, books, and the occasional trendy recycled clothing store sit cheek by jowl.

Sacramento Street | Laurel Heights ⚲B2–C2: Chock full of antique stores, children's shops, and a growing number of smartish boutiques featuring designers, both established and up-and-coming – not for the faint of wallet.

South Park | SoMa ⚲F3: Dotted around SF's 'Multimedia Gulch' are numerous stores selling home furnishings, off-price designer fashions, skate and bike gear, and records.

24th Street | Noe Valley
⚲C5–D5: Handicrafts, folk art, antiques, books, natural fibre fashions, and educational toy stores in a friendly residential area where baby strollers abound.

Union Street | Cow Hollow ⚲C2: Union Street attracts as homogeneous a crowd as nearby Chestnut Street, but the consumer pickings are far richer and quirkier – especially those designed to adorn the body and accessorize the home.

Union Square | Downtown ⚲E2: A densely populated shoppers' mecca of department stores, designer temples, luxury brands, chain flagships, theme stores, and a clutch of independent, only-in-San Francisco boutiques, as well as bookstores, art galleries, and mega-music stores.

Upper Grant Avenue | North Beach ⚲E1: An influx of talented young designers and creative retailers has made this three-block crawl in North Beach the NoLita of San Francisco – with interesting spill-over shops on nearby Columbus Avenue.

Valencia Street | Mission ⚲D4–D5: Vintage books, used clothing, up-and-coming designers, masses of music (vive le vinyl), recycled furnishings, funky gifts, and folk art emporia line this burgeoning Mission district strip. This is the closest San Francisco has to New York's happening East Village.

When it comes to retail, SF prides itself on individuality. Look beyond the main boulevards where big brands hold court, and treat yourself in the one-of-a-kind boutiques.

retail therapy

↓ department stores

Gumps

Since 1861, Gumps has been providing the well-heeled with high-end china, flatware and glassware, and a superlative collection of Oriental treasures – including jade and luscious freshwater pearls – under the watchful eyes of a large golden Buddha. In the last few years this retail *grande dame* has endeavoured to shake her fusty image by adding innovative lines to the mix, such as new and antique garden ornaments ideal for the country home. $$$

135 Post Street (at Grant Ave) ☎ 982-1616
🚌 2, 3 🌓 *10am–6pm Mon–Sat.* 💳 AE/MC/V

Macy's

Guided by the principle that more is better, Macy's, at 700,000 sq ft, is the second largest department store in the country. For tireless shoppers who relish football-field-sized floors of overstuffed racks, this is nirvana; others succumb to claustrophobia. Nevertheless, the persistent will find dozens of designer and private labels (and frequent sales) with little emphasis on cutting-edge names. There is a large selection of shoes, accessories, and cosmetics. Menswear, electronics, and home furnishings are housed in their own stores across the street. $–$$$

170 O'Farrell Street (at Stockton St)
☎ 397-3333 🚌 30, 38, 45 🚇 PH, PM
🌓 *10am–8pm Mon–Sat; 11am–7pm Sun.* 💳 all

Neiman-Marcus

Sardonically referred to as 'Needless Markup', this venerable chain doesn't really charge more, it just carries a tonier selection of goods, including the city's largest collection of Kate Spade's eye-catching handbags – from raw silk to raffia – and power shoes by the likes of Prada, Blahnik, and Gucci. Cosmetics include some of the trendier boutique

lines and the ever popular Kiehl's plant-based lotions (supermodels reportedly go ga-ga over the lip balm). Men's and women's clothing is comprised of the usual solid gold names as well as less pricey casualwear. $$–$$$

150 Stockton Street (at Geary St) ☎ 362-3900
🚌 30, 38, 45 🚇 PH, PM 🌓 *10am–7pm Mon–Sat (to 8pm Thu); 12–6pm Sun.* 💳 AE

Nordstrom

This Seattle-born chain is known as much for its friendly customer service as its wearables. The five-star shoe department offers the latest profiles at all price ranges, and smaller sections are laid out like individual boutiques. Treading a clear path between two extremes, the clothing is current without being scary and there is a good selection of suits for the career-inclined. $–$$$

SF Shopping Centre, 865 Market Street (at 5th St)
☎ 243-8500 🚌 6, 7, 9, 66, 71 🚇 F, J, K, L, M, N
🌓 *9.30am–9pm Mon–Sat; 10am–7pm Sun.*
💳 AE/MC/V

Saks Fifth Avenue

There have been obvious efforts to pump up the volume on style and the payoff is hanging on the second floor, with designers such as Alberta Ferretti, JP Gaultier, Prada Sport, and the gang. Two floors up you can feast on a smorgy of Miu Miu, Anna Sui, and the reigning doyenne of street chic, Katayone Adeli. The boys get their own store down the street, where the selection is just as yummy and includes YSL's new boy wonder, Hedi Slimane, whose fearless, modernist designs have transformed the label into one of the hottest on the block. $$–$$$

384 Post Street (at Powell St); 220 Post Street (bet. Grant & Stockton Sts) ☎ 986-4300
🚌 2, 3 🚇 PH, PM 🌓 *10am–7pm Mon–Fri (to 8pm Thu); 12–7pm Sun.* 💳 all

↓ fashion

men & women

AB Fits

Graduate from Gap and look to this post-industrial North Beach temple of jeans for guidance. The owners have a doctorate in fit, the selection to back up their expertise, and endless patience. Slip in and out of the two dozen or so brands such as Diesel, Replay, and the beautifully loomed inky blue jeans by Hollywood Ranch Market with sterling silver buttons and a price tag to match. $$

1519 Grant Avenue (at Union St) ☎ 982-5726 🚌 12, 15, 30, 41, 45 ⏱ 11am–7pm Tue–Sat; 12–5pm Sun. 💳 AE/JCB/MC/V

Agnès B

This French export found an instant niche by offering classic shapes in multiple colours and patterns. Separates for women include variations on the cropped cardigan, pretty mohair pullovers, cotton shirts printed with pink roses, and classic pants that fit like a dream. Upstairs in the men's lair the sailor-striped cotton T's, soft knitted tops, oilskin jackets, dress shirts, and hipster suits continually stun with the amount of style they deliver for the price. $$

33 Grant Avenue (bet. Geary & Market Sts) ☎ 772-9995 🚌 6, 7, 38, 71 🚇 F ⏱ 11am–7pm Mon–Sat; 12–6pm Sun. 💳 AE/MC/V

Diesel

This is the closest you may come to knowing what it feels like to be in a rock video, so play it to the hilt. As the music throbs remember to look cool, distant, and a teeny bit bored while taking in the street-urchin-goes-to-Hollywood-via-Milan line of tops, jeans, and underwear. Or opt for the super trendy (and very wearable) StyleLab line, with its cropped-to-the-knee pants and millennial fabrics. $$

101 Post Street (at Kearny St) ☎ 987-7077 🚌 2, 3, 15, 30, 45 ⏱ 10am–8pm Mon–Sat (to 7pm Sat); 12–6pm Sun. 💳 AE/MC/V

Jeremy's

If your idea of discount shopping is stuffed racks and communal dressing rooms, think again. Inside this airy SoMa space, Jeremy Kidson rounds up delectable designer strays not adopted by the department stores. Bits and pieces of Prada, Vivienne Westwood, Alberta Ferretti, Chanel, and many lesser known (and priced) prodigies fill the racks, which always include an impressive selection of cardigans and pullovers. The shoe selection harbours numerous treats, including Miu Miu and Costume National. $–$$

2 South Park (at 2nd St) ☎ 882-4929 🚌 15, 42 ⏱ 11am–7pm daily (to 6pm Sat; to 5pm Sun). 💳 AE/MC/V

Susan

Over-indulging in this candy box of a store won't make you fat, but it might make you broke. A longtime champion of Japanese designers, Susan buys Yohji Yamamoto's exquisitely crafted pieces and Comme des Garçons' eccentric collectables. Nearby racks hold must-have pieces for women by Marni, mod squad boys Martin Margiela and Helmut Lang, Dolce & Gabbana, Lacroix et al. $$$

3685 Sacramento Street (bet. Locust & Spruce Sts) ☎ 922-3685 🚌 1, 3 ⏱ 10.30am–6.30pm Mon–Sat (to 6pm Sat). 💳 AE/MC/V

Ultimo

The Geary Street entrance leads to sartorial splendour for women; Maiden Lane opens onto Jil Sander for him and her. In a clean, uncluttered setting view the latest by Bluemarine, Dolce & Gabbana, Marc Jacobs, JP Gaultier, Randolph Duke and the like, with lesser-priced pieces by Daryl K and the mistress of the boot-cut pant and downtown gal Katayone Adeli thrown into the mix. And if you happen to stumble into one of their end-of-season sales you've won the fashion lottery. $$$

140 Geary Street (bet. Grant & Stockton Sts) ☎ 273-7077 🚌 30, 38, 45 ⏱ 10am–6pm Mon–Sat; 12–5pm Sun. 💳 all

Wilkes Bashford

Try not to get lost in this warren of *haute couture*, attitudes, and prices. While SF's social aristocracy has elected this as its store of choice, mere mortals can feel invisible among the private and trophy label pieces. For the cooler stuff (Dolce, Etro, and new designers) head straight to the top floor and note your escape options – these are some of the most persuasive salespeople around. $$$

375 Sutter Street (at Stockton St) ☎ 986-4380 🚌 2, 3, 30, 45 🚇 PH, PM ⏱ 10am–6pm Mon–Wed & Fri–Sun. 💳 AE/DC/JCB/MC/V

women's fashion

Betsey Johnson

Seductive, sexy, sometimes soft, sometimes trashy girly-wear (at very pretty prices) is Betsey's trademark. And the gilded flea-market-flash decor of the two stores is right in line with her clothing. Stretchy velvet minis, ruffled blouses, flowing hip huggers, rose-patterned slips, sassy faux fur coats, platform boots, and feathered boas – where else can you get fitted for a wedding and an S&M date all under one roof? $–$$

2031 Fillmore Street (bet. Pine & California Sts) ☎ 567-2726 🚌 1, 2, 3, 22 ⏱ 11am–7pm Mon–Sat; 12–6pm Sun. 💳 AE/MC/V

shops

→ more shops

Diana Slavin

This haberdashery for women draws acolytes from afar with clean, tailored clothing inspired by menswear. The quality of Diana's pieces is reflected in the imported fabrics, the drape of the jackets, and the hang of her signature trousers. Blouses and evening dresses share the same spare sensibility without sacrificing femininity. Sunglasses from Cutler & Gross and Clergerie shoes add an elegant touch. $$–$$$

3 Claude Lane (off Bush St) ☎ 677-9939
🚇 2, 3, 15 ◑ 11am–6pm Tue–Fri; 12–5pm Sat.
☐ AE/MC/V

Dosa/Workshop

With its Arabian-princess palette in shot silk and other natural fibres, Dosa's brand of fashion is instantly recognizable. At her eponymous Cow Hollow boutique, the collection is set off with slim-cut trousers by NY Industry, confections by Catherine, stretchy tops by Velvet, and city chick shoes. Sister store Workshop [→94] down the street cranks it up with bejewelled cashmere sweaters, Colette Dinnigan's glamour girl slips and dresses, baubles with attitude, and an entire cottage out back filled with lingerie. $$

2063 Union Street (bet. Webster & Buchanan Sts) ☎ 931-9939 🚇 22, 45 ◑ 11am–6pm Mon–Sat; 12–5pm Sun. ☐ AE/MC/V

The Grocery Store

This den of seduction carries many of the diffusion lines of designers touted by sister store Susan [→89] and is the only SF retailer with Y's – the lower-priced collection of Yohji Yamamoto. It also stocks the ultracool Y-Sacs briefcases and airline bags. The rest of the store is an urban Eden, with Helmut Lang jeans, Margiela Group 6 tops and dresses, D&G separates, and other temptations, including John Smedley's comfy cotton underwear and alpaca and wool mix sweaters from Ireland. $–$$

3615 Sacramento Street (at Locust St)
☎ 928-3615 🚇 1 ◑ 10.30am–6.30pm Mon–Fri (to 6pm Sat). ☐ AE/MC/V

MAC

One of the first retailers to bring cutting-edge fashion to San Francisco, Modern Appealing Clothing has evolved along with its gregarious owners. The women's store now sells the kind of pretty and comfortable clothes the post-label queen craves. Priced for hoarding are Finis' delicious slip skirts and cami tops, tie-dyed in shades like cotton candy and mandarin orange. Petro Zillia's ankle-grazing mohair cardigan is heart-stopping and there's always a must-have handbag. $–$$

1543 Grant Avenue (bet. Union & Filbert Sts) ☎ 837-0615 🚇 15, 30, 45 ◑ 11am–6pm Mon–Sat; 12–5pm Sun. ☐ AE/MC/V

Metier

It's not just what Sheri Evans buys, it's how she mixes it up that makes Metier the dreamiest store Downtown. Imagine Anna Molinari's collectable flowered sweaters and dolce vita dresses, fantasy velvet wraps by Georgina von Etzdorf, crisp hipster pants by Chaiken & Capone, the largest gathering of Suzi Johnson's genius Souchi sweaters, embroidered Indian shawls, and the best-edited collection of antique and contemporary jewellery in the city. And don't forget the killer selection of handbags and wallets by Il Bisonte. $–$$$

355 Sutter Street (bet. Stockton & Grant Sts) ☎ 989-5395 🚇 2, 3, 30, 45 ◑ 10am–6pm Mon–Sat. ☐ AE/MC/V

Six Brady

Shopping at Six is good clean fun. The looks are sharp and urban, from Michael Star's famously hued T's and Katayone Adeli's low-slung pants and boat-neck sweaters to the cheap-and-cheerful stretchy ones of Easel, and colour-drenched cashmere cardigans plus the occasional gamine dress by SoHo's Catherine. $$

6 Brady Street (at Market St) ☎ 626-6678
🚇 6, 7, 14, 26, 42, 66, 71 🚉 F, J, K, L, M, N
◑ 11am–6pm Tue–Sat (to 6.30pm Thu–Sat); 12–5pm Sun. ☐ AE/MC/V

big names

San Francisco isn't New York, where every fashion deity has his or her flagship Valhalla. But a stroll around the Union Square area will yield enough stars to satisfy label slaves – with other titans of the trade (Calvin, Miuccia, Donna) on offer in the nearby department stores and boutiques. Many local movers and shakers head to **Giorgio Armani** *to get outfitted for A-list affairs and transatlantic travels, seeking his understated, perfectly draped designs. For casual days and nights they check in at* **Emporio Armani**. *Others saunter into* **Ralph Lauren** *whose classicism confers a pedigree along with clean-cut eveningwear and jodhpurs. Now occupying an entire coveted corner of Union Square is* **Gucci** *– where pretty young things and trustafarians come to worship at the house that Tom*

built. At **Versace** *the late designer lives on in the extroverted, 'see-me, feel-me' body-hugging designs, while around the corner, chez* **Chanel**, *the spirit of Coco is channelled through Karl Lagerfeld. Crocodile bags and scenic scarves and ties fly out the door at* **Hermès**, *whose trademark orange shopping bag has become as covetable as the Kelly Bag. Also benefiting from new fashion direction and several breaths of fresh air are three venerable houses:* **Bottega Veneta**, **Louis Vuitton**, *and* **Coach** *– keeping leather boys and girls smiling. Not open for breakfast but dishing up plenty of ice is* **Tiffany's**, *with its ever popular modernist baubles by Elsa Peretti. Finally, over at* **Jil Sander**, *the Frau's ultra-minimal masterpieces are arrayed reverently in an appropriately austere setting.*

chain stores

Today, many of the hottest items are 'reinterpreted' before they've barely tripped off the runway – making it all the more affordable to be a fashion diva. And some companies have created empires that dish up good, clean American clothing that's safely stylish if not terribly scintillating. What would Americans do without the SF-based holy trinity, **Banana Republic**, **Gap**, and **Old Navy** (listed in descending order of price). As ubiquitous (and predictable) as Starbucks, they deliver big-style bang for the buck – and as many shades of khaki as Eskimos have words for snow. In the same vein, **J Crew** deftly taps into the American mythology with jeans, khakis, piles of affordable activewear, and well-designed shoes for both sexes. As part of its ongoing challenge to stay ahead of the pack, local favourite **Levi's** has opened its own store to showcase its edgy new streetwear as well as interactive experiences undreamed of by Mr Strauss. Pushing the design boundaries at super-low prices, the cool kids check out **Urban Outfitters**, and stockpile low-slung pants, floaty skirts, embroidered pillows, and homewares. Sexy, shapely girly clothes and club-worthy outfits backed with eye-catching ad campaigns are the specialty at **Club Monaco** and **Bebe**. And season after season **Laundry Industry** offers the kind of well-made, modern silhouettes favoured by city girls with interesting jobs. Boys get theirs at **Abercrombie & Fitch**, which underwent a dramatic transformation from stuffy safari outfitters to dressers of muscled young things. Those who want to match their Range Rovers head for **Eddie Bauer** or **Timberland** – which has a well-priced range of good sturdy shoes for hiking. For something to wear under that polar fleece, there's the mass merchant of Lycra **Victoria's Secret**. And post-modern preppies looking to go places stop at **Brooks Brothers**, which is starting to attract legions of women with its softer-side-of-Wall-Street designs and luxe fabrics. All these brands and more have their flagship stores on and around Union Square; a few have smaller outposts around town.

men's fashion

BillyBlue

GQ once wrote 'BillyBlue might be a tiny store, but it isn't small town.' In fact, it's modelled on those fabulous shops in Europe where the owner hand-picks everything, according to his or her personal taste. Billy Bragman is an Italophile, so many of the designers he touts end in an 'a' (Vestimenta, Arlotta, Zanella, Agnona, Altea). The selection looks polished and pulled together without any hint of gigolo slickness, and the store attracts its share of celebrity devotees. $$$

54 Geary Street (bet. Grant & Kearny Sts)
☎ 781-2111 🚍 15, 30, 38, 45 🕐 10am–6pm Mon–Sat. 💳 AE/MC/V

Citizen

This Castro shop spans the gamut from streetwear to suits in a relaxed, unimposing way that neither intimidates nor causes you to re-mortgage your house. Easy-to-wear and build-upon pieces from Kenneth Cole, French Connection, DKNY, Gene Meyer, and BCBG set the tone, with shoes by Giraudon, Ferré, and Calvin Klein. Super-hip bags from UK's Custard Shop and Energie reflect the utilitarian chic that Citizen embraces. $$

536 Castro Street (bet. 18th & 19th Sts)
☎ 558-9429 🚍 24 🚇 K, L, M 🕐 10am–8pm Mon–Sat; 11am–7pm Sun. 💳 AE/D/JCB/MC/V

MAC

Modern Appealing Clothing's men's store is a family operation with heart and humour. It also represents one-stop shopping for that preferred SF look: switched-on casual. James Bondian suits from Ike and Dean, Kenzo pullovers, Ryan Roberts' beefy knitwear, and flat-front gaberdine pants with rust-on-burgundy striping by Brit-wits Parke Ronan – all offer modern clothes with a vintage sensibility. And the ties – from Paul Smith, Kenzo, and Savile Row tailor Timothy Everest – will drive you mad with desire and indecision. $$

5 Claude Lane (bet. Sutter & Bush Sts)
☎ 837-0615 🚍 2, 3, 15 30, 45 🕐 11am–7pm Mon–Sat; 12–5pm Sun. 💳 AE/MC/V

Nomads

Someone has to outfit San Francisco's YUWs (young urban warriors), and Nomads rises to the challenge. Shirts, pants, and jackets by Adriano Goldschmied and Catherine Joseph are cut with just the right amount of slouch, suitable for upwardly mobile skaters and art-boys alike. $$–$$$

556 Hayes Street (bet. Laguna & Octavia Sts)
☎ 864-5692 🚍 21 🕐 11am–7pm daily (to 6pm Sun). 💳 AE/MC/V

Rolo

Not so much a store as a sprawling retail empire, there are four Rolos specializing in urban, edgy streetwear, loosely organized around price point. The two stores on Castro Street (Rolo and Rolo Undercover) hit the two most affordable tiers, with jeans by Lucky and Stussy at the former and Tom of Finland and Prototype at the latter. On Market Street there's designer sportswear, jeans by Diesel and G-Star, and more prestigious labels. And Downtown at the flagship store there's a smattering of everything – including a tiny taste for the ladies. $$

25 Stockton Street (at Market St)
☎ 989-7656 🚍 30, 45 🕐 10am–8pm Mon–Sat; 11am–7pm Sun. 💳 AE/MC/V

↓ vintage clothing

Ever since the 60s when hippies favoured Victorian ruffs and 20s flapper-girl gear, San Francisco has been a vintage-style mecca. It turns out the hippies knew their stuff. The highest concentration of retro outfitters can be found in their former 'hood, Haight-Ashbury. For bargain basement vintage, **Aardvark's Odd Ark** has virtually all the post-war styles. The glitzier **Wasteland** caters to movie and rock stars – from the literal to the wannabes. **Held Over** is a little more grounded – that is if an entire rack of pristine Scandinavian milkmaid dresses is your idea of reality! They also have a great selection of vintage T-shirts. The art deco crowd shop at **Departures – From the Past** for rhinestones, ball gowns, and men's formalwear, while **Guys & Dolls Vintage** is where the swing kids find the best in gabardine suits, circle skirts, and capri pants. A handpicked selection of women's costume jewellery, bags, and shoes are fit to match. **Ver Unica** is a tiny specialist in designer and one-of-a-kind finery through the decades. Bags and shoes top the list of unbeatables and the condition of the fairly priced items is tops. **Trixie's** is the place to pull together your San Francisco-girl look – a little of this, a little of that. **Crossroads Trading Co** takes on a little of each decade – even the 90s; Levi's from all eras are big here. And if there's something you really need, chances are **American Rag** has it – in triplicate; vintage ethnic wear and pure Americana are specialties. Hankering after something more of the moment – such as last season's barely worn Miu Miu skirt? Then wend your way to **GoodByes** in squeaky-clean Laurel Heights. This is where the socialites and shopaholics sell their barely worn threads so they can buy more, more, *more*.

The **Geneva Swap Meet** is a flea market on the grounds of an old drive-in movie theatre in Daly City. It makes for a great place for a Sunday's sift through the contents of people's attics – old furs, jewellery, and paintings are among some of the staples.

Aardvark's Odd Ark
1501 Haight Street (at Ashbury St) ☎ 621-3141 🚌 6, 7, 43, 66 ◑ 11am–7pm daily (to 8.30pm Fri & Sat). ▭ AE/D/MC/V $–$$

American Rag
1305 Van Ness Avenue (bet. Sutter & Bush Sts) ☎ 474-5214 🚌 47, 49 ◑ 10am–9pm Mon–Sat; 12–7pm Sun. ▭ AE/MC/V $–$$$

Crossroads Trading Co
1901 Fillmore Street (at Bush St) ☎ 775-3282 🚌 2, 3 ◑ 11am–7pm Mon–Sat (to 8pm Fri & Sat); 12–6pm Sun. ▭ MC/V $–$$

Departures – From the Past
2028 Fillmore St (bet. California & Pine Sts) ☎ 885-3377 🚌 3, 22 ◑ 11am–7pm Mon–Sat; 12–6pm Sun. ▭ AE/MC/V $$

Geneva Swap Meet
607 Carter Street (at Geneva Ave), Daly City ☎ 587-0515 🚌 15 ◑ 7am–4pm Sat & Sun. ▭ none $

GoodByes
3464 Sacramento St (at Walnut & Laurel Sts) ☎ 346-6388 🚌 1, 3 ◑ 10am–6pm Mon–Sat (to 8pm Thu); 11am–5pm Sun. ▭ D/MC/V $–$$

Guys & Dolls Vintage
3789 24th Street (at Church St) ☎ 285-7174 🚇 48 J ◑ 11am–7pm Mon–Sat (to 6pm Sat); 12–6pm Sun. ▭ AE/D/MC/V $$

Held Over
1543 Haight Street (at Ashbury St) ☎ 864-0818 🚌 6, 7, 43, 66 ◑ 11am–7pm daily. ▭ MC/V $$

Trixie's
1724 Fillmore Street (bet. Sutter & Post Sts) ☎ 447-4230 🚌 2, 3, 22 ◑ 11am–7pm Tue–Sat; 12–6pm Sun. ▭ MC/V $–$$

Ver Unica
148 Noe Street (at Henry St) ☎ 431-0688 🚇 24 J, K, L, M, N ◑ 12–8pm daily (to 6pm Sun). ▭ AE/MC/V $$–$$$

Wasteland
1660 Haight Street (bet. Belvedere & Clayton Sts) ☎ 863-3150 🚌 6, 7, 43, 66, 71 🚇 N ◑ 11am–7pm daily. ▭ AE/JCB/MC/V $$–$$$

↓ beauty

In San Francisco, designer cosmetics are sold almost exclusively in department stores. One exception is the Parisian pleasure palace **Sephora**, where every brand of make-up, fragrance, and skincare product you've heard of (and several you haven't) are displayed along with explanatory info almost like a museum of beauty. Best of all, you can paint, dab, draw, and blend to your heart's content without interference, unless you desire it. Visit the Fragrance Organ to test your 'nose' on around 500 aromas. Don't forget to grab a few free samples. Two popular cosmetic lines have their own freestanding stores. **MAC** attracts legions of make-up artists with its painterly palette and glam-rock shades. And SF-based **Benefit** sells its light-hearted brand of beauty in three locations around town. For products to pamper body and soul, explore the wonderful world of Kiehls, sold at Neiman Marcus [→88] (as well as selected stores around town). With coriander body lotion, mango liquid soap, and Moroccan jasmine body oil, this counter is an olfactory Eden.

Benefit
2219 Chestnut Street (at Fillmore St) ☎ 567-1173 🚌 22, 30, 43 ◑ 10am–6pm daily. ▭ AE/MC/V $

MAC
1833 Union Street (bet. Laguna & Octavia Sts) ☎ 771-6113 🚌 45 ◑ 11am–8pm Sun–Fri (to 6pm Sun); 10am–7pm Sat. ▭ AE/MC/V $$

Sephora
1 Stockton Street (at Ellis St) ☎ 392-1545 🚌 6, 7, 30, 45, 66 🚇 F, J, K, L, M, N ◑ 10am–8pm Mon–Sat; 11am–7pm Sun. ▭ AE/D/MC/V $$–$$$

↓ shoes

Gimme Shoes opened in an iffy part of town 15 years ago and it is now hard to over-state its impact on the feet of SF men and women. Today there are stores in three wealthy areas (Hayes Valley – the original outlet – Downtown, and Pacific Heights), giving residents easy access to a sublime mix of the haute (Prada, Kelian, Clergerie), the hip (Costume National, Dirk Bikkembergs, Ann Demeule-meester), and the happening (Freelance, Satore, Miu Miu). Over in North Beach at **Insolent**, chic little blacks flats and heels by Sigerson Morrison whisper as seductively as the young Jane Birkin in this sun-filled shop that also carries European lines like Mare and Espace. And for more examples of high-cachet foot-ware, look to department stores Neiman-Marcus, Saks, and Nordstrom [→88], as well as some of the trendier clothing boutiques – Villains Vault, Susan [→89], The Grocery Store [→90], Diana Slavin [→90], Rolo [→91], and Citizen [→91].

The young and trendy find all the extreme styles they crave in Haight-Ashbury, where **Luichiny** (sky-high platforms and Olive Oil Mary-Janes), **Shoe Biz** (fetish-influenced lace-ups and retro-styled sneakers), and **John Fluevog** (theatre of the absurd) keep the club kids dancing. And over in Hayes Valley, they check in at **Bulo**, with its English and Italian styles ranging from the sacred to the profane. Downtown, the chain store **Nine West** can't keep their current styles in stock because even fashionistas love a bargain when spring-ing for a one-season won-der. For good, hip, leather shoes with masses of endur-ing style for the price, **Kenneth Cole** is impossible to beat. At his newly expanded flagship store Downtown there's enough black leather coats, bags, and briefcases to give a PETA member a migraine, as well as urban sportswear with just the right amount of edge. Around the corner is

the local branch of **Joan & David**, where few trends are set – or violated – by the well-made boots, loafers, and sandals. Looking for trainers to impress? The best places to go hunting for the vintage-looking styles in coveted colours are at **Villains**, **Shoe Biz II**, and **Body Citizen**.

Body Citizen
4071 18th Street (at Castro St)
☎ 861-6111 🚃 24 🚇 F, K, L, M
🕐 10am–8pm Mon–Sat; 11am–7pm Sun. 💳 AE/D/MC/V $$

Bulo
437a Hayes Street (at Gough St)
☎ 864-3244 🚃 21 🕐 11.30am–6.30pm Mon–Sat; 12–6pm Sun. 💳 AE/D/MC/V $$

Gimme Shoes
416 Hayes Street (at Gough St)
☎ 864-0691 🚃 21 🕐 11am–6.30pm Mon–Sat; 12–6pm Sun. 💳 AE/D/MC/V $$–$$$

Insolent
1418 Hayes Avenue (at Green St) ☎ 788-3334 🚃 30, 45 🕐 11am–7pm daily (to 6pm Sun) 💳 AE/MC/V $$

Joan & David
1 Union Square (at Powell St)
☎ 397-1958 🚃 2, 3 🚇 PH, PM
🕐 10am–8pm Mon–Sat; 12–5pm Sun. 💳 AE/MC/V $$

John Fluevog
1697 Haight Street (at Cole St)
☎ 436-9784 🚃 6, 7, 43, 66, 71
🕐 11am–7pm Mon–Sat; 12–6pm Sun. 💳 AE/MC/V. $$

Kenneth Cole
2078 Union Street (at Webster St) ☎ 346-2161 🚃 45 🕐 10am–8pm Mon–Sat; 11am–6pm Sun. 💳 AE/MC/V $$

Luichiny
1529 Haight Street (at Ashbury St) ☎ 252-7065 🚃 6, 7, 43, 66, 71 🕐 11.15am–7pm daily (to 8pm Sat). 💳 all $–$$

Nine West
250 Stockton Street (at Post St)
☎ 772-1924 🚃 2, 3
🕐 10am–7pm Mon–Sat; 11am–6pm Sun.
💳 AE/JCB/MC/V $$

Shoe Biz
1446 Haight Street (bet. Ashbury & Masonic Sts)
☎ 864-0990 🚃 6, 7, 43, 66, 71
🕐 11am–7pm daily.
💳 AE/MC/V $

Shoe Biz II
1553 Haight Street (bet Ashbury & Clayton Sts)
☎ 861-3933 🚃 6, 7, 43, 66, 71
🕐 11am–7pm daily (to 6pm Sun). 💳 AE/MC/V $

Villains/ Villains Vault
1672 & 1653 Haight Street (at Belvedere St) ☎ 626-5939/864-7727 🚃 6, 7, 43, 66, 71
🕐 11am–7pm daily. 💳 all $

shops

outlet stores

Books Inc Outlet
A great selection of novelty, coffee table, cooking, and blank books at a discount – fiction and newer titles are few and far between. $$
160 Folsom Street (at Main St)
☎ 442-4830 🚃 1, 42 🚇 N
🕐 10am–5pm Mon–Sat.
💳 AE/D/MC/V

Esprit
Women and children's brand Esprit was conceived in San Francisco and this outlet carries seconds as well as first-class goods with dis-counts of up to 70%. $–$$
499 Illinois Street (at 16th St)
☎ 957-2550 🚃 15, 22, 48
🕐 10am–8pm Mon–Sat (to 7pm Sat); 11am–5pm Sun.
💳 AE/D/MC/V

Loehmann's
Do the names Calvin, Donna, and Miuccia ring a bell? This is where bargain-addicts find big-time labels at shrink-wrapped prices in the heart of Union Square. And trust your fashion radar: labels are sometimes removed from the

garments to cushion design-ers' WalMart-sized egos. $
222 Sutter Street (bet. Grant & Kearny Sts) ☎ 982-3215
🚃 2, 3, 30, 45 🕐 9am–8pm Mon–Sat (from 9.30am Sat); 11am–6pm Sun. 💳 D/MC/V

Nordstrom Rack
Everything from the luscious Nordie's eventually finds its way to this Colma outpost. The shoes are especially tempting – from Doc Marten's to Ferragamo's – marked way, way down. $
81 Colma Boulevard, 280 Metro Center, Colma
☎ 1-650-755-1444 🚃 15
🕐 10am–9pm daily (to 7pm Sun). 💳 AE/D/MC/V

Tower Records Outlet
Plenty of great deals on CDs that made it out the door at the regular stores and sur-vive here, waiting for rescue by the right customer. $
660 3rd Street (at Brannan St) ☎ 957-9660 🚃 15, 30, 42, 45 🕐 10am–5.30pm Mon–Sat; 12–5pm Sun.
💳 AE/D/MC/V

→ more shops

↓ accessories & lingerie

Alla Prima

You'll be tempted to touch everything in sight in this frothy shop. The bras, camis, bustiers, and panties seduce with hues of lavender ice, emerald, and cassis. The inclusive size range embraces both gamines and sex bombs alike. High designers Leigh Bontivoglio, Chantal Thomas, La Perla, and Cosabella share space with Ripcoste's ribbed tanks and thongs. $–$$$

1420 Grant Avenue (bet. Union & Green Sts) ☎ 397-4077 🚌 15, 30, 45 ◐ 11am–7pm Mon–Sat; 12–5pm Sun. 🚇 AE/MC/V

Canyon Beachwear

Tankinis. Bikinis. Maillots. If the thought of trying on bathing suits makes you break out in a cold sweat, stock up here. The sales assistants are friendly and supportive, and will find you a flattering, comfortable suit even if you're not a waif. All year round there are trendsetters by Cacharel, Calvin Klein, Delfina, and Parah – as well as matching sarongs. $$

1728 Union Street (bet. Octavia & Gough Sts) ☎ 885-5070 🚌 45 ◐ 11am–8pm Sun–Fri (to 6pm Sun); 10am–7pm Sat. 🚇 AE/MC/V

City Optix

Whether searching for little vintage rimless lenses or blistering hot pink aviators, a trip to City Optix is the best way to get framed. The Marina store offers many options, and custom lens colours that can match that baby blue Louis Vuitton clutch. The list of brands is endless. $$–$$$

2154 Chestnut Street (bet. Pierce & Steiner Sts) ☎ 921-1188 🚌 22, 28, 30, 43 ◐ 10am–6pm Mon–Sat; 12–5pm Sun. 🚇 AE/MC/V

de Vera

Everything here feels like a lost treasure waiting to be recovered. Necklaces, earrings, and bracelets that transcend any era are created by pairing the old and new in unusual ways (antique Venetian glass and Indian beads are favourites). Pieces from the legendary art glass collection provide a perfect backdrop for the jewellery. $$$

29 Maiden Lane (at Grant St) ☎ 788-0828 🚌 30, 38, 45 ◐ 10am–6pm Tue–Sat. 🚇 AE/DC/MC/V

Mapuche

As seen in Vogue... and on the arms of trendmeisters on both coasts. At the fringes of the Hayes Valley retail scene, this funky leather-shop-cum-showroom turns out some of the most happening leather handbags, wrist cuffs, and chokers around. Classic, in a cutting-edge kind of way. $$

500 Laguna Street (at Hayes St) ☎ 551-0725 🚌 21 ◐ 12–7pm daily (to 6pm Sun). 🚇 MC/V

Metier

A wonderland boutique, where Victorian-era jewellery looks right at home next to contemporary treasures: platinum lacework rings and earrings, Renaissance-inspired burnished gold pieces, and magical lockets minutely engraved with phrases and snatches of poetry. Don't miss Beth Orduna's epic chokers made from leather, chenille, and semiprecious stones. $–$$$

355 Sutter Street (bet. Stockton & Grant Sts) ☎ 989-5395 🚌 2, 3, 30, 45 ◐ 10am–6pm Mon–Sat. 🚇 AE/MC/V

N Peal

Slip into N Peal and try on one of their incomparable Pashmina shawls. Available in colours from ink blue to Schiaparelli pink, the wraps will likely ignite your desire for the pashmina blanket. Also available are cashmere wraps, sweaters, and other lighter-than-air methods of staying warm. $$$

110 Geary Street (at Stockton St) ☎ 421-2713 🚌 30, 45 ◐ 10am–6pm Mon–Sat. 🚇 all

Workshop

This Cow Hollow store is awash with colour and texture, from the velvet Sigerson Morrison shoes to Kara Varian Baker's South Sea Pearls. For a luscious surprise, explore the 'lingerie cottage', where you'll find all the chic little camis, teddies, and lacy bras you always see in magazines but can never find. Also a sensational mix of bathing suits. $$–$$$

2254 Union Street (at Fillmore St) ☎ 561-9551 🚌 22, 45 ◐ 10am–6pm Mon–Sat; 12–5pm Sun. 🚇 AE/MC/V

Zeitgeist

Vintage Bulovas, Gruens, Rolexes, and other fine wrist- and pocket watches are restored to their original timekeeping splendour under the auspices of a master watch- and clockmaker, who also repairs modern-day timepieces and jewellery. $$–$$$

437b Hayes Street (at Gough St) ☎ 864-0185 🚌 21 🚇 F, J, K, L, M, N ◐ 12–6pm daily. 🚇 MC/V

theme stores

Disney Store

Everyone has a favourite Disney character, from villain to princess. Get your Magic Kingdom items here: anything from coffee mugs to kids' clothes. $$–$$$

400 Post Street (at Powell St) ☎ 391-6866 🚌 2, 3 🚇 PH, PM ◐ 10am–6pm Mon–Sat (to 7pm Fri); 11am–5pm Sun. 🚇 all

Levi's Jean Store

The jeans that were invented in San Francisco finally have a freestanding store of their own. With all those width and length variations, it's about time! $$

300 Post Street (at Stockton St) ☎ 501–0100 🚌 2, 3, 30, 45 ◐ 10am–8pm daily (to 6pm Sun). 🚇 all

Niketown

What American sports devotee could miss Niketown? It is a veritable shrine to the world's greatest (and aspiring) athletes who don the trademark swoosh. $$–$$$

278 Post Street (at Stockton St) ☎ 392-6453 🚌 2, 3, 30, 45 ◐ 10am–8pm Mon–Sat (to 7pm Sat); 11am–6pm Sun. 🚇 AE/D/MC/V

Sharper Image

Executive gadgets are the specialties here: pens that stab, letter openers with killer blades, crossbows – stuff like that. $$–$$$

532 Market Street (at 2nd St) ☎ 398-6472 🚌 6, 7, 66, 71 🚇 F, J, K, L, M, N ◐ 10am–6pm Mon–Sat; 12–5pm Sun. 🚇 all

Warner Bros Studio Store

High quality clothing – from bomber jackets to denim shirts – and the usual cartoon action figures of Bugs Bunny and friends, all under one roof. $$

Pier 39, Embarcadero (at Stockton St) ☎ 397-9003 🚌 42 ◐ 9.30am–8.30pm daily. 🚇 all

↓ one-of-a-kind

ArtRock

In this shop-cum-museum rock and roll paraphernalia – psychedelic Fillmore posters, watches and clocks, T-shirts – are all up for grabs. $$–$$$

1155 Mission Street (bet. 7th & 8th Sts) ☎ 255-7390 🚍 14, 19, 26 🕐 11am–5pm Mon–Sat. 🚫 AE/MC/V

DLX

A cultural centre of sorts for skateboarders who come to share stories, watch skate videos, check out the boards, and get outfitted in de rigueur threads by Thunder, Spitfire, and Adrenalin. $$–$$$

1831 Market Street (at Guerrero St) ☎ 626-5588 🚍 6, 7, 26, 66, 71 🚇 F 🕐 11am–7pm daily (to 6pm Sun). 🚫 AE/MC/V

George

Hipster pet products with Homo sapiens eye appeal: red tartan collars; velveteen 'cat-trip' toys embroidered with flocks of birds; alpaca mice; made-from-scratch edible treats; cat-photo feeding mats; and a fabulous pink turtleneck sweater for · cutting-edge chiens. $$

2411 California St (at Fillmore St) ☎ 441-0564 🚍 1, 3, 22 🕐 11am–6pm daily (from 10am Sat, 12pm Sun). 🚫 AE/MC/V

Good Vibrations

'Sexual pleasure is everyone's birthright': this is the philosophy behind Good Vibrations, a friendly, women-owned shop selling safe sex supplies and other 'lurve' toys. The founder has been collecting vibrators for over 20 years, and the fruits of her labor are dis-

played here, in the only vibrator museum in the world. $$–$$

1210 Valencia Street (at 23rd St) ☎ 550-7399 🚍 26 🕐 11am–7pm daily. 🚫 AE/D/MC/V

Kitty Katty's

A slice of the Latin Quarter in the Castro, Flower Frankenstein's quirky shop has T-shirts, cards, stationery, colouring books, comics, and all kinds of très cool stuff. Everything bears the image of alter-ego Kitty Katty – a gitane-puffing, motorcycle-riding, beret-wearing, globe-trotting gal about town. She's hep, she's happening – and her favourite colour is scalding pink! $

3804 17th Street (at Sanchez St) ☎ 864-6543 🚍 22 🚇 F, K, L, M 🕐 10am–6pm daily. 🚫 D/MC/V

Paxton Gate

If you like dead things, this is the shop for you. It encloses a collection of oddities inspired by the garden and the natural sciences. Butterflies, stuffed bats and squirrels, as well as plants that don't need dirt or water to grow are on display at this unique shop. $$–$$$

824 Valencia Street (at 19th St) ☎ 824-1872 🚍 26 🕐 12–8pm Tue–Sun (to 9pm Fri & Sat). 🚫 AE/MC/V

Quantity Postcards

A mind-bending selection of new and old postcards with surreal scenes and San Francisco memorabilia fill the floor and walls of this delightful place. $

1441 Grant Avenue (bet. Union & Green Sts) ☎ 986-8866 🚍 15, 30, 45 🕐 11am–11pm Mon–Sat (from 12.30pm Fri & Sat). 🚫 AE/MC/V

Satin Moon

Even if the thought of getting within 10 ft of a sewing machine brings you out in hives, venture to this Richmond shop for the most beautiful and mind-blowing fabrics. Stylists are fond of taking a few yards and turning them into one-off shawls or instant bedspreads. And the buttons and ribbons are pure poetry. $$

32 Clement Street (bet. Arguello Blvd & 2nd Ave) ☎ 668-1623 🚍 2 🕐 11am–6pm Tue–Sat. 🚫 MC/V

Stormy Leather

The latest in PVC and leather goods, without the sleaze-factor. A completely clean and well-lit place for fetish supplies and street wear. $$–$$$

1158 Howard Street (bet. 7th & 8th Sts) ☎ 626-6783 🚍 14, 19 🕐 12–7pm Mon–Sat; 2–6pm Sun. 🚫 AE/D/MC/V

Studio 24

Mexican folk art as well as Latino cultural items like Day of the Dead figurines and votive candles brighten this one-of-a-kind storefront next to the Galeria de la Raza. $–$$

2857 24th Street (at Bryant St) ☎ 826-8009 🚍 9, 27 🕐 12–6pm Wed–Sun 🚫 AE/MC/V

Used Rubber USA

Never knew what they make out of old tyres? Try backpacks and book covers among other environmentally friendly and fashionable items. $$

597 Haight Street (at Steiner St) ☎ 626-7855 🚍 6, 7, 22, 66, 71 🕐 12–6pm daily. 🚫 AE/D/MC/V

↓ museum stores

Exploratorium

Educational children's games with a spin on science and fun are among the kooky items found here. Check out the Soccer Robot and the Spiraculum, a gyroscopic desk sculpture for the grown-up egghead in your life. $–$$

3601 Lyon Street (bet. Marina Blvd & Bay St) ☎ 561-0360 🚍 28, 30 🕐 10am–6pm daily (to 9pm Wed; to 5pm Thu–Tue in winter). 🚫 AE/MC/V

Mexican Museum Shop

This rather extensive gift shop, an adjunct to the museum, stocks colourful

folk art pieces and a fine selection of books and artefacts related to the history and culture of Chicano and Mexican people. $$

Building D, Fort Mason Center (at Laguna St & Marina Blvd) ☎ 441-0404 🚍 28 🕐 12–6pm Wed–Sun (from 11am Sat & Sun). 🚫 AE/MC/V

Mission Dolores Gift Shop

Mission Dolores' modest gift shop is well worth a peek for old-fashioned SF souvenirs and California Mission-specific books and tchotchkes. $

3371 16th Street (at Dolores St) ☎ 621-8203 🚍 22 🚇 J 🕐 9am–4.30pm daily. 🚫 MC/V

SFMOMA Store

Even purists find it impossible to leave this shop without picking up artisan earrings, a book on Monet's Giverny, a Picasso-style dish, or a fabulous fog dome (shake it up and see a miniature SFMOMA shrouded in fog). $$–$$$

151 3rd Street (bet. Mission & Howard Sts) ☎ 357-4000 🚍 5, 9, 14, 15, 30, 38, 45 🚇 F, J, K, L, M, N 🕐 10am–6pm daily (to 9pm Thu). 🚫 AE/MC/V

shops

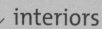

↓ interiors

Alabaster

Once a repository for all things pale – vintage ironstone tureens, French cellu- loid powder boxes, old hotel silver, ivory- coloured ostrich eggs, mother-of-pearl caviar dishes, and alabaster table lamps unearthed in Italy – this carefully curated store now includes traces of colour. Master tastemakers, the owners have added old spinning globes, framed African butterflies, burnished leather suitcases, and a selection of fine photography into the mix, which resides behind a creamy white Victorian storefront in trendy Hayes Valley. $$–$$$

597 Hayes Street (at Laguna St)
☎ 558-0482 🚋 21 ◑ 11am–6pm Tue–Sat; 12–5pm Sun. 🚌 AE/MC/V

Aria

A cross between a rich archaeological site and wonderful flea market, Aria is the vision of Bill Haskell, who appreciates the redemptive value of dust. A snapshot on any given day might catch industrial steel cases and desks from the 40s, Nelson lamps, Eames chairs, medical lab flasks, vintage circus and Tour de France photos, 30s office fans, Mexican santos shrines, architectural tools, Proust-era French inkwells, ceramic letters, and Murano glass blown into light-refracting fruit. $$

1522 Grant Avenue (at Sutter St)
☎ 433-0219 🚋 2, 3, 30, 45 ◑ 11.30am–6pm Mon–Sat; 12–5pm Sun. 🚌 all

de Vera

In the windows of Federico de Vera's shrine-like shop-cum-gallery, vintage and modern art glass catches the light and reflects back rich jewel and lollipop colours. Early 20th-century pieces from Austria, Murano, Peking, and elsewhere are displayed in graceful wooden cases along with investment-quality contem- porary glass and a scattering of luscious artefacts, like antique Thai bodhisattva. $$$

29 Maiden Lane (at Grant St)
☎ 788-0828 🚋 30, 45 ◑ 10am–6pm Tue–Sat. 🚌 AE/DC/MC/V

Fillamento

Tricked out like a model home you'd actually want to live in, Fillamento can give every room in your house a makeover. With a post-modern/Zen sensibility, its three floors are filled with everything from Phillipe Starck staplers to Japanese teak tea utensils – so Wallpaper-toting couples often register their wedding lists here. The top floor is furnished with arts-and-crafts influenced furniture. $$–$$$

2185 Fillmore Street (at Sacramento St)
☎ 931-2224 🚋 1, 3, 22 ◑ 10am–6pm Mon–Sat; 12–5pm Sun. 🚌 all

Interieur Perdu

In a 2000-sq ft space under a SoMa free- way, this enterprising store gathers antique finds from Normandy and Brittany. Individuals and retailers come miles to peruse the well-priced linens, hand-forged gardening tools, iron baby cradles, enamelware, café au lait bowls, tins, old toys, signs from long-gone shops, and stunning wrought-iron crosses. $$

340 Bryant Street (at 2nd St)
☎ 543-1616 🚋 15, 30, 42, 45 ◑ 11am–6pm Mon–Sat. 🚌 MC/V

Limn

While admiring the voluminous collec- tion of 20th-century furniture, lighting, art, and accessories you're bound to trip over at least one architect or designer intent on outfitting his or her own house. This is, after all, the place that introduced Memphis (and with it Ettore Sottsass) to America, and has relentlessly championed the likes of Noguchi, Eames, Rietveld, Starck, Thonet, and stacks of other modern design venerables ever since. $$–$$$

290 Townsend Street (at 4th St)
☎ 543-5466 🚋 15, 30, 42, 45 ◑ 9.30am–5.30pm daily (from 11am Sat & Sun). 🚌 AE/MC/V

Nest

The Fillmore Street Nest is packed with treasures: Tocca flowered linens, quilts that transform a bed, heavy glasses etched with sea creatures, Moroccan tea glasses, reproduction tin motorcycle toys, Chinese lanterns that catch the wind, Laku's fairy princess slippers, Venetian and Victorian-inspired chandeliers, milky white French ironware dishes, and homages to the Tour Eiffel. $$–$$$

2300 Fillmore Street (at Clay St)
☎ 292-6199 🚋 1, 3, 24 ◑ 10.30am–6.30pm Mon–Sat. 🚌 AE/MC/V

Zonal

Rustmeisters Russell Pritchard and Scott Kalmbach have parlayed the motto of 'Always Repair, Never Restore' into three stores replete with naturally distressed furnishings of wrought-iron and wood. People come in search of beds, gliders, finials, lamps, tables, and desks that proudly wear the hard-earned signs of age and evoke a dreamy nostalgia. Expanding the aesthetic is the new Home line: simply designed and beautifully priced couches, chairs, benches, and beds covered in clubby leather, and stainless- topped tables wrought from reclaimed wood (made to order, the pieces can be shipped all over the world). $$–$$$

568 Hayes Street (bet. Laguna & Octavia Sts)
☎ 255-9307 🚋 21 ◑ 11am–6pm daily. 🚌 AE/D/MC/V

↓ food & drink

Alemany Farmer's Market

Like a ticket around the world. Strange and exotic herbs, fruits, and vegetables from Vietnam to Surinam are on sale on this parking lot site. For the adventurous foodie. $$–$$$

100 Alemany Boulevard (at Crescent Ave) ☎ 647-2043 🚌 9, 14, 24, 49 🚋 J
🕐 6am–6pm Sat. 🍴 none

Bi-Rite

Restored to its past art deco splendour, this grocery store cures its own salmon; makes its own sausages, dips, and pasta sauces; and always has a spread of flavourful salads (all certified organic) and some of mama's freshly baked goods.

3639 18th Street (bet. Guerrero & Dolores Sts)
☎ 241-9773 🚌 22, 26 🚋 J
🕐 10am–9pm Mon–Fri; 9am–8pm Sat & Sun (to 7pm Sun). 🍴 MC/V

Bombay Bazaar & Ice Creamery

Pistachio and cardamom ice-cream as well as popular curry and tandoori dishes are all here at this Indian market, where you can also stock up with poppadoms, naan breads, and chutneys for home cooking. $

548 Valencia Street (at 16th St) ☎ 621-1717
🚌 22, 26 🕐 10am–7pm Tue–Sun. 🍴 AE/D/MC/V

Boulangerie

The patissiers at this Pacific Heights bakery render the classic French fare ever so artfully: the flaky pastries are flakier, the savoury things are soulful, and whatever your mood when you arrive, it will be several feet higher when you leave. $$

2325 Pine Street (at Fillmore St)
☎ 1-800-833-8869 🚌 1, 3, 22
🕐 8am–6pm Tue–Sat; 9am–4pm Sun. 🍴 none

Citizen Cake

Prozac for foodies: post-modern cakes, melting ginger-orange scones, sticky buns, the kind of bread people write poetry about, savoury sandwiches, and wood-fired oven pizzas – a snack this joint is worth most any detour. $$

399 Grove Street (at Gough St) ☎ 861-2228 🚌 21
🕐 7am–7pm daily (from 9am Sat & Sun). 🍴 AE/D/MC/V

Ferry Plaza Organic Farmer's Market

Every Saturday morning, food lovers gather to collect snap-dragon and basil, delicate asparagus, as well as dairy products and meat – cultivated at nearby farms. Restaurants set up informal booths for breakfast tasting and chefs demonstrate recipes. $$–$$$

Embarcadero (at Green St).
🚌 42 🕐 8.30am–1.30pm Sat. 🍴 none

La Palma Mexicatessen

From carne asada (grilled steak) to guacamole and fresh tortillas, the Mexican food here is fresh and packed to take away. $

2884 24th Street (at Florida St) ☎ 647-1500 🚌 27, 48
🕐 8am–6pm daily (to 5pm Sun). 🍴 MC/V

Lucca Ravioli

Homemade pasta, Italian deli goods, wines, and fresh breads: everything you need for lunch al fresco or dinner at home. $$

1100 Valencia Street (at 22nd St) ☎ 647-5581 🚌 26 🕐 9am–6pm Mon–Sat. 🍴 AE/MC/V

Maruwa Foods Inc

Looking for seaweed? Dried cuttlefish? Japanese grocery staples like rice crackers, teas, and soy products are here too. $$–$$$

1737 Post Street (at Webster St)
☎ 563-1901 🚌 2, 3, 22
🕐 10am–7pm daily (to 6pm Sun). 🍴 DC/JCB/MC/V

Napa Valley Winery Exchange

If your goal is to take home some of California's primo home-grown, this Downtown shop has the best bottlings of the valley and will ship practically anywhere. $$–$$$

415 Taylor Street (at Geary St)
☎ 1-800-653-9463 🚌 38
🕐 10am–7pm Mon–Sat.
🍴 AE/D/MC/V

Peet's Coffee & Tea

The darkest brew in a town known for good coffee; it was the inspiration for Seattle's Starbucks chain of cafés. $$

2156 Chestnut Street (at Pierce St) ☎ 931-8302 🚌 28, 30, 43 🕐 6am–8pm Sun–Fri (from 7am Sun); 7am–9pm Sat. 🍴 D/MC/V

Stella Pastry & Caffè

The place where North Beach Italian-Americans swear by the fine pastries, cakes, and other treats they dip in their espresso. $$

446 Columbus Avenue (bet. Green & Vallejo Sts)
☎ 986-2914 🚌 15, 30, 45
🕐 7.30am–6pm daily (to mid-night Sat & Sun). 🍴 MC/V

Sweet Inspiration

Old-fashioned fresh fruit tarts, chocolate cakes, and breakfast pastries, but with a modern twist, all baked on the premises. $$$

2239 Market Street (at Noe St)
☎ 621-8664 🚌 24 🚋 F, K, L, M
🕐 7am–11pm Mon–Fri; 8am–midnight Sat & Sun.
🍴 none

Trader Joe's

Locals shop here for gourmet staple foods, wine, beer, and spirits, as well as for the house-brand sauces and large discounts on packaged items like California dried fruits and frozen pot-stickers. $

3 Masonic Avenue (at Geary Blvd) ☎ 346-9964
🚌 38, 43 🕐 9am–9pm daily.
🍴 D/MC/V

Whole Foods

A high-end organic grocer, the real treats are at the deli, freezer, and bakery counters, where you'll find gorgeous meals to take away. $$–$$$

1765 California Street (at Franklin St) ☎ 674-0500
🚌 1, 42, 47, 49 🕐 9am–10pm daily. 🍴 AE/D/MC/V

Yank Sing Takeaway

The elegant Yank Sing dim sum restaurant has an adjacent takeaway for that pork bun or shrimp dumpling on the run. $$

427 Battery Street (bet. Clay & Washington Sts) ☎ 781-1111
🚌 1, 42 🕐 11am–3pm daily (to 4pm Sat & Sun).
🍴 AE/DC/MC/V

Yum-Yum Fish

This Franco-Japanese shop in the Sunset sells some of the freshest fish around. But the real prize for picnickers headed for nearby Golden Gate Park [→78] is the amazingly artful and astonishingly priced sushi which you can take away or consume at one of a few tables on-site. $

2181 Irving Street (bet. 21st & 22nd Aves) ☎ 566-6433
🚌 28, 71 🕐 10.30am–7.30pm Tue–Sun. 🍴 MC/V

→ more shops

↓ books

When it comes to bookstores, downtown San Francisco is a study in contrasts, from the monolithic, multi-storey **Barnes & Noble** and **Borders** to the infinitely more intimate **Alexander Book Co**, an old-fashioned independent that offers jewels of literature, biography, and history (and a literate staff). **Rizzoli** specializes in coffee-table art books and illustrated works, while the **SFMOMA Store** is strong on art, graphic design, and photography. For a really deep selection of both classic and contemporary photography, browse the **Friends of Photography Bookstore** at the Ansel Adams Center [→75]. And, down at the Civic Center, the evening author events and well-stocked shelves pack in bibliophiles and pick-up artists alike at **A Clean Well-Lighted Place for Books**.

San Francisco's celebration of diversity is reflected in the bookstores that thrive (or survive) by catering to the special interests of its denizens. **A Different Light** focuses on gay, lesbian, and transgender literature and non-fiction, while **Get Lost** and the **Rand McNally Map & Travel Store** cater to travellers planning their most exotic and far-flung treks. Architects and interior designers meanwhile make regular pilgrimages to **William K Stout** for both new and out-of-print titles, some quite rare. **Marcus Books** keeps works by African and African-American writers. And the **Limelight Film & Theater Bookstore** is a thespian magnet.

Mystery buffs and collectors of Sherlockiana flock to the **Mystery Bookstore** for old and new mysteries and detective fiction, and lovers of science fiction, fantasy, and horror get their fright fix (along with first-edition Stephen Kings) at **Borderlands**. Polyglots and foreign travellers find French, German, and Spanish language books and magazines at the **European Book Co**. And local favourite **Kayo Books** has racks of vintage pulp paperbacks and dimestore novels with fabulous melodramatic cover art from the 40s to the 70s.

'Free the Press from its Capitalist Owners' reads a sign at North Beach's **City Lights**, the best-known bookstore in all of San Francisco. Founded by Beat poet Lawrence Ferlinghetti, it has an intense collection of European fiction in translation, Latin-American literature, poetry, and literary 'zines.

High-end collectable antiquarian bookstores cluster around Union Square, but for a tempting mixture of the rare and merely previously read, head for the Mission district [→8–13], the capacious **Green Apple** in the Richmond district, and **Acorn Books** on lower Polk Street.

A Clean Well-Lighted Place for Books
601 Van Ness Avenue (at Turk St) ☎ 441-6670 🚍 42, 47, 49 ◑ 10am–11pm daily (to 9pm Sun). 🚭 AE/MC/V $$

Acorn Books
1436 Polk Street (bet. California & Pine Sts) ☎ 563-1736 🚍 19 ⓞ C ◑ 10.30am–8pm Mon–Sat; 12–7pm Sun. 🚭 AE/D/MC/V $$$

A Different Light
489 Castro Street (at 18th St) ☎ 431-0891 🚍 24 ◑ 10am–12pm daily. 🚭 AE/D/MC/V $$

Alexander Book Co
50 2nd Street (at Market St) ☎ 495-2992 🚍 2, 3, 9, 15, 71 🚇 F, J, K, L, M, N ◑ 9am–6pm Mon–Fri. 🚭 AE/DC/MC/V $$

Barnes & Noble
2550 Taylor Street (at Bay St) ☎ 292-6762 🚍 15, 30, 31, 45 ⓜ PH ◑ 9am–11pm daily. 🚭 AE/D/MC/V $$

Borderlands
534 Laguna Street (at Fell St) ☎ 558-8978 🚍 21 ◑ 12–8pm Tue–Sun. 🚭 MC/V $$

Borders
400 Post Street (at Union Sq) ☎ 399-1633 🚍 2, 3 ⓜ PH, PM ◑ 9am–11pm daily (to midnight Fri–Sun). 🚭 all $$

City Lights
261 Columbus Avenue (at Broadway) ☎ 362-8193 🚍 15 ◑ 10am–midnight daily. 🚭 AE/MC/V $$

European Book Co
925 Larkin Street (bet. Post & Geary Sts) ☎ 474-0626 🚍 2, 3, 7, 38 ◑ 10am–6pm Mon–Sat (to 5pm Sat). 🚭 all $$

Friends of Photography Bookstore
655 Mission Street (bet. 3rd & New Montgomery Sts) ☎ 495-7242 🚍 9, 15, 30, 45 🚇 F, K, L, M, N ◑ 11am–5pm Tue–Sun. 🚭 AE/MC/V $$

Get Lost
1825 Market Street (at Guerrero St) ☎ 437-0529 🚍 6, 7, 66, 71 🚇 F, K, L, M, N ◑ 10am–7pm Mon–Sat (to 6pm Sat); 12–5pm Sun. 🚭 none $$

Green Apple
506 Clement Street (at 6th Ave) ☎ 387-2272 🚍 2, 38 ◑ 9.30am–11pm daily (to midnight Fri & Sat). 🚭 MC/V $–$$

Kayo Books
814 Post Street (at Leavenworth St) ☎ 749-0554 🚍 2, 3 27 ◑ 11am–6pm Wed–Sun. 🚭 D/MC/V $–$$

Limelight Film & Theater Bookstore
1803 Market Street (at Octavia St) ☎ 864-2265 🚍 6, 7, 66, 71 🚇 F, J, K, L, M, N ◑ 11am–6pm daily. 🚭 MC/V $$

Marcus Books
1712 Fillmore Street (at Post St) ☎ 346-4222 🚍 2, 3, 22 ◑ 10am–7pm Mon–Sat; 12–5pm Sun. 🚭 AE/D/MC/V $$

Mystery Bookstore
4175 24th Street (at Diamond St) ☎ 282-7444 🚍 24 ◑ 11.30am–5.30pm Wed–Sun. 🚭 MC/V $$–$$$

Rand McNally Map & Travel Store
595 Market Street (at 2nd St) ☎ 777-3131 🚍 6, 7, 9, 66, 71 🚇 F, J, K, L, M, N ◑ 9am–7pm Mon–Fri; 10am–6pm Sat; 11am–5pm Sun. 🚭 AE/D/JCB/MC $$

Rizzoli
117 Post Street (at Kearny St) ☎ 984-0225 🚍 2, 3 ◑ 10am–7pm daily (to 6pm Sun). 🚭 AE/D/MC/V $$

SFMOMA Store
151 3rd Street (at Mission St) ☎ 357-4035 🚍 5, 9, 14, 15, 30, 38, 45 🚇 J, K, L, M, N ◑ 10.30am–6.30pm daily (to 9.30pm Thu). 🚭 AE/MC/V $$

William K Stout
804 Montgomery Street (bet. Pacific & Jackson Sts) ☎ 391-6757 🚍 42 ◑ 11am–6.30pm Mon–Sat. 🚭 MC/V $$

electronics & computers

Adolph Gasser

The city's most comprehensive selection of cameras. Most professional (and savvy amateur) photographers buy and rent new and used gear here – and avail themselves of the on-site lab. $–$$

181 2nd Street (bet. Howard & Mission Sts) ☎ 495-3852
🚌 14, 15 🕐 9am–6pm Mon–Sat. 🖃 AE/D/MC/V

Circuit City

A reasonably priced major chain that spans the gamut: CD players to camcorders to computers. $–$$

1200 Van Ness Ave (at Post St) ☎ 441-1300 🚌 2, 3, 42, 47, 49 🕐 10am–9pm daily (to 7pm Sun). 🖃 AE/D/MC/V

Franklin Covey

If your appointment book is powered by a microchip rather than a pen, and your Palm Pilot could use a little accessorizing, upgrading, or replacing, visit this den of seduction for digital junkies. $$

50 California St (at Davis St) ☎ 397-1776 🚇 1 🚋 C 🕐 8.30am–7pm Mon–Sat; 10am–5pm Sun. 🖃 AE/D/DC/MC/V

Good Guys

A solid and well-priced selection of TVs, VCRs, CD players, electronic products, and other essentials. $–$$

1400 Van Ness Ave (at Bush St) ☎ 775-9323 🚌 42, 47, 49 🕐 10am–9pm Mon–Sat (to 7pm Sun). 🖃 AE/D/MC/V

Macadam

San Francisco's resource for all things Apple – from the latest generation Macintosh computers and PowerBooks to all the groovy bells, whistles, and enhancements – at fairly competitive prices. $$

1062 Folsom Street (bet. 6th & 7th Sts) ☎ 863-6222
🚌 27, 42 🕐 9am–6pm Mon–Fri (to 5pm Thu); 10am–5pm Sat; 11am–4pm Sun.
🖃 AE/D/MC/V

San Francisco Stereo

A high-end store for state of the art DVD and DAT players and turntables – the place for what's hot in the world of home electronics. $$$

2201 Market Street (at Sanchez St) ☎ 861-1044
🚌 22 🚋 F, K, L, M 🕐 11am–7pm daily (to 6pm Sat, to 5pm Sun). 🖃 AE/D/DC/MC/V

Sony Style

A toystore for the wired generation, with everything from CDs, DVDs, and videogames to the latest Sony equipment and computers, in a jumping, interactive environment that will either turn you on or drive you stark, staring mad. $$–$$$

101 4th Street (bet. Mission & Howard Sts) ☎ 369-6050
🚌 14, 15, 30, 45 🚋 F, J, K, L, M, N 🕐 10am–10pm daily. 🖃 all

↓ cds, records & tapes

Music lovers won't be disappointed with the concentration of music stores on Castro, Market, and Haight streets. **Grooves** and **Record Finder** are the places for slabs of vintage vinyl – from the 50s to the 70s. **Medium Rare Records** specializes in show tunes, cabaret, and everything torchy and kitsch. **Jack's Record Cellar** swings toward old blues and soul 78s, 45s, and CDs, while **Groove Merchant** is known for rare soul and funk grooves. For Latin flavours stop off at the Mission's **Discolandia** or **Ritmo Latino**. At **Open Mind** good taste prevails, 'from Abba to Zappa', on CD and vinyl. **Aquarius** stocks CDs by and for indie-rockers which is ground zero for local rock activities, while **Recycled Records** is SF's old standby for vinyl and used CDs. For a nice and competitive selection of hip titles on vinyl and CD as well as perennials in all formats, head to **Mobster**. You will be bowled over by the unbelievably diverse selection of the new and used in all formats at **Amoeba Music**, the country's largest independent record seller, which also hosts free weekly gigs. **Virgin Mega-**

store is the best bet for new songs you just heard on the radio as well as for hard-to-find international imports; best of all, you can hear a tune or two at a listening post. Likewise at **Tower Records**, a good all-rounder open 'til midnight.

Amoeba Music

1855 Haight Street (at Shrader St) ☎ 831-1200
🚌 7, 43, 66 🕐 10.30am–10pm Mon–Sat; 11am–9pm Sun. 🖃 D/MC/V $–$$$

Aquarius

1055 Valencia Street (bet. 21st & 22nd Sts) ☎ 647-2272
🚌 14, 26, 49 🕐 10am–10pm Mon–Sat (to 10pm Fri & Sat).
🖃 MC/V $$

Discolandia

2964 24th St (bet. Alabama & Harrison Sts) ☎ 826-9446
🚌 27, 48 🕐 11am–6pm daily.
🖃 AE/D/MC/V $–$$

Groove Merchant

687 Haight Street (bet. Pierce & Steiner Sts) ☎ 252-5766
🚌 6, 7, 27, 66, 71 🕐 12–7pm Tue–Sun (to 6pm Sun).
🖃 MC/V $–$$

Grooves

1797 Market Street (at Guerrero St) ☎ 436-9933 🚌 6, 7, 66, 71 🚋 F, J, K, L, M, N 🕐 11am–7pm daily. 🖃 AE/MC/V $$

Jack's Record Cellar

254 Scott Street (at Page St) ☎ 431-3047 🚌 6, 7, 66, 71 🚋 F, K, L, M 🕐 12–7pm Wed–Sun. 🖃 AE/MC/V $$

Medium Rare Records

2310 Market Street (at 16th St) ☎ 255-7273 🚌 22, 24 🚋 F, K, L, M 🕐 11am–7pm Mon–Sat (to 9pm Fri & Sat); 12–7pm Sun. 🖃 AE/MC/V $$

Mobster

85 Carl Street (at Cole St) ☎ 242-0119 🚌 6, 43 🚋 N 🕐 11am–7pm daily. 🖃 AE/MC/V $$

Open Mind

342 Divisadero Street (at Oak St) ☎ 621-2244 🚌 6, 7, 24, 66, 71 🕐 11am–9pm Mon–Sat; 12–8pm Sun. 🖃 AE/D/MC/V $$

Record Finder

258 Noe Street (near Market St) ☎ 431-4443 🚌 22, 24 🚋 F, K, L, M 🕐 11am–8pm Mon–Sat (to 9pm Fri & Sat).
🖃 AE/D/MC/V $$$

Recycled Records

1377 Haight Street (at Masonic Ave) ☎ 626-4075 🚌 6, 7, 43, 66, 71 🕐 10am–8pm Mon–Sat; 11am–7pm Sun. 🖃 AE/MC/V $$

Ritmo Latino

2401 Mission Street (at 20th St) ☎ 824-8556 🚌 14, 26, 49 🕐 10am–9.30pm daily (to 10.30pm Fri & Sat). 🖃 D/MC/V $$

Tower Records

2280 Market Street (at Noe St) ☎ 621-0588 🚋 F, K, L, M 🕐 9am–midnight daily. 🖃 AE/D/JCB/MC/V $$

Virgin Megastore

2 Stockton Street (at Market St) ☎ 397-4525 🚌 6, 7, 30, 45, 66, 71 🚋 F, J, K, L, M 🕐 9am–11pm Mon–Sat (to midnight Fri & Sat); 10am–10pm Sun. 🖃 AE/JCB/MC/V $$

san francisco's
night-time
hot spots

The Presidio

marina

cow hollow

pacific heights

japantown

richmond

hayes valley

lower haight-ashbury

Golden Gate Park

upper haight-ashbury

sunset

castro

twin peaks

noe valley

🜋 directory

Castro ⚲*C4–C5*: Colourful, lively and still the global epicentre of gay culture, the Castro needs no excuse to party. Bears, daddies, dykes, and straights alike congregate nightly at the ever-festive 18th & Castro intersection.

Chinatown ⚲*E2*: Overshadowed as a boozing port of call by nearby North Beach, Chinatown's maze of dim and narrow streets merit an après-sun visit for dinner.

Civic Center ⚲*D3*: Sophisticates might begin their evening at one of the glorious performing arts halls here before heading to nearby Hayes Valley.

Downtown ⚲*E2*: The year round hub of tourist commotion, the area on and around Union Square offers a number of suitable if not particularly soulful places to dine and tip a cold one. Most

city residents come here after hours for productions at any one of the fine theatres in the zone.

Financial District ⚲*E2*: All but a ghost town once the suits head home, the Financial District still hides a few worthy restaurants and bars down its alleys.

Haight-Ashbury ⚲*B4–D4*: After dark a curious blend of hippy holdovers, swing cats, yuppies, and barflies scatter about the numerous watering holes along this avenue. The Lower Haight grows darker, tougher and all the more bike messenger-esque with numerous gritty bars, often jammed with anti-yuppie twentysomethings.

Hayes Valley ⚲*D3*: Nestled in the heart of an otherwise so-so area, quaint, young, and emerging Hayes Valley offers

some excellent eateries and a few fine bars.

Japantown ⚲*C2*: Not exactly a prime locale for nightlife, Japantown remains a good place to sample authentic Nippon cuisine. Kingpins should rent a lane at Japantown Bowl [→82], open late with an appropriately dive-y bar.

Marina & Cow Hollow ⚲*C1–C2*: A yupscale crowd frequents the numerous cosy bistros here, while in the bars, post-frat, MBA candidates chug beer, shoot pool, and flirt.

Mission ⚲*D4–D5*: All manner of bars, restaurants, and clubs line the bustling streets here. Cool restaurants, jazz clubs, punk clubs, dives, and swank lounges, are loaded with a cross section of Missionites young, brash, and

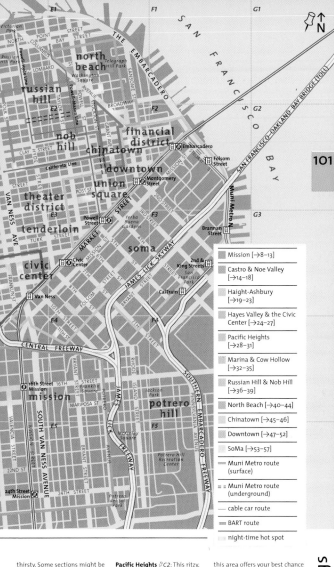

Mission [→8–13]

Castro & Noe Valley [→14–18]

Haight-Ashbury [→19–23]

Hayes Valley & the Civic Center [→24–27]

Pacific Heights [→28–31]

Marina & Cow Hollow [→32–35]

Russian Hill & Nob Hill [→36–39]

North Beach [→40–44]

Chinatown [→45–46]

Downtown [→47–52]

SoMa [→53–57]

—— Muni Metro route (surface)

= = Muni Metro route (underground)

—— cable car route

== BART route

night-time hot spot

thirsty. Some sections might be a tad scary (ie 16th & Mission), but this remains *the* hottest zone for nightlife.

Noe Valley ♪C5–D5: Quaint Noe Valley (essentially just 24th St) sleeps once the sun sets behind Twin Peaks, save a few local eateries and quasi-Irish taverns that cater to pint-chugging twenty-ish types.

North Beach ♪E1–E2: All at once sleazy, sexy, bluesy, yuppified, touristy and old world, North Beach ranks with the Castro and Mission as best place to do anything you want 'til day break. Fine dine, pick up guys, watch girls dance naked, hear live music, or sip champagne with the cigar set. You'll want for nothing here but a safe ride home.

Pacific Heights ♪C2: This ritzy, pricey strip has scant spirited spots to party but yields numerous appealing restaurants.

Potrero Hill ♪F4: Atop the steep hills of sprawling Potrero Hill are a number of worthy spots to eat, drink, and make merry.

Richmond ♪A3: Generally left off the revellers must-do list, this Asian and Russian populated district merits the trek for unparalleled views and ales at the Beach Chalet in Golden Gate Park [→78] or the equally world class sex-hungry singles scene at the South Pacific frat haunt, Trad'r Sam (6150 Geary Blvd).

Russian Hill & Nob Hill ♪D2–E2: Classy, kitschy, and loaded with some of the city's best locales,

this area offers your best chance to sample old-world bar elegance, take in stunning Bay vistas or sip pints in pseudo-Anglo pubs.

SoMa ♪E3: Ground zero for all dance-crazed San Franciscans with a hub of supercool pop rock lounges around 11th and Folsom. SoMa is where night owls – yuppy, gay, and hipster – come to shake their groove thangs.

Sunset ♪A5: The increasingly bustling area around 9th and Irving boasts a mini-treasure of excellent eateries and fine bars.

Tenderloin ♪D3–E3: Replete with hookers on every corner, the lovably seedy Tenderloin harbours a host of colourful booze-eateries and live music joints, all with a fittingly low-brow vibe. Expect a mixture of freaks, bar-flies, and adventurous hipsters.

getting your bearings

restaurants, cafés, bars & clubs

what's where

castro & noe valley

Barney's | $ [→111] ✆

The Café [→123–124] ○

Café du Nord [→119] ▯

Chow | $–$$ [→113] ✆

Firefly | $$ [→113] ✆

Hot 'n' Hunky | $ [→111] ✆

Lucky 13 [→121] ▯

Mecca | $$–$$$ [→108] ✆

Midnight Sun [→119] ▯

Miss Millie's | $–$$ [→108] ✆

The Pilsner Inn [→120] ▯

Zodiac Club | $$–$$$ [→107] ✆

chinatown

Li Po's [→121] ▯

downtown

Aqua | $$$ [→116] ✆

Café Claude | $–$$ [→112] ✆

Campton Place | $$$ [→104] ✆

C Bobby's Owl Tree [→121] ▯

Farallon | $$$ [→116] ✆

Fleur de Lys | $–$$$ [→104] ✆

Harry Denton's Starlight Room [→118] ▯

The Irish Bank [→120] ▯

Le Colonial | $$–$$$ [→114] ✆

Masa's | $$ [→105] ✆

Original Joe's | $–$$ [→111] ✆

Oritalia | $$–$$$ [→113] ✆

Plouf | $$–$$$ [→116] ✆

Postrio California | $$–$$$ [→110] ✆

The Red Room [→118] ▯

Rubicon | $$–$$$ [→105] ✆

Sear's Fine Foods | $–$$ [→108] ✆

Shalimar | $ [→115] ✆

The Waterfront | $$$ [→117] ✆

haight-ashbury (upper & lower)

Cha Cha Cha | $–$$ [→113] ✆

Club Deluxe [→119] ▯

EOS | $$–$$$ [→112] ✆

Finnegan's Wake [→120] ▯

Gold Cane [→120] ▯

Indian Oven | $–$$ [→114] ✆

Kate's Kitchen | $ [→108] ✆

Mad Dog in the Fog [→120] ▯

Nickie's BBQ [→123–124] ○

Noc Noc [→121] ▯

Persian Aub Zam Zam [→121] ▯

Storyville [→122 & 124] ○

Toronado [→120] ▯

hayes valley & the civic center

Alamo Square | $–$$ [→116] ✆

Carta | $–$$ [→113] ✆

Hayes & Vine Wine Bar [→121] ▯

Hayes Street Grill | $$–$$$ [→116] ✆

Jardinière | $$$ [→106] ✆

Justice League [→122 & 124] ○

Millennium | $$ [→117] ✆

The Orbit Room [→119] ▯

Suppenkuche | $–$$ [→113] ✆

Zuni Café | $$–$$$ [→109] ✆

marina & cow hollow

Baker Street Bistro | $–$$ [→110] ✆

Betelnut Pejiu Wu | $$ [→112] ✆

Café Marimba | $–$$ [→113] ✆

Doidge's | $–$$ [→108] ✆

Greens | $$ [→117] ✆

Horseshoe Tavern [→121] ▯

Irrawaddy | $–$$ [→114] ✆

Lhasa Moon | $–$$ [→115] ✆

Perry's | $–$$ [→111] ✆

PlumpJack Café | $$–$$$ [→110] ✆

mission & potrero hill

Blowfish Sushi To Die For | $$–$$$ [→115] ✆

Bottom of the Hill [→119] ▯

Burger Joint | $ [→111] ✆

Delfina | $$ [→105] ✆

Doc's Clock [→119] ▯

Elbo Room [→119] ▯ [→124] ○

El Rio [→120] ▯ [→123–124] ○

500 Club [→121] ▯

Gordon's House of Fine Eats | $–$$$ [→105] ✆

Herbivore | $ [→117] ✆

Latin American Club [→119] ▯

Liquid [→123–124] ○

Lone Palm [→118] ▯

Make-Out Room [→119] ▯

restaurant, café, bar & club chart

restaurants & cafés

Martuni's [→118] ▯

Panchita's Café | $–$$ [→113] ☞

Slanted Door | $ [→106] ☞

Slow Club | $$ [→108] ☞

Universal Café | $$–$$$ [→108] ☞

Watergate | $$ [→107] ☞

Woodward's Garden | $$–$$$ [→107] ☞

north beach & jackson square

Albona Ristorante Istriano | $$ [→114] ☞

Bimbo's 365 Club | [→122 & 124] ●

Black Cat | $–$$$ [→107] ☞

Broadway Studios | [→123–124] ●

Café Jacqueline | $$–$$$ [→107] ☞

Caffè Trieste | $ [→112] ☞

Cypress Club | $$$ [→109] ☞

Enrico's | $–$$$ [→110] ☞

Globe | $$–$$$ [→108] ☞

Helmand | $–$$ [→114] ☞

Kokkari | $$–$$$ [→106] ☞

L'Osteria del Forno | $–$$ [→113] ☞

Mario's Bohemian Cigar Store Café | $–$$ [→112] ☞

MC² | $$$ [→106] ☞

Moose's | $$–$$$ [→109] ☞

Rose Pistola | $–$$$ [→112] ☞

Tosca Café [→121] ▯

Vesuvio [→121] ▯

pacific heights

Café Kati | $$–$$$ [→112] ☞

The Meetinghouse | $$–$$$ [→106] ☞

Mifune | $–$$ [→113] ☞

Vivande Porta Via | $$ [→112] ☞

richmond & presidio heights

Brother's | $–$$ [→114] ☞

Chapeau! | $$ [→110] ☞

Ella's | $–$$ [→108] ☞

Kabuto Sushi | $–$$ [→115] ☞

Khan Toke Thai House | $–$$ [→114] ☞

Nagano Sushi | $–$$ [→115] ☞

Straits Café | $–$$ [→115] ☞

Ton Kiang | $–$$ [→116] ☞

russian hill & nob hill

Acquerello | $$$ [→107] ☞

Charles Nob Hill | $$$ [→104] ☞

The Dining Room | $$ [→104] ☞

La Folie | $$$ [→105] ☞

Sushi Groove | $–$$ [→115] ☞

The Terrace at the Ritz-Carlton | $$–$$$ [→108] ☞

Top of the Mark [→118] ▯

Yabbie's Coastal Kitchen | $$–$$$ [→117] ☞

soma & china basin

Asia SF [→123–124] ●

Bizou | $$–$$$ [→110] ☞

Boulevard | $$–$$$ [→109] ☞

Cat Club [→122–124] ●

Club Townsend [→123–124] ●

Covered Wagon Saloon [→123–124] ●

End Up [→122–124] ●

42 Degrees | $$–$$$ [→105] ☞

Fringale | $–$$$ [→111] ☞

Hamburger Mary's | $–$$ [→111] ☞

Hawthorne Lane | $$$ [→106] ☞

Hotel Utah [→119] ▯

Infusion [→118] ▯

Kate O'Briens [→123–124] ●

Kyo-Ya (The Palace) | $–$$ [→115] ☞

Le Charm | $$ [→111] ☞

Mercury [→123–124] ●

One Market | $$$ [→109] ☞

1015 Folsom [→122 & 124] ●

Paradise Lounge [→122 & 124] ●

Restaurant LuLu | $–$$ [→111] ☞

Seven01 Multimedia Café | $ [→112] ☞

Slim's [→122 & 124] ●

South Park Café | $–$$ [→112] ☞

The Stud [→120] ▯ [→123–124] ●

330 Ritch Street [→122–124] ●

Twenty Tank Brewery [→120] ▯

Up & Down Club [→122 & 124] ●

sunset

Ebisu | $–$$ [→115] ☞

Park Chow | $–$$ [→111] ☞

Organica | $–$$ [→117] ☞

tenderloin

Backflip [→118] ▯ [→123–124] ●

Edinburgh Castle [→120] ▯

Osaka Grill | $$ [→115] ☞

wine country

Chez Panisse | $$–$$$ [→109] ☞ Berkeley

French Laundry | $$$ [→105] ☞ Yountville

key

☞	restaurant/café
▯	bar
●	club
$	main courses up to $10
$$	main courses up to $20
$$$	main courses above $20

Inventive and impeccably fresh cuisine is almost as synonymous with San Francisco as the Golden Gate Bridge. Ingredients culled from the Bay Area's own backyard are put through the global spin cycle to emerge as something entirely new, sparking food revolutions around the country.

chow baby

↓ big bucks

Campton Place 340 Stockton Street (at Sutter St) | Downtown

There's something about this serene hotel dining room that hot young chefs read as a call to action. It jump-started the careers of several who have gone on to fame and fortune. Current chef Laurent Manrique's personal vision includes Southern French and Basque-influenced dishes in luxurious tasting menus. Breakfasts were a big thing when the hotel opened in 83, and the habit persists – a case in point is the corned beef hash topped with quivering poached eggs.

☎ 955-5555 🚇 2, 3, 30, 45 🚍 PH, PM ◑ 7am–2pm daily (from 12pm Sat; from 11am Sun); 6–10pm Sun–Thu (to 9.30pm Sun); 5.30–10.30pm Fri & Sat. ♦ 68 ♿ ▯ ▤ Ⓥ Ⓡ 2 wks Ⓢ $29, $70, $110 ▤ all $$$ ($27–$34)

Charles Nob Hill 1250 Jones Street (at Clay St) | Nob Hill

Chef Ron Siegel is this year's media darling. Despite his obvious culinary chutzpah, there's nothing jarring about the jewel-like plates that arrive in the ultra-luxe Nob Hill dining room, whether it's little ramekins of white corn soup dotted with caviar, or silky sweetbreads married with lobster (the ingredient, incidentally, with which Siegel saw off his opponent at the 'Iron Chef' competition in Japan).

☎ 296-7465 🚇 1, 27 🚍 C, PH, PM ◑ 6–10pm Mon–Sat. ♦ 80 ♿ ▯ ▤ Ⓥ Ⓡ 4–6 wks Ⓢ $61, $69, $75 ▤ all $$$ ($26–$34)

The Dining Room Ritz-Carlton Hotel, 600 Stockton Street (at California St) | Nob Hill

It may have all of the civilized trappings of any Ritz-Carlton, but don't let that lull you. The harpist's repertoire has been known to include 'Stairway to Heaven' and the wine director always has a roguish glint in his eye as he uncorks a quirky bargain. Current chef Sylvain Portay, late of Le Cirque in New York, has a less flamboyant style than his predecessor, although his lamb chops with fried fennel and his squid ink risotto are showstoppers, as is his crayfish bisque. The outstanding selection on the cheese cart deserves a special mention.

☎ 296-7465 🚇 30, 45 🚍 C, PH, PM ◑ 6–10pm Mon–Sat. ♦ 80 ♿ ▯ ▤ Ⓥ ✎ harpist Mon–Sat Ⓡ 3 wks Ⓢ $61, $69, $75 ▤ all $$ (set menus only)

Fleur de Lys 777 Sutter Street (at Taylor St) | Downtown

It's haute cuisine under the big top. Long one of the city's fine-dining stalwarts, Fleur de Lys has undergone a remodelling, updating the fabric-tented dining room. The exquisite New French cuisine has evolved with the tastes of its clientele over the years, but chef Hubert Keller's dishes remain highly stylish and visually stunning. Lately, Keller's fixed-price vegetarian menu commands the most enthusiasm. The accompanying wine list and service are suitably smooth.

☎ 673-7779 🚇 2, 3 🚍 C ◑ 5.30–9.30pm Mon–Thu; 6–9pm Fri & Sat. ♦ 134 ▯ ▤ Ⓥ Ⓡ 4 wks Ⓢ $80 ▤ DC/MC/V $–$$$ ($9.75–$62)

La Folie 2316 Polk Street (at Union St) | Russian Hill

Roland Passot has been on everyone's lips lately for his wildly successful brasseries, but he's still doing what he does best almost every night in the kitchen of La Folie. An unpretentious storefront in an unlikely area provides the setting for Passot's technical wizardry. Plates are architectural, vertical, with vibrant swirls of vegetable-heavy sauces and fancy garniture. Passot's wife and brother (the wine waiter) preside over the intimate room.

☎ 776-5577 🚗 19, 45 🅿 PH ◖ 5.30–10pm Mon–Sat. 🍴 62 ♿ 🚭 🗐 V R 2–4 wks Ⓢ $55, $75 🍽 all $$$ ($30.50–$42.50)

French Laundry 6640 Washington Street (at Creek St) | Yountville

It used to be that you rented one of a handful of tables here for an extra special culinary experience. Seating has expanded (it's still the Bay Area's toughest reservation), but it's no less entertaining. The stone laundry house in Napa Wine Country is the rustic setting for world-acclaimed chef Thomas Keller's playfulness: sometimes that's 'tongue and cheek salad' (braised beef cheeks and veal tongue), 'oysters and pearls' (oysters with tapioca), or even a tiny ice cream cone filled with tuna tartare and a dollop of crème fraîche.

☎ 1-707-944-2380 🚗 most easily accessible by car ◖ 11am–1pm Fri–Sun; 5.30–9.30pm daily. 🍴 62 ♿ 🚭 🗐 🌱 V R 2 months Ⓢ $80, $95 🍽 AE/MC/V $$$ (set menus only)

Masa's 648 Bush Street (at Powell St) | Downtown

Rosy seared foie gras and a glass of Château d'Yquem. Maybe some caviar or a bit of shaved truffle. It's that kind of place. 'What's to become of us?' San Francisco foodies whimpered when the longtime chef took off to open his own place in Las Vegas. His sous chef has moved into the driver's seat to steer the stately hotel restaurant around any bumps. The red silk drapes covering the walls add a touch of romance.

☎ 989-7154 🚗 2, 3 🅿 PH, PM ◖ 6–9.30pm Tue–Sat. 🍴 65 ♿ 🚭 🗐 V R 1 wk Ⓢ $75, $80 🍽 all $$ (set menus only)

Rubicon 558 Sacramento Street (at Montgomery St) | Downtown

Cork dorks swoon over the wine list. The rest of us just think it's cool to hang out in a place backed by Robin Williams, Robert De Niro, and Francis Ford Coppola (not that they ever show up). The original chef left to open her own digs, but the kitchen has kept the faith. The chic interior is lent some warmth by dishes like roast chicken and homey lamb shanks.

☎ 434-4100 🚗 1, 15 🅿 C ◖ 11am–2.30pm Mon–Fri; 5.30–10.30pm Mon–Sat. 🍴 160 ♿ 🚭 🗐 V R 2 wks Ⓢ $31, $45, $65, $90 🍽 all $$–$$$ ($19–$29)

↓ talk of the town

Delfina 3621 18th Street (bet. Dolores & Guerrero Sts) | Mission

The buzz is pretty fierce for a place this small and unassuming. Like the increasingly chichi neighbourhood around it, Delfina has all the allure of a diamond in the rough. Since it opened, the little Mission eaterie has been swamped with Italophiles eager to tuck into *ribollita da Delfina* (sautéed patties made from thick minestrone soup), calamari with white beans, or buttermilk *panna cotta*, all offered at crazy-reasonable prices.

☎ 552-4055 🅿 J ◖ 5.30–10pm Mon–Sat (to 11pm Fri & Sat). 🍴 30 ♿ V R 3 wks 🍽 AE/MC/V $$ ($10–$15)

---

42 Degrees 235 16th Street (at Illinois St) | China Basin

The only reason to visit this hinterland is for 42 Degrees' nurtured Med-Cal cuisine. Inside feels like a scene from *The Cotton Club*, albeit set in a contemporary speakeasy – lots of concrete, metal, and dark drapes and, of course, jazz, which ushers in vittles like watercress salad with duck confit, walnuts, and pomegranate, or lamb shank with eggplant.

☎ 777-5558 🚗 15 ◖ 6–10.30pm Wed–Sun. 🍴 100 ♿ 🚭 🗐 🌱 V R 1 wk 🍽 AE/MC/V $$–$$$ ($19–$28)

Gordon's House of Fine Eats 500 Florida Street (at Mariposa St) | Mission

Perfect for the indecisive, this ultra-hip 'Multimedia Gulch' meeting place has even been called schizophrenic. The menu is divided into categories of distinct personalities, with Healthful, Comfort, Luxury, Local Showcase, and Continental dishes all jostling for attention. 'Comfort' may mean matzo ball soup or short ribs, and 'Luxury' describes dishes like sultry *coquilles St-Jacques*, but it's all served in a bustling, industrial-chic atmosphere. Live jazz, gospel, country, or bluegrass music most nights after 9pm.

☎ 861-8900 🚗 27 ◖ 11.30am–10pm Fri–Wed (to 11pm Tue & Wed; to midnight Fri & Sat). 🍴 120 ♿ 🚭 🌱 🎵 jazz Tue–Sat R 1 wk 🍽 DC/MC/V $–$$$ ($8–$15)

→ more restaurants & cafés

Prices quoted correspond to the cost of a main course

Hawthorne Lane 22 Hawthorne Street (at Howard St) | SoMa

David and Anne Gingrass were once the co-chefs at Wolfgang Puck's Postrio. They've gone on to open their own place, a soaring, warehouse-style restaurant with open ducts and exposed beams that has been among the city's most coveted reservations since Day One. The wine list is thought-provoking, the service expert, but it's the Gingrass' Cal-Asian sensibility (miso-glazed black cod) that has lured the Clinton family along with countless other luminaries to this tiny lane off Howard Street.

☎ 777-9779 🚌 15, 30, 45 ◑ 11.30am–2pm Mon–Fri; 5.30–10pm Mon–Sat (to 11.30pm Fri & Sat). 🍴 200 ♿ ▯ 📋 ✎ piano jazz 6–10pm nightly Ⓡ 2 wks ▭ DC/MC/V $$$ ($24–$29)

Jardinière 300 Grove Street (at Franklin St) | Civic Center

An obvious choice before or after the theatre, ballet, or opera, Jardinière improves the effect of any little black dress. The interior, brainchild of fabled restaurant designer Pat Kuleto, is over-the-top dramatic – a dark, two-level, domed dining room glitters with little lights, while live music and a gorgeous bar crowd keep the place hopping. This is fancy cocktail territory (the Cosmopolitan is *de rigueur*), and namesake chef Traci Des Jardins presides over a sophisticated, changing French-Californian menu that includes lobster strudel and fois gras with pear salad and toasted brioche.

☎ 861-5555 🚌 21 🚇 J, K, L, M, N ◑ 5.30–10.30pm daily (to midnight Tue–Sat). 🍴 175 ♿ ▯ 📋 Ⓥ ✎ jazz nightly Ⓡ 3 wks Ⓢ $75 ▭ all $$$ ($22–$30)

Kokkari 200 Jackson Street (at Front St) | Jackson Square

When Evvia [→66] opened in 95 in Palo Alto, diners didn't know what to make of Greek chic. Folks figured it out, though, because Evvia's owners used the same formula with Kokkari and it's been a hit with the savvy stylish crowd from the outset. The kitchen is overseen by a (gulp) Frenchman, but he still has a way with moussaka, oregano-redolent lamb chops, and grilled octopus salad. Desserts like yogurt sorbet with orange granita or rice pudding and berries are some of the best in the city.

☎ 981-0983 🚌 42 ◑ 11.30am–2.30pm & 5.30–10pm Mon–Fri (to 11pm Fri); 5–11pm Sat. 🍴 170 ♿ ▯ 📋 Ⓥ Ⓡ 2 wks ▭ all $$–$$$ ($14.95–$28.95)

MC² 470 Pacific Avenue (at Montgomery St) | Jackson Square

Is this multimillion-dollar hotspot really all that hot? Well, everything is relative. Some people are underwhelmed by the sleek, minimalist interior and the equally no-nonsense cuisine. Others are smitten by the pure wash of light over exposed bricks and gleaming metal structures in the landmark Barbary Coast Building – the backdrop for simple, Zen-like dishes such as local sardines with grilled aubergine, monkfish with niçoise veggies, or fennel salad with tomatoes and shaved Parmesan.

☎ 956-0666 🚌 15, 42 ◑ 11.30am–2pm Mon–Fri; 5.30–10pm Mon–Sat (to 9pm Mon & Tue; to 9.30pm Wed; to 10.30pm Fri & Sat). 🍴 180 ♿ ▯ 📋 Ⓥ Ⓡ 1 day ▭ all $$$ ($22–$27.50)

The Meetinghouse 1701 Octavia Street (at Bush St) | Pacific Heights

Vanilla-coloured wainscoting and rows of apothecary drawers set just the right Shaker-chic mood for homemade biscuits and mint-chip ice-cream sandwiches. Never mind the begrudging looks of locals who covet the tiny Meetinghouse as their own personal discovery. It's worth arm wrestling a Pacific Heights matron for John Bryant Snell's contemporary American menu, which might include rock shrimp and scallion johnny cakes, pan-roasted range chicken with wild mushrooms, or grilled pork chop with apple sauce.

☎ 922-6733 🚌 2, 3 ◑ 5.30–9.30pm Mon–Sat (to 10pm Fri & Sat). 🍴 40 ♿ Ⓥ Ⓡ 5 days ▭ all $$–$$$ ($17–$25)

Slanted Door 584 Valencia Street (at 17th St) | Mission

This Vietnamese restaurant has created as big a stir as anyone can remember, especially for an ethnic restaurant in the Mission district. Foodies are all restively elbowing for a crack at the imperial rolls, green papaya salad, and 'shaking beef' over lettuce. Slanted Door has actually managed to bring national attention to traditional Vietnamese street foods, yet the noisy little bistro is still one of the city's best bargains. The interior is architecturally hip, the wine list far-reaching and masterful.

☎ 861-8032 🚌 22, 26 ◑ 11.30am–3pm & 5.30–10pm Tue–Sun. 🍴 120 ♿ ▯ Ⓥ Ⓡ 3 wks ▭ MC/V $ ($3.95–$6.10)

Watergate 1152 Valencia Street (bet. 22nd & 23rd Sts) | Mission

No, the name isn't a reference to *that* Watergate; you won't find any 'Deep Throat' moles waiting to give you the inside lowdown on menu additions. The chef prefers his exposés on the plate, in the form of tantalizing French-Asian cuisine that is drawing huge queues to a neighbourhood already rife with instant-hit restaurants. With its elegant, dark good looks, Watergate appears to have lasting power: Watergate manages to successfully tread the fine line between classic and trendy, with offerings such as roasted lobster with barley risotto cake, braised lamb shanks with shaoxing wine sauce, and sautéed foie gras with grapes and verjus sauce.

☎ 648-6000 🚌 26, 48 Ⓑ 24th Street 🕐 5.30–10pm Fri–Tue (to 11pm Fri & Sat). 👤 180 ♿ 🖥 ▤ 🎴 Ⓥ Ⓡ 2 days 🍴 all **$$** ($14–$20)

Zodiac Club 718 14th Street (at Church St) | Castro

It's an astrology-themed restaurant, so if someone asks you your sign it's unlikely to be a shopsworn pick-up. Each cosmic character gets its own cocktail, and the lively Mediterranean food – Romesco-marinated shrimp and crayfish in parmesan or chive risotto with wilted bitter greens – will suit no matter which house your moon is in. The decor is the real attraction here for the young crowd – purple and silver, with swathes of billowing material, give the dining room a space-age supper club feel.

☎ 626-7827 🚌 22 🚇 F, J, K, L, M 🕐 6pm–midnight daily (to 1am Fri & Sat). 👤 44 ♿ 🖥 ▤ Ⓥ Ⓡ 1 wk MC/V **$$–$$$** ($12–$21)

↓ romantic rendezvous

Acquerello 1722 Sacramento Street (at Polk St) | Russian Hill

Acquerello has just celebrated its tenth anniversary, not bad for a tiny, formal Italian restaurant smack in the middle of what's sometimes ungenerously called 'Polk Gulch'. The success is owed to the setting (this was once a lovely chapel), plus the award-winning Italian wine list, and co-owner Suzette Gresham-Tognetti's zealous examination of the regional culinary treasures of Italy. The restaurant has brought back longtime favourites: Parmesan *budino*, rabbit pappardelle, and fillet of beef atop sweet caponata.

☎ 567-5432 🚌 1, 42, 47, 49 🚇 C 🕐 5.30–10.30pm Tue–Sat. 👤 45 ♿ Ⓡ 1 wk Ⓢ $60 🍴 all **$$$** ($25–$30)

Café Jacqueline 1454 Grant Avenue (bet. Union & Green Sts) | North Beach

Big puffy, billowy soufflés that defy gravity and make everyone go 'oooh' – that's what Jacqueline Margulis has been doing in her tiny, intimate North Beach digs for over two decades. What could be more romantic than sharing a bit of such decadence? Margulis can be seen in the back, whisking egg whites in copper bowls before adding brie and broccoli or, for her king of soufflés, a generous drizzle of Grand Marnier.

☎ 981-5565 🚌 15, 30, 45 🕐 5.30–11pm Wed–Sun. 👤 24 🖥 ⏤ on patio 🎴 Ⓥ Ⓡ 1 wk 🍴 all **$$–$$$** ($20–$50)

Woodward's Garden 1700 Mission Street (at Duboce Ave) | Mission

This gem under a freeway in a seedy part of SF feels just like home once you step inside – seating for about 20, a kitchen inches away from your table, and quiet. Your attention will be focused on the heat of the stove and the newfangled American cuisine it turns out: duck breast with grilled polenta, cherry-onion marmalade, and braised chard.

☎ 621-7122 🚌 14, 49 Ⓑ 16th Street 🕐 sittings from 6/6.30pm & 8/8.30pm Tue–Sun. 👤 22 ♿ Ⓡ 3 days 🍴 MC/V **$$–$$$** ($14.50–$24)

↓ hip hangouts

Black Cat 501 Broadway (at Kearny St) | North Beach

Unlike Hard Rock Cafés or Twins, Black Cat is a themed restaurant where you have to work pretty hard to figure out the theme. In fact it's homage to the 'heyday of San Francisco's bohemian nightlife'. This is where classic Chinatown grub meets the noodles of North Beach and other idiosyncratic traditional SF dishes. Prolific restaurateur Reed Hearon's hipper-than-thou nightspot has the trappings of a diner (black-and-white tile, red leather booths), and includes the Blue Bar jazz lounge downstairs.

☎ 981-2233 🚌 15, 30 🕐 5.30pm–1.15am daily. 👤 120 ♿ 🖥 🍷 on patio 🎴 Ⓥ 🎵 jazz Ⓡ 2 wks 🍴 all **$–$$** ($8.95–$18.50)

restaurants & cafés

more restaurants & cafés

Prices quoted correspond to the cost of a main course

↓ breakfast/brunch

Doidge's 2217 Union Street (at Fillmore St) | Marina

It's homey, it's loud, and you get ten different choices for toast with your perfectly cooked eggs.
☎ 921-2179 🚌 22, 45 🕐 8am–1.45pm daily (to 2.45pm Sat & Sun). 🚶 40 Ⓥ Ⓡ 2 days 🍽 MC/V $–$$

Ella's 500 Presidio Avenue (at California St) | Presidio Heights

Chicken hash and cheesy fried cornmeal. Go during the week to avoid the crowds.
☎ 441-5669 🚌 1, 3, 43 🕐 7am–9pm Mon–Fri; 9am–2pm Sat & Sun. 🚶 37 Ⓥ 🍽 MC/V $–$$

Kate's Kitchen 471 Haight Street (at Fillmore St) | Haight-Ashbury

It's worth braving the wait to get at the flanched farney garney (biscuits topped with eggs),
the red flannel hash, or the hush puppies.
☎ 626-3984 🚌 6, 7, 22, 66, 71 🕐 8am–2.45pm Mon–Fri (from 9am Mon); 9am–3.45pm Sat & Sun.
🚶 85 ♿ Ⓥ 🍽 none $

Miss Millie's 4123 24th Street (at Castro St) | Noe Valley

Breakfast, Noe Valley-style, from lemon-ricotta pancakes to omelettes packed with tomato,
basil, and feta.
☎ 285-5598 🚌 24, 48 🕐 9am–2.30pm & 6–10pm Wed–Fri; 9am–2pm & 6–9pm Sat & Sun.
🚶 63 ♿ Ⓥ 🍽 MC/V $–$$

Sear's Fine Foods 439 Powell Street (bet. Post & Sutter Sts) | Downtown

World-famous stacks of Swedish pancakes are the main draw, but the rest of the fare is also
spot on. Hangover heaven.
☎ 986-1160 🚌 2, 3 🚋 PH, PM 🕐 6.30am–3.30pm daily. 🚶 177 ♿ 🗐 Ⓥ Ⓡ 1 day 🍽 none $–$$

The Terrace at the Ritz-Carlton 600 Stockton Street (bet. Pine & California Sts) | Nob Hill

Impress your date with a really chic brunch that includes live jazz and a caviar station.
It's pricey, but worth the splurge.
☎ 773-6198 🚌 30, 45 🕐 6.30am–10pm daily. 🚶 126 ♿ 🖵 🗷/🗐 Ⓥ 🎵 piano jazz 🍽 all $$–$$$

Globe 290 Pacific Avenue (bet. Battery & Front Sts) | North Beach

You know a restaurant is worthy of your patronage when chefs from all over the city
flock there for R'n'R after their own tours of kitchen duty. There's a distinctive vibe at
Globe: elite hipsters; elite chefs; elite service. Don't be intimidated. Just tune into the
chatter as it bounces off the industrial bar and brick walls. It's tiny, so you'll hear just
about everyone fawning over the innovative Cal cuisine.

☎ 391-4132 🚌 42 🕐 11.30am–3pm & 6pm–1am daily (to 11.30pm Sun). 🚶 50 ♿ 🖵 🗐 Ⓥ Ⓡ 1 wk
🍽 all $$–$$$ ($17–$36)

Mecca 2029 Market Street (bet. Dolores & 14th Sts) | Castro

This really is a destination for pilgrims seeking the height of cool. The interior is a
sexy mix of industrial (grey insulation ceilings) and opulent (velvet drapes and
buttery black leather booths), seen at its best late at night. Although it's smack in
the middle of the Castro, it appeals to gay and straight in search of a fab martini,
oysters, or banana coconut cream pie.

☎ 621-7000 🚇 F, J, K, L, M, N 🕐 6–11pm daily (to midnight Sat & Sun). 🚶 165 ♿ 🖵 🗐 🗷 Ⓥ
🎵 jazz Mon Ⓡ 1 wk 🍽 AE/MC/V $$–$$$ ($16–$23)

Slow Club 2501 Mariposa Street (at Hampshire St) | Mission

Film buffs and ghouls will remember that this was the name of the bar in *Blue Velvet*.
Bearing very little resemblance, this Slow Club is nonetheless a chic hang-out –
a study in gun-metal grey and shiny black. Located in the burgeoning 'Multimedia
Gulch', the little bistro offers a daily-changing menu of small and large plates. The
best choice is often the antipasti platter – maybe grilled red and yellow peppers, wax
beans with chili flakes and fennel seeds, balsamic-roasted onions, and mixed olives.

☎ 241-9390 🚌 9, 27 🕐 11.30am–2.30pm Sun–Fri (from 10am Sun); 6.30–10pm Tue–Sat (to 11pm
Fri & Sat). 🚶 45 ♿ 🖵 🗷 sidewalk area Ⓥ 🍽 MC/V $$ ($12–$16)

Universal Café 2814 19th Street (at Bryant St) | Mission

It started as a coffee roastery, and everyone's glad it didn't stay that way. A casual café
at lunchtime, in the evening Universal turns into the fiefdom of chef Cheryl Brown-
Harriman, who specializes in the kind of earthy, unpretentious fare that makes the food
cognoscenti swoon. There are chicken livers, brisket, pot roast with a stew of winter
vegetables – all served in a funky, industrial dining room.

☎ 821-4608 🚌 27 🕐 7.30am–10pm Tue–Fri; 9am–10pm Sat & Sun (to 9.30pm Sun). 🚶 40 ♿ 🖵 🗷
Ⓥ Ⓡ 4 days 🍽 all $$–$$$ ($12–$21)

Zuni Café 1658 Market Street (at Franklin St) | Hayes Valley

When you purvey the archetypal roast chicken, french fries, and Pacific oysters, you can afford to have a bit of attitude. And many of Zuni's employees do. Never mind, though, because there are few more enjoyable places in the city to people-watch, sip a little something, and familiarize yourself with one of the big guns of San Francisco gastronomy. Owner Judy Rodgers has established herself in the pantheon of local food gods, and she makes a damn fine hamburger.

☎ 552-2522 🚌 6, 7, 66, 71 🚊 J, K, L, M, N ◐ *11am–11pm Mon; 11.30am–midnight Tue–Sat.* 👤 160 ♿ 🖥 🖋 Ⓥ Ⓡ 1 wk 🚭 AE/MC/V **$$–$$$** ($14–$21)

↓ sf originals

Boulevard 1 Mission Street (at Steuart St) | SoMa

It's no surprise that the collaboration of chef Nancy Oakes and designer Pat Kuleto has been successful. What *is* surprising is that it's still one of the city's hottest tables. Dark wood panelling, exposed-brick ceilings, and outsize flower arrangements suit the historic building, taking you back to a more 'civilized' era. American food such as roasted loin of lamb with wild mushroom relish captures that same vibe, but with a strictly contemporary attitude when it comes to appetizers and side dishes.

☎ 543-6084 🚌 2, 6, 7, 14, 21, 31, 32, 66, 71 🚊 F, J, K, L, M, N ◐ *11.30am–2pm Mon–Fri; 5.30–10pm daily (to 10.30pm Thu–Sat).* 👤 150 ♿ 🖥 📖 Ⓥ Ⓡ 6 wks 🚭 all **$$–$$$** ($20–$30)

Chez Panisse 1517 Shattuck Avenue (at Cedar St) | Berkeley

It's not in San Francisco, but Chez Panisse has cast its big shadow across the Bay for 25 years. Rookies often make the pilgrimage over the bridge only to whine, 'Is that it?' Well, they've missed the point. The mother of California Cuisine, Chez Panisse's style relies on immaculate produce expertly and simply rendered edible: delicacies include Maine lobster chanterelle salad with orange oil dressing, and ripe figs sliced into a tangle of lightly dressed greens. The main dining room downstairs features a single fixed-price menu each day, and the upstairs café offers à la carte dining.

☎ 1-510-548-5525 🚇 to Berkeley ◐ *6–9.15pm Mon–Sat (Café 11.30am–3pm & 5–10.30pm Mon–Thu; 11am–4pm & 5–11.30pm Fri & Sat).* 👤 50 ♿ 🖥 Ⓥ Ⓡ 2–4 wks Ⓢ $39–$69 🚭 **$$–$$$** (set menus only)

Cypress Club 500 Jackson Street (at Montgomery St) | Jackson Square

What does a 40s-style supper club gone crazy look like? The Cypress Club. But don't spend too much time gazing up at the huge, electric-hued breast lamps – it could stunt your growth. The interior is no less luxuriously phantasmagorical than the day it opened, although critics contend the food has slipped in recent years. Still, it's the perfect place to look cool, sip cocktails, or sample one of the extreme, architectural desserts complete with flying buttresses and corkscrewed sugar doodahs.

☎ 296-8555 🚌 15, 42 ◐ *4.30–11pm daily.* 👤 130 ♿ 🖥 Ⓥ 🎷 jazz nightly Ⓡ 5 days Ⓢ $65 🚭 all **$$$** ($23–$30)

Moose's 1652 Stockton Street (bet. Union & Filbert Sts) | North Beach

Washington Square Park has not been the same since the neon-blue Moose sign went up. Parking has become nearly impossible, a fact that doesn't seem to trouble the revellers crammed in every night. The suave dining room, flawless service, live music, and chef Brian Whitmer's slick eats (think veal chop with pancetta-braised greens and roasted figs) give North Beach diners in search of something other than straight Italian a top-notch alternative.

☎ 989-7800 🚌 30, 45 ◐ *11.30am–2.30pm Tue–Sun (from 10am Sat & Sun); 5.30–10pm Sun–Thu (from 5pm Sun); 5–11pm Fri & Sat.* 👤 120 ♿ 🖥 📖 Ⓥ 🎷 jazz occasionally Ⓡ 1 wk 🚭 all **$$–$$$** ($14–$29)

One Market 1 Market Street (at Steuart St) | SoMa

Bradley Ogden is the original champion of rib-sticking American cuisine. He's won every award, written best-selling cookery books, and fathered numerous restaurants. He probably doesn't spend much time now behind the stove at One Market, his posh Downtown eatery. A series of chefs has kept the standard high with pot roast, 'prime rib' of pork, and chocolate bread pudding. Co-owner Michael Dellar's wine knowledge informs an encyclopedic list.

☎ 777-5577 🚌 1, 2, 6, 7, 14, 21, 31, 32, 66, 71 🚊 F, J, K, L, M, N ◐ *5.30–9pm Mon–Sat (to 10pm Fri & Sat).* 👤 250 ♿ 🖥 📖 Ⓥ 🎷 piano jazz Mon–Sat Ⓡ 1 wk Ⓢ $25, $55, $85 🚭 all **$$$** ($21.95–$29.50)

→ more restaurants & cafés

PlumpJack Café 3127 Fillmore Street (at Filbert St) | Cow Hollow

PlumpJack was destined for success. It's co-owned by hunky city supervisor Gavin Newsom and San Francisco scion Bill Getty; offers a far-reaching and modestly priced wine list (thanks to its nearby wine shop); and purveys glorious hearty stews and braised meat dishes that harken to the French countryside. So, naturally, the Marina spot is packed to the gills with wholesome-looking, food-loving yuppie types.

☎ 563-4755 🚍 22, 28, 43, 45 🕐 11.30am–2pm Mon–Fri; 5.30–10pm Mon–Sat. 👤 50 ♿ 🖥 🎴 Ⓥ Ⓡ 3 wks ▦ AE/MC/V **$$–$$$** ($13–$22)

Postrio California 545 Post Street (at Mason St) | Downtown

Maybe it's no accident that Postrio's kitchen is always tag-team executive-cheffed. The Rosenthal brothers are currently at the helm of Wolfgang Puck's opulent Downtown favourite. Perhaps it requires two vigilant divas presiding over the staff to turn out food for this dramatic, oversized paean to LA luxury which always has a waiting list for reservations. Two distinct dining levels showcase whimsical decorations and stellar views of other well-heeled diners. Postrio offers breakfast, lunch, and dinner – the finest efforts seem to be the East-West dinner entrées and the magnificent desserts.

☎ 776-7825 🚍 2, 3, 4, 76 🕐 PH, PM 🕐 7–10am Mon–Fri; 9am–2pm Sun; 11.30am–2pm Mon–Sat; 5.30–10pm daily. 👤 180 ♿ 🖥 Ⓥ Ⓡ 6 wks Ⓢ $65, $70 ▦ all **$$–$$$** ($12–$30)

↓ club med

Baker Street Bistro 2953 Baker Street (at Lombard St) | Cow Hollow

Just listen: lamb stew printanier, blanquette de veau, escargots forestier – it's the sound of San Franciscans trying to pronounce their favourite 'je ne sais quoi' at Baker Street Bistro. The many, cramped dining rooms are presided over by a gracious owner while the chef struts her stuff in the kitchen. The prix-fixe, four-course menu is one of the city's best deals at $14.50, and the à la carte menu has to-die-for duck liver pâté, mousseline of scallops, and crème brûlée.

☎ 931-1475 🚍 28, 43 🕐 10am–2pm Tue–Sun (to 2.30pm Sat & Sun); 5.30–10.30pm Tue–Sat; 5–9.30pm Sun. 👤 40 ♿ 🎴 sidewalk area Ⓥ Ⓡ 2 days Ⓢ $14.50 ▦ all **$–$$** ($8.75–$14.50)

Bizou 598 4th Street (at Brannan St) | SoMa

No one does beef cheeks like Loretta. Loretta Keller's rustic French/Italian/Spanish menu makes a virtue of necessity. Pork shoulder and other historically second-class cuts are given tender, seasonal treatment in a gracious, sophisticated setting. The place can get airstrip-loud when busy – which is often – in the close-set dining room and bar warmed by fresh flowers and luminous yellow walls.

☎ 543-2222 🚍 15, 30, 42, 45 🕐 11.30am–2.30pm Mon–Fri; 5.30–10pm Mon–Sat (to 10.30pm Fri & Sat). 👤 70 ♿ 🖥 Ⓥ Ⓡ 4 days Ⓢ $25, $100 ▦ all **$$–$$$** ($14–$25)

Chapeau! 1408 Clement Street (at 15th Ave) | Richmond

Quick French lesson: *chapeau* means hat; *chapeau!* means something like congratulations, or hats off. Either way the crowds cram into this tight-packed French bistro with an exceptionally far-reaching wine list, warm service, and bargain-priced prix-fixe menus. The food doesn't necessarily cover new ground, but it's ground that everyone seems to like to traverse on a regular basis. That's the land of *brandade*, roast duck, and crème brûlée. Your bill, of course, arrives in a hat.

☎ 750-9787 🚍 2 🕐 5–10pm Tue–Sun (to 10.30pm Fri & Sat). 👤 50 ♿ Ⓥ Ⓡ 1 wk Ⓢ $27, $33, $25 ▦ all **$$** ($15–$19)

Enrico's 504 Broadway (at Kearny St) | North Beach

This was the preferred hangout of beatniks, pimps, politicians, Hells Angels, and revolutionaries in the 50s and 60s. In homage to Enrico Banducci (the garrulous North Beach proprietor of the old comedy club cum restaurant Hungry i that launched the careers of Lenny Bruce, the Smothers Brothers, even Bill Cosby), this new version of Enrico's Sidewalk Café is universally welcoming. Go people-watching on the patio and revel in the menu of Italian staples and small plates.

☎ 982-6223 🚍 12, 15, 30 🕐 11.30am–11.30pm daily (to 12.30am Sat & Sun). 👤 130 ♿ 🖥 🎴 Ⓥ 🎷 jazz daily Ⓡ 1 wk ▦ all **$–$$$** ($8.95–$23.95)

↓ burgers

Barney's 4138 24th Street (at Castro St) | Noe Valley

This chain makes burgers out of chicken, turkey, even tofu. Advice: go beef.
☎ 282-7770 🚍 24, 48 🕐 11am–10pm Mon–Fri (to 10.30pm Fri); 10am–10.30pm Sat; 10am–9.30pm Sun. 🚻 104 ♿ ⌘ ▣ ▤ MC/V $

Burger Joint 807 Valencia Street (at 19th St) | Mission

Quality burgers, hand-cut fries and Haagen-Dazs ice cream shakes are the BJ staples.
☎ 824-3494 🚍 26 Ⓑ 16th Street 🕐 11am–11pm daily. 🚻 48 ♿ ▣ ▤ none $

Hamburger Mary's 1582 Folsom Street (at 12th St) | SoMa

The contained chaos in this 70s landmark lesbian joint won't spoil the fat mushroom burgers.
☎ 626-1985 🚍 9, 42 🕐 11.30am–10.30pm Tue–Fri & Sun (to midnight Fri); 10am–midnight Sat. 🚻 99 ♿ ▣ ▤ ▤ all $–$$

Hot 'n' Hunky 4039 18th Street (at Hartford St) | Castro

The clientele or the burgers? It's at the centre of the Castro, but the Macho Man weighs in at three quarters of a pound. You decide.
☎ 621-6365 🚍 24 Ⓕ F, K, L, M 🕐 11am–midnight daily (to 1am Fri & Sat). 🚻 60 ▣ ▤ none $

Original Joe's 144 Taylor Street (bet. Turk & Eddy Sts) | Downtown

Brave the sketchy area at the edge of the Tenderloin for this old timer, if only to say you got your hands around a three-quarter-pound steak burger.
☎ 775-4877 🚍 31 🕐 10.30am–12.15am daily. 🚻 130 ▣ ▤ all $–$$$

Perry's 1944 Union Street (at Laguna St) | Marina

It may not be the groovy pick-up spot it once was, but the burgers aren't resting on their laurels.
☎ 922-9022 🚍 41, 45 🕐 8.30am–10pm daily. 🚻 300 ♿ ▣ 🔊 ▣ ▤ all $–$$

Fringale 570 4th Street (at Bryant St) | SoMa

Sure, duck confit may only be stringy leg meat cooked and preserved in its own fat, but what Gerald Hirigoyen manages to make of it is a miracle. A casual French joint boasting reasonable prices, Fringale is always crowded with Francophiles and those on the prowl for perfect rack of lamb or crème brûlée. Waiters are shipped over from France, only to head off elsewhere when their English gets too comprehensible.

☎ 543-0573 🚍 15, 30, 42, 45 🕐 11.30am–3pm Mon–Fri; 5.30–10.30pm Mon–Sat. 🚻 50 ♿ ▣ Ⓡ 3 wks ▤ AE/MC/V $–$$$ ($8–$21)

Le Charm 315 5th Street (bet. Folsom & Harrison Sts) | SoMa

A gem hidden in an un-chic industrial street in SoMa, this tiny bistro is an attractive option for couples looking for romance as well as families. Fresh flowers and butter-yellow walls make for a warm atmosphere, and the food is reassuringly French too: steamed mussels, sautéed escargots, salad niçoise, and the like, all cooked with great care by a husband and wife team. Sit outside in good weather.

☎ 546-6128 🚍 27, 42 🕐 5–9.30pm Mon–Fri; 5.30–10pm Sat. 🚻 45 ♿ ⌘ Ⓡ 3 days Ⓢ $20, $23 ▤ AE/MC/V $$ ($11–$15)

Park Chow 1240 9th Avenue (at Lincoln St) | Sunset

It's next to Golden Gate Park, it's solid chow, it's super cheap. What more do you need to know? The original Chow restaurant in the Castro was such a hit that the owner decided to do it again. It's not just the spaghetti and meatballs that packs this place every day, or the burgers, the pizzas, or the pecan pie, it's the warm atmosphere, complete with fireplace and heated deck, and good honest value. No reservations.

☎ 665-9912 🚍 71 Ⓝ N 🕐 10am–10pm daily. 🚻 74 ♿ ⌘ ▤ MC/V $–$$ ($5.95–$12.50)

Restaurant LuLu 816 Folsom Street (at 4th St) | SoMa

One of the original SoMa culinary meccas, LuLu dazzles locals with robust Provençal dishes centred around a wood-fired oven, rotisserie, and grill. Hearty meats come on platters (rosemary-scented chicken, pork loin with fennel); side dishes come separately (broccoli rabe with chili flakes and garlic). The decor is open and spare. Ask to be seated in the smaller room if you want to avoid the buzz from the boisterous multi-generational crowds. The same team has opened Zibibbo in Palo Alto and Azie (French-Asian cuisine), next door, and launched a successful line of sauces and condiments.

☎ 495-5775 🚍 30, 45 🕐 11.30am–10.30pm daily (to 11.30pm Fri & Sat). 🚻 250 ♿ ▣ 🔳 ▣ Ⓡ 1 wk ▤ all $–$$ ($9.95–$18.50)

restaurants & cafés

⊙ more restaurants & cafés

↓ cafés

Café Claude 7 Claude Lane (bet. Kearny & Grant Sts) | Downtown
A croque monsieur and a little attitude? Mais, oui!
☎ 392-3505 🚌 2, 3, 15 🕐 11.30am–11pm Mon–Sat. 🍴 80 ♿ 🚱 ▣ ▾ ▭ all $–$$

Caffè Trieste 601 Vallejo Street (bet. Grant & Columbus Sts) | North Beach
What's left of beatnik North Beach comes here to write poetry and sip espresso at sidewalk tables, while inside waiters serenade you with Italian opera.
☎ 392-6739 🚌 30 🕐 6.30pm–midnight daily. 🍴 150 ♿ 🚱 ▤ ▾ ▭ none $

Mario's Bohemian Cigar Store Café 556 Columbus Avenue (at Union St) | North Beach
Where beatniks sip cappuccinos, share grilled focaccia sandwiches, and tell their tales.
☎ 362-0536 🚌 15, 30, 45 🕐 10am–midnight daily (to 11pm Sun). 🍴 60 ♿ 🚱 ▾ ▭ none $–$$

Sevenoi Multimedia Café 701 Mission Street (at 3rd St) | SoMa
Free Internet access is the lure at this new nook inside Yerba Buena Center for the Arts [→73].
☎ 243-0930 🚌 15, 30, 45 🚇 F, J, K, L, M, N 🕐 11am–6pm Tue–Sun (to 8pm Thu & Fri). ♿ 🍴 35 ▭ none $

South Park Café 108 South Park (bet. 2nd & 3rd Sts) | SoMa
Tiny and very French. Sit at an outdoor table with a bowl of café au lait and read Voltaire.
☎ 495-7275 🚌 15, 30, 42 🕐 11.30am–2.30pm Mon–Fri & 6–10pm Mon–Sat. 🍴 40 ♿ 🚱 ▭ all $–$$

Rose Pistola 532 Columbus Avenue (at Union St) | North Beach

When it opened in 96 Rose Pistola was hailed the best new restaurant in the country by the James Beard Foundation. Although locals have begun to grumble that prices have gotten bloated, the hype has not died down and the place is still hopping. Ligurian cuisine accompanied by a sturdy Sangiovese can be charming, while raw artichoke with shaved parmesan, paired with a white truffle oil-slathered focaccia, is satisfaction guaranteed.

☎ 399-0499 🚌 15, 30, 45 🅿 PM 🕐 5.30–10.30pm daily (to 11.30pm Fri & Sat). 🍴 110 ♿ 🚱 ▤ ∅ ▾ 🎵 jazz 10pm Thu–Sat 🆁 2 wks ▭ all $–$$$ ($10–$25)

Vivande Porta Via 2125 Fillmore St (bet. California & Sacramento Sts) | Pacific Heights

The name means 'food to go'. Yup, they do that: olive oils, pastas, fancy condiments, pungent cheeses, Italian tortas, and cured meats are all sold here. But why cook when you can just pull up a chair? It's cramped and you can't book, but Vivande Porta Via has long been one of the city's most beloved little trattorias. Homemade pastas, risottos, and simple salads are just a warm-up for the always-delicious desserts.

☎ 346-4430 🚌 1, 3, 22 🕐 11.30am–10pm daily. 🍴 45 ♿ 🚱 ▾ ▭ all $$ ($11.50–$19)

↓ east meets west

Betelnut Pejiu Wu 2026 Union Street (at Buchanan St) | Marina

In the mood for Asian, just can't decide which kind? Take a trip over to Betelnut and you won't have to. The modern, stylish and always packed hotspot specializes in recreating authentic dishes from Thailand, China, Japan, Singapore, Malaysia and so on. Get ensconced at a sidewalk table, throw back a couple of Asian beers, and plough through a pile of small plates such as steamed buns or fried anchovies with peanuts and chilies.

☎ 929-8855 🚌 45 🕐 11.30am–11pm daily (to midnight Fri & Sat). 🍴 136 ♿ 🚱 ∅ ▾ ▾ 🆁 1 wk ▭ DC/MC/V $$ ($10.95–$15.95)

Café Kati 1963 Sutter Street (at Fillmore St) | Pacific Heights

Sometimes a dish arrives and all you can think is that chef Kirk Webber must have too much time on his hands. Diminutive, architectural fantasyscapes – fish preparations with delicate ginger- and soy-based sauces, or a vertical Caesar salad – it's all edible, in fact, it's dinner. Webber was doing East-West fusion before most of these Johnny-come-latelies had ever fired up a burner. This little neighbourhood restaurant has a huge following and a cosy, romantic interior that nurtures convivial conversation.

☎ 775-7313 🚌 2, 3, 22 🕐 5.30–10pm Tue–Sun. 🍴 70 ♿ 🚱 ▾ 🆁 5 days ▭ MC/V $$–$$$ ($17.95–$22.95)

EOS 901 Cole Street (at Carl St) | Haight-Ashbury

Many swear that the wine list is the primary draw at EOS. Clearly they haven't spent enough time with the smooth East-West fare. The decor is sleek industrial, with an upstairs mezzanine and a lively wine bar next door. Creations run the gamut from the expected (tea-smoked duck) to the wacky (blackened catfish with lemongrass risotto).

☎ 566-3063 🚌 6, 43 🚇 N 🕐 5.30–10pm daily. 🍴 70 ♿ 🚱 ▾ 🆁 1 wk ▭ AE/MC/V $$–$$$ ($18–$28)

Firefly 4288 24th Street (at Douglass St) | Noe Valley

If fireflies were found in California, they might feel menaced by the huge metal version of their species that functions as this Cal-Asian restaurant's sign. It's a comfortable spot to chat with friends while exploring a menu that changes every couple of weeks. Veggies will always find something to stir their loins, as will organic food hounds. Everyone else will swoon over the shrimp and scallop pot-stickers.

☎ 821-7652 🚌 48 ◑ 5.30–10pm daily. 🧍 50 ♿ Ⓥ Ⓡ 1 wk 💳 AE/MC/V $$ ($12.75–$17.75)

↓ global village

Café Marimba 2317 Chestnut Street (at Scott St) | Marina

There are many reasons to stop in at this Marina hotspot, some of which can be sampled in the daily selection of three salsas. It's a great introduction to the authentic and sophisticated regional dishes of Mexico. Of course, there are lots of regulars who don't give a damn for the nuances of Oaxacan mushroom tacos, they just want another 'rita.

☎ 776-1506 🚌 28, 30, 43 ◑ 11.30am–10pm Tue–Sun (to 11pm Fri & Sat). 🧍 85 ♿ Ⓤ Ⓥ Ⓡ 2 days 💳 all $–$$ ($8–$13)

Carta 1772 Market Street (at Octavia St) | Civic Center

Like Hillary Clinton's fashion sense, this restaurant is all over the place. Every two months the kitchen shifts gears, trotting out food from a different part of the world, whether it's the sunny flavours of the Med (calamari and lemon fritti), Indian (onion pakoras), or the American South (succotash). The charming restaurant appeals to the National Geographic, food-as-anthropological-survey set. A new lounge serves food until midnight.

☎ 863-3516 🚌 1, 6, 7, 14, 26, 66, 71 🚇 F, J, K, L, M, N ◑ 12–10.30pm Mon–Sat (to 11pm Fri & Sat; from 5pm Sun). 🧍 120 ♿ Ⓤ ✿ Ⓥ ✎ piano jazz nightly Ⓢ $24.95, $29.95 💳 all $–$$ ($8–$18)

Oritalia 586 Bush Street (at Stockton St) | Downtown

If San Francisco is the epicentre of Fusion cuisine, Oritalia may be where the tectonic plates meet. A seismic shift occurred when Oritalia moved from its longtime Fillmore digs to a new, velvet-draped spot. The much-expanded restaurant is a slick emporium of elegant riffing with Japanese, Mediterranean, and even New Orleans ingredients and flavours.

☎ 782-8122 🚌 2, 3, 30, 45 🅿 PH, PM ◑ 5.15–10.45pm daily. 🧍 120 ♿ Ⓤ Ⓥ Ⓡ 4 days 💳 all $$–$$$ ($16.75–$26.50)

Panchita's Café 3115 22nd Street (at Valencia St) | Mission

Now expanded and dolled up, Panchita's allures are not just skin-deep. The owner took time off in 98 to hone his skills at the Culinary Institute of America. The results? Warm-roasted chili salsa scooped up with thin tortilla chips, raw fresh black clams, white corn tamales fat with a filling of garbanzo beans, and smooth fried plantains and cream.

☎ 431-4232 🚌 14, 26, 49 🅱 24th Street ◑ 9am–11pm daily (to 2am Fri & Sat). 🧍 40 Ⓥ 💳 MC/V $–$$

↓ cheaper eats

Cha Cha Cha 1801 Haight Street (at Shrader St) | Haight- Ashbury
Throbbing Caribbean music, dreadlocked, patchouli-wearing crowds, and zingy tapas.
☎ 386-5758 🚌 7, 43, 66, 71 ◑ 11.30am–4pm & 5–11pm daily (to midnight Fri & Sat). 🧍 100 ♿ Ⓤ Ⓥ 💳 MC/V $–$$

Chow 215 Church Street (at Market St) | Castro
How do they do it? Everything – pizza, butterscotch banana pie – is tasty. Everything is cheap.
☎ 552-2469 🚌 22 🚇 F, J, K, L, M 🅱 Church Street ◑ 11am–10pm Mon–Fri (to 11pm Fri); 10am–11pm Sat & Sun (to 10pm Sun). 🧍 80 ♿ Ⓤ Ⓥ 💳 MC/V $–$$

L'Osteria del Forno 519 Columbus Avenue (bet. Green & Union Sts) † North Beach
A North Beach favourite, it traffics in life-sustaining focaccia and baked pastas.
☎ 982-1124 🚌 15, 30, 45 🅿 PM ◑ 11.30am–10pm Wed–Mon (to 10.30pm Fri & Sat; from 1pm Sun). 🧍 28 ♿ Ⓤ Ⓥ 💳 none $–$$

Mifune Japan Center, 1737 Post Street (bet. Laguna & Webster Sts) | Pacific Heights
Fifty-five different noodle combinations, examples of which are cast in plastic at the front of this Japantown institution.
☎ 922-0337 🚌 2, 3, 38 ◑ 11.30am–9pm Sun–Thu; 11am–10pm Fri & Sat. 🧍 82 ♿ 🈚 Ⓡ 2 days 💳 all $–$$

Suppenkuche 601 Hayes Street (at Laguna St) | Hayes Valley
The best German beers and a nuanced German menu are served up at long communal tables.
☎ 252-9289 🚌 21 ◑ 10am–2.30pm Sat–Sun; 5–10pm daily. 🧍 65 ♿ 🈚 Ⓡ 1 wk 💳 AE/ MC/V $–$$

Prices quoted correspond to the cost of a main course

restaurants & cafés

more restaurants & cafés

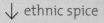

↓ ethnic spice

restaurants & cafés

Albona Ristorante Istriano 545 Francisco Street (at Taylor St) | North Beach

If Italy is a boot, the Istrian peninsula is where the boot meets the flouncy skirt, near Croatia. The owner is from there, and has for years taught the locals the charms of Istrian cuisine. Albona is on the edge of North Beach, in a homey room where you will find the likes of sweet caponata or roasted pork stuffed with sauerkraut, apples, and prunes.

☎ 441-1040 🚌 30 🍴 PM ◑ *5–10pm Tue.–Sat.* 👥 45 ♿ Ⓥ Ⓡ 2 wks 🍽 all **$$** ($13.25–$17.75)

Brother's 4128 Geary Boulevard (bet. 5th & 6th Aves) | Richmond

Brother's II down the street is a little slicker, but the Korean families that pack this location don't seem to notice the lack of decor as they toss a little mackerel or a short rib onto the small grills embedded in each table. It's Korean barbecue at its best, with lots of pungent side dishes (kimchee will make you sweat on sight). Not a good place for the single diner as barbecuing requires two people. Filling, inexpensive soups are also worth exploring.

☎ 387-7991 🚌 38 ◑ *11–3am daily.* 👥 72 ♿ Ⓥ 🍽 MC/V **$–$$** ($10–$17)

Helmand 430 Broadway (bet. Montgomery & Kearny Sts) | North Beach

With some of the most expert service in town, the Helmand has carved out a serious spot for Afghan food in the heart of North Beach. It's like Indian cuisine jazzed up with other Asian and Middle Eastern influences. Leek-stuffed ravioli comes with a meat sauce dotted with mint; candied pumpkin gets a swirl of yogurt; and savoury lamb is served with fluffy piles of cardamom-scented rice.

☎ 362-0641 🚌 15, 30 ◑ *5.30–10pm daily (to 11pm Fri & Sat).* 👥 70 ♿ 📱 🍷 Ⓥ Ⓡ 2 days Ⓢ $30 🍽 AE/MC/V **$–$$** ($9.95–$15.95)

Indian Oven 233 Fillmore Street (at Haight St) | Haight-Ashbury

An open kitchen at the back of the downstairs dining room is the site of all the tandoori drama. It's not the latest, cutting-edge Indian, but the North Indian staples are all competently rendered and moderately priced. The vegetarian thali – small bowls of legumey stew – is life-sustaining after the long wait for a table (though a new upstairs dining room has improved on the lack of space).

☎ 626-1628 🚌 6, 7, 22, 66, 71 ◑ *5–11pm daily.* 👥 80 ♿ Ⓥ Ⓡ 1 day 🍽 all **$–$$** ($7–$16)

Irrawaddy 1769 Lombard Street (bet. Octavia & Laguna Sts) | Marina

Burma's cuisine draws from the most sultry aspects of its neighbours, India, China, and Thailand – fried garlic, preserved ginger, green tea leaves, coconut milk curry sauces, and wheat noodles appear in the complex 'salads' and garnishes central to Burmese cooking. Irrawaddy's decor has lifted it above other SF Burmese restaurants: shimmering, silky pillows, and low tables invite intimate conversation, spiced by the heady aroma of coconut shrimp curry.

☎ 931-2830 🚌 28, 30, 43 ◑ *5–10pm daily.* 👥 50 ♿ Ⓥ Ⓡ 1 wk 🍽 AE/MC/V **$–$$** ($5.75–$14.95)

Khan Toke Thai House 5937 Geary Boulevard (at 24th Ave) | Richmond

Take your shoes off, then make your way through the romantically lit dining room, hung with intricate wooden carvings, and pull up a cushion at a low table (padded back supports and leg wells under tables make for more ergonomic seats). What follows is one of the most elegant Thai meals in town. The curries are aromatic and balanced, the spicy squid salad is calmed by mint, and the green papaya packs a chili punch.

☎ 668-6654 🚌 38 ◑ *5–10.30pm daily.* 👥 157 ♿ 🍷 Ⓥ Ⓢ $17.95 🍽 AE/MC/V **$–$$** ($5.95–$11.95)

Le Colonial 20 Cosmo Place (bet. Jones & Taylor Sts) | Downtown

The exterior is vaguely Spanish but inside it's pure colonial Vietnam, with rattan chairs, ceiling fans, and the upscale ambience of an old plantation. Don't miss the rice-paper-wrapped starters, filled with beef, pork, or shrimp, wrapped in basil and dipped in a delicate peanut sauce. For entrées, try the spare ribs or sea bass. The awning-covered front breezeway is heated, so you can bask in tropical warmth even when the fog rolls in.

☎ 931-3600 🚌 2, 3 ◑ *5.30–10pm daily (to 11pm Fri & Sat).* 👥 360 ♿ 📱 🍷 🎷 Ⓥ 🗝 jazz Fri, DJs Fri & Sat Ⓡ 1 wk Ⓢ 50 🍽 all **$$–$$$** ($15–$28)

↓ sushi

Blowfish Sushi to Die For 2170 Bryant Street (at 20th St) | Mission
Even the hip SoMa crowd enthuses about Blowfish's creative rolls and sake selection.
☎ 285-3848 🚌 9, 27 🕙 *11.30am–2.30pm Mon–Fri; 5.30–11pm daily (to midnight Fri & Sat).*
👤 70 ♿ 🚾 🍴 all $$–$$$

Ebisu 1283 9th Avenue (bet. Lincoln & Irving Sts) | Sunset
Choose a seat at the bar where you can see what specials are still wriggling.
☎ 566-1770 🚌 71 📍 N 🕙 *11.30am–2pm daily (to midnight Sat & Sun); 5–10pm Mon–Fri (to midnight Thu & Fri).* 👤 60 ♿ 🈂 🍴 all $$–$$

Kabuto Sushi 5116 Geary Boulevard (at 15th Ave) | Richmond
Sachio Kojima kibbitzes with the best of them, serving up fab barbecued eel and conch.
☎ 752-5652 🚌 2, 28, 38 🕙 *5.30–11pm Tue–Sun (to 10pm Sun).* 👤 60 ♿ Ⓥ Ⓡ 1 day
🍴 MC/V $–$$

Kyo-Ya (The Palace) 2 New Montgomery Street (at Market St) | SoMa
Super pricey, super fresh, it's best for no-holds-barred expense account binges.
☎ 546-5090 🚌 2, 6, 7, 9, 66, 71 📍 F, J, K, L, M, N 🕙 *11.30am–2pm Tue–Fri; 6–10pm Tue–Sat.*
👤 100 ♿ 🚾 Ⓥ Ⓡ 1 wk 🍴 all $–$$

Nagano Sushi 3727 Geary Boulevard (bet. Arguello St & 2nd Ave) | Richmond
Another Richmond fave, Nagano posts a daily board of imaginative special rolls.
☎ 221-9811 🚌 38 🕙 *11am–3pm; 5–11pm daily.* 👤 50 🍴 MC/V $–$$

Sushi Groove 1916 Hyde Street (bet. Union & Green Sts) | Russian Hill
Prices are a bit higher, but produce is organic, stunt-sushi (eg sea urchin) fresh, and the decor elegant.
☎ 440-1905 🚌 1, 45 📍 PH 🕙 *5.30–10pm daily (to 10.30pm Fri & Sat).* 👤 35 ♿ Ⓥ Ⓡ 2 days
🍴 all $–$$

Lhasa Moon 2420 Lombard Street (at Scott St) | Marina

A simple, comfy eaterie, it's the city's only Tibetan restaurant. The fare may remind you of India, but with little touches that make it also somehow Chinese. *Momos* are reminiscent of Chinese dumplings, filled with vegetables, beef, or chicken, and stews come stocked with hearty lentils or lamb with hand-rolled pasta noodles. *Bocha*, a tea brewed with milk and salty butter, is something of an acquired taste.

☎ 674-9898 🚌 28, 43 🕙 *11am–2pm Thu & Fri; 5–10pm Tue–Sat (to 10.30pm Fri & Sat); 4.30–9.30pm Sun.* 👤 45 ♿ Ⓥ Ⓡ 1 day 🍴 AE/MC/C $–$$ ($7.50–$11.50)

Osaka Grill 1217 Sutter Street (bet Polk & Van Ness Sts) | Tenderloin

The clean, spare room is outfitted with *hibachi* tables seating six, where diners cluster to witness the skills of *teppanyaki* masters. The tabletop hibachi griddle is responsible for exceptional sea bass with ginger sauce and grilled scallops, but the kitchen still sends out a mean miso soup as well as satisfying teriyaki and tempura classics.

☎ 440-8838 🚌 2, 3, 19, 42, 47, 49 🕙 *11.30am–2pm Mon–Fri; 5.30–10pm daily.* 👤 65 ♿ 🈂 Ⓥ Ⓡ 1 wk
💲 $16, $35 🍴 all $$ (set menus only)

Shalimar 532 Jones Street (at Geary St) | Downtown

Indian food lovers have been crawling out of the woodwork since this low-rent spot opened in the area between Downtown and the Tenderloin. For pocket change you can eat like a rajah, gorging on *murg korma shahi* (chicken simmered in yogurt, spices, and saffron), or several varieties of tandoori chicken, lamb, and beef. The naan bread and daal may be worth remortgaging your house for. You won't have to, as nothing on the menu is over $8. Take a cab and keep your wallet close if you come here at night.

☎ 928-6654 🚌 27, 38 🕙 *12–3pm & 5–11.30pm daily.* 👤 49 ♿ Ⓥ 🍴 none $ ($3.50–$7.95)

Straits Café 3300 Geary Boulevard (bet. Commonwealth & Parker Sts) | Richmond

Influences from China, Malaysia, India, and Indonesia inform a menu that can be at once homey, spicy, sweet, even zany. Chris Yeo brought Singaporean cuisine to San Francisco with much noise in 87. The name? Singapore, off the southern tip of the Malay peninsula, was once part of a British Crown Colony known as the Straits Settlements. Knock back a Singapore Sling and eat fragrant satays and addictive roti bread in a small dining room decorated with a trompe l'oeil street scene complete with hanging laundry and shuttered windows. .

☎ 668-1783 🚌 38 🕙 *11.30am–3pm & 5–10pm Mon–Thu; 11.30am–11pm Fri–Sun.* 👤 94 Ⓡ 3 days
♿ 🚾 Ⓥ 🍴 all $–$$ ($9–$20)

restaurants & cafés

more restaurants & cafés

Prices quoted correspond to the cost of a main course

Ton Kiang 5821 Geary Boulevard (bet. 22nd & 23rd Aves) | Richmond

Technically, this place specializes in Hakha cuisine, with its pickled vegetables and claypot dishes (all hail the rock cod with tofu). The uninformed will just think it serves some of the finest dim sum in the city. It's a big, slightly bland, Hong Kong-style dining room on two levels, with waiters scurrying all over offering Shanghai meat dumplings, translucent little shrimp dumplings, and all manner of temptation.

☎ 752-4440 🚌 38 🕐 10.30am–10pm Mon–Sat (to 10.30pm Sat); 9am–10pm Sun. 🪑 200 ⏚ 🖵 🗏 Ⅴ 🟰 all $-$$ ($7.50–$16.32)

↓ catch of the bay

Alamo Square 803 Fillmore Street (bet. Grove & Fulton Sts) | Hayes Valley

Although it's relatively new to the city scene, this restaurant looks as if it's been here forever. Shabby chic with mustard and maroon pillows tossed on a long banquette, Alamo Square has the kind of neighbourhood Zeitgeist groove that usually takes years to acquire. The menu is refreshingly simple: pick a fish, pick a preparation, and have them drizzle it with heavenly beurre blanc or bearnaise. For $13.50, it may be one of the best deals around.

☎ 440-2828 🚌 22 🕐 10am–2pm daily; 5.30–10pm Mon–Sat; 5–9.30pm Sun. 🪑 40 ⏚ 🖵 Ⅴ Ⓢ $11.50 🟰 MC/V $-$$ ($10–$15)

Aqua 252 California Street (at Battery St) | Downtown

When it opened in 91, Aqua brought a novel kind of New York-chic to Downtown. Towering flower arrangements defined a spare, dramatic interior and the kitchen sent out studied dishes in which fish and shellfish covered new territory. Other upmarket fish emporia have opened since then, but current chef Michael Mina has kept standards high. Entrées are as composed and daring as the desserts, with dishes like grilled tuna layered with foie gras in a Pinot Noir sauce topping the bill.

☎ 956-9662 🚌 1, 15, 42 🅟 C 🕐 11.30am–2pm Mon–Fri; 5.30–10.30pm Mon–Sat (to 11pm Fri & Sat). 🪑 120 ⏚ 🖵 🗏 Ⅴ Ⓡ 2 wks Ⓢ $68 🟰 all $$$ ($29–$42)

Farallon 450 Post Street (at Powell St) | Downtown

A hyper-stylish restaurant that celebrates creatures from the underwater world, it's as edifying as a trip to the Monterey Bay Aquarium, but way more delicious. The ichthyophiles will be just as happy with the decor as the food – there are jellyfish light fixtures, resin kelp columns, and lots of caviar-esque black beads. The food is less whimsical, more serious, with a focus on spare-no-expense ingredients (corn ravioli with foie gras and truffles, truffled mashed potatoes with crab and sea urchin sauce). The desserts (try the huckleberry, blueberry and hazelnut cake with peaches and crème anglaise ...) are among the best in town.

☎ 956-6969 🚌 2, 3 🅟 PH, PM 🕐 11.30am–10.30pm daily (to 11pm Thu–Sat). 🪑 180 ⏚ 🖵 🗏 Ⓡ 2 wks Ⓢ $22 🟰 all $$$ ($23–$33)

Hayes Street Grill 320 Hayes Street (bet. Franklin & Gough Sts) | Hayes Valley

A piece of fish. Maybe grilled, maybe sautéed. Then add a sauce. Herb butter? A little hollandaise? That's the concept. Hayes Street Grill looks quaint and Old World in its simplicity, and the food is unswervingly straightforward. Regulars swear by the local sand dabs (white fish), the calamari fritto misto, and the french fries. It's been a San Francisco favourite for pre- or post-theatre dining since 79, and the helpful waiting staff will make it their business to get you to that performance on time.

☎ 863-5545 🚌 21, 47, 49 🕐 11.30am–2pm Mon–Fri; 5–9.30pm daily (to 10.30pm Fri & Sat; to 8.30pm Sun). 🪑 70 ⏚ 🖵 Ⓡ 3 wks 🟰 all $$-$$$ ($15–$22)

Plouf 40 Belden Street (bet. Pine & Bush Sts) | Downtown

'Plouf' (French for 'splash') describes the satisfying sound of mussels being dropped into broth. Seafood prevails at this sleek, noisy, modern French bistro, a favourite haunt of the Financial District elite. Start with a pile of mussels in one of the seven delicious sauces available (from marinière to crayfish and tomato), then have the generous seafood salad, and you might well be satisfied. Then again, the main dishes are tasty – order anything that swims.

☎ 986-6491 🚌 2, 15 🕐 11.30am–3pm Mon–Fri; 5.30–10.30pm Mon–Sat (to midnight Thu–Sat). 🪑 45 ⏚ 🖵 🌿 Ⓡ 3 days 🟰 all $$-$$$ ($13–$23)

The Waterfront Pier 7, Embarcadero (at Broadway) | Downtown

Chef Bruce Hill is arguably a master of the fusion rage, and his combination of delicacies like sesame-crusted scallops with escargot and fennel tortellini; or house-smoked sturgeon with roasted beet salad, wasabi cream, and osetra caviar can be truly sublime. Downstairs is more casual (cheaper); upstairs is for fine dining among the scenesters – everyone from politicos to Hollywood waywards. Views of the Pacific are good all around, but the downstairs café has outdoor seating (and heat lamps).

☎ 391-2696 🚍 32 ◑ 11.30am–2pm daily; 5.30–10pm Sat & Sun. 👤 110 ♿ 🖵 ▤ 📶 Ⓥ Ⓡ 2 wks Ⓢ $22 ▤ all $$$ ($22–$36)

Yabbie's Coastal Kitchen 2237 Polk Street (bet. Green & Vallejo Sts) | Russian Hill

One can only imagine that chef Mark Lusardi left his amazing fish recipes behind when he retired from Yabbies last year. Polk Street denizens, even the twenty-something set, still can't get enough of the perfectly rendered scallops, crayfish, halibut etc served nightly in the glass-decorated 70-seat restaurant. Perfection takes time (more time here than anywhere, it seems), but the attractive staff, all *cum laude* graduates of charm school, will distract you with wine and chitchat.

☎ 474-4088 🚍 19, 45, 47, 49 ◑ 6–10pm daily (from 5.30pm Sun). 👤 70 ♿ 🖵 Ⓥ Ⓡ 1 wk ▤ MC/V $$–$$$ ($16–$21)

↓veg-out

Greens Building A, Fort Mason (bet. Buchanan & Beach Sts) | Marina

This place taught San Franciscans that vegetarian doesn't have to mean denial. The approach is luxurious, pampering, and certainly not a study in asceticism. It's been the city's destination vegetarian spot for over 20 years, as much for the gorgeous Golden Gate views, ground-breaking wine list, and light-suffused room, as the vegetarian food. Try the perfect green salads bedecked with tiny jewel-coloured beets, or the crisp-crusted pizzas sprinkled with herbs and blanketed with pungent cheeses and roasted veggies. Weekend brunch is the most popular meal.

☎ 771-6222 🚍 28, 47, 49 🚇 PH ◑ 11.30am–2pm & 5.30–9.30pm Tue–Sat; 5.30–9.30pm Mon; 10am–2pm Sun. 👤 125 ♿ Ⓥ Ⓡ 2 wks ▤ D/MC/V Ⓢ $40 (only Sun) $$ ($12–$18)

Herbivore 983 Valencia Street (at 21st St) | Mission

Voluptuous colour photographs of dewy fruits and vegetables adorn the walls, getting you in the mood for a plate of tofu-ricotta and mushroom lasagne, or maybe a little grilled seitan (wheat protein) with a pile of friendly veggies and a lemon-garlic sauce. It's seat-yourself and often busy, so it may be a moment or two before you can dig into the strictly vegan (and mostly organic) goods. Service is young and pierced, like a lot of the clientele of this relaxed Mission favourite.

☎ 826-5657 🚍 14, 26, 49 ◑ 11am–10pm daily (to 11pm Fri & Sat). 👤 180 ♿ 📶 Ⓥ ▤ MC/V $ ($3.25–$7.95)

Millennium 246 McAllister Street (at Larkin St) | Civic Center

Planet-friendly, of course, is the buzz word for the next millennium and for this restaurant – a sophisticated Civic Center eatery with a mission. They even have that Margaret Mead quote on the wall: 'Never doubt that a small group of thoughtful, committed citizens can change the world. Indeed, it's the only thing that ever has.'. From smoked portobello mushroom with a sweet Moroccan dressing to grilled rosemary polenta with crushed fresh tomatoes, it's all vegetarian, all the time.

☎ 487-9800 🚍 5, 19 ◑ 5–9.30pm daily. 👤 77 ♿ Ⓥ Ⓡ 1 wk ▤ DC/MC/V $$ ($13.95–$16.50)

Organica 1224 9th Avenue (at Irving St) | Sunset

No vegetables had to suffer here to bring you dinner. It's all raw, nothing cooked, hardly anything even chopped. It used to be called Raw, under different ownership, but it's maintained the same high standards for food and unbelievably low standards for service (truly comical). The 'raw-sagna', 'raw-violi' and cabbage-wrapped burritos are the safest way to go, although the 'burger' specials on air-dried gruel crackers are an experience.

☎ 665-6519 🚍 71 🚇 N ◑ 12–10pm Tue–Sun. 👤 36 ♿ Ⓥ ▤ none $–$$ ($7–$13)

restaurants & cafés

SF may be something of a slave to cocktailing fashion, but for every neon vodka-infusion joint or swank swing lounge, it offers up a bevy of spirited watering holes as diverse as its many neighbourhoods.

high spirits

↓ shaken & stirred

Harry Denton's Starlight Room

Elegant to the core, this luxurious supper club on the 21st floor of the equally refined Sir Francis Drake Hotel is local icon Harry Denton's pièce de resistance. Dress up, act your age, bring big bills, run up big bills, and sip Denton's trademark chocolate martini in a deep velvet booth. Or two–step the night away with city lights twinkling beneath you. Pure old school decadence.

450 Powell St (bet. Post & Sutter Sts), Downtown ☎ 395-8595 ◼ 2, 3 ◼ PH, PM ◑ 4.30pm–2am daily. ◔ 4.30–8pm daily. ▱ all ♿ ✆ ⚒ swing Mon; top 40 dance Tue–Sun ◐ nightly

Infusion

This 'Multimedia Gulch' watering hole is named after the in-house vats of vodka that are steeped with pineapple, cucumber, strawberries, and other flavouring agents. It's a tasteful, unpretentious place to start the evening sipping and nibbling on fab hors d'oeuvres. On weekends, you may want to stay on for the live jazz.

555 2nd Street (bet. Bryant & Brannan Sts), SoMa ☎ 543-2282 ◼ 15, 42 ◑ 11.30–12am Sun–Fri (to 1am Thu & Fri; from 5pm Sun); 5pm–1am Sat. ▱ all ♿ ✆ ⚒ Fri & Sat

Lone Palm

This neighbourhood joint, with its glass brick façade and white tablecloths, veers on the sleek side of retro, physically resembling a lounge that film noir actress Barbara Stanwyck might slip into to avoid a sugar daddy. In those days, it would have been quiet and swank, but Lone Palm fills with upscale former bohemians who tend to get loud while drinking their Manhattans.

3394 22nd Street (at Guerrero St), Mission ☎ 648-0109 ◼ 26, 48 ◼ J ◑ 24th Street ◑ 6pm–2am Sat–Thu (from 7pm Sun & Mon; from 5pm Fri). ▱ none ♿

Martuni's

A swanky though slightly camp piano bar in an up-and-coming area. Frequented by a mix of gay, straight, young, and old, this surprisingly low-key martini bar gives you a chance at 15 minutes of fame to sing along with the fantastic piano man.

4 Valencia Street (at Market St), Mission ☎ 241-0205 ◼ 26 ◼ F, J, K, L, M ◑ 4pm–2am daily. ▱ MC/V ♿ ⚒ nightly

The Red Room

A glow of red, not surprisingly, is the dominant colour of this popular edge-of-Union-Square spot. It's a cozy, impressively designed little place that can barely accommodate the throngs of stylish locals and tourists who line up to get in and drink a fittingly rosy Cosmopolitan.

827 Sutter Street (bet. Jones & Leavenworth Sts), Downtown ☎ 346-7666 ◼ 2, 3, 27 ◑ 5pm–2am daily. ▱ MC/V ♿

Top of the Mark

Behold the magical panorama from the Golden Gate Bridge [→70] to the Transamerica Pyramid [→71] from this well-behaved old world wonder. Savour caviar and sip pricey cocktails in your finest rags (Levis a no-no) as smooth jazz fills the lounge and your senses overload. Arrive early for a window seat.

Mark Hopkins Inter-Continental, 999 California Street (at Mason St), Nob Hill ☎ 392-3434 ◼ 1 ◼ C ◑ 3pm–12.30am Mon–Sat (to 1am Fri & Sat; from 10am Sun). ▱ all ♿ ✆ ⚒ nightly

↓ hipster havens

Backflip

Part of the Phoenix Hotel, this swimming pool-inspired spot is all baby blue and sparkly, and the feel is space age Vegas. Early in the evening, you'll want to sip on a Blue Hawaii between nibbles of California cuisine, but later you'll be swaying to the sounds of late-night club DJs.

601 Eddy Street (bet. Larkin & Polk Sts), Tenderloin ☎ 771-3547 ◼ 19, 31 ◑ 7pm–2am Tue–Sat (from 9pm Sun). ▱ all ♿ ✆ ⚽ ◐ nightly

Doc's Clock

This remodelled Mission district bar has rapidly become a social hotspot for San Francisco's hipster crowd. Thankfully, it hasn't sold out completely or lost its charm. Mellow atmosphere and a well-stocked jukebox help round out this neighbourhood hang out.

2575 Mission St (bet. 21st & 22nd Sts), Mission ☎ 824-3627 🚌 14, 49 Ⓜ 24th Street ◐ 6pm–2am daily (from 8pm Sun). ◷ 4–7pm daily. 🍴 none ♿

Latin American Club

One of a string of bars that define the youthful flavour of the Valencia Street corridor. Once a watering hole for Latino thugs, it now favours a basic-drinkin' crowd with one foot in grunge and the other in a cushy Silicon Valley day job.

3286 22nd Street (at Valencia St), Mission ☎ 647-2732 🚌 26 Ⓜ 24th Street ◐ 6pm–2am daily (from 5pm Fri; from 4pm Sat). 🍴 none ♿

The Orbit Room

This coffee shop by day, mod hang-out by night has a circa 50s space age decor that draws a diverse, yet always cool crowd. During the day, you'll find sombre writers tapping the great American novel on their laptops. In the evening, the digerati crowd mellow out after a hard day of making money on the Net. And at night, rockabilly cats roll up on vespas and knock back some of the strongest martinis in town.

1900 Market Street (at Laguna St), Civic Center ☎ 252-9525 🚌 6, 7, 26, 66 🚇 F, J, K, L, M, N ◐ 7.30–2am Mon–Thu (from 7am Fri & Sat); 9am–midnight Sun. 🍴 none ♿ ♨ ⚘

↓ music on tap

Bottom of the Hill

This is the best local music venue in town with big indie acts rolling in all the time. Hipsters rock out and smoke like chimneys on the patio between sets. Check local listings for shows and covers and try the $5 all you can eat Sunday BBQ.

1233 17th St (bet. Missouri & Texas Sts), Potrero Hill ☎ 621-4455 🚌 22 ◐ 3pm–2am Mon–Sat (from 2pm Fri; from 8.30pm Sat); 3–10pm Sun. ◷ 3–6pm Mon–Fri. 🍴 MC/V ♿ ♨ ⚘ ♪ nightly

Café du Nord

Dark wood panelling gives this sprawling basement speakeasy the look of an old world men's club. The warm interior serves as a backdrop for a striking range of live events – soul DJs, swing bands, cabaret, salsa, and performance art. Drinks are first rate, the pool table conspicuously placed, and the crowd stylish but not intimidating.

2170 Market Street (bet. Church & Sanchez Sts), Castro ☎ 861-5016 🚌 22 🚇 F, J, K, L, M, N ◐ 4pm–2am daily (from 6pm Sun–Tue). ◷ 4–7pm Mon–Fri. 🍴 all ♿ ♨ Wed–Sat ♪ Tue–Thu ☉ Sat–Mon

Club Deluxe

Ground zero for the West Coast swing revival, supremely cool cats in vintage zoot suits and fedoras pass through Deluxe's shiny silver doors to pretend it's the 40s all over again. Understandably attitudinal but still among the best places to jump to Louie Prima cover bands and soak in the retro air with a top notch Cosmopolitan or martini. Cover charges can be steep.

1511 Haight Street (at Ashbury St), Upper Haight-Ashbury ☎ 552-6949 🚌 7, 43, 66, 71 ◐ 4pm–2am daily (from 3pm Sat; from 2pm Sun). 🍴 none ♿ ♨ Wed–Sun ☉ Tue

Elbo Room

Eclectic nightly jams including DJs, jazz fusion, and rockabilly in the Elbo's upstairs lounge avert the clientele stale factor in this consistently popular Mission joint. Hipsters and frat guys peacefully coexist in the dimly lit downstairs bar, raging, if rarely intermingling, in drunken harmony.

647 Valencia Street (bet. 17th & 18th Sts), Mission ☎ 552–7788 🚌 26 ◐ 5pm–2am daily. ◷ 5–9pm daily. 🍴 none ♿ ♨ nightly ☉

Hotel Utah

A woody and cozy SoMa tavern with a gorgeous balcony fashioned from the bow of an old ship, offering birds-eye views of the tiny stage where local acts of a folky/ countrified variety strum and holler nightly. Refreshingly free of the haughtiness you'll find elsewhere in the local music scene.

500 4th Street (at Bryant St), SoMa ☎ 421-8308 🚌 9, 30, 45 ◐ 11.30–2am daily (from 6pm Sat & Sun). ◷ 4.30–7.30pm Mon–Fri. 🍴 MC/V ♿ ♨ ♪ nightly

Make-Out Room

This surprisingly handsome neighbourhood spot tends to bottleneck with young patrons at the bar and the boothed front, but the back of this place is a roomy area with tables and a stage backed with a glam red velvet curtain. Live music, of an eclectic variety, is the main lure.

3225 22nd Street (at Mission St), Mission ☎ 647-2888 🚌 14, 26, 49 Ⓜ 24th Street ◐ 6pm–2am daily. ◷ 6–8pm daily. 🍴 none ♿ ♪ nightly

↓ gay thirst

Midnight Sun

This trendy gay video bar serves up the best in dance music, camp film clips, and comedy on two large video screens. Clientele ranges from club boys popping in for a quick pre-club drink to professional types just off work. This is a big pick-up joint, but don't be surprised if all eyes are on the video screens and not on you.

4067 18th Street (bet. Castro & Hartford Sts), Castro ☎ 861-4186 🚌 24 🚇 F, K, L, M ◐ 12pm–2am daily. ◷ 3–7 pm Mon–Fri. 🍴 none ♿ ☉

↷ more bars

The Pilsner Inn

The Pilsner is pleasantly devoid of the frenetic pick-up atmosphere of most Castro pubs. But that's not to say you won't make a few new friends. The back patio is mighty conducive to conversation and the jukebox, pumping everything from indie Britpop to punk rock, sets the perfect backdrop for that Saturday evening beer.

225 Church Street (at Market St), Castro ☎ 621-7058 🚊 22 🚇 F, J, K, L, M, N ◑ *9pm–2am daily.* 🍴 none ♿ ⚲

The Stud

A staple of the gay scene since the 60s, The Stud has managed to stay on top, and stay around, in a fickle scene. Go late (most nights pick up closer to 11 or midnight) and soak up the carnival-like atmosphere.

399 9th Street (at Harrison St), SoMa ☎ 252-7883 🚊 19, 27, 42 ◑ *5pm–2am daily.* ◒ *5–9pm daily.* 🍴 none ♿ ⚲ Fri ◉ *nightly*

↓ brew crews

Toronado

An absolute must for the beer connoisseur, this visually unspectacular Lower Haight neo-saloon offers around 110 varieties of malt and hops goodness. Take your taste buds globe trotting from the yuppiest, almond-berry California microbrew to the rarest of Cameroonian palm wines.

547 Haight Street (bet. Fillmore & Steiner Sts), Lower Haight-Ashbury ☎ 863–2276 🚊 6, 7, 22, 66, 71 ◑ *11.30–2am daily.* ◒ *4–6pm daily.* 🍴 none ♿ ⚲ Sat & Sun

Twenty Tank Brewery

This brewpub is the club hang-out for the Downtown after-dark crowd. Any night of the week, you'll find a wide mix of twenty- and thirtysomethings competing for the limited tables while downing some of the many microbrews on tap or enjoying the house specialty Nachos.

316 11th Street (bet. Folsom & Harrison Sts), SoMa ☎ 255-9455 🚊 9, 42 ◑ *11.30–1.30am daily.* 🍴 AE/MC/V ♿ ⚲

↓ take a dive

El Rio

On those rare, warm nights, make a beeline for El Rio. Essentially two bars connected by probably the city's biggest patio, this dive-esque watering hole boasts cheap margaritas and eclectic entertainment, from outdoor movie screenings to free belly dancing lessons and gritty garage rock in the back cabana on Saturdays.

3158 Mission St (bet. 26th & Cesar Chavez Sts), Mission ☎ 282-3325 🚊 14, 27, 49 ◑ *3pm–2am daily (to midnight Sun & Mon).* ◒ *3pm–midnight Mon.* 🍴 none ♿ ⚲ Wed, Sat & Sun

Gold Cane

A haven of themeless sanity on Haight Street, the Gold Cane ranks among the best and most accessible dive bars in town. With kind bartenders and a laid-back environment, it packs up late on weekend nights with a cross-section of red-nosed regulars, career drinkers, and college kids looking to shoot stick, toss Liar's Dice, or puff smokes on the patio.

1569 Haight Street (bet. Ashbury & Clayton Sts), Upper Haight-Ashbury ☎ 626-1112 🚊 7, 43, 66, 71 ◑ *12pm–2am daily.* 🍴 none ♿ ⚲

↓ the pub experience

Edinburgh Castle

Pints, plays, and pipes. If you're longing for Scottish culture, you'll find it here in this always-lively Tenderloin bar. The beer flows on tap and on any given night you'll find either a troupe of performers presenting live drama or a bagpipe artist squeezing out the tunes. Fish'n'chips also served!

50 Geary Street (bet. Polk & Larkin Sts), Tenderloin ☎ 885-4074 🚊 19, 38 ◑ *5pm–2am daily.* ◒ *5–7pm Mon–Fri.* 🍴 MC/V ♿ ⚲ indie rock Thu & Fri; special events Sat ◉ Wed ◒

Finnegan's Wake

Nestled in cute Cole Valley, this friendly yuppie pub compensates for its underwhelming looks with a warm and social atmosphere and a mean Irish coffee. A few blocks off the Haight, but figuratively worlds away, Finnegan's is cozy and chatty even on weekends when throngs of dart-tossing late twentysomethings duck in.

937 Cole Street (bet. Carl & Parnassus Sts), Upper Haight-Ashbury ☎ 731-6119 🚊 6, 43 🚇 N ◑ *11.30–2am daily.* 🍴 none ♿ ⚲

The Irish Bank

After a hard day of banking and business merging, Downtown suits unwind at this cool slice of pseudo-Dublin. Pouring argubly the best Guinness in town, this alley tavern comes complete with authentic Irish barkeepers, belly-warming bangers and mash, and, when crowded (usually 5–10pm), tapped kegs on the street outside.

10 Mark Lane (bet. Bush & Sutter Sts), Downtown ☎ 788-7152 🚊 2, 3, 15 ◑ *11–2am daily.* 🍴 all ⚲⚲

Mad Dog in the Fog

Guzzle Bass beneath the soccer flags as festive Lower Haight hooligans root on Man United via satellite hookup. This nearly spot-on UK bar recreation hosts weekly pub quizzes and serves an authentically greasy breakfast on weekends guaranteed to soak up a hangover.

530 Haight Street (bet. Fillmore & Steiner Sts), Lower Haight-Ashbury ☎ 626-7279 🚊 6, 7, 22, 66, 71 ◑ *11.30–2am daily.* ◒ *11.30am–7pm Mon–Fri.* 🍴 none ⚲⚲ ⚲

↓ a taste of the unusual

C Bobby's Owl Tree

King of the kitsch bars, the Owl Tree's theme is, you guessed it, owls. Dangling from the ceiling and stuck to the walls, dozens of faux hooters hover about this divey ex-brothel and the resulting effect is as cool as it is creepy. As yet the place is unspoiled by hipsters.

601 Post Street (at Taylor St), Downtown ☎ 776-9344 🚌 2, 3 ◑ 3pm–2am daily. ◐ 4–8pm daily. 🗖 none ♿

Li Po's

A bizarre and surreal experience is guaranteed in this cavernous (and some say haunted) former opium den in the heart of Chinatown. Old Chinese men play dice in the intimate red booths while hordes of thirsty youngsters flood in from nearby North Beach ensuring a lively buzz.

916 Grant Avenue (at Washington St), Chinatown ☎ 982-0072 🚌 1, 15, 30, 45 🚇 PH, PM ◑ 2pm–2am daily. 🗖 none

Noc Noc

If Dali or Doc Seuss were to open a bar, odds are it might look something like this fanciful Haight Street beer and wine joint. Tall, trippy chairs, a seemingly melting ceiling, splintered mirrors, and the house partiality to goth and ambient make for a totally psychedelic boozing experience.

557 Haight Street (bet. Fillmore & Steiner Sts), Lower Haight-Ashbury ☎ 861-5811 🚌 6, 7, 22, 66, 71 ◑ 5pm–2am daily. ◐ 5–7pm Mon–Fri. 🗖 MC/V ♿ ◒ nightly

Persian Aub Zam Zam

Bruno the bartender is dictator supreme here. Some tips for passing his impossible test: don't order anything but one of his sublime gin martinis; don't kiss your partner; and don't dare to sit at any of the tables (which are always empty). In fact, if the bar stools are all taken, don't even go in. First-timers are usually kicked out anyhow. Curious? Feeling lucky? Sporadic hours to say the least.

1633 Haight Street (at Belvedere St), Upper Haight-Ashbury ☎ 861-2545 🚌 7, 43, 66, 71 ◑ variable, usually from 4pm. 🗖 none ♿ ◒ ▨

↓ singles spots

500 Club

Head for the mammoth neon cocktail glass to find what is arguably the Mission's purest meat-market. Once the domain of elite hipsters, the 500 has since been duly gentrified but ploughs on nonetheless. On weekends, expect lewd drunkenness and a shameless good time.

500 Guerrero St (at 17th St), Mission ☎ 861-2500 🚌 22, 26 🚇 J ◑ 2pm–2am Mon–Fri (from 12pm Sat & Sun). ◐ 5–7pm daily. 🗖 none ♿

Horseshoe Tavern

A rambunctious frat guy sports bar where cheesy pick-up artists bombed on Jaegermeister shots shoot pool, booty-dance to New Wave hits, or practice other such Marina mating rituals. Not exactly a hotbed of socio-political awareness, but as fine a place as any to get drunk (and laid).

2024 Chestnut Street (at Fillmore St), Marina ☎ 346-1430 🚌 30, 43 ◑ 10–2am daily. 🗖 none ♿

Lucky 13

Don't let the façade fool you. The spooky name and black cat above the doorway are just for show at this pool bar just outside the Castro. The young clientele leans toward the post-frat crowd, and things get pretty lively as the night wears on. Pick-up potential grows as the beer flows. And these boys and girls love their beer!

2140 Market Street (bet. Church & Sanchez Sts), Castro ☎ 487-1313 🚌 22 🚇 F, J, K, L, M, N ◑ 4pm–2am daily (from 2pm Sat & Sun). 🗖 none ♿ ◒ ▨

↓ sip & socialize

Hayes & Vine Wine Bar

While the name may suggest the seedy legend of Hollywood, the tenor of wine sipping is more suited to the nearby opera house. It's a crisply modern, comfortably swank place for a before- or after-performance glass of wine or champagne.

377 Hayes Street (bet. Franklin & Gough Sts) Hayes Valley ☎ 626-5301 🚌 21, 42, 47, 49 ◑ 5pm–midnight Mon–Sat (to 1am Fri & Sat); 4–10pm Sun. 🗖 MC/V ♿ ◒

Tosca Café

Tosca is one of those SF legends that has maintained its integrity since its North Beach doors opened in 1919. The dusky place, with its vinyl booths, opera juke box, and Venice murals still attracts a crowd of local literati, politicians, socialites, touring rock and movie stars, and just plain locals. The famous house cappuccino tastes like spiked Swiss Miss, but the standard cocktails are perfectly satisfying.

242 Columbus Avenue (bet. Broadway & Pacific Sts), North Beach ☎ 986-9651 🚌 15, 30 ◑ 5pm–2am daily. 🗖 none ♿

Vesuvio

This literary hot spot used to be the boozing and pontificating venue-of-choice for Kerouac and the San Francisco Beat poets – and the decor stays true to the era, complete with antique advertisements and photos. Drop in for a drink on your way to check out the other North Beach beat attraction, City Lights bookstore.

255 Columbus Avenue (at Broadway St), North Beach ☎ 362-3370 🚌 15, 30, 45 ◑ 6–2am daily. ◐ 3–7pm Mon–Thu. 🗖 none ♿

night fever

San Francisco's booming nightlife mirrors its all-over-the-map mix of inhabitants. The weekly roster at each venue can change radically from night to night, infested with ex-frat boys on the make one night, and trannie showgirls or death metal rockers the next. And the music can be just as different.

top venues

clubs

Bimbo's 365 Club

This swanky, spacious club is decked out with all the lustrous trappings of its past glamour days. A lavish see-and-be-seen lobby entrance gives way to a high-ceilinged room with a massive dance floor, and romantic, candle-lit tables dotting the perimeter. There's live music most nights, with some of the best swing, big band, and jazz bands around. Increasingly, Bimbo's showcases alternative acts.

Cat Club

Whether you're a glam rock groupie or into the leather 'n' whip scene, the wildly popular Cat Club, with two dance floors and a state-of-the-art DJ station, will cater to your every whim – it's just a matter of picking the right night [→Wed, Sat, Sun].

End Up

If your evening's itinerary includes some all-night imbibing, chances are you'll end up at End Up, and be eternally grateful for its existence. Here you can share the pounding dance floor with a bevy of like-minded partyers until the wee hours of the morning. Sundays and Fridays are gay nights, while other nights of the week are mixed [→Mon, Sun].

Justice League

This long-running nightspot [→131], renowned for its live music sessions, packs in a cool, urban, dance-hungry crowd who come to groove to hip-hop, reggae, and jazz bands, and DJ house and techno nights. A large, round, easy-access bar is the centrepiece of the massive, warehouse-style dance floor.

1015 Folsom

This three-storey, six-bar club is – to its fans – the be-all-and-end-all grand altar to electronica and techno where every night a hypnotic barrage of lights and lasers syncs with the music. One of the busiest clubs on the west coast, it draws top international DJs who spin their thumping techno magic for the dancing masses. Fridays bring a ravey, more underground crowd, while Saturday is more mainstream [→Sat].

Paradise Lounge

This swish, cavernous 11th Street institution, with its three stages and bars, plays host to the best and worst local rock would-bes. Quieter acts swing the upstairs lounge while louder alternative groups blast from the two downstairs risers. Check listings for shows.

Slim's

If live music is your thing, Slim's is the place to be [→131]. Musicians agree that there's no better SF venue to play than here, where a superior sound system and ample stage make the music the star of the show. And there are great views of the stage no matter where you decide to kick back. The bands are mostly rock and indie, often with a bluesy, rootsy bent.

Storyville

From the red velvet walls lined with photos of jazz icons down to the cozy fireplaces, this sophisticated yet comfortable joint has real class, and showcases everything from traditional jazz acts to hip-hop and reggae bands. There are two stages and a large dance floor. Free snacks (and live jazz) are on offer during happy hour (5–9pm Fri).

330 Ritch Street

This smooth supper club – a beacon of light in the middle of SF's Multimedia Gulch – draws swing kids, techies, and clubsters with its retro allure and adventurous range of music from Latin to swing to funk and soul. Come for dinner (entrées between $8–$15) and make a night out of it [→Wed, Thu, Sat].

Up & Down Club

With its curved bar, low leather banquettes, and dim, swanky lighting, this happening club serves up a blend of eccentric sophistication – and the very latest in jazz, hip-hop, and soul shows. The low-key vibe draws a good mix of hipsters and after-work crowds.

monday

Club Dread @ End Up

One of the mellow nights at this long-standing staple. Mainly straight, with a young, reggae-loving crowd (also on Wed).

Grateful Dead Jam @ Nickie's BBQ

The legacy lives on at this chilled Haight club bar. If you're looking for old school hippie culture, this is where it's at.

Joy @ Liquid

A hopping gay night that actually lives up to the hype. Intimate atmosphere, pretty people, and the hardest hitting house, techno, and trance anywhere.

tuesday

Lucifer's Hammer @ Covered Wagon Saloon

Not for the weak at heart, Lucifer's Hammer spins hard core heavy metal and thrash for metal heads of all shapes and sizes.

Taboo @ Liquid

Liquid may be the tiniest club in the city, but that doesn't stop it from throwing a groovy house night where you can forget that it's still only the middle of the week.

Trannyshack @ The Stud

A midnight drag show, and half-price drink specials for trannies help make this the biggest drag night in town.

wednesday

Bondage-a-go-go @ Cat Club

A fetish party for the S&M and leather set. DJs spin industrial and goth, while revellers live out their darkest fantasies.

College Night @ The Stud

Disco and 80s alternative tunes keep the clean-cut young boys dancing at San Francisco's oldest gay nightclub.

Seance @ Backflip

Bringing new life to the sketchy Tenderloin district is hip drum 'n' bass-heavy Seance. Tarot readers, belly dancers, and mystic decor put the trip in the trip-hop.

Swing & Lounge @ 330 Ritch Street

Pompadoured boys and retro-girls jump, jive, and wail to SF's swing revival in this cozy club tucked away in South Park.

thursday

Eclipse @ Mercury

The city's nightlife élite schmoozes to house and trance tunes every other Thursday at this upscale club. Attitude and club kid ID cards essential.

Pan Dulce! @ Asia SF

A strictly gay Latin dance club featuring the hottest salsa mixes and coolest Latino boys – plus many admirers of both.

Popscene @ 330 Ritch Street

DJs spin Brit-pop for a barely legal crowd of indie-rockers sporting Beatle do's, Blur T-shirts, and much attitude.

Stinky's Peep Show @ Covered Wagon Saloon

And now for something completely different: a rock 'n' roll carnival experience, featuring, among other things, go-go girls.

friday

Club Q @ Club Townsend

Ladies night at SF's biggest warehouse club every first Friday of the month. An under-35 lesbian crowd dances to the tricks of super-spin-meistress Page Hodel.

Club Nzinga @ El Rio

Join all the other free spirits who swarm to this racially diverse night of world music. Salsa, merengue, and African beats keep the crowds grooving all night long.

Swing Dancing @ Broadway Studios

Rockabilly boys and girls strut their stuff at this dance studio turned nightclub that offers lessons earlier in the night.

saturday

Area @ Cat Club

This R'n'B, hip-hop, and funk club caters to an upscale (well-dressed only) crowd that gets down to soul 'til the early hours.

DJ Phil B @ The Café

Always a line, but never a cover. The ever popular Café turns out alternative and R'n'B dance mixes to the gay crowds who gather here for a spot of people-watching.

Housepitality @ Kate O'Briens

Downtown's hippest Irish pub plays house music for a mixed crowd. Check other slammin' dance nights at Kate's (Eklectic on Thu & Fever on Fri).

clubs

more clubs | directory

clubs

Release @ 1015 Folsom

Mainstream early on, then packed with rave-friendly clubbers as the night turns into day, this arty club features three dance floors and techno in all its incarnations.

Sounds of San Francisco @ 330 Ritch Street

This series of rotating clubs brings the best live bands and local DJs each week – from rock to retro, to soul and swing.

Universe @ Club Townsend

A must for all gay newcomers. This all-night house scene with sweaty shirtless men and hefty drink prices is the ultimate in testosterone-heavy partying.

sunday

Dub Mission @ Elbo Room

Tribal, dub, and reggae grooves rule the upstairs dance floor at this trendy, Mission venue. Crowd is mixed with an emphasis on the hippie/college crew.

Pleasuredome @ Club Townsend

The longest running gay party in SF, packed with muscle-bound party boys from dusk 'til dawn. The music is pure house, the vibe pure energy.

Sixxteen @ Cat Club

Glam rock lives on into the new millennium at one of the best kept secret nightclubs in SF. Largely a local hard rocker crowd.

T-Dance @ End Up

A great place to party into the wee hours. Mainly gay, but also for techno heads not yet ready to call it a night.

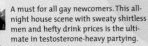

venue directory

Asia SF
201 9th Street (at Howard St)
☎ 255-2742 **w** sanfrancisco.
sidewalk.com/detail/48224
❑ ➡ 19 ◐ 5pm–2am Thu-Sat.
❑ $6–$15 ♟ gay (Thu)
➡ AE/DC/MC/V

Backflip
Phoenix Hotel, 601 Eddy Street
(at Larkin St) ☎ 771-3547
w www.sftrips.com ❑ ➡ 19, 31
◐ 5pm–2am Tue–Sun (from 10pm Sun). ❑ $2–$5 ♟
➡ AE/DC/MC/V

Bimbo's 365 Club
1025 Columbus Avenue
(at Chestnut St) ☎ 474-0365
❑ ➡ 15 ◐ PH ◐ times vary depending on the show.
❑ $12–$28 ♟ none

Broadway Studios
435 Broadway (bet. Kearny & Montgomery Sts) ☎ 291-0777
❑ ➡ 15 ◐ 9pm–1am Tue-Sat (to 2am Fri & Sat). ❑ $5–$10
♟ MC/V

The Café
2367 Market Street (bet. 17th & 18th Sts) ☎ 861-3846
❑ ➡ 24 ♟ F, J, K, L, M, N
◐ 12.30pm–2am daily.
❑ free ♟ ➡ none

Cat Club
1190 Folsom Street (at 8th St)
☎ 431-3332 ❑ ➡ 19
◐ 9pm–4am Wed–Sun.
❑ $2–$12 ◐ ♟ ➡ none

Club Townsend
177 Townsend Street (bet. 2nd & 3rd Sts) ☎ 974-6020
❑ ➡ 15, 42 ◐ 9pm–6am Fri & Sun; 9.30pm–7am Sat.
❑ $7–$12 ♟ gay ➡ none

Covered Wagon Saloon
917 Folsom Street (bet. 5th & 6th Sts) ☎ 974-1585 **w** sanfrancis co.sidewalk.com/detail/81342
❑ ➡ 27 ◐ 4.30pm–2am Mon–Sat (from 8pm Sat).
❑ $4–$5 ♟ ➡ none

Elbo Room
647 Valencia Street (bet. 17th & 18th Sts) ☎ 552-7788
w www.elbo.com ❑ ➡ 26
◐ 5pm–2am daily. ❑ $4
♟ ➡ none

El Rio
3158 Mission Street (bet. Cesar Chavez & Valencia Sts)
☎ 621-4410 ❑ ➡ 14, 49
◐ 24th Street ◐ 3pm–mid-night daily (to 2am Wed–Sat).
❑ free–$7 ♟ ➡ none

End Up
401 6th Street (at Harrison St)
☎ 357-0827 **w** www.theend up.com ❑ ➡ 27, 42
◐ 10pm–4am Wed–Fri; 9pm–4am Sat & Sun (from 5.30pm Sun).
❑ $6–$10 ♟ gay ➡ none

Justice League
928 Divisadero Street (bet. Grove & Hayes Sts)
☎ 289-2038
w www.sfstation.com /clubs/justiceleague.htm
❑ ➡ 5, 21, 24 ◐ 9pm–2am daily (from 8pm Sat & Sun).
❑ $5–$10 ♟ gay (Thu)
➡ none

Kate O'Briens
579 Howard Street (bet. 1st & 2nd Sts) ☎ 882-7240
❑ ➡ 42 ◐ 11.30–2am daily.
❑ free ♟ ➡ AE/MC/V

Liquid
2925 16th Street (at S Van Ness St) ☎ 431-8889 ❑ ➡ 14, 22, 49 ◐ 7pm–2am daily.
♟ ❑ $2–$3 ➡ none

Mercury
540 Howard Street (bet. 1st & 2nd Sts) ☎ 777-1419 ❑ ➡ 15, 42 ◐ 9.30pm–2am Thu-Sat (to 3am Fri & Sat). ❑ $10–$15
◐ ♟ ➡ AE/MC/V

Nickie's BBQ
460 Haight Street (bet. Fillmore & Webster Sts)
☎ 621-6508
w www.nickies.com
❑ ➡ 6, 7, 22, 66, 71 ◐ 9pm–2am Thu-Tue. ❑ $3–$5 ♟ ➡ none

1015 Folsom
1015 Folsom Street (at 6th St)
☎ 431-1200 **w** www.1015.com
❑ ➡ 27, 42 ◐ 10pm–6am Wed–Sun. ❑ $5–$10 ◐ ♟
➡ none

Paradise Lounge
1501 Folsom Street (at 11th St)
☎ 621-1912 ❑ ➡ 9, 42
◐ 8pm–2am daily.
❑ free–$10 ♟ ➡ MC/V

Slim's
333 11th Street (bet. Folsom & Harrison Sts) ☎ 522-0333
❑ ➡ 9, 27, 42 ◐ 7pm–2am daily. ❑ free–$25 ♟ ➡ MC/V

Storyville
1751 Fulton Street (bet. Central & Masonic Sts) ☎ 441-1751
w www.citysearch.com
❑ ➡ 5, 43 ◐ 7pm–2am Tue–Sat (from 6pm Fri & Sat).
❑ $5–$10 ➡ AE/MC/V

The Stud
399 9th Street (at Harrison St)
☎ 863-6623 **w** members@aol.com/thestudbar/site.html
❑ ➡ 19, 27, 42 ◐ 5pm–3am daily (to 2am Sun & Mon).
❑ free–$8 ♟ ➡ none

330 Ritch Street
330 Ritch Street (bet. Brannan & Townsend Sts) ☎ 522-9558
w www.blasto.com/330ritch
❑ ➡ 15, 30, 42, 45
◐ 6pm–2am Wed–Sun.
❑ free–$10 ◐ ♟ ➡ AE/MC/V

Up & Down Club
1151 Folsom Street (bet. 7th & 8th Sts) ☎ 626-8862 ❑ ➡ 19
◐ 9pm–2am Thu–Sun.
❑ $5–$10 ♟ ➡ AE/MC/V

Operatic warbling or a cabaret drag show? Heckling the latest comedian or a thought-provoking theatre performance? Whatever your pleasure, SF can quench your thirst for it.

that's ententainment

↓ tune in

television

Most San Franciscans wouldn't readily admit to watching the TV much – that's something those *ordinary* Americans (or worse still, Angelenos) do. But don't be fooled, even the local sophisticates put in quality couch potato time. Most residents (and all hotels) have a basic cable service – around 40 channels, encompassing the major networks, specialty channels (Comedy Central, Nickelodeon, American Movie Classics, etc), plus educational and public access. Public access, at 53 and 54, is where you'll find local 'Look, ma, I embarrass myself in public now!' weirdness. Bay TV (35) is the slicker side of locally-slanted programming; then there's MTV (21), all-sports ESPN (14), and CNN (17). Local and national news can be found on many channels between 5pm and 7pm and from 10pm to midnight. The main non-cable TV networks are NBC (4), ABC (7), CBS (5), WB (20), Fox (2), and national public TV station KQED (9). American TV is somewhat prudish – graphic violence, let alone explicit sex and nudity, are seldom found outside the 'premium' (non-basic cable) channels that show uncut recent movies and XXX flicks.

radio

There are plenty of 24-hour radio stations to soundtrack your stay in SF. KFOG's (104.5) 'world class rock' and KITS, aka 'Live 105' (105.3), provide mainstream guitar crankage, with the latter skewing more towards younger artists. 'Alice' (KLLC, 97.3) is on the mellower side. For truly alternative and punk sounds, try college station KUSF (90.3). Oldies (that is to say, tunes from the 60s and 70s) are the staple at KBGG (98.1) and KFRC (99.7). The area's main classical station is KDFC (102.1) while, just up the dial, KMEL (106.1) and KBLX (102.9) lead the R&B/hip-hop contingent, and KJAZ (92.7), as you might expect, plays jazz. You can get your country music fix from KYCY (93.3). The local National Public Radio station, KQED (88.5), provides an upscale mix of chat, culture, and news.

the papers

San Franciscans have long bemoaned the fact that the city's two major daily papers are not up to speed with the well-educated population. The morning *Chronicle* is fairly conservative and unsophisticated in editorial slant, although its entertainment coverage contains competent reviews. The afternoon *Examiner* is marginally better, albeit thinner due to its much smaller circulation. Both papers will give you a passable fix of local, national, and international news; for something more in-depth, pick up the *Los Angeles* or *New York Times*. The *Chron* and *Ex* already team up to put out a single, larger Sunday edition: soon, however, courtesy of a long-rumoured corporate buyout, they will merge to create SF's only daily.

listings mags & the free press

A somewhat livelier, more youthful and insider-ish perspective on city life can be found in two major free weeklies: the *SF Bay Guardian* and *SF Weekly*. Both hit street-corner bins, café counters, and other locations on Wednesdays, and each provides a good source for entertainment listings, restaurant mini-reviews, local trends, and more. The *Guardian*, around since the late 60s, is still a proud bastion of old-school leftie political rabble-rousing, while the *Weekly*, owned by a national corporation, has a less distinctive overall tone but some good columnists. The weekly *Bay Area Reporter* (out on Thursdays) is the city's leading gay paper, followed by the marginally more lesbian-inclusive *Bay Times*. These are free, and can be found on the street or at businesses primarily in the Castro, the Mission, or on Polk Street. There's also the *Metropolitan*, a monthly local arts magazine, and a slew of smaller, more erratic publications detailing the city's club and music scenes.

websites

With Silicon Valley encroaching ever more onto the streets of San Francisco, naturally there is no lack of websites charting Bay Area events, resources, and businesses. Among the largest are: w *www.sanfrancisco.com* w *www.sfgate.com* w *www.citysearch.com*. All are very useful all-purpose info stops, with descriptions and directions for restaurants, entertainment, and city sights. The city-sponsored w *www.artsmonthly sf.org* lists upcoming arts events and has links to its sponsors' sites. You can log onto the internet for free at any of the city's 30-odd neighbourhood branch libraries – the main one is at Larkin Street (bet. Grove & Fulton Sts) – or at many of the city's cafés [→149].

→directory 131–132

↓ reeling in the bay

Ever picturesque, San Francisco is the film location that won't quit – you may experience cinematic *déjà vu* while huffing up fabled 'crooked street' Lombard [→71], site of Steve McQueen's screeching car chase in *Bullitt*, or gazing down the old Fort Point plunge that tempted suicidal Kim Novak in Hitchcock's *Vertigo*. And with city residents including Robin Williams and Francis Ford Coppola, San Francisco is as much in the movies as it is a great place to watch the latest releases.

Counting on a sophisticated, eager audience, more obscure features often open here well before they test the waters in New York or Los Angeles. But for more mainstream fare, two glossy new multiplexes from AMC and Sony will serve the urge for such celluloid delights as *Scream 5*, or the latest Julia Roberts' lovefest. The **AMC 1000** has 12 screens, while the Sony **Metreon**'s [→80] 15 screens include one dedicated to the jumbo IMAX® format.

Predictably, this 'plex-building has had a chilling effect on the few remaining single-screen emporiums. First-run independent and foreign films turn up at a handful of remaining single-screen houses (the **Bridge**, **Clay**, and **United Artists Vogue**), but primarily at a trio of mini-plexes. The **Embarcadero Center Cinema** has the benefit of bigger screens and better viewing angles, while things get cozier at the **Lumiere**, which plays new films mostly for one-week runs, and the mini-theatre **Opera Plaza**, whose four screens are the usual last stop before a non-mainstream premiere flick exits town.

Further off the beaten track, the **Castro Theatre**'s [→70] main competition is the **Roxie Cinema** – an ugly box near the scruffy Mission and 16th Street nexus of hipdom, that nonetheless programmes some of SF's most delectable celluloid. Left-leaning documentaries, Hong Kong action flicks, and racy oldies from Hollywood's censorship-free 'Pre-Code' era are often found here. New kid on the Mission block, however, is the **Foreign Cinema**, an exciting restaurant/film venue showing sub-titled films like *La Dolce Vita* on a big wall outside while serving excellent French food. For truly underground fare, keep your eyes peeled for Saturday night programmes at the Mission Street venue **Artists Television Access**. The San Francisco Cinematheque also screens experimental videos and films at both the **SF Art Institute** in North Beach and the **Yerba Buena Center for the Arts** [→73].

At present, there's no consistent midnight movie outlet to satisfy that late-night flick lust – but peruse local media for occasional wee-hour schedulings at the **Roxie**, **Lumiere**, and **Bridge**. If you're in the mood to mix psychotronic cinema and loosening libations, however, hail a cab out to Potrero Hill's well-hidden **Werepad**. This artists'-studio-cum-neo-60s-luv-lounge serves up martinis along with 10.30pm weekend showings of such exploitation obscurities as *The Touchables* and *Hot Rods to Hell*.

festivals

It may not boast anything as media-swamped as Cannes, but SF has long sustained a bevy of specialized annual film fests. Most celebrated is the springtime **SF International Film Festival** ☎ 931-3456, which casts a broad net to capture old and new work from around the globe. Scheduled to close in synch with the city's massive Gay Pride Day in June, the **SF International Lesbian & Gay Film Festival** ☎ 703-8650 is the world's oldest festival of its type, embracing crossover hits like *The Adventures of Priscilla*, as well as more specialized bills, such as *Toughtitties* and *Fun in Girls' Shorts*. Audience participation runs famously high.

The **Jewish Film Festival** ☎ 552-3378 is a late-summer session at the Castro Theatre that frequently challenges audiences with many a debate-fuelling flick. In March, you can also find film buffs and filmmakers admiring and/or arguing with one another at the **SF Asian American Film Festival** w www.naatanet.org/festival which blankets the 'Asian diaspora'. Early fall brings the **Film Arts Festival** ☎ 552-3456 to the Roxie – a showcase for largely US independents and documentary makers.

Other festivals include the **SF American Indian**; **Irish**; **Latino**; and **Bi** (as in Bisexual). Most run for just a week, and they tend to migrate around the calendar from year to year (and from venue to venue). Check the local media for schedules.

tickets & reviews

$ Admissions at multiplexes top out at $8.50 for adults, $4.50 for children; art and rep houses are $2 or $3 cheaper. Student, senior, and early-afternoon discounts apply at most venues. Most SF cinemas are cash-only at the door.

⊙ Screening times vary; mainstream commercial theatres feature daily matinées, while reps add daytime shows on weekends and Wednesdays only.

❶ Daily movie guides run in the *Chronicle* and *Examiner*, with full-length film reviews on opening days; capsule reviews for all current features appear in the *Chronicle*'s Sunday 'Pink Section' and the *Examiner*'s Friday 'Style' section. Hipper and wider coverage can be found in the free *SF Bay Guardian* and *SF Weekly*.

↓ treading the boards

San Francisco has been a hub of theatrical activity since its wild 'Barbary Coast' days in the 19th century, when lucky gold prospectors returned here to blow their new-found wealth on wine, women, and, yes, high kulcha. Homegrown theatre bloomed late, if explosively, in the late 60s when Bill Ball founded the American Conservatory Theater (ACT). It reached its heyday in the 70s and 80s and some argue the theatre scene has since slumped. But there's still plenty happening, from top-flight Broadway shows to drag-camp extravaganzas. The biggest venues are the splendid early 20th-century theatres **Orpheum** and **Golden Gate**, which, along with the smaller **Curran**, are where cash cows like *Rent* or *Cabaret* reel in the masses. Touring dramas, comedies, revues, or headlining solo performers usually stop at one of a clutch of medium-sized houses around the Union Square area, such as the **Marines Memorial**, **Stage Door**, **Alcazar** theatres, and **Theatre on the Square**. Also located in the same Union Square nexus, the **Lorraine Hansberry** is the area's

leading forum for African-American playwrights.

On the non-profit front, the area's largest repertory institution is the American Conservatory Theater (ACT), whose mix of plays old and new is staged at the remodelled **Geary Theatre**. Their shows are always polished, but for a more dynamic experience you may want to travel across the Bay to the equally prestigious **Berkeley Repertory Theatre**, where programming choices are often bolder. The **Magic Theatre** has changed a lot since its early days, when writers Sam Shepard and Michael McClure participated in a world-premieres-only policy. The fare is less risky these days, but still stimulating, with a slant towards quirky American playwrights.

The majority of interesting small-scale theatre happens in the Mission and SoMa districts, at **New Langton Arts**, **Intersection for the Arts**, and a few other pocket-sized spaces. The larger **BRAVA Theatre Center** focuses on politically-tinged works by and about women and other 'minority' groups, while

Potrero Hill's **Theatre Artaud** hosts A Traveling Jewish Theatre and the Theatre of Yugen (specialist in contemporary Japanese drama).

Not surprisingly, you might find gay themes being explored at just about any venue, but **Theatre Rhinoceros** got there first. Its 112-seat main stage and tiny basement studio offer an uneven, but often delightful, mix of works. The **New Conservatory Theatre Center**, meanwhile, has been dubbed the 'Nude Conservatory' for its slant towards comedies featuring as many unclad male thespians as possible.

festivals

Each summer, the indoor theatres quieten down and a glut of alfresco Shakespeare commences, led by the **California Shakespeare Festival** ☎ 1-510-548-9666 – four Bardic works staged from June to September in a scenic (if often frigid) setting amid the East Bay hills. The more on-the-ball **Shakespeare Santa Cruz Fest** ☎ 1-831-459-2159 plays a shorter season (mid-Jul to late Aug) in a cozy redwood-grove amphitheatre on the University of California Santa Cruz campus. Free **Shakespeare in the Park** ☎ 422-2221 performs one play per summer, travelling from park to park from July, ending at Golden Gate Park [→78] in September.

An alternative to all that metered verse is the **SF Mime Troupe** ☎ 285-1717, which for nearly 40 years has been anything but mute, with their vigorous, left-leaning political satires (one per year, touring area parks for free Jul–Sep). The **SF Fringe Theatre Festival** ☎ 673-3847 descends upon small venues in the Downtown area for 11 days in mid-September. Anything goes here – from classical plays to children's shows.

tickets & reviews

💷 The primary ticket agencies handling major shows are **BASS** and **Ticketmaster**, and both apply a service charge for phone or internet reservations. Repertory and mid-to-small-sized theatres handle their own tickets, with 'rush' and student, senior, etc discounts often available. Big-name touring shows run as high as $70 a pop, though lesser seats and midweek nights can be had for as little as $20. The better rep theatres charge $18–$45, small venues' prices are often in the low teens.

Nearly every theatre, except those running the 'Best of Broadway' musicals and plays, participates in the half-price, day-of-show tickets on sale at the **TIX Bay Area Booth** on Union Square, where you can also purchase full price advance tickets to most shows. A list of available tickets is posted daily for in-person purchase only.

🕐 The biggest shows and plays usually run from Tuesday or Wednesday to Saturday at 8pm, with 2pm Sunday matinees. Smaller scale performances usually cluster closer around the weekend at the same times.

❶ The *Chronicle*'s notorious 'Little Man' (jumping-out-of-seat for a rave review, an empty seat for a dud) rates all the major current shows in Sunday's 'Pink Section', while the *Examiner* prints capsule reviews on Fridays. The free papers give better input on the smaller scale and more experimental productions.

theatre

comedy, cabaret & performance arts | dance | poetry & lit

→directory 131–132

↓ stand & deliver

comedy

Comedy was all the rage in the 80s, when a slew of stand-up talents rose from SF's club scene to national prominence on TV's Johnny Carson or David Letterman shows, each hoping to be the next Robin Williams or Whoopi Goldberg. The scene has quietened down since, though occasionally a local, like Margaret Cho or the politically acerbic Will Durst, breaks out to make some waves via a few of the old venues that still keep the faith. Among them are the **Punch Line** on Battery Street, or **Cobb's Comedy Club** at Fisherman's Wharf, both comfy rooms serving up TV-embraced headliners (George Lopez, Paula Poundstone, Tree) and rising hopefuls to well-lubricated crowds.

The really big names either play single dates at music venues or settle in for longer runs at downtown legit houses like **Theatre on the Square**, the **Marines Memorial**, or the **Alcazar**.

cabaret

While the mainstream comedy scene has shrunk, there's new life in establishments that cater to gay and lesbian comics or sketch comedy ensembles à la Monty Python. For both, try the primarily gay **Josie's Cabaret & Juice Joint** in the Castro, or the Mission's alternative performance space **The Marsh**. Some hilarious talent has developed among improv comedy troupes, most notably Bay Area Theatresports and True Fiction Magazine, a group that performs regularly on 'WestCoast Live' [→83].

Cabaret is another field that has taken a back seat in recent years, and the principal remaining venue is the **Plush Room**, a smooth little joint that welcomes the likes of velvet-toned thrush Weslia Whitfield and erstwhile *West Side Story* firecracker Rita Moreno. **Piaf's** also books touring talent and show tune revues. If you've got a yearning for musicals, seek out erratic programmes at **Josie's Cabaret & Juice Joint** and the **New Conservatory Theatre Center**, which also hosts 42nd Street Moon Productions – their 'Lost Musical Series' digs up old, forgotten Broadway shows from as far back as 1910.

North Beach plays host to a venerable tourist tradition in the form of Beach Blanket Babylon at **Club Fugazi**. The longest running musical revue in history, this is a nightly high-gloss, high-octane camp show that has spoofed pop culture in song and silliness for over 25 years.

performance arts

If your taste is more for the experimental and multidisciplinary, pint-sized venues such as **The Lab, The Marsh** (both in the Mission), and SoMa's **Venue 9** are the likeliest outlets. Queer, tribalist, and feminist underground performance of any genre is staged at fringy **848 Community Space** and the women-run **Luna Sea**.

Highly visual, if unclassifiable, theatre is contrived by such migrating troupes as Antenna and Nightletter Theatre. The warehouse-like **Theatre Artaud** on Potrero Hill is most frequently host to such expansive multidisciplinary efforts.

festivals

The year's biggest comedy event is **Comedy Day** ☎ 643-9009, a free afternoon of stand-up in Sharon Meadow at Golden Gate Park [→78] in late summer. Check tomorrow's stars at the **SF Stand-Up Comedy Competition** ☎ 383-8394 (mid-Sep–mid-Oct) at various venues. And East meets West as NYC's Mabel Mercer Foundation mounts its next **West Coast Cabaret Convention** ☎ 1-212-980-3026, a biennial event, in June 2000.

Performance art is among the many theatrical genres showcased at the multivenue, 11-day **SF Fringe Theatre Festival** ☎ 673-3847, as well as at the **Queer Arts Festival** ☎ 552-7709 (Jun–Jul) and **Dancers' Group Edge Festival** ☎ 824-5044 in May. The **Afro Solo Arts Festival** ☎ 771-2376 spotlights African-American poets and dancers each August at locations around town and, in spring, the Lorraine Hansberry Theatre offers the **Lift Every Voice** ☎ 474-8800 festival of black theatre and music.

tickets & reviews

🎟 Most comedy events can be booked through **BASS**, or directly through venue box offices. National headliners, which are more likely to sell out, can run up to $25; club bills are in the $8–$15 range. Cabaret venues generally handle their own tickets. Performance art programmes are ticketed ($8–$20) through venue box offices, and the smaller, experimental venues may take cash only.

♠ Except for the biggest names, seating is most often first-come, first served; arrive at least a half hour before the scheduled start time.

❶ Comedy and cabaret typically have shows at 8 or 9pm on weekdays, with a late show added on weekends.

❶ The Sunday *Chronicle* as well as free weeklies *SF Bay Guardian* and *SF Weekly* have extensive performance listings, though cabaret and performance art get better coverage in the *Bay Area Reporter* and *Bay Times*.

↓ on your toes

The Big Kahuna of the Bay Area dance scene is the San Francisco Ballet, which approaches its 70th anniversary with a more lustrous global reputation than ever. The internationally drafted corps does brilliantly by a repertoire that includes much Balanchine, Tudor, and Robbins, plus select ultra-modern pieces by the likes of William Forsythe and Mark Morris. SFB's season runs from late January to early May at the **War Memorial Opera House** [→71].

Major touring companies appear largely under the wing of SF Performances (at **Herbst Theatre**) and Cal Performances (at **Zellerbach Hall** on the UC Berkeley campus). On their fall-to-spring schedules, you'll find national and international luminaries, such as the Dance Theatre of Harlem, Ballet Folklorico de Mexico, and Merce Cunningham.

For a more experimentally inclined homegrown dance scene, keep an eye out for On Site, Joe Goode Performance Group, Margaret Jenkins, the neo-classical Lines Contemporary Ballet,

and ODC/San Francisco. All generally perform at **Yerba Buena Center for the Arts** [→73] or **Cowell Theatre**. These venues also host Smuin Ballets/SF, whose sexed-up 'pop' dances irk some critics but thrill their fan base. Edgier, smaller-scale dance can be seen at **Dancers' Group Studio Theatre** and **ODC Performance Gallery**, while the **Theatre Artaud** hosts magnum opuses by local and occasional national dance and performance-art troupes.

San Francisco's diverse ethnic population makes for a vast range of multicultural dance on frequent display, from Japanese *butoh* to Latin and African folk idioms, flamenco, and hip-hop. These companies compete en masse for spots in the annual **San Francisco Ethnic Dance Festival** ☎ 474-3914, a three-week blowout in June in the Palace of Fine Arts [→71]. More experimental trends are charted at **Dancers' Group Edge Festival** ☎ 824-5044 each May, while Japan's enigmatic, achingly slow modern idiom is showcased at the **SF Butoh Festival** ☎ 648-1177 (two weeks in late July).

tickets & reviews

💲 SF Ballet handles its own tickets, which range from $8 (standing) to $100. They can be booked by phone or picked up at the War Memorial Opera House box office. Other companies at major venues are generally purchasable through **BASS**, **Ticketmaster** or at the **TIX Bay Area Booth**, which offers half-price, day-of-show tickets. Performances for touring ensembles are usually in the $20–$35 range and larger local companies around $12–$25. Most performances only last a few days. This means a stampede on tickets if a favourable review appears.

❶ The Sunday *Chronicle* and Friday's *Examiner* list each performance, but on the whole dance coverage is fairly weak in both. To get an angle on what's happening at grassroots, you're better off picking up the *SF Weekly* or *SF Bay Guardian*.

↓ word up

Ever since the days of the Beat Generation, much of SF's literary reputation has lain upon North Beach, the neighbourhood where the likes of Ginsberg and Kerouac spent their time busting rhymes and slugging wine. You'll still see plenty of bearded poets scribbling notes in the bars and cafés, and a trip to the landmark beatnik bookstore **City Lights** [→41] is still *de rigueur*. But North Beach is by no means the only place to get your word fix.

Readings happen all over town, every night of the week, and are usually free. Check out *Poetry Flash*, a free monthly publication that includes interviews,

reviews, and plenty of listings. Also look at the 'Spoken Word', sections of the weekly papers, and the 'Datebook' section of the *Chronicle*.

One event that's given spoken word a broader appeal is the poetry slam – loud and feisty affairs that take place regularly at the **Transmission Theatre** and the **Justice League**. Slams have brought greater attention to poetry than any number of polite coffee-house readings and have helped spotlight local writers and readers, such as Justin Chin and Beth Lisick.

Coffee houses take a little of the action now, with

open-mike spots, which are featured at nearly every other coffee bar. A few nightclubs dabble in this territory as well, and one of the city's longest running open-mike slots takes place on Sundays at **Above Paradise**, which is the upstairs half of the music club Paradise Lounge [→122]. It is hosted by Jennifer Joseph, publisher of local *Manic D Press*, and the crowd's a rowdy but friendly mix of spluttering drunks, crusty regulars, and jelly-legged newcomers. Other places to look for some verbal pearls are the comfortably funky **Annie's Cocktail Lounge**, where readings take place on Mondays, and the Scottish

→directory 131–132

dance | poetry & literature

→ more poetry & lit | classical music & opera | music | directory

pub **Edinburgh Castle** [→120], which has sporadically hosted excellent evenings with visiting authors such as Irving Welsh and Patrick McCabe. Bookstores offer more sober events of a similar nature, and most publish monthly calendars that give the lowdown. **A Clean, Well-Lighted Place for Books** and **Booksmith** have regular readings and discussions. Others to check include **City Lights** for poetry; **A Different Light** for gay and lesbian authors; and **Modern Times** for social/political writers. If you're here in early November, the annual **San Francisco Bay Area Book Festival** ☎ 487-4541 is packed full of readings, signings, and other literary merriment.

↓ classic chords

classical music

Ground zero for classical music is the Civic Center nexus, where the ultra-modern **Davies Symphony Hall** plays host to the San Francisco Symphony. Since 95 it has been under the baton of Michael Tilson Thomas, who is especially keen on 20th-century American composers, such as John Adams, Aaron Jay Kernis, and Lou Harrison. Their works are served up alongside the usual European heavyweights.

Two organizations bring in stellar vocalists, chamber ensembles, and instrumental soloists from around the globe: San Francisco Performances at **Herbst Theatre** and **Yerba Buena Center for the Arts**; and Cal Performances across the Bay at Berkeley's **Zellerbach Hall** and **Hertz Hall**. Both schedule recitals from September to June. Also of note in the East Bay is the Berkeley Symphony Orchestra, which performs four major concerts a year at Zellerbach Hall under musical director Kent Nagano, who mixes a classical repertoire with more modern work.

Among the many SF-based chamber groups are the Pacific Mozart Ensemble, San Francisco Early Music Society, California Bach Society, and Kronos Quartet. You may also come across the Women's Philharmonic, which focuses on female composers, the famously conductor-free New Century Chamber Orchestra, and the SF Gay Men's Chorus.

opera

The **War Memorial Opera House**, just across the street from the Davies Symphony Hall, is home to the San Francisco Opera (SFO), regarded as sacred by some, considered lumbering by others. The repertoire is fairly conservative – Puccini, Rossini, Mozart, and Verdi, with few 20th-century works – and productions are lavish, if at times rather creaky. More modestly scaled alternatives to SFO can be had from Berkeley Opera, which stages several productions each year at the **Julia Morgan Theatre**, and **Pocket Opera**, a company that performs condensed, English-language versions of popular staples at venues around the city.

festivals

San Francisco's rich array of performing schedules occupies most of the year between fall and late spring, leaving a slender gap in summer for the **Stern Grove Festival** ☎ 252-6252, a series of free concerts usually held at 2pm on Sundays. Set in an outdoor eucalyptus-grove amphitheatre [→78] often crowded with picnic- and binocular-toting hordes (get there early!), the festival includes performances from the SFO and the SF Symphony.

To top its regular fall season, the **SFO** usually plans an early-summer festival, like 99's full Ring Cycle. The **Symphony** also holds a special series in June, such as 99's Stravinsky Festival, as well as hosting a nighttime **'Summer in the City'** pops series ☎ 864-6000 at Davies Symphony Hall. The latter leans toward light classical fare and stars Broadway belters such as Bernadette Peters.

tickets & reviews

Tickets for the San Francisco Opera and San Francisco Symphony are available through their box offices and websites; the latter also feature handy on-line seating charts. The Opera also sells through **BASS**, but book as early as you can.

💲 A night at the opera can cost as much as $145 or as little as $10; $10 rear standing-room tickets go on sale at the box office at 10am daily, and two hours before showtime. Symphony tickets are $20–$80; 40 seats go on sale two hours before most concerts. Touring 'name' recitals are in the $20–$35 range, local artists are usually under $20.

🎤 At the War Memorial Opera House – where all operas are English-supertitled – try to avoid extreme side seats which will cut your stage view and seats beneath balcony overhangs (for acoustic reasons).

🕐 Classical performances begin around 8pm (longer operas as early as 6.30pm), with Sunday matinées at 2 or 3pm.

👑 Dress up or down as you like (there's usually a drag queen around to waylay attention from you, anyway).

❶ The Sunday *Chronicle* 'Pink Section' and Friday's *Examiner* offer event listings, but you might also pick up the *Bay Area Reporter*. Two websites w www.sfcomposersforum.org and radio station-sponsored w www.kdfc.com offer event listings.

↓ sounds of the city

You may still get away with wearing flowers in your hair in San Francisco, but be warned, that was over three decades back, and while you might still find the odd Deadhead around, things have moved on and the 'San Francisco Sound' has been replaced by a scene that is extraordinarily diverse.

Even after all these years, the **Fillmore** remains a fab place to see and hear music. There's still a greeter at the top of the stairs and even free apples – courtesies held over from the club's 60s heyday. It's booked by local concert promotion company Bill Graham Presents, as is the **Warfield**, an old Downtown theatre that draws various types of good acts but can get uncomfortably crowded. **Slim's** [→122] is a no-frills place with a solid sound system. It brings in all manner of touring bands, but also regularly showcases local artists, such as the swamp-blues-turn-table outfit Go-Go Market. Featuring a similar roster is the **Great American Music Hall**, a beautiful turn-of-the-century space that was once a ballroom and a brothel. The most glam venue is **Bimbo's 365 Club** [→122], an original 40s-era supper club with a spacious dance floor and eclectic beats.

Justice League [→122] handles most of the major hip-hop and turntable shows, but also keep an eye out for the monthly Future Primitive Sound Session – a DJ extravaganza that lands at various locations. For indie gigs, **Bottom of the Hill** [→119] gets crowded fast, but it's where many of the best artists wind up.

The hip but comfy **Make-Out Room** [→119] has a great draught beer selection and live music a couple of times a week. Metal heads can shake their locks at Lucifer's Hammer, a Tuesday night showcase at the **Covered Wagon Saloon** [→123], while, on the other side of the tracks, country music hangs on by its fingernails – though Nashville this ain't.

During the 50s, the Fillmore district was the fulcrum of a swinging jazz scene. Those days have passed and the best jazz places are now across the Bay. Local groups can still be heard in the city at **Jazz at Pearl's** and **Blue Bar**, downstairs from Black Cat [→107]. Jazz can also be heard at **St John Coltrane African Orthodox Church**, an honest-to-god church with an open-door policy towards anyone who wants to worship with the regulars and get in the groove with the band that plays during Sunday services. The churches in Fillmore and neighbouring Western Addition district are also a haven for gospel music lovers.

For blues, head to the **Boom Boom Room**, John Lee Hooker's smart new club. **Café du Nord** [→119] and **Biscuits & Blues** are other places for slide guitar and songs of woe, but a Sunday night excursion to North Beach dive **The Saloon** to hear the wail of Johnny Nitro and the Door-slammers is mandatory.

festivals

The ever popular **Blues Festival** ☎ 979-5588, packs a two-day bill with national and local bands each September. The **Jazz Festival** ☎ 398-5655 is a world-class event each fall, with bookings in several venues throughout the city. The city's longest-running jazz fest, however, is the **Asian-American Jazz Festival** ☎ 379-8879. During a recent outing, Duke Ellington's *Far East Suite* was performed with the addition of a Chinese mouth organ, bamboo flutes, and a gong. Rock 'n' roll fests have proved less stable, but the recently founded **Nadine's Wild Weekend** ☎ 821-6299 – which takes place over a long weekend each summer – has fared rather better.

music

→ more directory

🎸 venue directory

venue directory

Berkeley Repertory Theatre
2025 Addison Street
(bet. Shattuck Ave &
Milvia St), Berkeley
☎ 1-510-845-4700

Bimbo's 365 Club
1025 Columbus Ave
(bet. Chestnut & Francisco
Sts) ☎ 474-0365

Biscuits & Blues
401 Mason Street
(at Geary Blvd)
☎ 292-2583

Blue Bar
501 Broadway (at
Kearny St) ☎ 981-2233

Booksmith
1644 Haight Street
(bet. Clayton &
Cole Sts)
☎ 863-8688

Boom Boom Room
1601 Fillmore Street
(at Geary Blvd)
☎ 673-8000

Bottom of the Hill
1233 17th Street (bet.
Missouri & Texas Sts)
☎ 621-4455

BRAVA Theatre Center
2789 24th Street
(at York St)
☎ 647-2822

Bridge Theatre
3010 Geary Boulevard
(bet. Cook & Blake Sts)
☎ 352-0810

Café du Nord
2170 Market Street
(bet. Church &
Sanchez Sts)
☎ 861-5016

Castro Theatre
429 Castro Street
(at Market St)
☎ 621-6120

City Lights
261 Columbus Street
(at Broadway)
☎ 362-8193

Clay Theatre
2261 Fillmore St (bet.
Clay & Sacramento Sts)
☎ 352-0810

Club Fugazi
678 Green Street
(bet. Columbus &
Powell Sts)
☎ 421-4222

Cobb's Comedy Club
2801 Leavenworth St
(at Beach St)
☎ 928-4320

Covered Wagon Saloon
917 Folsom Street
(bet. 5th & 6th Sts)
☎ 974-1585

Cowell Theatre
Fort Mason Center
Pier 2, Laguna Street
(at Marina Blvd)
☎ 441-3687

Curran Theatre
445 Geary Blvd (bet.
Taylor & Mason Sts)
☎ 551-2000

Dancers' Group Studio Theatre
3221 22nd Street
(at Mission St)
☎ 824-5044

Davies Symphony Hall
Van Ness Avenue
(at Grove St)
☎ 864-6000

Edinburgh Castle
950 Geary Boulevard
(bet. Polk & Larkin Sts)
☎ 885-4074

848 Community Space
848 Divisadero St (bet.
Market & Fulton Sts)
☎ 922-2385

Embarcadero Center Cinema
1 Embarcadero Center,
Sacramento Street
(at Battery St)
☎ 352-0810

Fillmore
1805 Geary Boulevard
(at Fillmore St)
☎ 346-6000

Foreign Cinema
2534 Mission Street
(bet. 21st & 22nd Sts)
☎ 648-7600

Geary Theatre (ACT)
405 Geary Street
(at Mason St)
☎ 749-2228

Golden Gate Theatre
1 Taylor Street
(at Market St)
☎ 551-2000

Great American Music Hall
859 O'Farrell Street
(bet. Polk & Larkin Sts)
☎ 885-0750

Herbst Theatre
401 Van Ness Avenue
(at McAllister St)
☎ 392-2545

Hertz Hall
UC Berkeley Campus
(at Bancroft Way),
Berkeley
☎ 1-510-642-4864

Intersection for the Arts
446 Valencia Street
(bet. 15th & 16th Sts)
☎ 626-3311

Jazz at Pearl's
256 Columbus Street
(at Broadway)
☎ 291-8255

Josie's Cabaret & Juice Joint
3583 16th Street
(at Market St)
☎ 861-7933

Julia Morgan Theatre
2640 College Avenue
(at Derby St), Berkeley
☎ 1-510-845-8542

Justice League
628 Divisadero Street
(bet. Grove & Hayes
Sts) ☎ 289-2038

The Lab
2948 16th Street
(bet. Mission St &
Van Ness Ave)
☎ 864-8855

Lorraine Hansberry Theatre
620 Sutter St (bet.
Taylor & Mason Sts)
☎ 474-8800

Lumiere
1572 California Street
(at Polk St)
☎ 352-0810

Luna Sea
2940 16th Street
(bet. Van Ness Ave
& Mission St)
☎ 863-2989

Magic Theatre
Fort Mason Center,
Building D, Laguna St
(at Marina Blvd)
☎ 441-8822

Make-Out Room
3255 22nd Street
(bet. Mission &
Valencia Sts)
☎ 647-2888

Marines Memorial Theatre
609 Sutter Street
(at Mason St)
☎ 771-6900

The Marsh
1062 Valencia Street
(bet. 21st & 22nd Sts)
☎ 641-0235

Metreon
4th Street
(bet. Mission &
Howard Sts)
☎ 369-6200

Modern Times
888 Valencia Street
(bet. 19th & 20th Sts)
☎ 282-9246

New Conservatory Theatre Center
25 Van Ness Avenue
(bet. Oak & Fell Sts)
☎ 861-8972

New Langton Arts
1246 Folsom Street
(bet. 8th & 9th Sts)
☎ 626-5416

ODC Performance Gallery
3153 17th Street
(at Shotwell St)
☎ 863-9834

Opera Plaza
601 Van Ness Avenue
(at Turk St)
☎ 771-0183

Orpheum Theatre
1192 Market St (at
Hyde St) ☎ 551-2000

Piaf's
1686 Market Street
(at Gough St)
☎ 864-3700

Plush Room
940 Sutter Street
(bet. Leavenworth &
Hyde Sts)
☎ 885-2800

Pocket Opera
☎ 989-1855

Punch Line
444 Battery Street
(at Washington St)
☎ 397-7573

Roxie Cinema
3117 16th Street
(at Valencia St)
☎ 863-1087

St John Coltrane African Orthodox Church
351 Divisadero Street
(at Oak St)
☎ 621-4054

The Saloon
1232 Grant Street
(bet. Vallejo St &
Broadway)
☎ 989-7666

SF Art Institute
800 Chestnut Street
(bet. Leavenworth &
Jones Sts) ☎ 771-7020

Slim's
333 11th Street
(bet. Folsom &
Harrison Sts)
☎ 621-3330

Stage Door Theatre
420 Mason Street
(bet. Post & Geary Sts)
☎ 788-9453

Theatre Artaud
450 Florida Street
(at 17th St)
☎ 437-2700

Theatre on the Square
450 Post Street (bet.
Powell & Mason Sts)
☎ 433-9500

Theatre Rhinoceros
2926 16th Street
(bet. Mission St &
South Van Ness Ave)
☎ 861-5079

Ticketmaster
☎ 951-7900
w www.
ticketmaster.com

TIX Bay Area Booth
Union Square
(at Stockton St)
☎ 433-7827

Transmission Theatre
314 11th Street
(at Folsom St)
☎ 621-1911

United Artists Vogue
3290 Sacramento St
(at Presidio St)
☎ 221-8183

Venue 9
252 9th Street (bet.
Folsom & Howard Sts)
☎ 626-2169

Warfield
982 Market Street
(bet. 5th & 6th Sts)
☎ 243-8510

War Memorial Opera House
301 Van Ness Avenue
(at Grove St)
☎ 621-6600

Werepad
2340 3rd Street (bet.
20th & 22nd Sts)
☎ 824-7334

Yerba Buena Center for the Arts
701 Mission Street
(bet. 3rd & 4th Sts)
☎ 978-2787

Zellerbach Hall
UC Berkeley Campus
(at Bancroft Way),
Berkeley
☎ 1-510-642-9988

san francisco agenda

An eventful guide to what is going on throughout the year

summer

San Francisco Ethnic Dance Festival

[→129]

North Beach Festival

One of SF's many annual neighbourhood street fairs, this festival focusing on Italian culture is the country's oldest.

🌙 *weekend mid-June*
Grant St (bet. Broadway & Filbert St), North Beach ☎ 989-2220
� 15, 42 🅿 PH, PM 💲 free

Haight Street Fair

Psychedelia, patchouli oil, and tie dye flow freely during this annual ode to Haight-Ashbury's hippy heyday. Highlights of the street festival are arts and crafts, rock 'n' roll bands, and more tofu burgers than you can shake an incense stick at.

🌙 *Saturday mid-June*
Haight St (bet. Masonic & Stanyan Sts), Haight-Ashbury
☎ 661-8025 � 6, 7, 21, 43, 66, 71
🚆 N 💲 free

SF Lesbian, Gay, Bisexual, & Transgender Pride Celebration & Parade

Put on your best spike heels and wave your rainbow flag at this enormous cheer for diversity, humanity, and gayness. The month-long Pride festivities include a film festival and a two-day fair highlighted by a huge Sunday morning parade – one of SF's most memorable moments.

🌙 *June*
Festival: Civic Center; parade: Market St (from Beale to 8th Sts)
☎ 864-3733 w www. sf-pride. org � 5, 9, 19, 21, 26 🚆 F, J, K, L, M, N 💲 free

SF International Lesbian & Gay Film Festival

[→126]

Stern Grove Festival

[→130]

Fourth of July Waterfront Festival

The entire city hits the streets for this patriotic celebration. The evening fireworks are the main highlight, and, fog permitting, you can see them from most high points in SF. Ground zero is to the west of Pier 39; Telegraph Hill is a more appealing spot.

🌙 *4 July*
Fireworks visible from anywhere in town ☎ 777-8498
w www.sfgate.com 💲 free

California Shakespeare Festival

[→127]

Shakespeare Santa Cruz Fest

[→127]

SF Butoh Festival

[→129]

Shakespeare in the Park

[→127]

Jewish Film Festival

[→126]

Afro Solo Arts Festival

[→128]

Summer in the City

[→130]

A la Carte, à la Park

This outdoor food and drink festival features tastings from various local restaurants, wineries, and breweries, and some hot music to help it all go down.

🌙 *Labor Day weekend (Sep)*
Sharon Meadow, Golden Gate Park ☎ 762-2277
w www.sfgate. com
� 5, 7, 21, 66, 71 🚆 N 💲 $9

Blues Festival

[→131]

autumn

Folsom Street Fair

Leash up your slave and polish your piercings for this untamed leather-boy extravaganza. Oh, right, and there's music, dancing, and food as well.

🌙 *late September*
Folsom St (bet. 7th & 12th Sts), SoMa ☎ 861-3247
w www.folsomstreetfair.com
� 9, 19, 27, 42 💲 free

SF Fringe Theatre Festival

[→127]

SF Stand-Up Comedy Competition

[→128]

Castro Street Fair

This celebration of the Castro neighbourhood and its gay and lesbian community is tamer than its Folsom Street cousin but plenty colourful and festive.

🌙 *first weekend in October*
Castro Street (bet. 19th & Market Sts), Castro ☎ 467-3354
w www.castrostreetfair.org
🚆 24, 48 🚆 F, K, L, M 💲 free

San Francisco Open Studios

Participating artists open their studio doors to the public and, of course, hope to sell some pieces in the process. Studios are spread throughout the city, and the event focuses on a different set of neighbourhoods each weekend.

🌙 *October*
various venues ☎ 861-9838
w www.sfopen studios.com
💲 free

Jazz Festival

[→131]

Fleet Week

Depending on how you feel about exhibition fighter jets (the Blue Angels) roaring through the SF cityscape – not to mention dodging hordes of partying navy boys on shore leave – you'll either embrace or despise this annual military spectacle.

🌙 *weekend mid-October*
Blue Angels visible from anywhere in town
☎ 1-650-378-4745
w www.fleetweek.com 💲 free

Exotic Erotic Halloween Ball

The largest indoor masquerade ball in the world is less sexually outlandish than it supposedly was in the 'good old' days, but it's still a fun dress-up party. A similar bash is held on New Year's Eve.

🌙 *late October*
Cow Palace, 2600 Geneva Ave (at Santos St), Daly City
☎ 469-6065
w www.exoticeroticball.net
🚆 9, 15 💲 $10–$25

Halloween

The 'official' event usually happens in the Civic Center, but the real party is in the Castro, where all manner of lions, tigers, and bears let their freak flags fly high.

🌙 *31 October*
Civic Center & Castro (bet. 18th & Market Sts) ☎ 826-1401
w www.xq.com/cuav/halloween
Civic Center: 🚆 5, 9, 19, 21, 26, 66 🚆 F, J, K, L, M, N (Castro: 🚆 24, 33, 35, 48 🚆 F, K, L, M) 💲 free

Film Arts Festival

[→126]

San Francisco Bay Area Book Festival

[→129–130]

winter

MacWorld Expo

This annual Macintosh computer trade show and convention packs in as many millionaire wannabes as it does technology geeks, but you never know what innovation may be revealed.

🌙 *early January*
Moscone Center, Howard Street (bet. 3rd & 4th Sts)
☎ 974-4000
w www.macworldexpo.com
🚆 14, 15, 30, 45 💲 $29 in advance, $45 on door

events

more events

events

Chinese New Year Parade & Celebration

Witness Chinese dragons snake down city streets during the annual Chinese New Year celebration. Firecrackers fly and lion dancers weave along Grant Avenue during the two-week festival which includes the Miss Chinatown USA Pageant, a community street carnival, and a huge, colourful parade that is the city's most popular.

◗ late Jan–early Feb
various locations around Downtown & Chinatown
☎ 982-3000
w www.chineseparade.com
🎫 free

California International Antiquarian Book Fair

The world's largest rare book fair alternates each year between San Francisco and Los Angeles.

◗ next SF fair: February 2001
Concourse Exhibition Center, Brannan Street (at 8th St)
☎ 551-5190 w www.california bookfair.com 🚌 19, 27, 42
🎫 two-day ticket $5; three-day ticket $10

spring

St Patrick's Day Parade

A week of local events – some solemn, many merry – lead up to a grand parade through town. SF turns green as the streets fill with shamrock and leprechauns.

◗ 17 March
Market Street (from 2nd St to City Hall) ☎ 661-2700 🚌 5, 9, 19, 21, 26 🚇 F, J, K, L, M, N 🎫 free

Whole Life Expo

A New Age trade show focusing on nutrition, alternative healing practices, and a touch of the psychic stuff that made California famous in the 70s.

◗ second weekend in April
Concourse Exhibition Center, Brannan St (at 8th St)
☎ 721-2484
w www.wholelifeexpo.com
🚌 19, 27, 42 🎫 three-day pass: $20 in advance; $24 on day

SF Asian American Film Festival

[→126]

Cherry Blossom Festival

A family-friendly street fair celebrating Japanese culture and the arrival of spring. The Taiko drumming performance and the final grand parade are the highlights.

◗ mid-April
Fillmore & Post Sts, Japantown
☎ 563-2313 🚌 5, 21, 42, 47, 49
🎫 free

Dancers' Group Edge Festival

[→128]

Lift Every Voice

[→128]

Bay to Breakers

More than 100,000 'runners', most in costume, journey across town from bay to ocean in this wacky street race.

◗ third Sunday in May
from Embarcadero through Golden Gate Park to Ocean Beach ☎ 808-5000 ext 2222
w www.baytobreakers.com
🎫 $20 in advance; $25 on day

Cinco de Mayo

This celebration of Mexico's 1862 victory over the French has become a street festival packed with music, food, and beer. Some decry its growing commercialism, but that hasn't stopped the Mission district from partying on.

◗ 5 May
24th Street, Mission ☎ 826-1401
w www.carnaval.com
🚌 9, 22, 26, 27, 49 🎫 free

Carnaval San Francisco

Carnaval festivities, long over in Rio, get revived at this two-day celebration of Latin-American culture highlighted by a huge parade and loads of samba music and dancing.

◗ last week in May
street party on Harrison Street (bet. 16th & 22nd Sts), Mission
☎ 826-1401
w www.carnaval.com
🚌 9, 22, 26, 27, 49 🎫 free

spectator sports

Boasting five Superbowl wins, the San Francisco 49ers are heralded as one of the best teams in the National Football League. Their excellence is matched only by the fierce loyalty of their fans who have the uncanny ability to cheer through the freezing winds that rattle through 3Com Park (formerly known as Candlestick Park). Tickets can be hard to come by, so call early. The football season runs Sep–Dec, culminating in the Superbowl on the third Sunday in Jan.

As for baseball, the home team is the San Francisco Giants, known for their never-say-die prowess on the field. In April 2000 they will be moving into a new home, Pacific Bell Park. With stupendous views of the Bay Bridge and the SF skyline – and a prime SoMa location – the park is worth the ticket price even if you're not a baseball aficionado. Not to be outdone, the East Bay steps up to the plate with the tough and scrappy Oakland A's, noted for the mix of young blood and seasoned veterans. They play in the Oakland's Network Associates Coliseum (also home to the Oakland Raiders football team). The season runs Apr–Oct.

San Francisco's basketball team is the Golden State Warriors who play at the Oakland Arena. They have seen more bad days than good in the past few years, but they still have their diehard fans and, if they're playing against a famous team (say, the Chicago Bulls), games will sell out, so call ahead for a schedule. The basketball season runs Nov–Apr.

If there's one sport where it's better to be there in person, it's ice hockey, the better to see all the fights... er, the magnificent manoeuvres on ice. Although they've never reached the Stanley Cup, the San Jose Sharks are a team with fighting (and staying) power, and it's well worth seeing them battle it out over the puck. They play at the San Jose Arena. The hockey season runs Oct–Apr.

San Francisco 49ers

3Com Park, Daly City ☎ 656-4900
w www.sf49ers.com 🚌 'Ballpark' from different parts of SF
🎫 from $50; also available from Ticketmaster (☎ 421-8497) ♿
◗ ticket office: 9am–5pm Mon–Fri.

San Francisco Giants

Pacific Bell Park (bet. King, 2nd, & 3rd Sts) ☎ 467-8000 or ☎ 1-800-544-2687
w www.sfgiants.com 🚌 15, 30, 42, 45 🚇 N 🎫 from $7 ♿ ◗ ticket office: 8.30am–5.30pm Mon–Fri.

Golden State Warriors, Oakland A's & Oakland Raiders

Oakland Coliseum Complex (Oakland Arena & Oakland's Network Associates Coliseum), 700 Coliseum Way, north of Hegenberger Rd, off I-880
☎ 1-510-569-2121 🎫 from $20; also available from Bass
(☎ 1-800-352-0212) ◗ ticket office: 8.30am–5pm Mon–Fri.

San Jose Sharks

San Jose Arena, 525 W Santa Clara Street (at Autumn St)
☎ 1-408-287-7070 w www.sj sharks.com 🎫 from $17; also available from Ticketmaster (☎ 1-408-998-8497) 🚆 CalTrain from 4th & King to Diridon/Cahill station ◗ ticket office: 9.30am–5.30pm Mon–Fri; 9.30am–1pm Sat.

There are countless hotel rooms in SF to welcome the never-ending influx of visitors. You can usually find the big-name hotels just by pointing a finger at some of the tallest buildings in town. But there are also several smaller, more unique, places to stay. From chic and hip, to fun and funky, just about every niche is covered by the city's many hoteliers. While rooms here may be more expensive than in most cities, you typically get a lot for your money.

hotels

sleep easy

what's where

more hotels

prices – lowest quoted for double room in peak season (unless otherwise stated)

↓ dead famous

Fairmont Hotel 950 Mason St (bet. Sacramento & California Sts), Nob Hill 94108

This is one of the anchors of the Nob Hill fab hotels. Almost unchanged since it opened, shortly after the 1906 earthquake, today the emphasis is on service, with a seemingly-one-employee-to-each-guest ratio. A tower behind the original building brings the room-count to 600, each one a home-away-from-home: comfortable, quiet, private, and moderately sized. A good choice for those looking for a slice of traditional San Francisco. Visit the adjacent Tonga Room [→38] for a kitschy tropical atmosphere.

☎ 772-5000 or 1-800-527-4727 **F** 781-3929 **w** www.fairmont.com 🖼 1 🕔 C, PH, PM
🛬 600 🖵 🖩 📟 🎴 ↔ 🖉 📡 🖵 **P** free 🕭 🍴 all $$$ singles: from $249; doubles: from $289

hotels

Huntington Hotel 1075 California St (at Taylor St), Nob Hill 94108

This unassuming 12-floor brick building atop Nob Hill was given a recent revamp. The small lobby and refined Big Four adjacent restaurant retain an early-San Francisco atmosphere. While some of the rooms lack sunlight, they are all comfortable and designed by notable SF designers. A few celebs have favourite rooms here. Mostly, though, it's business-types and discriminating world travellers.

☎ 474-5400 **F** 474-6227 **w** www.slh.com/huntington 🖼 1 🕔 C
🛬 14 🖵 🖩 📡 🖵 **P** free 🕭 🍴 all $$$ singles: from $230; doubles: from $255

Mark Hopkins Inter-Continental 1 Nob Hill (at California & Mason Sts), Nob Hill 94108

During World War II, US soldiers would share a last romantic moment with their loved ones here. The following day the women would return to the hotel's top-floor lounge to watch them sail out the Golden Gate. The views are not the only reason this hotel has its landmark status. Rooms are large and elegant, and range from money-no-object suites to business-oriented and less opulent. Lots of guests stay here to relive a bygone era.

☎ 392-3434 or 1-800-662 4455 **F** 421-3302 **w** www.markhopkins.citysearch.com 🖼 1 🕔 C, PH, PM
🛬 390 🖵 🖩 ↔ 🖉 📡 🖵 **P** free 🕭 🍴 all $$$$ singles: from $220; doubles: from $425

Palace Hotel 2 New Montgomery St (at Market St), SoMa 94105

Opened in 1875, this opulent building quickly became known as the arbiter of old-school luxury. US presidents, including Teddy and Franklin Roosevelt, were drawn here. It burned to the ground in 1906 but was quickly rebuilt to its lavish standards. Popular with business people and families alike, the average-size rooms are decorated with antiques and historic San Francisco photographs. Refurbishment restored the original splendour in the Garden Court, a glass-ceilinged atrium where high tea is served daily.

☎ 512-1111 or 1-800-325-3535 **F** 543-0671 **w** www.sfpalace.com 🖼 2, 3,6, 7, 9, 38, 66, 71
🖼 F, J, K, L, M, N 🛬 551 🖵 🖩 📟 🎴 ↔ 🖉 📡 🖵 **P** 🕭 🍴 all $$$$ singles: from $330; doubles: from $350

Westin St Francis 335 Powell St (bet. Geary & Post Sts), Downtown 94102

The anchor of Union Square, the St Francis manages to feel small and intimate despite its looming 1200 rooms. The place crawls with tourists, but is still beloved by locals, many of whom might be found lounging to live jazz over after-work cocktails in the Compass Rose, the old-world-style lobby bar. The hotel is run by the Westin company and the rooms have an air of corporate anonymity. Still, some San Francisco vibe remains.

☎ 397-7000 **F** 774-0124 **w** www.westin.com 🖼 2, 3 🖼 F, J, K, L, M, N 🕔 PH, PM
🛬 1192 🖩 🎴 ↔ 🖉 📡 🖵 **P** free 🕭 🍴 all $$$ singles: from $219; doubles: from $239

↓ last word in luxury

Campton Place 340 Stockton St (bet. Sutter & Post Sts), Downtown 94108

Oh so chic, with a rarefied atmosphere that might dissuade tourists despite its prime location. The hotel's 117 rooms are large and well appointed with technological innovations: modem ports, faxes etc. In the tradition of fine European manors, attention is paid to the smallest detail: in-house French laundry service; valets will pack and unpack for you, and shoes will be shined. The restaurant downstairs is popular with ladies who lunch.

☎ 781-5555 or 1-800-235-4300 **F** 955-5536 **w** www.camptonplace.com 🖼 2, 3, 30, 45 🖼 F, J, K, L, M, N
🕔 PH, PM 🛬 117 🖵 🖩 📟 🎴 🖵 **P** 🕭 🍴 all $$$$ singles: from $275; doubles: from $365

Clift Hotel 495 Geary St (at Taylor St), Downtown 94102

The Clift provides a boutique-ish feel and hospitality. NYC's hotelier Ian Schrager has stepped in with Philippe Starck to put his stamp on it. One of the grand San Francisco hotels, the Clift draws well-seasoned travellers and newcomers. Regulars include travelling performers; special 'theatre suites' even have two baths, so couples trying to make a curtain can dress at the same time. Good for families too. The Redwood Room [→51] downstairs is one of San Francisco's most venerable bars.

☎ 775-4700 **F** 441-4621 **w** www.clifthotel.com 🖪 38 🖪 F, J, K, L, M, N
🚶 326 💻 🖳 📧 ⏰ ↔ ⊘ ⊘° 🖵 🅿 🛏 🖭 AE/DC/JCB/MC/V **$$$** singles & doubles from $255

Hotel Palomar 12 4th St (at Market St), SoMa 94103

Never mind the fact that at street level, this brand new hotel is actually an Old Navy store, because five floors above the retail level is nestled a sanctuary of tranquil luxury. The atmosphere is sophisticated. Boldly decorated rooms have large bathrooms and comfy sofas. The place is aimed at those who like civility without stuffiness.

☎ 348-1111 or 1-877-294-9711 **F** 348-1529 **w** www.hotelpalomar.com 🖪 9, 30, 45 🖪 F, J, K, L, M, N 🚇 PH, PM
🚶 198 💻 🖳 📧 ≋ ⊘ ⊘° 🖵 🅿 free 🛏 🖭 all **$$** singles & doubles from $150

Mandarin Oriental 222 Sansome St (bet. Pine & California Sts), Downtown 94104

Housed in the top 11 floors of the twin-towered First Interstate skyscraper, this tranquil hotel offers stunning views from all of its rooms. Many have marble baths set next to windows overlooking the city and bay. Rent the Oriental Suite for a unique hotel experience. The lobby is quiet and sophisticated and the restaurant, Silks [→50], on the second floor, is among the city's best. Popular with business types and Japanese nouveaux riches.

☎ 276-9888 **F** 433-289 **w** www.mandarin-oriental.com 🖪 15, 42 🖪 F, J, K, L, M, N 🚇 C
🚶 158 💻 🖳 📧 ⏰ ↔ ⊘ ⊘° 🖵 🅿 free 🛏 🖭 all **$$$$** singles: from $395; doubles: from $415

Prescott Hotel 545 Post St (at Mason St), Downtown 94102

It's an expensive way to snag a table at the impossibly jammed Postrio [→110] restaurant downstairs, but people have been known to check in to receive preferential seating. The clamour over the restaurant overshadows the hotel's quiet, luxurious appeal. The rooms bear little resemblance to the high-profile Hollywood glamour downstairs, and are quietly sophisticated and refined. If you're looking to impress, book the Mendocino Penthouse, complete with grand piano and roof-top jacuzzi.

☎ 563-0303 or 1-800-283-7322 **F** 563-6831 **w** www.prescotthotel.com 🖪 2, 3
🚶 164 📧 ↔ ⊘ ⊘° 🖵 🅿 free 🛏 🖭 all **$$$** singles & doubles from $235

Ritz-Carlton 600 Stockton St (bet. Pine & California Sts), Nob Hill 94108

Considered by many to be the finest hotel San Francisco has to offer, this landmark Nob Hill hotel has the feel of a grand museum, with giant oil portraits, antiques, and original 18th-century still lifes gracing the walls. Rooms are large and have feather twin or king-size beds, with Egyptian cotton linen. Service from the multilingual staff is impeccable. Bonuses include daily high tea, an indoor pool, and a fitness centre. The hotel's renowned restaurant, The Dining Room [→104], is a five-star culinary experience.

☎ 296-7465 or 1-800-241-3333 **F** 291-0147 **w** www.ritzcarltonsanfrancisco.com 🖪 9, 30, 45 🖪 F, J, K, L, M, N
🚇 C 🚶 336 💻 🖳 📧 ⏰ ↔ ⊘ ⊘° 🖵 🅿 free 🛏 🖭 all **$$$$** singles & doubles from $400

↓ designer label

Hotel Monaco 501 Geary St (at Taylor St), Downtown 94102

You know you've arrived when the bellmen who take your bags are better dressed than you; their felt-fedoras are the giveaway, and a reminder that the Monaco (being branded across the US) aims to make a stylish impression. The rooms are fairly large and flamboyant colours and patterns vie for attention. The 34 suites are super-luxuriant, complete with whirlpool tubs. Big, canopied beds are ultra comfy; the amenities cutting-edge. Whimsical touches include Nintendo games on the TV, and an available pet goldfish to keep during your stay – no need to feed it!

☎ 292-0100 or 1-800-214-4220 **F** 292-0149 **w** www.hotelmonaco.com 🖪 27, 38 🖪 F, J, K, L, M, N
🚶 201 💻 🖳 📧 ⏰ ↔ ⊘ ⊘° 🖵 🅿 🛏 🖭 all **$$$** singles & doubles from $239

more hotels

hotels

Prices exclude all taxes

Hotel Triton 342 Grant Ave (at Bush St), Downtown 94108

More stylized than stylish, this fun, trendy boutique near Union Square is a regular haunt for film and music types, as well as hip gays and lesbians. A few of the small, but startlingly furnished rooms have been designed by, or in honour of, showbiz luminatti, including Jerry Garcia, Carlos Santana, and the set designer from *Rent*. Twenty-four of the 140 rooms are 'eco-chic', with natural cotton linens, energy-efficient lighting, biodegradable soaps, and water filtration systems.

☎ 394-0500 or 1-800-433-6611 **F** 394-0555 **w** www.hotel-tritonsf.com 🚇 2, 3, 15, 30, 45 🚋 F, J, K, L, M, N 📞 140 ⬚ 🗎 📶 🖉 🖳 **P** free ♿ 🛏 all **$$** singles & doubles from $179

Phoenix Hotel 601 Eddy St (at Larkin St), Tenderloin 94109

The fact that the accommodation is little more than motor-lodge-style rooms with nicer beds, cooler paint jobs, and more stylish amenities hasn't stopped celeb rockers like REM, Ben Harper, and Sonic Youth from making this a favourite crash pad. The Phoenix's 41 bungalow guest rooms and three suites (which include adjacent 'tour manager' suites) are situated around a tropical-themed courtyard with a decorated swimming pool. Like an oasis in this somewhat sketchy part of town, people are drawn to its funky charm. Locals line up for the ultra-fashionable Backflip Lounge [→118].

☎ 776-1380 or 1-800-248-9466 **F** 885-3109 **w** www.sftrips.com 🚇 19, 31 🚋 F, J, K, L, M, N 📞 44 📶 🖉 🖳 □ **P** free 🛏 all **$$** singles & doubles from $129

W Hotel San Francisco 181 3rd St (at Howard St), SoMa 94103

Living up to the hype created by San Francisco's first ground-up hotel in 10 years is indeed a monumental task. But the latest version of the growing W chain seems up to the chore. The cutting-edge design is defined by stark, clean lines with surfaces polished smooth. Window seats in the rooms create a sense of comfort, as do the luxurious linens. The service – swift, professional, and matter-of-fact – is exemplified in the 'Whatever Whenever' button on the room phones.

☎ 777-5300 **F** 817-7823 **w** www.whotels.com 🚇 15, 30, 45 🚋 F, J, K, L, M, N 📞 423 ⬚ 🗎 🔞 📶 ↔ 🖉 🖳 □ **P** free ♿ 🛏 all **$$$$** singles & doubles from $369

↓ themes & variations

Abigail Hotel 246 McAllister St (bet. Polk & Larkin Sts), Civic Center 94102

A characterful, fun, sophisticated, European-style hostelry near the Civic and Performing Arts Centres. Built in 1926 and frequented by visiting actors and singers, the Abigail is now favoured by bohos who like the intimate feel of the rooms and the excellent vegetarian restaurant, Millennium [→117].

☎ 861-9728 **F** 861-5848 **w** www.sftrips.com 🚇 5, 19 🚋 F, J, K, L, M, N 📞 61 ⬚ 🔞 🖳 **P** ♿ 🛏 AE/DC/MC/V **$** singles & doubles from $85

Hotel Bijou 111 Mason St (at Eddy St), Downtown 94102

It ain't Hollywood, but San Francisco has quite a cinematic history in its own right, and the Bijou celebrates that fact in fine form. Each of the 65 bright, colourful rooms is named after a movie filmed in the city, like *Vertigo* or *What's Up Doc*. The concierge will even plan a movie-led day for you. Or, just watch one of the San Francisco-themed films shown each night in the hotel's charming mini-theatre off the lobby.

☎ 771-1200 **F** 346-3196 **w** www.sftrips.com 🚇 27, 31 🚋 F, J, K, L, M, N 🕑 PH, PM 📞 65 **P** ♿ 🛏 all **$$** singles from $139

Hotel Serrano 405 Taylor St (at O'Farrell St), Downtown 94102

A handsome new hotel in the Theater District that was built into a historic landmark 1920s Spanish Revival building that formerly housed a not-so-handsome hotel. During the remodel attention was paid to visual stimuli, and rich, bold colours abound in the whimsical lobby and in the eclectic-looking guest rooms. In order to keep guests amused, the hotel has adopted a 'board game theme' so make the most of backgammon, chess, and checkers in your room. One notable rarity here: your pet, if well-behaved, can join you.

☎ 885-2500 or 1-877-294-9709 **F** 351-7654 **w** www.serranohotel.com 🚇 27, 38 🚋 F, J, K, L, M, N 🕑 PH, PM 📞 236 ⬚ 🗎 ↔ 🖳 □ **P** ♿ 🛏 all **$$$** singles: from $190; doubles: from $205

Inn at the Opera 333 Fulton St (at Franklin St), Civic Center 94102

Smack in the heart of the city's Performing Arts Center, Inn at the Opera is popular with visiting divas. The hotel runs the theme of its location through each of the 48 spacious, elegant rooms and aptly named Symphony or Opera suites, many of which have living rooms with sofa beds. All are equipped with the comforts of home: microwaves, fridges, TVs, and VCRs. Singer Tony Bennett called it the 'most romantic hotel I know.'

☎ 863-8400 or 1-800-325-2708 **F** 861-0821 **w** www.citysearch.com 🚍 5, 21
◆ 48 ➰ ℗ 🛎 🖥 **P** ♿ 🍴 AE/DC/MC/V **$$** singles & doubles from $175

↓ big business

Hotel Nikko 222 Mason St (bet. Ellis & O'Farrell Sts), Downtown 94102

Whether you're on business or your business is exploring the city, the Nikko's the place. It is positioned centrally between the Yerba Buena Gardens and Union Square and the amenities are well thought out. Decor is sleek and Japonesque modern, with spacious, comfortable, and practical rooms with large desks. If you don't find what you need in the room, the hotel's business centre is equipped with computers, email and Internet access, modem lines, scanners, printers, and everything else you might require. The Nikko can even provide someone to act as your personal valet. The restaurant, Anzu, offers both fresh sushi and prime steaks, sort of an upscale surf 'n' turf.

☎ 394-1111 **F** 394-1106 **w** www.nikkohotels.com 🚍 27, 38 🚃 F, J, K, L, M, N
◆ 525 ➰ 🖥 🈳 ≋ ↔ ⌁ ℗ 🛎 **P** free ♿ 🍴 all **$$$$** singles: from $270; doubles: from $310

Pan Pacific San Francisco 500 Post St (at Mason St), Downtown 94102

One of the most stunning hotels in the city, with a soaring atrium that extends the entire height of the John Portman-designed skyscraper. The rooms are large and beautiful, with full marble bathrooms. When it comes to business, everything is covered, including three telephones in each room, fax machines, and laptops delivered on request. Chauffeur-driven Rolls Royces will take you anywhere within two miles of the place. Throw in the personal valet service, and this is a good choice for those travelling on the company's platinum card.

☎ 771-8600 **F** 398-0267 **w** www.panpac.com 🚍 2, 3 🚃 F, J, K, L, M, N 🚍 PH, PM
◆ 330 ➰ 🖥 🈳 ↔ ⌁ ⌁ ℗ 🛎 **P** free ♿ 🍴 all **$$$$** singles & doubles from $320

↓ chic boutiques

Commodore Hotel 825 Sutter St (at Jones St), Downtown 94109

Artsy neo-bohemians and those who like to imitate them adore the no-nonsense and very urban atmosphere of the Commodore. The rooms represent great value for money, being large with full bath and shower, walk-in closets, and furnishings created by local designers. Downstairs, The Red Room [→118] is one of the city's coolest (if not one of its smallest) bars; drenched entirely in red, from the barstools to the giant-size Cosmopolitans. Next door, the Titanic Café serves excellent, American-style breakfast.

☎ 923-6800 or 1-800-338-6848 **F** 923-6804 **w** www.sftrips.com 🚍 2, 3, 27 🚃 F, J, K, L, M, N
◆ 113 🖥 **P** ♿ 🍴 all **$$** singles & doubles from $129

Hotel Diva 440 Geary St (bet. Mason & Taylor Sts), Downtown 94102

Who needs Hollywood Boulevard? You'll step across the cement handprints of such celeb divas as Carol Channing, Joan Collins, and Lily Tomlin to enter this fun, small-calibre-chic hotel near Union Square and the Theater District. The chrome-and-glass-styled rooms feel stark, minimalist, futuristic even, but have all the requisite modern amenities and are large enough for families.

☎ 885-0200 **F** 346-6613 **w** www.hoteldiva.com 🚍 38 🚃 F, J, K, L, M, N 🚍 PH, PM
◆ 111 ➰ 🖥 ↔ ⌁ **P** free ♿ 🍴 all **$$** singles & doubles from $199

hotels

→ more hotels

hotels

Hotel Rex 562 Sutter St (at Powell St), Downtown 94102

While it doesn't quite carry the cachet of New York's famed Algonquin, the Rex endeavours to create a similar literary experience. Youngish, informed travellers stay here for comfort and value more than for the occasional literary gatherings, however. The 94 average-sized rooms are indeed studied, with clean lines and polished furniture (including a writing desk, naturally). The lobby has an impressive antiquarian bookstore to one side and a sleek bar to the other.

☎ 433-4434 **F** 433-3695 **w** www.citysearch.com/sfo/hotelrex.com 🚌 2, 3 🚇 F, J, K, L, M, N 🚇 PH, PM
🛏 94 ↔ 💻 **P** 🚫 🍽 all $$$ singles: from $185; doubles: from $225

Nob Hill Lambourne 725 Pine St (bet. Powell & Stockton Sts), Nob Hill 94108

Like an office away from home, the Nob Hill Lambourne is a stylish, modern retreat with just 14 rooms and six suites, each appointed to serve as a room for the night and an office. Laptops, colour printers, modems, and other business equipment can be borrowed at no extra charge. All rooms have workstations, fully stocked kitchenettes, stereos, and VCRs. A tempting assortment of massage and spa treatments is available to ease the stress of a hard day's work.

☎ 433-2287 or 1-800-274-8466 **F** 433-0975 **w** www.sftrips.com 🚌 30, 45 🚇 F, J, K, L, M, N 🚇 PH, PM
🛏 20 ⚭ 🐾 **P** free 🍽 all $$$ singles & doubles from $210

↓ hideaways

Archbishop's Mansion 1000 Fulton St (at Steiner St), Hayes Valley 94117

Set on one corner of Alamo Square (aka Postcard Row), this imitation French château was built for the Archbishop of San Francisco in 1904. Today it operates as a quaint B&B, but does not forsake its history. Tours of the place are available to non-guests. A magnificent three-storey staircase capped by a huge stained-glass dome sweeps upward to the 15 extravagant guest rooms – each has been named after a famous opera character. Some rooms have a fireplace and whirlpool bath. All rooms have at least a queen-size bed and are decorated with fine French antiques.

☎ 563-7872 or 1-800-543-5820 **F** 885-3193 **w** www.archbishopsmansion.com 🚌 5, 21, 22
🛏 15 🔞 **P** free 🍽 all $$ singles & doubles from $159

El Drisco 2901 Pacific Ave (at Broderick St), Pacific Heights 94115

El Drisco's elegance lies in its simplicity. Its no-nonsense approach to style and service (as well as its stunning bay and city views) have made it the choice of visiting dignitaries and heads-of-state, including presidents Eisenhower and Nixon. Today, savvy politicos and designer types like the hotel's large, well-appointed rooms which after a recent $5 million restoration are prepared for the 21st century with high-speed modem ports, two-line phones etc. Parking can be next to impossible.

☎ 346-2880 **F** 567-5537 **w** www.eldriscohotel.com 🚌 3, 24
🛏 43 ↔ 🐾 🚫 🍽 AE/D/DC/MC/V $$$ singles & doubles from $220

Hotel Bohème 444 Columbus Ave (bet. Vallejo & Green Sts), North Beach 94133

If you walk by too quickly you'll miss this cute 15-room hostelry smack in the heart of North Beach. The entrance is but an awning-covered door squeezed between a bakery and a café, but it opens to reveal a cosy retreat. The Bohème pays homage to the Beat Generation that thrived all around it during the 50s. Check out the collection of black and white photos from the era. The quite spacious rooms have queen-size beds and colour TV with cable. Many visitors return here.

☎ 433-9111 **F** 362-6292 **w** www.hotelboheme.com 🚌 15, 30, 41, 45 🚇 PM
🛏 15 **P** 🍽 all $$ singles & doubles from $149

Hotel Juliana 590 Bush St (at Stockton St), Chinatown 94108

Those looking for proximity to Union Square without all the traffic will like the under-rated Juliana. The recently renovated hotel is enjoying renewed notoriety since a longtime popular restaurant, Oritalia [→113], moved in downstairs. The rooms are bright, colourful, and flooded with natural light. For more space, rent one of the 25 one-bedroom suites. European-style touches include a complimentary glass of wine each evening, valet service, and a free limo ride to the Financial District in the morning.

☎ 392-2540 or 1-800-328-3880 F 391-8447 W www.julianahotel.com 🚌 9, 30, 45 🚇 F, J, K, L, M, N 🚋 PH, PM 👥 107 💻 📠 📺 🏋 ⬛ 🅿 ⬛ all $$ singles: from $189; doubles: from $199

Hotel Majestic 1500 Sutter St (at Gough St), Pacific Heights 94109

This beautiful hotel on the outskirts of Pacific Heights invites a clandestine rendezvous. The five-storey Edwardian-style building bears a regal presence in this residential neighbourhood. Its recent restoration earned an honour from the California Heritage Council. Guests are looked after by slavishly attentive staff. Rooms are large with four-poster queen-size beds and European antiques. Olivia de Havilland lived here during the 30s. The restaurant is routinely recommended on local 'most romantic' lists.

☎ 441-1100 or 1-800-869-8966 F 673-7331 W www.worldres.com 🚌 2, 3 ◈ 57 💻 📺 🏋 ♿ 🅿 ⬛ free ♿ all $$ singles & doubles from $175

Inn on Castro 321 Castro St (at 16th St), Castro 94114

Those looking to entrench themselves in the heart of San Francisco's gay culture need look no further than this lovable B&B. Set discreetly in a perfectly revamped Edwardian-style building, it offers a quiet escape from the head-spinning pace of the Castro district. Each room is stylishly decorated, using motifs from Chinese kitsch to contemporary whimsy; all but one have private bathrooms. Choose some up-to-date gay literature from your shelf and make yourself at home in the intimate living room downstairs; you never know who you might meet.

☎ 861-0321 F 861-0321 W www.innoncastro.com 🚌 24 🚇 F, K, L, M ◈ 8 ⬛ AE/D/DC/MC/V $$ singles: from $120; doubles: from $150

Queen Anne Hotel 1590 Sutter St (at Octavia St), Pacific Heights 94109

Popular with tourists who are after inn-style charm, but don't want to give up the security of a large hotel. Built at the turn of the century by Jim Fair (better known for the Fairmont [→136] on Nob Hill), the building was a school for society-bound young girls; the 48 rooms still contain some furnishings from that time. Rooms, indicative of the era, are a bit small, but each has a private bath, and a queen- or king-size bed.

☎ 441-2828 F 775-5212 W www.queenanne.com 🚌 2, 3 ◈ 48 🏋 🔧 🅿 ♿ ⬛ all $$ singles: from $165; doubles: from $180

Red Victorian B&B 1665 Haight St (bet. Cole & Belvedere Sts), Haight Ashbury 94117

Eccentric, fun, quirky, and comfortable, this 18-room bed-and-breakfast reflects all the characteristics of its hippy dippy neighbourhood. Artist Sami Sunchild is the proprietor at this turn-of-the-century property, the last surviving hotel on Haight Street, and she maintains the artistic bent: the lobby and common areas double as an art gallery. Each room is decorated in a different theme, including 'Summer of Love' and 'Flower Power'. Great value for money given room size, service, and location.

☎ 864-1978 F 863-3293 W www.redvic.com 🚌 7, 43, 66 🚇 N ◈ 18 ⬛ AE/D/DC/MC/V $ singles: from $70; doubles: from $86

Sherman House 2160 Green St (bet. Webster & Fillmore Sts), Cow Hollow 94123

Built in 1876 by the founder of the Sherman Clay Music Company, the wonderfully restored halls still echo with music. The three-storey recital hall has hosted many private concerts by the world's top musicians. The 14 rooms are fairly large and are exquisitely furnished with antiques from the Jacobean, Beidermeier, and Second Empire eras. Service is impeccable and discreet. Popular with celebs who can come and go virtually undetected. Definitely not for those in search of nightlife.

☎ 563-3600 F 563-1882 W www.theshermanhouse.com 🚌 22, 41, 45 ◈ 14 🏋 🔧 🅿 free ⬛ AE/DC/MC/V $$$$ singles & doubles from $385

more hotels

Washington Square Inn 1660 Stockton St (bet. Union & Filbert Sts), North Beach 94133

Fifteen rooms with three things in common: location, location, location. Smack in the middle of North Beach, walking distance to countless restaurants, nightspots, and attractions, this fun inn is evocative of rural France, with half the pretension and twice the sociability. Rooms are a decent size, and packed full of beautiful furnishings, from huge armoires to thoughtfully placed baskets of flowers.

☎ 981-4220 or 1-800-388-0220 F 397-7242 W www.wsisf.com 🚌 15, 41, 45 ◈ 15 🅿 free ♿ ⬛ all $$ singles & doubles from $120

Prices exclude all taxes

↓ cheaper sleeps

Handley Union Square Hotel 351 Geary St (at Powell St), Downtown 94102

An excellent choice for families, in fact the hotel itself is family run. Besides being great value for money, given its Union Square location, the Handley also has Downtown's only outdoor swimming pool – adults, fear not, the pool is not always overrun by splashing tikes. Rooms are big, if uneventful. There is also a full selection of business amenities and plenty of on-site parking.

☎ 781-7800 **F** 781-0269 **w** www.handlery.com ▤ 38 ▨ F, J, K, L, M, N 🅟 PH, PM
🌢 377 ⏸ ▤ ▧ ⌀ 🖳 🅿 ♻ 🖻 all **$$** singles: from $159; doubles: from $169

Hotel Del Sol 3100 Webster St (at Lombard St), Cow Hollow 94123

Never has 50s Americana looked so chic. In fact, it is a former motor lodge that has been revamped to be a fun, cheery hostelry with a knowing wink. As if to celebrate California's sunny disposition, the hotel is splashed in vibrant colour, has a crystal-blue outdoor swimming pool, and palm trees in the hammock-strung courtyard. While they retain their original layout, the rooms are upgraded to a current boutique-style standard; sleek, modern furniture, and all the e-culture amenities.

☎ 921-5520 or 1-877-433-5765 **F** 931-4137 **w** www.sftrips.com ▤ 28, 43
🌢 57 ⏸ ▤ ▧ ⌀ 🅿 free 🖻 AE/D/DC/MC/V **$** singles & doubles from $99

Hotel San Remo 2237 Mason St (bet. Francisco & Chestnut Sts), North Beach 94133

The rooms are bright, flowery, comfortable and old-fashioned – a little like sleeping at your grandma's house. Even so this Italianate Victorian hotel is a popular draw with budget travellers and young backpacker types who don't want to skimp on originality. What's more, it's just steps away from the heart of North Beach. The bar, shipped here from Cape Horn more than a century ago, is a fun place to hang out. Shared bathrooms!

☎ 776-8688 or 1-800-352-7366 **F** 776-2811 **w** www.sanremohotel.com ▤ 15, 30 🅟 PM
🌢 62 🖳 🅿 🖻 AE/DC/JCB/MC/V **$** singles: from $50; doubles: from $60

Willows Inn 710 14th St (at Church & Market Sts), Castro 94114

An undiscovered gem popular with gays and lesbians wanting to maintain a low profile on a lowish budget. The 12 rooms of this quiet B&B have the look of a refined European country cottage, with California Gypsy Willow furniture designed especially for each one. Guests share a bathroom, but each room has a washbasin.

☎ 431-4770 **F** 431-5295 **w** www.willowssf.com ▤ 22 ▨ F, J, K, L, M
🌢 12 ⏸ ▧ ↔ ⌀ 🅿 free 🖻 AE/DC/MC/V **$** singles: from $82; doubles: from $90

↓ away in the wine country

Auberge du Soleil 180 Rutherford Hill Rd, Rutherford 94573

When you need to escape everything – including yourself – this is a Wine Country retreat on a par with an out-of-body experience. The 'Inn of the Sun' offers 31 guest rooms and 19 suites, each private, serene, almost Zen-like, most with a fireplace and a view. Three tennis courts, a gym, a pool with sun deck, and complete spa services with skilful masseuses all help if you're ready to check out of the rat race.

☎ 1-707-963-1211 **F** 1-707-963-8764 **w** www.aubergedusoleil.com 🚗 most easily accessible by car
🌢 50 ▤ ▧ ↔ ⌀ ⌀ ⌀ 🖳 🅿 free ♻ 🖻 AE/DC/MC/V **$$$$** singles & doubles from $350

Sonoma Mission Inn & Spa 18140 Highway 12, Boyes Hot Springs 95476

This is Sonoma's only full-service resort, and it is simply the best way to get the complete Wine Country package. A spa and country club, the place was built in the 20s on the secluded site of a natural hot spring. The town has encroached a bit since, but the spa remains a private respite from the hubbub. The location is key, just an hour's drive from San Francisco and it's like the Italian countryside. Rooms are luxurious and feature all mod cons. In addition to full spa facilities, there is an 18-hole golf course and two good restaurants. This place is popular, so book early.

☎ 1-800-862-4945 [Sonoma] **F** 1-707-996-5358 **w** www.sonomamissioninn.com
🚗 most easily accessible by car 🌢 198 ▤ ↔ ⌀ ⌀ ⌀ 🖳 🅿 free ♻ 🖻 AE/DC/MC/V
$$$ singles: from $195; doubles: from $275

↓ arriving & departing

San Francisco is served by three airports –
San Francisco, Oakland, and San Jose, though
Oakland and San Jose are largely domestic.
In addition there are two coach stations, a
commuter network train station in the centre,
and the city is linked to two mainline train
stations in the East Bay by a shuttle bus service.

by air

San Francisco International Airport (SFO) receives the majority of international and domestic arrivals at its three terminals. There are excellent
Airporter bus services, door-to-door vans and taxis, and some bus/train
options into the city centre. A direct BART link is planned for Dec 2001.

transport options

Airporter bus services

45–50 mins non-stop to/from
numerous Downtown hotels.
Airport pick-up is from the
blue columns on the central
island outside the lower
levels of all terminals.

🕐 6.30am–11.30pm,
every 30 minutes.

💺 $10

☎ 495-8404

door-to-door vans

30 mins–1 hour to/from
Downtown. A number of van
services will drop off/pick up
at up to 3 addresses. Airport
pick-up is from the central
island outside the upper
levels of all terminals. Check
when it is leaving, how many
addresses it is stopping at,
and the exact price.

🕐 see below.

💺 $10–$15 per person

Door-to-Door Airport Express
🕐 5am–11pm ☎ 775-5121

Lorrie's Airport Service
🕐 5.30am–11.30pm
☎ 334-9000
Quake City Shuttle
🕐 24 hours ☎ 777-4899
Supper Shuttle
🕐 24 hours ☎ 558-8500

taxis

30–45 minutes to/from
Downtown. Airport pick up is
at yellow columns on central
island outside baggage claim
levels in all terminals.

🕐 24 hours.

💺 $32–$40 (metered)
plus 15% tip

Limo 2000
☎ 1-650-737-8500
Luxor Cab Co
☎ 1-650-344-1414
All New Yellow Cab Co
☎ 1-800-919-2227

local buses & BART

SamTrans buses 292 and KX
connect SFO to the Transbay
Terminal in SoMa. SamTrans
buses BX and 193 connect SFO

to Colma and Daly City BART
stations respectively. Then
BART to SF. No luggage is
allowed on board the KX.
💺 buses $1–$3
💺 BART $2.10–$2.25
SamTrans ☎ 1-800-660-4287
BART ☎ 989-2278

shuttle bus & CalTrain

SFO shuttle bus to/from Mill-
brae station, then CalTrain to/
from CalTrain Depot in SoMa.
💺 free & $2
SFO Shuttle bus
☎ 1-800-736-2008
CalTrain ☎ 1-800-660-4287

☎ useful numbers

**Airport Ground Transportation
Info** 1-800-736-2008
**Airport Info Booth, International
Terminal** 1-650-876-7880
British Airways 1-800-247-9297
Marriott Hotel 1-650-692-910
Virgin Atlantic 1-800-862-8621
SF Airport Hilton 1-800-445-8667
**Oakland International Airport
Visitors Service** 1-510-577-4015
**San Jose International Airport
Information** 1-408-277-4759

by rail

The CalTrain rail system links San Francisco to the South Bay and Silicon
Valley. For all other California and out-of-state destinations, trains leave
from either Oakland or Emeryville Amtrak stations in the East Bay.

train essentials

▶ Call CalTrain or Amtrak for
information on fares and
special offers.

▶ CalTrain and Amtrak tickets
can be booked by credit card
(or with cash on collection)
using their phone or online
reservation system.

▶ The San Francisco CalTrain
station is in SoMa near the 4th
& King Streets Muni Metro
station. Taxis and buses are
also available.

▶ A free shuttle service links
the two East Bay Amtrak stations to Downtown.

▶ North American (Canada
and USA) and USA rail passes
are available offering unlimited
stops for up to 30 days of
travel. For details call Amtrak.

▶ The California Zephyr runs
from San Francisco to Chicago,
reputedly one of the most
beautiful train journeys in the
US. The Coast Starlight runs
in part along the coast from
LA to Seattle via SF (Emeryville). Call Amtrak for details.
[→59 for more information
on day trip destinations].

useful numbers &
addresses

Amtrak Ticket Office
The Ferry Building
Market Street (at Embarcadero)
☎ 1-800-872-7245
w www.amtrak.com
Emeryville Amtrak Station
5885 Landregan Street (at Haruff
St), Emeryville ☎ 1-510-450-1080
Oakland Amtrak Station
245 2nd Street
(at Broadway), Oakland
☎ 1-510-238-4306
San Francisco CalTrain Station
700 4th Street (at King St)
☎ 495-1659 or 1-800-660-4287

transport

→ more transport

by coach

The Greyhound Bus company runs a nationwide service linking all the major cities and some smaller towns. Green Tortoise Adventure Travel – an alternative coach company – runs a less comprehensive service covering the West Coast and special adventure trips. Coaches from both companies operate from SoMa's Transbay Terminal.

coach essentials

▸ It is not possible to make reservations on Greyhound coaches. Passengers are treated on a first-come-first-served basis and you are advised to purchase tickets (at the Transbay Terminal) at least one hour before departure.

▸ The Greyhound Ameripass provides unlimited travel for between seven and 60 days of consecutive travel.

▸ Reservations and confirmations are necessary for Green Tortoise coaches, but walk-ons are possible, especially for short trips. Passengers pay the driver on departure with cash or travellers' cheques only.

▸ Ticket prices for both coach companies are similar. An adult return to Los Angeles is $69–$70, and to Santa Cruz $20.

▸ Green Tortoise Adventure Travel destinations include Yosemite, the Northern California Loop, the Grand Canyon, Baja California, and the Southern National Parks. Coaches are equipped with bunks and (outdoor) cooking facilities.

useful numbers

Greyhound Bus Company
☎ 1-800-231-2222
w www.greyhound.com
Green Tortoise Adventure Travel
494 Broadway (at Kearny St)
☎ 956-7500
w www.greentortoise.com
Transbay Terminal
425 Mission Street (at 1st St)
☎ 495-1659

at the wheel

You won't need a car in central San Francisco, as it is easy to get around on foot and public transport is good. Traffic can be heavy especially at peak times (7–9am and 5–7pm Mon–Fri), above all on the bridges, and the one-way system in the city centre can be frustrating. A car is, however, just about essential for many of the best day trips [→58–67] outside the city.

car hire

▸ Car rental shuttles for most companies at the airport depart from the central island outside the upper level of all terminals. Commuter traffic can make the journey into the city centre a long one.

▸ Shop around for the best car hire deals. You will get better prices if you book at least one week in advance. Summer weekly rates are between $139 and $349.

▸ Check for discounts. Internet reservations are often cheaper. Many airlines and credit card companies offer special deals.

▸ All companies charge sales tax and a vehicle licensing fee surcharge on top of the quoted price. Many companies offer unlimited mileage, others charge extra per mile over a certain number of miles. Check other surcharges.

▸ You will need to be over 25 and in possession of a valid driver's licence and credit card (some accept a cash deposit).

▸ Check you have been provided with a full tank of gas/petrol and make a note of all scratches etc on the car before departure. Refill the tank yourself before you return the car to avoid steep refill charges.

▸ Most rental cars will be automatic.

car hire numbers

Avis ☎ 1-800-831-2847 (airport and city centre)
Bob Leech Auto Rental
☎ 1-800-325-1240 (well-priced independent at airport).
Budget ☎ 1-800-527-0700 (airport and city centre)
City Rent A Car ☎ 861-1312 (city centre, airport pick-ups)
Hertz ☎ 1-800-654-3131 (airport and city centre – includes sports cars)
Payless ☎ 1-650-737-6134 (airport)
Rent-a-Wreck ☎ 1-800-732-7368 (airport and city centre – older cars and good prices)
Specialty Car Rental
☎ 1-800-400-8412 (city centre, airport pick-ups – includes sports cars)

rules of the road

▸ Drive on the right.

▸ A flashing red light (found along cable car and streetcar routes) means stop and proceed when it is safe.

▸ Pedestrians have the right-of-way at corners and cross-walks.

▸ A right turn can be made at a red light – after you have yielded to pedestrians/vehicles – except where there is a sign 'No turn on red' or a red arrow.

▸ At intersections marked by four-way STOP signs, the car that arrived first has priority.

▸ Safety belts are compulsory in front and rear seats.

▸ The speed limit in central San Francisco is 25mph.

parking

▸ Finding an on-street parking place can be problematic. There are multi-storey car parks around Union Square (these can be expensive), as well as a number of cheaper open-air lots in SoMa. Many Downtown hotels and restaurants have pricey valet parking.

▸ Parking meters take quarters ($0.25). Maximum stay and hourly cost vary.

▸ Ticketing ($20–$275) and towing ($130 plus hefty storage charges after four hours) are very common. If you are towed call City Tow ☎ 621-8605.

▸ Check for street signs which give details of parking conditions. You can usually park for up to two hours in permit only areas without a permit. Check for coloured curbs: red means no stopping; blue: disabled; yellow: commercial loading; green: ten-minute parking. Never park in front of a fire hydrant.

▸ When parking downhill turn the front wheels into the curb. When parking uphill, turn the front wheels away from the curb and roll the car back until the rear of one front wheel touches it. Failure to curb your wheels will result in a ticket.

▸ Always park facing the same direction as the traffic.

↓ out & about

The only real problem with getting out and about in San Francisco is making the decision on just how to do it – you are spoilt for choice. Most of the city is accessible by foot, bike, or various forms of public transport (see over), making it easy to dispense with the cost of hiring a car. Explore on foot; hire a bike; hop on a cable car; relax on a ferry; negotiate the Muni Metro and bus system; venture on the BART, or, if all else fails, do it the easy way and hail a taxi.

general information

public transport

The subway-to-surface metro system, historic streetcars, diesel buses, electric trolley buses, and famous cable cars are collectively known as Muni. An additional underground train system, BART, links the city with the East Bay and the Northern Peninsula. Muni street & transit maps are available in stores for $2.

travel passes & tickets

The best deal is the Muni Passport which allows unlimited travel on metro, buses, and cable cars for one ($6), three ($10), or seven ($15) days of consecutive travel. It also entitles you to discounts at various museums and on ferry tours. An ongoing weekly Muni pass is $9, but cable cars cost an additional $1 per journey, while a $35 monthly pass covers all Muni (including cable cars), as well as BART and CalTrain within the city. These passes are not for sale at Muni/BART stations, but in various shops and outlets, including the cable car ticket booths at Powell & Market and Hyde & Beach in Victorian Park. You must have a valid ticket or pass when travelling and may be required to show it to an inspector; failure to do so can result in a fine. ID is required for youth, senior, and disabled concessions.
Muni Information ☎ 673-6864

disabled travellers

Many buses and stations are equipped with Braille and raised letter identification signage. There is also a talking timetable ☎ 923-6336. All underground stations have lifts – check in advance that these are functioning. The attendant will assist with ticket purchase and will open the gate at the ticket barriers on request. All Metro streetcars and BART trains are wheelchair accessible from underground stations; surface stations vary, so call the information line. Certain buses have 'kneelers' which lower the front of the bus to aid those who have difficulty with steps. For information on access to public transport call the Disabled Access Information Line ☎ 923-6142.

kids

Children under 5 generally travel free. Those aged 5–12 (17 on Muni) qualify for youth discounts but may need to show proof of date of birth.

walking

Central San Francisco is easily negotiated on foot and it is a good idea to spend your first day here doing just that. Some of the hills, however, are very, very steep, so getting from A to B may take longer than you anticipated. At corners or intersections with STOP signs, pedestrians have the right of way: all vehicles have to come to a complete stop and cannot proceed until you have crossed. Be cautious, however, as motorists and pedestrians don't always obey the rules.
For details on the many organized free walking tours around the city, contact:
City Guides ☎ 557-4266
w www.wenet.net/users/jhum

transport

cycling & motorcycling

bicycle/motorcycle essentials

▸ Cycling and motorcycling are good ways to get around the city and especially to explore Golden Gate Park [→78], the Presidio [→78], and Marin County [→60–61].
▸ Traffic is heavy in the city centre and there are few bicycle lanes.
▸ Bicycles are permitted on certain BART and CalTrain trains and on a handful of buses (check in advance), but not on Muni Metro.
▸ A shuttle bus for cyclists operates on the Bay Bridge at commute times. For details call ☎ 1-510-286-0876.
▸ When cycling at night you must by law display a white headlight and a red rear light.

▸ Motorcyle helmets are required by law.
▸ Bicycles can be hired from $5 an hour, $25 a day, and $125 a week; scooters from $50 a day; motorcycles between $75–$150 a day depending on size. Your credit card details will be taken as deposit and ID will be required.
▸ Most rental companies will also rent helmets, bags etc and supply maps and route suggestions.
▸ For suggested rides in and around San Francisco, check out w www.bayinsider.com/recreation/cycling/rides
▸ [→144 for rules of the road].

hire outlets

Adventure Bicycle Company
968 Columbus Avenue
(bet. Lombard & Chestnut Sts)
☎ 771-8735
American Bike Rental
2715 Hyde Street (at North Point St) ☎ 931-0234
Avenue Cyclery
756 Stanyan Street (at Waller St)
☎ 387-3155
Eagle Rider Motorcycle Rental (Harleys)
1060 Bryant Street (bet. 8th & 9th Sts) ☎ 503-1900
Park Cyclery
1794 Waller Street (at Stanyan St)
☎ 221-3777

bicycle tours

For organized bicycle tours around the city and all over northern California, contact:
Wheel Escapes ☎ 586-2377
w www.wheelescapes.com

→ more transport

transport options	◐	💲
🚌 Muni buses		
Muni buses include diesel and trolley buses. Their distinctive white and orange colours are easy to spot. Those bearing X, AX, and BX usually run only during peak hours. Owl Service buses run on a reduced schedule through the night. There are nine lines. Phone Muni for more information.	5–1am daily. Busy routes run every 5–10 mins during peak hours. Owl Service buses run 1–5am daily, every 30 mins.	$1: this includes a transfer ticket allowing two additional boardings within 90 minutes in any direction. Youth, seniors, and disabled $0.35. You can also buy ten Muni tokens (with transfers) for $8.
🚋 Muni Metro		
These subway to surface streetcars run on six lines: F (Market); J (Church); K (Ingleside); L (Taraval); M (Oceanview); and N (Judah). Five of them (J, K, L, M, and N) run underground along Market Street making the same stops as BART (at Embarcadero, Montgomery St, Powell St and Civic Center). After the Van Ness stop, they diverge travelling under- and overground: J goes via Church Street through Castro and Noe Valley, N through Sunset to Ocean Beach. K, L, and M continue southwest along Market Street. The N also operates along the Embarcadero between Market Street and the CalTrain Depot. The historic route F runs colourful vintage streetcars from around the world overground along Market Street from First Street to Castro Street.	5am–midnight Mon–Fri; 8am–midnight Sat & Sun (to 8pm Sun). Every 6–20 mins.	$1 (see above)
🚋 Muni cable cars		
SF's 125 year-old cable cars run on three routes: **Powell-Hyde**: from Powell Street (at Market St) to Victorian Park (at Hyde & Beach Sts); **Powell-Mason**: from Powell Street (at Market St) to Bay (at Taylor St); **California**: from California Street (at Market St) to Van Ness Avenue (at California St).	6–12.30am daily. Approx every 10 mins.	$2, or $1 for seniors/ at certain times.
Ⓑ BART (Bay Area Rapid Transport)		
BART is an underground/overground train system with five lines linking the city, the East Bay, and the Northern Peninsula. BART provides a fast and efficient service to Berkeley, Oakland, and Oakland airport and is a good way to avoid traffic jams on the Bay Bridge. The BART makes stops at Embarcadero, Montgomery Street, Powell Street, Civic Center, and 16th and 24th Streets in the Mission.	4am–midnight Mon–Fri, 6am–midnight Sat, 8am–midnight Sun/hols. Check on the website or through the info number for train frequency to your destination.	The minimum single fare is around $1.10 and the maximum around $4.
🚕 taxis		
Yellow taxis don't tend to cruise the streets much except in busy areas such as the Castro and North Beach, so it is better to order one by phone – well in advance (particularly if calling from a residential area) as they can take time to arrive. There are no taxi ranks, but there are usually taxis in front of major hotels.	24 hours	Prices vary but usually average about $2 per mile.
⛴ ferries		
The Blue & Gold Fleet takes passengers on bay cruises and to Alcatraz, Angel Island, Tiburon, and Sausalito. Ferries depart from Piers 39 (bay cruise) and 41 (all others) at Fisherman's Wharf. Golden Gate Ferries go to Sausalito from the Ferry Building on Embarcadero at Market Street. The Red & White Fleet offers tours of the bay. Ferries depart from Pier 43.5 at Fisherman's Wharf. The Blue & Gold and Red & White Fleets also offer dinner package tours and boat/coach tours of Marin County, the Wine Country, Carmel, and Monterey [→59].	For departure times and frequency contact the individual companies.	Prices listed are adult returns: Blue & Gold Fleet: Alcatraz $12.25; Angel Island $11; Sausalito/ Tiburon $12; tour of the bay $17. Golden Gate Ferries: Sausalito $9.60. Red & White Fleet: tour of the bay $17.

transport

☎	❗
Muni Information provides advice on what number buses/trains to take 673-6864 **Muni Lost & Found** 923-6168 [→59, 144 for buses out of SF]	► If there is no bus shelter marking a stop, there will be pole signs or yellow bands on adjacent utility poles. ► Bus numbers and names are displayed on the front and sides of the vehicle. ► You will need exact change for the fare boxes on board, although they do accept single dollar bills as well as coins. ► Avoid travelling at rush hour if you can (7–9am and 5–7pm Mon–Fri): the system gets very crowded and there are sometimes delays. ► Smoking is not permitted.
(see above)	► The Downtown underground stations are shared between Muni Metro and BART, but have separate platforms, so ensure you enter the right part of the system. It is usually well signposted. ► To access the Muni Metro platforms insert your pass or money (in exchange for a ticket) into the ticket barrier. On exiting, simply push the turnstile. ► The barriers only accept exact fare coins for tickets, but there are always change machines nearby. ► The attendants in the booths cannot provide tickets or change but will offer help and information. ► Ensure you know what line your destination is on, as streetcars are announced by their name only; stops en route are not given. ► The platforms are much longer than the streetcars, so follow the crowds who usually seem to know where the train is going to stop. ► Avoid travelling at rush hour (7–9am and 5–7pm Mon–Fri). ► Smoking is not permitted.
(see above)	► There are usually huge queues at Powell Street, while the California line is less crowded. ► To avoid the crowds go for an early morning or evening ride. ► Purchase tickets on board or at the ticket booths (Powell at Market or Hyde at Beach in Victorian Park). ► Transfers are neither issued or accepted on cable cars. ► Smoking is not permitted.
BART San Francisco 989-2278 **w** www.bart.org **BART Lost & Found:** 1-510-464-7090	► Tickets are available from ticket machines (located in each station) which also display fare charts. It is best to have the exact fare as some machines won't give change, while others only provide up to $4.95 in change. There should be change machines nearby. Charge-a-Ticket machines accept credit cards, but there is a minimum $20 purchase. ► You will need to insert your ticket in the ticket gate on entering and leaving the BART station. ► Smoking, eating, and drinking are forbidden on trains or at stations. ► Bikes are allowed on trains except at certain times of day (usually rush hour). Check in advance. ► Avoid travelling at rush hour (7–9am and 5–7pm Mon–Fri).
Luxor Cab Co 282-4141 **Veterans Taxicab Co** 552-1300 **Yellow Cab Co-operative** 626-2345	► Hailing a taxi may be easier from a nearby hotel via the doorman. ► Taxis tend to arrive promptly for airport trips. ► There are usually a number of taxis around the Transbay Terminal, CalTrain Depot, and Ferry Building. ► Your taxi should display licence details. ► All taxi fares are metered. A 15% tip is expected.
Blue & Gold Fleet 705-5555 **Golden Gate Ferries** 923-2000 **Red & White Fleet** 673-2900	► Don't be too despondent if it is foggy: the fogs often burn off by lunch time, and the weather can sometimes be better at your destination – for example in Sausalito – than in the city itself. ► For departure times and frequency, contact the individual companies. ► The ferries can get very booked up and the ticket office queues can be huge, particularly for Alcatraz – it is wisest to book in advance by phone with a credit card.

→back cover and sheet map for transport options around San Francisco

bare essentials

admission charges

Admission charges vary but expect to pay $7.50 for a ticket to a major museum [see individual listings for prices →72–79]. Most museums are free (and busy!) once a month. There are also passes allowing you to visit many attractions at a discount [→68–69]. Among these are CityPass ($27.75), and Golden Gate Park Explorer Pass ($14) which can both be purchased from any participating attraction. A Muni Travel Passport [→145] also entitles you to some discounts.

CityPass ☎ 1-800-824-4795 **w** www.citypass.net
Golden Gate Explorer Pass ☎ 750-7145
Muni Passport Info Line ☎ 923-6050

banks

Banks usually offer a better exchange rate than bureaux de change [→bureaux de change]. Most will cash US dollar travellers' cheques if you have photo ID [→travellers' cheques], but few will exchange hard foreign currency. Opening hours are usually 9am–6pm Mon–Fri, but outside the Downtown area banks may close as early as 3pm. Banks are closed on public holidays. Most banks and some shops have cashpoint machines (ATMs) where you can obtain cash [→credit & debit cards]. Check ATM rates.

Bank of America has a foreign exchange branch in the *International Terminal, SF Airport* ☎ 1-650-742-8080 ◑ 7am–11pm daily.
Another branch is at 1 Powell St (at Market St) ☎ 953-5102 ◑ 9am–6pm Mon–Sat (to 2pm Sat).
Wells Fargo Bank will cash travellers' cheques 1 Montgomery Street (at Market St) ☎ 396-7152 ◑ 9am–6pm Mon–Fri.

Western Union handles international money transfers ☎ 1-800-325-6000 ◑ 24 hours.

bars

Opening times vary, but are usually from mid-morning to 2am (it is illegal to sell alcohol after this time, even in clubs), with last orders around 1.30am. There might be an entrance fee if there is live music. Tip at bars – $1 per drink is the norm, 15% if you are buying a round. The legal age for entering a bar and buying an alcoholic drink is 21. Some places will not sell alcohol to anyone who looks under 30, so carry photo ID. Smoking is not allowed in bars.

bureaux de change

Check commission and minimum charges before exchanging money and cashing travellers' cheques [→travellers' cheques] as rates vary. For changing money out of banking hours:
American Express 333 Jefferson St (at Jones St) ☎ 775-0240 ◑ Jun–Sep: 10am–9pm daily; Oct–May: 10am–6pm daily (to 9pm Fri–Sat, from 11am Sun).
Thomas Cook Foreign Exchange 75 Geary Street (at Grant St) ☎ 362-3453 ◑ 9am–5pm Mon–Fri; 10am–4pm Sat.

children

Transport: children under 5 travel free on most city transport systems; older children are entitled to discounts [→145].
Admission prices: there are discounts for children (6–11) and youths (12–17). Children 5 and under are often free, except at kids' venues.
Restaurants & bars: most sizeable restaurants provide seating and special menus for children.
Hotels: most hotels will allow children under

12, often under 18, to share their parents' room at no extra charge. Many provide cots or 'cribs', for a fee – reserve them in advance. Baby-sitters can be arranged.
Baby changing: many shops, restaurants, and museums have baby changing facilities.
Childminders: contact *Children's Council of San Francisco* ☎ 243-0700 for a list of registered baby-sitting agencies.
Listings: children's activities are listed in the weekly *Bay Guardian* and Sunday *Chronicle*'s 'Pink Section', and in the monthly *Bay Area Parent* among others.

clubs

Clubbing hours are 11pm–2am (to 3–4am on the weekend). No alcohol is served after 2am.
Admission prices depend on the night of the week. As a rule, bigger clubs charge about $10, whereas local hot spots charge decidedly less. Very few clubs accept credit cards.
Dress codes vary, but are almost always relaxed.
Club listings can be found in the 'Pink Section' of the Sunday *Chronicle*, in SF's free newspapers, *The SF Weekly* and *The SF Bay Guardian*, and the free gay zines *Odyssey* and *Cream Puff*. Also, check out local websites **w** www.blasto.com and **w** www.citysearch.com
Drink prices differ greatly from club to club, and sometimes even from the person served before you. At SF clubs, the bartender rules the house, so be polite and tip well.
Age restrictions: most clubs are over 21 only – check by calling the venue.

conversions

Clothing	Women's				Men's			
US	6	10	14	16	36	40	44	46
British	8	12	16	18	36	40	44	46
European	36	40	44	46	46	50	54	56

Shoes	Women's				Men's			
US	5	6	7	8	7	8	9	10
British	4	5	6	7	6	7	8	9
European	37	38	39	40	40	42	43	44

courier services

The US post office offers two courier services: Global Priority Mail (4–5 day delivery) and Express Mail (2–3 day delivery) [→postal services]. Services are also offered by:
Federal Express ☎ 1-800-225-5345
UPS ☎ 1-800-782-7892

credit & debit cards

Credit cards are a near essential item for the traveller to the US. Hotels, car hire companies, etc often require one for security even if you pay the bill in cash or travellers' cheques. American Express, Diners Club, Discovery, Japanese Credit Bureau, MasterCard, and Visa are widely accepted. You can also use a credit or debit card to withdraw cash from any ATM (cashpoint machine) displaying your credit card symbol, or to buy dollars in a bank. Check rates with your bank or card company in advance – it is often cheaper to use a debit (cashpoint) card rather than a credit card to withdraw cash from ATMs. To report lost or stolen cards:
American Express ☎ 1-800-992-3404
Diners Club ☎ 1-800-234-6377
Discovery ☎ 1-800-347-2683
JCB ☎ 1-800-522-8788
MasterCard ☎ 1-800-307-7309
Visa ☎ 1-800-336-8472

currency

The United States dollar ($) is made up of 100 cents. There are $1, $5, $10, $20, $50, and $100 'bills' (notes). There are also bronze pennies (1c) and nickels (5c), dimes (10c), and quarters (25c) all of which are silver-coloured.

customs

Foreigners will be asked to fill in a customs declaration form during the flight. Many foodstuffs and all seeds and plants are prohibited.

dentists

Free dental treatment is not available, so keep receipts for insurance claims.
San Francisco Dental Office offers a 24-hour emergency service. *Suite 323, 131 Steuart Street (bet. Mission & Howard Sts)* ☎ *777-5115*
San Francisco Dental Society Referral Service offers a 24-hour referral service ☎ *421-1435*

disabled visitors

General information on travelling to San Francisco and northern California can be found at **w** www.accessnca.com
Hire cars: for a good selection of cars with hand controls contact:
Avis ☎ *1-800-331-1212*
Hertz ☎ *1-800-654-3131*
Disability Access Co-ordinator: (access to public buildings) ☎ *558-4000*
Hotels: *The Lodging Guide, San Francisco* publishes a survey on hotel accessibility available from the visitors centre [→tourist information].
Parking: Disabled parking spots are marked by blue signs and kerbs. For a temporary parking permit ($6) contact the DMV ☎ *557-1179*
Public Transport: contact Muni for access information and a copy of the *Muni Access Guide.*
Muni ☎ *923-6142*
BART ☎ *992-2278*
Taxis: Paratransit Taxi Service offers a discount service geared towards the disabled ☎ *543-9651*

driving

You can drive in the US with an overseas driving licence. Car hire firms often impose age restrictions and will only hire to 25+ year olds. [→144]

duty free

Duty free allowances on entering the US are 200 cigarettes, 100 non-Cuban cigars, 1 litre of alcohol, and gifts up to $400 in value. Check at return destination on tax-free limits for goods bought in the US.

earthquakes

Information on what to do in an earthquake can be found in the *Pacific Bell White Pages* or at the US Geological Survey website (**w** www.quake.wr.usgs.gov/). In the unlikely event of an earthquake, take cover under a sturdy piece of furniture. Do not use stairs or lifts while the building is shaking. If outside, stay away from buildings, trees, lights, and power lines.

electricity

Mains electricity is supplied at 115–120 volts. UK/European 220-volt appliances need an adaptor with universal voltage, available from department stores. Stereos and computer equipment will also need transformers.

email & internet

Internet cafés allow you to surf the net and may also offer office facilities. Most will help you set up a hotmail account to access emails.

Club i *850 Folsom Street (bet. 4th & 5th Sts)* ☎ *777-2582* ⌧ *free with food* ◑ *7am–midnight Mon–Sat (to 2am Fri & Sat); 10am–10pm Sun.*
Seattle Street Coffee *456 Geary St (bet. Mason & Taylor Sts)* ☎ *922-4566* ⌧ *$10/hour* ◑ *6.30am–11pm daily.*
Seven01 Multimedia Café *701 Mission St (at 3rd St)* ☎ *243-0930* ⌧ *free with food or a museum ticket* ◑ *11am–8pm Tue–Sun (to 5pm Tue).*
Local libraries offer free Internet access for a limited time, usually 15 minutes [→125].

embassies & consulates

Australian Consulate General
1 Bush St (bet. Battery & Market Sts) ☎ *362-6160*
British Consulate General
Suite 580, 1 Sansome St (at Sutter St) ☎ *981-3030*
Canadian Consulate General
555 Montgomery Street, Suite 1288 (bet. Clay & Sacramento Sts) ☎ *834-3180*
Consulate General of Ireland
Suite 3830, 44 Montgomery Street (bet. Post & Sutter Sts) ☎ *392-4214*
New Zealand Consulate General
1 Maritime Plaza (at Clay & Fillmore Sts) ☎ *399-1255*
South African Consulate General
Los Angeles ☎ *1-310-657-9200*

emergencies & medical matters

Call ☎ *911* for fire, police, and ambulance (24 hours – emergencies only). For emergency medical attention, dial 911 or go to the nearest Emergency Room (ER), where you will be asked for your insurance and/or payment details [→insurance]. Hospitals with ERs include:

California Pacific Medical Center *2333 Buchanan St (at Washington St)* ☎ *923-3333*
Davies Medical Center *Castro & Divisadero Streets (at Duboce Ave)* ☎ *565-6060*
Saint Francis Memorial Hospital *900 Hyde Street (bet. Pine & Bush Sts)* ☎ *353-6300*
SF General Hospital *1001 Potrero Avenue (at 23rd St)* ☎ *206-8111*
UCSF Mount Zion Medical Center *1600 Divisadero St (at Sutter St)* ☎ *885-7520*
For non-emergency treatment, your hotel may be able to recommend a doctor.

help & advice lines

AIDS Hotline ☎ *1-800-590-2437*
Alcoholics Anonymous ☎ *621-1326*
Better Business Bureau gives information on consumer protection ☎ *243-9999*
Drug Abuse & Crisis Intervention ☎ *1-800-234-0246*
Gay-Lesbian Switchboard & Counseling Services ☎ *1-510-841-6224*
Rape Crisis Center ☎ *647-7273*
Suicide Prevention ☎ *781-0500*

hotels

Charges: expect to pay 14% tax on the price of your room. Do try to negotiate the price, or book through your travel agent or airline as they may get a better rate. There may be an additional charge for housekeeping ($5–10), depending on length of stay.
Check-out time is usually midday.
Reservations are particularly recommended between June and October. A deposit equal to one night's stay allows you to arrive after 6pm. Always determine the hotel's cancellation and refund policies before making a booking.
SF Visitors Bureau offers a toll-free hotel reservations line and an online hotel reservation system ☎ *1-888-782-9673*
w www.sfvisitor.org

practical information

➔ more practical information

immigration visas & entry requirements

Control on entry to the US is strict. Visa requirements vary, so check with the US Embassy before you go. Canada, Australia, New Zealand, the UK, Ireland, and most Western European countries do not need a visa under the 90-day 'visa-waiver' scheme. All that is required is a passport valid for six months from your entry date. During the flight to the United States you will have to complete a form to present to immigration control on arrival. Part of this form will be attached to your passport, and you will need to show it on departure. No vaccinations are required.

insurance

Comprehensive medical insurance is a must as there is no free treatment and costs are high.

left luggage
[→146–147]

lost property

Report all lost items to the police to validate insurance claims [→police]. Lost passports should also be reported to your consulate [→embassies & consulates]. For items lost in airports, taxis, or on public transport, contact the relevant company [→transport].

maps

The *Muni Street & Transit Map* ($2) is useful, as is GM Johnson's *Greater San Francisco Map Book* ($8.95) which combines detailed street city maps with coverage of areas of interest south of the city. The SF Visitors Bureau and many hotels and shopping malls provide free maps.

measurements

The imperial system is used.

imperial : metric	metric : imperial
1 inch = 2.5 cm	1 mm = 0.04 inch
1 foot = 30 cm	1 cm = 0.4 inch
1 mile = 1.6 km	1 m = 3.3 ft
1 ounce = 28 g	1 km = 0.6 mile
1 pound = 454 g	1 g = 0.04 oz
1 pint = 0.6 l	1 l = 0.26 (US) gallon
1 (US) gallon = 3.8 l	1 l = 0.22 (UK) gallon

medicine & chemists

Many medicines are available only on prescription, including some things that can be bought over the counter in other countries. Other medicines can be bought at chemists, drugstores, or pharmacies, and supermarkets. Note that drug names and brand names are often completely different in the US from those in other English-speaking countries. Keep all receipts for insurance claims. 24-hour chemists include
Walgreens ☎ 1-800-925-4733
498 Castro Street (at 18th St) ☎ 861-3136
3201 Divisadero St (at Lombard St) ☎ 931-6417
Rite Aid 5280 Geary Boulevard (bet. 16th & 17th Sts) ☎ 668-2041

newspapers & listings magazines
[→125]

office & business services

Most hotels have business facilities. If not, Kinko's offers photocopying, printing, scanning, laminating, binding, etc, as well as PC and Mac rental. There are branches all over the city, including one Downtown at 201 Sacramento Street (at Davis St) ☎ 834-0240 ◑ 24 hours. [→email & Internet]

opticians

Site for Sore Eyes offers prescription glasses in one hour, eye tests, or exams:
901 Market Street (at 5th St) ☎ 495-2020
◑ 9am–7.30pm Mon–Sat; 11am–5.30pm Sun.
UCSF offers contact lenses, and laser correction:
400 Parnassus Ave (at Stanyan St) ☎ 476-3700

photography

Discount Camera offers new and used equipment, on-site photo lab, repair, and rental.
33 Kearny St (bet. Post & Market Sts) ☎ 392-1100
◑ 8.30am–6.30pm Mon–Sat; 9.30am–6pm Sun.

police

In an emergency dial ☎ 911. To contact the police about a crime that has already taken place ☎ 553-0123, or check the telephone directory's government pages for the number of your local police station.
Central Police Station 766 Vallejo Street
(at Stockton St) ☎ 553-1532

postal services

To send a postcard outside the US, you'll need a 50¢ stamp, while 60¢ will cover the basic international letter rate. The postboxes are dark blue: pull the handle down to use.

Post offices ◑ 9am–5.30pm Mon–Fri, some open on Saturday mornings.

The General Post Office offers 30-day poste restante services on post marked with your name and 'General Delivery'. You will need to show photo ID on collection.
450 Golden Gate Avenue (at Larkin & Polk Sts)
☎ 1-800-275-8777 (general enquiries)
There is a post office in the basement of Macy's
170 O'Farrell Street (at Stockton St) ☎ 397-3333

public holidays

New Year's Day – 1 Jan
Martin Luther King Day – 3rd Monday in Jan
President's Day – 3rd Monday in Feb
Easter Monday – (bet. Mar & Apr)
Memorial Day – last Monday in May
Independence Day – 4 July
Labor Day – 1st Monday in Sep
Columbus Day – 2nd Monday in Oct
Election Day – 1st Tuesday in Nov
Veterans Day – 11 Nov
Thanksgiving – 4th Thursday in Nov
Christmas Day – 25 Dec

religion

Baptist: Baptist Hamilton Square Church
☎ 673-8586; Buddhist: Buddhist Church of SF
☎ 776-3158; Evangelical: SF Evangelical Free Church ☎ 391-0699; Jewish: Beyt Tikkun, SF Jewish Community Center ☎ 575-1432;
Muslim: Islamic Society of SF, Masjid Darusalam ☎ 863-7997; Roman Catholic: Old Saint Mary's Cathedral ☎ 288-3800

restaurants

Reservations: recommended for well-known and well-reviewed restaurants, many of which can be booked up for weeks in advance.
Prices: vary enormously. On the whole, eating out is cheaper than in other major cities. Credit cards are accepted in most of the medium/large restaurants.
Tax & tipping: a sales tax of 8.5% will be added to your bill. A minimum 15% tip is expected. For easy calculation, double the sales tax.
Opening times: lunch is served from 11am–2.30pm and dinner from 6–10pm. Some places stay open from mid-morning to the evening.

safety

Crime levels in San Francisco are fairly low. Take the usual precautions when visiting: don't carry passports or much cash and don't leave valuables on show in a car. Be careful at night in the Tenderloin, 6th and 7th Streets in SoMa, and 16th and Mission Streets in the Mission.

shopping

Opening times vary, but are usually 10am–6pm and malls stay open until around 8pm. Many shops are open 7 days a week (Sunday hours may be shorter), and some of the super-markets and pharmacies stay open 24 hours a day [→medicine & chemists].
Payment can be made in US dollars, travellers' cheques, or by credit card. A discount may be offered or negotiated for cash purchases.
Tax & export [→taxes]
Returns stores do not have to offer refunds/exchanges. Each store has its own policy on both returns and guarantees.
Sales are in November and June, but some stores have a permanent sale rail. Keep an eye on the newspapers for details of current or upcoming sales.

smoking

Smoking is forbidden in public spaces including bars, restaurants, and cafés, but often permitted on restaurant/hotel terraces or in gardens.

students

Student discounts are available on some travel systems, at museums, etc with identification. The most widely accepted form of ID is the International Student Identity Card. In SF, the card is available from: **STA Travel**, *51 Grant Avenue (bet. Grant & Kearny Sts)* ☎ 391-8407 ◑ 9am–7pm Mon–Sat. ⑤ $20

taxes

An 8.5% sales tax is levied on most purchases (food bought in shops rather than restaurants is one exception). Hotel taxes are 14%.

telephoning

Phone sounds: continuous tone = ready to dial; repeated short beeps = engaged; 'beep beep…beep beep…beep beep' = ringing tone.
Payphones accept coins. There is a flat fee of $0.35 for all local calls.
Phonecards provide a number to dial on a touch-tone phone which allows you to charge a call to your card.
International Phonecards, available from convenience stores, are easy to use, and allow you to call home at a fraction of the prices charged by hotels. Call the freephone number on the card and tap in the PIN number provided to set up a temporary account.
Private phone rates vary – there are often three rates – the day rate, and the cheaper evening and night/weekend rates.
Freephone 800 numbers are free of charge.
Mobile phones can be rented by the day or week. Some firms charge for both equipment and calls, others just (higher rates) for the calls. Local calls start at around $1.45 per minute, international calls at around $2.50.
Auto Symphony Cellular Phone Rentals
International Terminal, SF Airport
☎ 1-650-866-3200
Action Cellular Rent a Phone *99 Osgood Place (bet. Pacific & Broadway Sts)* ☎ 929-0400
Area codes: San Francisco and North Bay
☎ 415; East Bay ☎ 510; South Bay ☎ 650. Always dial a 1 in front of the area code.

From July 2000, all San Francisco telephone numbers become 11-digit numbers. Locally dialled numbers (given as seven digits in this guide) must therefore be prefixed by the 1-415 area code (eg: 1 + 415 + seven digits).

International calls: ☎ 011 followed by the country code (Australia ☎ 61; New Zealand ☎ 64; South Africa ☎ 27; United Kingdom ☎ 44), the area/city code (usually without the initial 0), and the telephone number.
Operator: ☎ 0; **International operator**: ☎ 01.
Directory enquiries within your area: ☎ 411.
International directory enquiries: ☎ 00.
Phone Directories: the *Pacific Bell White Pages* (with separate sections for government, business, and residential listings), and the *Yellow Pages*, are widely distributed.

television & radio

[→125]

time

Clocks are set to Pacific Standard Time, GMT +8. They go forward by one hour to Daylight Saving Time on the first Sunday of April, and back again on the last Sunday in October.

tipping

Porters expect $1–$1.50 per bag, room service. Table service at cafés and restaurants, taxi drivers, and hairdressers expect 15% of the bill.

tourist information

San Francisco Convention and Visitors Bureau provides advice, free brochures, and maps. *Hallidie Plaza, 900 Market Street (at Powell St)* ☎ 391-2000 ◑ 9am–5pm daily (to 3pm Sat & Sun).
☎ 391-2001 (for listings recorded message)
☎ 392-0328 (TDD/TTY information line)
w www.sfvisitor.org
Information Booth *International Terminal, SF Airport* ☎ 1-650-876-7880

transport

[→143–147]

travel agents

STA Travel offers cheap flights [→ students]
Two reliable travel agents are:
Montgomery Travel Services *220 Montgomery Street (bet. Pine & Bush Sts)* ☎ 391-2287
Travel Connection *260 Stockton Street (at Post St)* ☎ 397-3977 ◑ 9am–6pm Mon–Fri; 10am–4pm Sat.

travellers' cheques

Travellers' cheques are the safest way to carry money – cheques in US dollars are the most widely accepted. The best places to cash travellers' cheques are bank-operated bureaux de change, American Express, or Thomas Cook [→bureaux de change].

weather

SF has a mild climate. Temperatures rarely rise above 70°F (21°C) or fall below 40°F (5°C). From June to August, dense fog hangs over the city until around midday and returns in the early evening. For weather reports
☎ 837-5000 (ext 1112), or check out the National Weather Service's website at
w www.nws.mbay.net

websites

[→125]

practical information

general index

more index

general index

➔ more index

general index

↓ shopping index

↓ eating index

159

↓ acknowledgements

Conceived, edited & designed by
Virgin Publishing Ltd
London W6 9HA
Tel: 020-7386 3300

Project Editor: Ella Milroy
Designer: Lisa Kosky
Assistant Editor: Sylvia Tombesi-Walton
DTP Designer: Jane Webber
Consultant: Bonnie Wach
Researcher: Helen Westwood
Design & editorial assistance: Laurie Armstrong (San Francisco Convention & Visitors Bureau), Robert Callwell (Muni) Mike Ellis, Claire Fogg, Sam Jobling, Tony Limerick, Naomi Peck, Sally Prideaux, Michele Repine, Clare Tomlinson, Ingrid Vienings, Fiona Wild, Trond Wilhelmsen
Series Editor: Georgina Matthews
Proof Reader: Stewart Wild
Index: Hilary Bird
Design concept: Paul Williams
Jacket concept: Debi Ani
Jacket: Button Design Co

Maps
Cartographic Editor: Dominic Beddow
Cartographers: Simonetta Giori, Jethro Lennox, Caspar Morris
Draughtsman Ltd, London
Tel: 020-8960 1602
mail@magneticnorth.net

Photography
Photographer: Lori Eanes
Additional photography: Ella Milroy [3c, 4b, 19b, 43c, 47b, 53t, 60c, 63t, 71c1, 71c2, 71b1, 88t]

Reproduced by Colourwise
Printed by Proost, Belgium

Features were written and researched by the following:
Getting Your Bearings – Areas: AnneLise Sorensen | Area Introductions: Deborah Bishop (Mission, Hayes Valley & the Civic Center, Pacific Heights, North Beach, SoMa); Danielle Svetcov (Castro & Noe Valley, Haight-Ashbury, Marina & Cow Hollow, Russian Hill & Nob Hill, Chinatown, Downtown) | Area Shopping: Deborah Bishop (Mission, Haight-Ashbury, Hayes Valley & the Civic Center, Pacific Heights, North Beach, Downtown, SoMa); Denise Sullivan (Castro & Noe Valley, Marina & Cow Hollow, Russian Hill & Nob Hill, Chinatown) | Area Restaurants

& Cafés: Danielle Svetcov | Area Bars & Clubs: Greg Heller | Getting Your Bearings – Around San Francisco: AnneLise Sorensen | Marin County, Wine Country, South of the City, Berkeley: Kristan Lawson & Anneli Rufus | Landmarks: Evan Elliot | Sights, Museums & Galleries: Elgy Gillespie; Glen Helfand; AnneLise Sorensen | Parks, Beaches & Views: Elgy Gillespie | Kids: Candi Strecker | Games & Activities: AnneLise Sorensen | Body & Soul: AnneLise Sorensen | Getting Your Bearings – Shopping: Deborah Bishop | Shopping listings: Deborah Bishop (department stores, fashion, beauty, shoes, accessories & lingerie, interiors, books); Denise Sullivan (vintage clothing, outlet stores, theme stores, one-of-a-kind, museum stores, food & drink, cds, records & tapes, electronics & computers) | Getting Your Bearings – Nightlife: Greg Heller | Restaurants & Cafés: Laura Reiley (additional copy from Evan Elliot, Danielle Svetcov, Bonnie Wach) | Bars: Joel Enos | Glen Helfand; Greg Heller | Clubs: Joel Enos; AnneLise Sorensen | Media, Cinema, Theatre, Comedy, Cabaret & Performance Arts, Dance, Opera & Classical Music: Dennis Harvey | Music, Poetry & Literature, Events: Kurt Wolff | Spectator Sports: AnneLise Sorensen | Hotels: Rob Farmer | Transport: Elizabeth Stubbs | Practical Information: Elizabeth Stubbs

Acknowledgements:
Virgin Publishing Ltd would like to thank all galleries, museums, shops, restaurants, bars and other establishments who provided photographs.

Virgin Publishing Ltd is grateful to the following for permission to reproduce their photographs.
(t=top, b=bottom, c=centre):
Asian Art Museum (1993): Seated Buddha, Avery Brundage Collection [72t] | California Academy of Sciences: Susan Middleton [75] | Kristan Lawson [3b, 60t] | Monterey Bay Aquarium: Kevin Candland [66t] | MH de Young Memorial Museum [73t] | Napa Valley Conference & Visitors Bureau [3b, 62t] | Robert Harding Picture Library: [64t] | San Francisco Convention & Visitors Bureau: [61t, 71b2, 80t]; Phil Coblentz [74t]; Kerrick James [70t2, 70b2, 71t1]; David Sanger [70b1]; Carol Simowitz [71c1]; Mark Snyder [70t1]; Vano Photography [70c2]; Carl Wilmington [78t] | Rosicrucian Egyptian Museum [65t] | Barbara Bargetto [65c] | San Mateo County Convention & Visitors Bureau [64c] | Sonoma County Tourism Program [63c]

Great care has been taken with this guide to be as accurate and up-to-date as possible but details such as addresses, telephone numbers, opening hours, prices and travel information are liable to change. The publishers cannot accept responsibility for any consequences arising from the use of this book. We would be delighted to receive any corrections and suggestions for inclusion in the next edition. Please write to:

Virgin Travel Guides
Virgin Publishing Ltd
Thames Wharf Studios
Rainville Road
London W6 9HA
Fax: 020-7386 3360
Email: travel@virgin-pub.co.uk

eating index | acknowledgements

⊻ key to symbols

☎ telephone number
F fax
W worldwide web
👁 things to see
❶ hot tips
⟳ good points
◑ opening times
♿ wheelchair access
   (phone to check details)
🛍 shop
🍴 restaurant/café *or*
   food available
🍸 bar
☆ entertainments
⚷ hotel
£ price
🕐 frequency/times
► picture arrow
🗺 map reference
▫ small museum/venue
▫ mid-sized museum/
   venue
▫ large museum/venue

💳 **credit cards**
   AE = American Express
   D = Discovery
   DC = Diners Club
   JCB = Japanese Credit
        Bureau
   MC = MasterCard
   V = Visa
   all = AE/D/DC/JCB/MC/V
   are accepted
★ recommended *(featured
   in listings section)*

sights, museums, galleries & parks

▶ forthcoming openings
📼 recorded information line
☞ guided tours
🎧 audio guides
👦 kids' activities/age group
⊙ sports & activities

key to area maps

white streets = streets
with lots of shops,
restaurants, bars etc

grey block =
important building

shops

$ cheap
$$ moderate
$$$ expensive

restaurants & cafés, bars & clubs, entertainment

$ cheap (main courses under
   $10 excluding taxes)
$$ moderate (main courses
   $10–$20 excluding taxes)
$$$ expensive (main courses
   over $20 excluding taxes)
🪑 capacity/seating
Ⓢ set menu
🚬 smoking allowed
👶 children allowed
▤ air conditioning
🌳 outdoor area/garden
Ⓥ good vegetarian selection
🎵 live music
⊙ DJs
📺 satellite/cable TV
Ⓡ reservation required
○ happy hour
👔 dress code
👫 gay/mixed crowd

hotels

🛏 number of beds
☕ breakfast included
▤ air conditioning
24 24-hour room service
≋ swimming pool
↔ fitness facilities
✎ business facilities
🌳 outdoor area/garden
🅿 parking (on or off site)
$ under $100
$$ $100–$200
$$$ $200–$300
$$$$ $300 plus

transport

🚌 city bus
🚆 Muni Metro/Muni Metro
   station
🚋 cable car
Ⓑ BART/BART station
🚌 coach/coach station
🎠 overground train station
🚗 taxi/car
✈ airport
⛴ ferry/cruise boat
③ highway
95 US interstate